Books by Page Smith

❋

JAMES WILSON, FOUNDING FATHER
JOHN ADAMS
THE HISTORIAN AND HISTORY
AS A CITY UPON A HILL — THE TOWN
IN AMERICAN HISTORY

Daughters
of the
Promised Land

Page Smith

Daughters of the Promised Land

WOMEN IN AMERICAN HISTORY

*Being an examination of the strange history of the female sex
from the beginning to the present with special attention
to the women of America, illustrated by
curious anecdotes and quotations
by divers authors, ancient
and modern.*

Little, Brown and Company
BOSTON   TORONTO

LIBRARY OF CONGRESS CATALOG CARD NO. 79–117037

FIRST EDITION

Published simultaneously in Canada
by Little, Brown & Company (Canada) Limited

PRINTED IN THE UNITED STATES OF AMERICA

Dedicated to my daughters, Ellen and Anne;
to the ladies of Cowell College; to the women in my life,
my mother, Ellen,
and my wife, Eloise;
and to Mary, Barbara, Frances, Sarah,
Jacquey, Hattie, Lee, Maxine, Betty, Liz, Claire, Dorothy,
Jean, Jane, Janet, Margie, Eve, Ruth, Freya, Alice,
Betsy, Hermia, Lois, Helen, Fawn, Rosalind, Ginny, Libby,
Linell, Pat, Nancy, Ann, Marcelle, Beatrice, Clarissa, Josephine,
Ida, LaVerne, Maria, Emma,
Marilyn, Virginia, Kim, Bertie, Tatty, Cleon,
Eleanor, Emmy, Carol, Gretchen,
Eunice, Laura, Fredericka, Mitzi, Vee, Marion,
Susan, Edna, Dixie, Matilda, Cette, Marjorie, Madeline, Sandra,
Gay, Peggy, Haddie, Kathy, Allen, Priscilla,
Hillary, Genevieve, Maile, Elaine,
Lucille, Connie, Rosanna,
Florence, Louise,
Teddy, Della, Gina, Kitty, Julia,
Ella, Janis, Maggie, Judy, Emily, Phoebe, Phyllis,
Flora Mae, Amanda, Sandy, Kris, Sheila,
Charlene, Candy, Julie,
Giselle, Sushila,
Daphne,
Corda

Introduction

❈

Although I was told in my childhood that to begin with an apology was bad form, I feel I must express some uneasiness at my presumption in undertaking a subject at once so vast and so obscure. I am reminded of Henry Adams's observation that "the proper study of mankind is woman and, by common agreement since the time of Adam, it is most complex and arduous." It was also Adams who wrote: "The study of history is useful to the historian by teaching him his ignorance of women; and the mass of his ignorance crushes one who is familiar enough with what we call historical sources to realize how few women have ever been known." Fortunately for this work, there is a very considerable body of material having to do with the history of American women, far more, in fact, than I could ever hope to encompass.

I was about to express a ritual apology for writing a generalizing book before all the monographs were in, so to speak. But it occurred to me that the generalizing works must and of course do precede monographic studies. Otherwise who knows what to write the monographs about? We are constantly making false analogies to science so I might as well make a proper one. Scientists, observing inconsistencies or "incompleteness" in what appear to be well-authenticated "laws" or axioms, propose a new and more comprehensive theory to reconcile the heretofore unnoticed or suppressed inconsistencies. Such theories, while generally accepted on the basis of their ability to explain what was previously inexplicable, may wait some time for empirical "proof" in the form of confirming experiments or observations.

This book is full of theories or hypotheses about the role and importance of women in American history. I like to think that a number of graduate students, wandering about like lost sheep looking for dissertation topics will subject these hypotheses and others suggested by them to monographic scrutiny. I do not much care whether they find me right or wrong so long as in so doing they help to illuminate the role of women in American history. My aim is thus a relatively modest one: I wish only to establish that American women have indeed a history, moving, dramatic, absorbing and in fact essential to any proper understanding of the larger history of the American people.

Many people have been most helpful in the preparation of this volume. As with everything I have written, Eugen Rosenstock-Huessy has been both an inspiration and an essential source of ideas and insights. Douglass and Virginia Adair contributed a most important item. Richard Randolph, Bert Kaplan, Ruth Frary, Malcolm Maccoby, Norman O. Brown, George Boas, Fox Butterfield, Peter Laslett, Jasper Rose, Bill Callan, Anne Scott, Donald and Emily Clark, Mary Dzyvendazk, and Anne Thimann all contributed in significant ways — through conversation, ideas, suggestions, through calling books or articles to my attention or lending them to me. I should make special mention of Sarah Boutelle and Mary Holmes whose ideas have been particularly helpful. I am much in debt to Ruth James, director of the Arthur and Phoebe Schlesinger Archives of American Women at Radcliffe, and to Elizabeth Duvall, bibliographer of the Sophia Smith Collection at Smith College. They both took special pains to assist my researches. Wendy Watson helped in the preparation of the manuscript and in criticisms and suggestions. The manuscript profited greatly from Charlotte Cassidy's scrupulous and devoted attentions.

The writing of this book owes nothing to my wife. She viewed the whole enterprise with undisguised skepticism, interrupted me frequently to ask if the Joneses would make good dinner partners with the Browns or whether the Thompsons will go with the Johnsons, seduced me from my labors with delicious meals (so that my girth grew with my book), and, most unnerving of all, said periodically: "How you could pretend to know anything about women! . . ." Which of course I don't.

Contents

Daughters
of the
Promised Land

1

The Beginnings:

Ishtar and Her Sisters

American women obviously belong to a larger category of womankind, with a history extending over a good many thousands of years and every area of the globe where human life has existed. It thus seems essential to review, however briefly, what is known (and it is certainly far too little) about the life, the roles, and the contributions of women to the strange, slow progress of the race from the earliest moment of which we have knowledge down to the time when this story properly begins — the settlement of the first English men and women in North America.

It would not be overstating the matter, I suppose, to say that there is no more compelling nor more complex theme in all history. We might recall Winston Churchill's aphorism applied to a far more mundane topic — "a riddle wrapped in a mystery inside an enigma." One thing seems clear enough: from the most primitive societies to the most sophisticated, men have regarded women with mixed feelings of awe, astonishment, devotion, fear, and even, on occasion, horror. If we observe primitive tribes we find in many of them some basis for the notion that the true fall was the fall from a matriarchal to a patriarchal society. Early man, who struggled to keep from being overwhelmed by the inscrutable and terrible forces of nature, saw the generative powers of women as a central part of the natural world. It indeed may have been that primitive man did not connect the act of intercourse with the birth of a child; the events were too far separated in time for him to readily establish their relationship. The earliest and most central taboos were directed at women and seem to have been concerned primarily with menstruation, which to primitive man must have been an awesome mystery.

We know that among the higher animals the females' "season" disrupts social life and pits rival suitors against each other, although such behavior is more dangerous among domesticated than among wild animals, who, as Konrad Lorenz points out, generally discharge the hostilities generated by courting rivalry through ritual acts of aggression, breaking off short of lethal encounters. The taboos prohibiting contact with menstruating women may have been, as Briffault has argued, efforts to bring some kind of order and regularity into sexual relations by at least establishing a period of the month when intercourse was forbidden.[1]

It is certainly clear that the female periods of menstruation were associated with the phases of the moon by primitive peoples, and in many languages the word for menstruation and moon are the same. The word menstruation means in fact "moon change." German peasants call the menstrual period "the moon," and in France it is referred to as *le moment de la lune*.[2] The Maori speak of menstruation as *mata marama* (moon sickness) and many primitives believed that the moon caused conception; women who did not wish to conceive were careful not to sleep or lie in the moonlight. The moon was feminine in its coolness, in its cyclical nature, in its growth, which seemed analogous to the swelling of a pregnant woman.

Earth and moon goddesses were familiar divinities in a number of ancient societies and in most, if not all, worship of the moon apparently preceded and later coexisted with worship of the sun. Commonly the sun, with its regularity, came to incorporate the masculine principle and the moon the feminine. The sun represented the principle "of work and achievement and of conscious understanding and discrimination, the Logos"; the moon, "of the unconscious . . . the Eros, powerful and fateful, and incomprehensible."[3] Like the cup and the chalice, the quarter moon appears in innumerable representations of the female principle, or the moon goddess.

The goddess Astarte or Ishtar was the presiding deity in Babylon and it was against her orgiastic cults that Moses and the prophets of Israel contended. Most of these myths involved the yearly death and resurrection of the son of the moon goddess (Ishtar's son was Tammuz, "the Green One"), and the profound ambivalence of the man toward the feminine principle, however represented, is shown by the fact that many of the goddesses had their origin as animal gods and even after their evolution into overtly feminine goddesses retained the aspect of cruelty and destruction as well as of fecundity and maternity. Ishtar's proper title was "Ishtar, Queen of Heaven and Queen of All the Stars, also Queen of the Underworld, Destroyer of Life and Goddess of the Terrors of the Storm."[4]

Cybele's son, Attis, was about to be married when his mother struck him mad. Attis, in turn, castrated himself before the great goddess. This occasion was commemorated in festivals which involved orgiastic eruptions culminating in acts of self-immolation by young men in a religious frenzy. Some castrated themselves before the goddess and threw their parts on her statue. "Others ran bleeding through the streets and flung the severed organs into some house which they passed. This household was then obliged to supply the young man, now become a eunuch priest, with women's clothes."[5]

In Egypt, Isis was the wife and sister of Osiris. When Set, the god of the underworld, killed Osiris, Isis searched for, found and reassembled all the parts of her husband's body except the phallus. This she made a replica of and by means of it bore a child, Horus the Younger. Isis thus became the figure representing renewal and immortality, and her cult survived into the Hellenistic period, when its most famous recruit was Lucius Apuleius.

In the earliest days of Greek religion Selene alone represented the moon. Later she was replaced by Aphrodite the Bright Moon and Hecate the Dark Moon, and they in turn by Hecate the Three-headed, a figure made up of Artemis, Selene, and Hecate representing the moon in its three phases — waxing, full, and waning.

Other threefold goddesses of the moon are to be found in the three Celtic Bridgets and the Three Ladies of Britain. Always there is emphasis on the dark side of the moon, the cruelty, deceitfulness and terror of the moon goddesses, echoing the basic anxiety of the man about his mate or mistress. The elaborate rituals, the taboos, the complex structure of myth served to reassure the man in his relations with the woman, to support and reinforce his own confidence and manliness. The man's instincts seem generally to have been innovative, the woman's conservative. Her sexuality was a constant reminder of his own vulnerability. Against her deliberate seductions he had fragile and unreliable defenses. She must have seemed to him at times as terrible and insatiable as nature herself.

We know of primitive peoples in modern times whose social organization is matrilineal, and it would be natural that women should dominate societies where paternity was often in doubt but the identity of the mother beyond question. The Marxists, drawing on Briffault and J. J. Bachofen, have argued that two developments led directly to the overthrow of matriarchal society: the acquisition of power in the form of property and the desire of the fathers to be able to establish a reasonable claim to having sired specific sons and heirs to whom their property could devolve.

The process was doubtless far more complicated, but if ancient symbols and mythologies have any meaning at all it is clear enough that much of man's tribal life centered on ways of coping with the anima of the female. The rites of passage, characteristic of all primitives, often involving circumcision and symbolic sex acts, were clearly intended to strengthen the psyche of the young man in anticipation of his frightening encounter with the woman. Until the sexual impulse was domesticated, tamed, contained and subordinated to the common needs of hunting, fighting and planting, the beginnings of civilized life were impossible.

There seems to have been a kind of alternation in the history of the higher ancient societies. Initially "mother right," or more broadly the power and efficacy of women, might be conspicuous. Gradually this "right" diminished, perhaps in response to the shift from tribal, nomadic life to urban life. The organization and rationalization of society seems always, at least in its initial stages, to represent a loss of status for women. It may well be that the degree of repression of women or their confinement to a very narrow and subordinate role was in reverse ratio to the power that their sexuality, their irrationality and mystery (a mystery containing, as we have suggested, a large element of fear, perhaps even terror) had presented in an earlier stage of the society. This would help to account for the pattern of religious prostitution that often emerged.

THE BEGINNINGS

Woman's sexuality was clearly, in a sense, divine. It was the agency of human life, the model of that fecundity in nature which supported that same life; it was compelling and disruptive as well. To separate sexuality from the mothering function so essential to orderly social life may have seemed a necessity in ancient societies. In any event such a pattern is unmistakable. Once masculine dominance had been established, women were treated as a conquered tribe, which in a sense they were. The war between the sexes is not a new one. The psychological depths of that encounter are represented by the ubiquitousness of the goddesses — the mother goddess, the moon goddess, Ishtar, Cybele, Bridget, Venus, Athena, Aphrodite, Shakti (the mate of Shiva, or however she may be represented) — as well as, in many instances, her destructiveness. In a number of ancient myths, the mother goddess brings a devastating flood which destroys all or a large part of the world.* Also, she not infrequently murders or connives in the killing of her son, whom she then restores to life. The mythic persons of the goddess and her consort re-enact this warfare, sometimes moving from masculine to feminine power as in the assertion of Isis' primacy over Osiris, or in the opposite direction as male deities struggle to assert themselves.

The worship of Ishtar, Cybele, Aphrodite, or Venus all involved forms of sacred prostitution. In Briffault's words, "The explanation of the sensual and sexual character of religious rites lies in the notion that every function of woman, whether as mother, as wife, as supplier of food, as cultivator of the soil, as sorceress, witch, prophetess, or priestess, postulates her union with the god who is the bestower of these powers. The indecency so conspicuous a feature of all heathen religions has everywhere reference to that union, in some form or other, of women with divine beings."[6]

Temple prostitutes in their relations with anonymous men were enacting this ritual and in Babylon every woman was required, Herodotus tells us, to come at some time to the temple of Ishtar and wait there until a man claimed her as a sexual partner. For some of the less prepossessing, he notes, the wait could be long indeed.

Although it seems that the worship of a goddess as principal deity

---

* If one accepts the notion of Jungian archetypes one is tempted to see the determination of Western man to conquer the moon, by means of a phallus-shaped projectile, as the most recent stage of this age-old warfare between the sexes.

did not necessarily reflect a corresponding regard for her earthly counterparts, we find that under the code of Hammurabi women did enjoy broad legal rights. In Babylon, as in most of the ancient world, marriage was a purchase. A girl was the property of her father and she was sold to her husband, although it was more typically the case that the girl had to bring with her a considerable dowry. If the wife was childless she might choose a servant girl to provide her husband with a child. If the wife refused the husband might take a concubine, in which case the wife became free. To the price offered for the bride was added the bride's dowry and both together came to the husband, although the dowry remained the property of the wife and passed from her to her children. If a husband wished to divorce his wife he could do so by returning her dowry. The wife received custody of the children and her father was responsible for their upbringing. Women, moreover, could be elders, secretaries, and judges as well, of course, as priestesses, hierodules, consecrated women and temple maidens.

Relatively little is known about the status of women in Egyptian culture. Perhaps the most frequently quoted lines on the subject simply urge a husband to be solicitous for the welfare of his wife: "If thou art prosperous, thou shouldst found thy household and love thy wife as is fitting. Fill her belly; clothe her back; ointment is the prescription for her body. Make her heart glad as long as thou livest, for she is a profitable field for her lord."[7] The emphasis seems to be on the wife's material value and offers no very encouraging picture of life even for a woman of wealth. Certainly the queens of the pharaohs had a central role to play in the pageantry of the royal household, but aesthetically compelling as the pictures and statues of many of them are, they seldom emerge as potent or powerful figures.

Amenhotep III (1417–1379 B.C.) broke with convention in featuring his beautiful wife, Tiy, and emphasizing his devotion to her as a woman, and Amenhotep IV (1379–1362 B.C.) went further with his exquisite sister-wife Nefertiti in "visible and publicized devotion." This was a period of both decadence and revolutionary change, and a kind of high tide of Egyptian feminism was marked by acceptance of the idea that the pharaoh's queen, Nefertiti, could become a divinity. Amenhotep IV pushed the revolution by building a new capital at Amarna and replacing Amon the Hidden One with

Aton the Sun God, whose temples were open to the sky. So, in a curious way, it might be said that feminine status, at least in the royal establishment, reached its highest point at a time when the feminine principle in the image of the divine Isis was superseded by the aggressively masculine deity Aton, a shift of emphasis as well from the life-giving power of the Nile to the splendor of the sun and the principle of universality.

While replacement of a matriarchal society by one dominated by men must have been the precondition of most higher forms of civilized life, feudal societies which were agricultural and essentially tribal, such as the Greeks of the Homeric age, witnessed a near balance between men and women, each with specific and honorable roles and a workable equilibrium between sexuality and order. Masculine and feminine roles were more sharply polarized, more dramatic and more formal. Sexual tensions and anxieties certainly existed, but they were suppressed or ritualized. In a feudal society with its preoccupation with problems of descent and devolution and its desire to preserve the status quo, the woman's quality of conserver is specially valued.

Werner Jaeger assures us that women held a higher social position at the close of the Homeric period than at any other time in Greek history.[8] The woman was honored for her useful role in the economy, for her talents as an arbiter of disputes, for her importance as a mother whose children will carry on the family name, as the faithful and devoted consort of a great warrior, the preserver of morality and tradition.

In Hesiod, on the other hand, writing in the seventh century B.C., we see reflected the basic suspicion and even hostility of the peasant toward the generalized feminine principle. The story of Pandora is a classic tale of the troublemaking potential of women, of their curiosity and mischievousness.

If we take Ionia as our model it is abundantly clear that the position of Greek women suffered a constant erosion from the age of Homer to the time of Periclean Athens. (We must except Sparta, which remained an authoritarian, feudal, agricultural society.)[9] Women were treated as little better than chattels. Even the life of a slave might be preferable to that of a Greek wife. She was relegated to special quarters in her husband's house; she had only the most

constricted social life, and had few legal rights. (Polybius was astonished when he went to Rome to find that Roman wives were included
in social events.) It is only slightly overstating the case to say that one
of the most sophisticated and creative societies in history was founded
on slavery, the subordination of wives, and homosexuality. When
Plato wrote his symposium on the nature of Eros, the starting point is
the love of one man for another, and the greatest feminine voice of
the Hellenic age was Sappho, whose love poems were addressed to
the girls who formed her circle.

The dramatic feminine figures of the Iliad and Odyssey do not
reappear until the Greek dramas of the fifth century. Medea, Antigone, Clytemnestra, Jocasta, and Cassandra are only the most notable
in a gallery of remarkable women whose passion for justice or for
their loved ones, for husbands, sons, brothers or lovers, forms the
central theme of the plays in which they appear. The subordinate
position of women is the harder to explain since the Greeks had an
unusually rich array of goddesses who were every bit as human as
their earthly charges and who showed no womanly inhibitions in
their relations with the gods. Jaeger casts some light on the paradox
by pointing out that the split in the Greek mind between the realm of
spirit and of the senses was so sharp that it was late in the Hellenic
era before Greek men "came to believe that erotic passion could gain
such importance as to invade their spiritual nature and interpenetrate
the whole of life . . . Only a woman was capable of the utter
abandonment of soul and senses alike which we should consider
worthy of the name of love."[10]

Demosthenes in the fourth century B.C. describes the categories of
Greek women in these terms: "Hetaerae we keep for the sake of
pleasure; concubines [female slaves] for the daily care of our persons; wives to bear us legitimate children and to be the trusted guardians of our households."[11]

Aristotle apparently viewed the union of male and female as little
better than a necessary evil. They must come together "in order to
reproduce." "That which is able to plan and to take forethought is by
nature ruler and master, whereas that which is able to supply physical
labor is by nature ruled." This is the rationale for slaves, Aristotle
argues, and for the subordination of women. It is a mark of the
inferiority of a society if men and women are treated as equals

("association there is a partnership between slaves, female and male"). In the Aristotelian logic, nature assigns, among higher orders of life, "a single function to a single thing. An instrument is at the peak of perfection when it serves a single end, not a number of ends."[12] Hence the division of female functions between hetaerae, concubines and wives.*

The legal restraints on the Greek woman were as repressive as the social ones. She could not hold office or attend the assembly; she could not own property or conduct legal business; she was the ward from birth to death of her nearest male relative. While unwanted infants of both sexes were exposed to death, many more girls than boys seem to have been the victims of that barbarous practice.

In summary, the Ionian Greeks, following the example of the Oriental world, divided the female into sexual and maternal functions. The life of the Greek mother was severely circumscribed; the life of the hetaera was exciting and glamorous; that of the mistress and concubine less exciting but superior in many ways to the situation of the wife. This "division of labor" was ratified by particular feminine deities: Aphrodite, sexual love; Artemis, chastity; Hera, the faithful wife; Demeter, mother of Persephone, the figure of fertility and fruitfulness. The multiplicity of goddesses made possible the fragmenting of Greek women.

Moreover, for the Greeks the most exalted love was that between men. Obviously homosexual relations posed far less risk than heterosexual ones. The mystery and fearfulness of the "other" was diminished in such liaisons; they could be idealized more readily than disorderly and often frightening relations with members of the opposite sex. Homosexual love cast thus a shadow over all the possibilities of spiritualized love between men and women.

In Rome, the situation of women was substantially different. They had wider legal rights and somewhat more social status — they were not, for example, excluded from social gatherings like their Greek sisters — but they were in effect owned by their fathers and subsequently by their husbands, and their primary function was to produce legionaries and senators. Yet Roman women were determined and

---

* Plato was, to be sure, willing to give women a place in sports and war though this concession was at the cost of their giving up domestic functions, since in Plato's view they were a bad influence on growing boys.

aggressive ladies and they exerted constant pressure for reform. Livy
tells us of the debate in the senate in 195 B.C. over repeal of the
Oppian law when women demonstrated in the streets, and he quotes
Cato on the decline of morals: "If every married man had been
concerned to ensure that his own wife looked up to him and respected
his rightful position as her husband, we should not have half this
trouble with women *en masse.* Instead, women have become so
powerful that our independence has been lost in our own homes and
is now being trampled and stamped underfoot in public. We have
failed to restrain them as individuals, and now they have combined to
reduce us to our present panic . . . Woman is a violent and uncon-
trolled animal and it is no good giving her the reins and expecting
her not to kick over the traces . . . What they want is complete
freedom, or, not to mince words, license . . . Suppose you allow
them to acquire or to extort one right after another, and in the end to
achieve complete equality with men, do you think that you will find
them bearable? Nonsense. Once they have achieved equality, they will
be your masters."

A more liberal spirit prevailed and the law was repealed. But at
least one later historian, Valerius Maximus, looked back on this as an
unhappy day for Rome.

In the last fifty years of the republic the Roman woman of the
upper classes was an important figure in the smart set of a luxurious
and decadent city. In Baldsdon's words: "Women of wealth, birth,
charm and talent, unfettered by any moral restraint, hungry for
animal pleasure or hungry for power — hungry, perhaps, for both —
the large stage of late Republican society had room for them."

The pages of Plutarch, Tacitus and Livy are sprinkled with the
most lurid accounts of feminine debauchery. Julia, the daughter of
Augustus, was charged with multiple adulteries and banished; Agrippina, the daughter of Julia and Agrippa, "devoted her life to vice."
Valeria Messalina, "lovely, gay, lascivious and foolish," was the first
wife of Claudius.[13] She carried on a notorious affair with her lover
Silius, and then in a gesture of ultimate depravity and contempt
participated in a marriage ceremony with him. Messalina and her
lover were murdered and Claudius married Agrippina (the younger).
The marriage, was under law, an incestuous one, but the senate oblig-
ingly changed the statute. Agrippina, who yielded to no one in

depravity, was, appropriately enough, the mother of Nero. After her son became emperor at the age of sixteen, Agrippina, seasoned in every vice, intervened in all the affairs of state. According to Tacitus, "on a number of occasions in broad daylight when he [Nero] was tipsy after dinner [Agrippina] appeared before him elaborately made up, with the unmistakable suggestion of incest. She kissed him with indecent passion, and wheedled him to her criminal purpose."[14]

From the Flavians through the Antonines, the women of the imperial court, the wives, the daughters, mothers, nieces, mistresses mixed freely in court intrigues and, profligate or virtuous, were powerful and important figures. Wives were praised for being "old-fashioned, content to stay at home, chaste, dutifully obedient, friendly and amusing, careful over money, not overdressed, religious without being fanatics."[15] That they were not always so we may conclude from Juvenal's gallery of Roman wives. He sketches the daughter of a distinguished family who talked of little else, the wife who thought it smart to look and talk like a courtesan or a prostitute, the wife who did her best to alienate her husband from his oldest friends, the wife who took all her troubles to her mother and formed an alliance against her husband, the querulous nagging wife, the gossip, the bluestocking, the wife who engaged in athletics to the neglect of her household duties and the one who was "stage-struck or games-struck," the woman of affairs, the unfaithful wife, and the strongly masculine wife.[16]

Juvenal directed his barbs against such women because they were conspicuous and important persons in Latin society, and this in itself tells an important story. Rome added to the gallery of human types a number of classic figures: Cincinnatus, the simple farmer who left his plow to lead a victorious army; Fabius, master of the tactics of evasion; Cato, guardian of public morals. It added, as well, a number of victorious and courageous wives and mothers: Cornelia, the wife of Tiberius Sempronius Gracchus and mother of the two tribunes Tiberius and Caius; Cornelia, the devoted wife of Pompey; Julia, aunt of Julius Caesar, eulogized by her nephew, her descent traced back to Venus; the mourning Octavia, wife of Marcellus.

In Roman as in Greek society the functions of mother/wife and sexual partner were usually clearly distinguished. The prostitutes of Rome were famous, and in the later empire it has been estimated that there were at least forty-five licensed brothels in Rome. The most vivid reminder of such institutions is to be found at Insula 12, No. 18, in Pompeii (where there were at least six others), the walls of which graphically illustrate the types of entertainment available to its patrons.

The courtesans were, of course, another matter. They were ladies distinguished by their beauty and talent. It was for them Ovid wrote his *Art of Love*. Handsomely maintained by wealthy and important men, they, in most instances, lived with their mothers or were married to husbands who profited from their exactions.

In many households slave girls constituted a kind of harem readily available to their masters. Concubinage was encouraged by law and accepted by Roman wives. Concubines were often women with whom a man wished to live as in marriage but whom for practical reasons (perhaps she was of inferior social position or had no dowry) he did not wish to marry. A married man did not, as a rule, have a concubine, but rather a mistress or slave girl. The status of concubine was reserved for unmarried women often of good character. An indeterminate state which sometimes ended in marriage, it allowed Roman legionaries to live, as husband and wife in all but law, with women they were forbidden to marry. Freedwomen might live in concubinage with slaves whom they were not allowed to marry.

Holy and religious women also made up an important segment of the feminine population of Rome. The vestal virgins are the most famous of these. They were originally young women of exemplary character selected to keep alive the sacred flame of the hearth goddess Vesta. Like most other institutions of Rome, that of the vestal virgins became in time corrupted, and the younger Pliny tells us that in A.D. 215 Caracella "satisfied his evil humor by seducing a vestal virgin and then ensuring that she and two others were buried alive." The principal duties of the vestal virgins, besides tending the sacred flame, were ceremonial ones concerned primarily with "the earth and the fundamentals of living."[17] Their purity was taken to be the guarantee of the soundness of Rome. It is certainly significant that in a society in which sexuality was such a potent element the central religious figures should have been virgins and their chastity related directly to the fate of the republic, and, later, the empire.

Greece and Rome have been discussed here at some length because

they provide a starting point for our consideration of the role and status of women. Feminine sexuality could be reconciled with an orderly and creative society only if the functions of women were separated and sharply defined, if, indeed, they were represented in different categories of women — hetaerae, concubines, mistresses, sacred prostitutes, wives — each category limited to its sphere: the wife to have for the most part a restricted social life; the mistress to forego any hope of legitimate offspring. This solution has, of course, an importance that extends far beyond its adoption in the ancient world. It is in fact the way that all societies of the Fertile Crescent, indeed of the entire Mediterranean world, of the Indic world and the Far East, structured themselves in relation to the role and status of women.

A society deserves to be judged by its highest achievements. While it is true that in Rome under the empire divorce, sexual license and dynastic maneuverings gave an unwholesome cast to the story of women, Rome did add to the classic human roles that of the noble matron. In the heyday of the republic the Roman mother was a potent and commanding figure, courageous, intelligent, devoted to the cause of her husband or the advancement of her sons. The creation of such an ideal type was certainly one of the most notable achievements of Latin culture. Indeed, the image of the Roman matron was a triumph over the devouring mother of Oriental religions. Bachofen has described the process by which Tanaquil, the Etruscan-Oriental hetaeric divinity, sexual and cruel, was converted by the Romans into the loyal wife of Tarquinius, "the model matronly patroness of the rights of women in the Roman state, an example of the nobility of the dutiful Roman wife." Bachofen, the earliest and most eloquent expositor of the notion of "mother right," traced the steps by which the sensual Oriental goddess was spiritualized, and found it the most significant transformation of the imaginative and religious life of the ancient world.[18]

2

Israel

Much of the history of the Hebrews recounts their struggles against the cultism of the societies that surrounded them. The less austere of the Israelites were constantly being seduced by the worshipers of Ishtar, Cybele, Mithras or Isis. Opposing these erotic gods and goddesses was an aggressively masculine deity, the Jehovah of the Old Testament, who destroyed the cities of the plain because they reeked of wickedness and iniquity. This grim patriarchal deity inveighed, through his prophets, against all moral laxity, and often his severest strictures were reserved for the jezebels, the whores and harlots who stewed the fleshpots. If we consider the world in which these warnings were uttered, it should be evident that these were not simply the libidinous fancies of repressive old men, i.e., the prophets, but the quite legitimate and characteristic anxiety of men about the sexuality of women as a threat to the order and stability of social life. At the same time women in Israel enjoyed higher status than in any ancient culture. The Old Testament offers us a gallery of vivid female portraits starting in Genesis with Sarah and Abraham.

Their story is familiar enough, and in its recounting of the chicanery, greed, cunning, and family rivalry of the "founding fathers," their quarrelsome wives and ungrateful children is the greatest and most human epic of ancient man. Most of the elements of the life of a simple, not to say primitive, tribal people are in Genesis — the obsession with the problem of succession and legitimacy seen in Sarah's sanctioning of her husband's relation with the slave girl Hagar for the purpose of producing a son; Abraham's concubines; the institution of the rite of circumcision; Sarah's determination to make Isaac the proper heir of Abraham rather than Ishmael; the arranged marriage between Isaac and Rebecca; Jacob's maneuvering, doubtless encouraged by his mother, to divest Esau of his birthright.

The "divers laws and ordinances" which were promulgated in the wake of the Ten Commandments covered the relationship of fathers and daughters, husbands and wives, slaves and masters. The laws governing the relationships between men and women are of special interest here. If a man seduces a girl to whom he is not engaged, he must "endow her to be his wife," and if her father opposes the marriage, he must nonetheless pay a dowry. No widow or fatherless child shall be "afflicted"; if she is, the Lord's wrath will be terrible — "I will kill you with the sword; and your wives shall be widows, and your children fatherless."

But behind all specific ordinances and laws was, of course, the injunction to have no other gods, to avoid contamination by other peoples — the Hittites, the Jebusites, the Amorites, and the Canaanites. Monotheism was the precondition of any ascetic morality. In a system of multiple gods, divinities could always be found or created under whose aegis any desire, however perverse, could be indulged. It was not that the Hebrews were so much better than their neighbors, it was only that they could be brought more readily to account; they could not take refuge with the goddess of love, or of the moon, or of hermaphroditic eroticism; they were responsible to a single stern and wrathful as well as loving deity. The Hebrews, in overcoming the goddesses of female sexuality, brought both men and women under one divine power. One Lord, presiding over all his children without regard to sex or age, calling them all to judgment provided the foundation for "feminine equality." That the Hebrew woman continued to be subject to the social customs and, to a degree, the legal restraints that circumscribed their Hittite or Jebusite or Greek or Egyptian sisters was, in the long run, far less important than the fact that she and her husband worshiped the same god, a god who did not discriminate on the basis of sex.

The struggle against the cultist gods of the Mesopotamian basin and the major deities of the eastern Mediterranean was not an easy one. When Moses lingered too long on Mount Sinai (which apparently had itself been the site of a shrine to the Mistress of Turquoise) his impatient charges prevailed on the priest Aaron to make a golden calf, symbol of Baal, son of Astarte, and shouted, "These are the gods, O Israel, which brought thee up out of the land of Egypt." They were, indeed, as the Lord told Moses, with obvious irritation, "a stiffnecked people."

The books of the law are the best index to the temptations against which the Hebrews contended: "Whosoever lieth carnally with a woman that is a bondmaid, betrothed to an husband, and not at all redeemed, nor freedom given her; she shall be scourged; they shall not be put to death because she was not free." "Do not prostitute thy daughter, to cause her to be a whore; lest the land fall to whoredom, and the land become full of wickedness." The danger of "falling into whoredom" obsessed the minds of the priests and prophets of Israel; it was of course no imaginary danger. Those commentators who view the anxieties of the Hebrew leaders and the early church fathers over female sexuality as the unhealthy fantasies of prurient old (or young) men have a very dim notion of its terrible potency. The prohibitions in Leviticus provide an inventory of the sexual aberrations of the ancient world. The injunction against a man giving any of "his seed unto Moloch" referred to masturbatory rites in honor of that dismal deity. There are equally stern injunctions against familiar spirits, witches and wizards, against incest (which, from the plotting of Lot's daughters, was by no means unknown). It is perhaps worth noting that the punishment for incestuous relations with one's sister was less severe than for such relations with mother or daughter-in-law; the violator and his victim were to be "cut off in the sight of their people"— ostracized. We also find the classic taboo against intercourse during a woman's menstrual period.

We know how sporadically the Hebrews observed the laws and how frequently they strayed. We know of Solomon's problems with his wives and concubines and of his underhanded tactics in getting Uriah out of the way so that he could enjoy the favors of his general's wife. We know that such scandalous behavior did not inhibit Solomon, or someone writing in his name, from offering a famous set of moral precepts in Proverbs, many of which have to do with relations between the sexes. It is "the strange woman" who is to be feared. She is the seductress, the tempter —"For the lips of a strange woman drop as an honeycomb, and her mouth is smoother than oil. But her end is bitter as wormwood, sharp as a twoedged sword. Her feet go down to death; her steps take hold on hell"; it is her mobility that makes her most dangerous. She is not known. She is contained by no social context. She is feminine sexuality without those restraints that mothers, wives, concubines, handmaidens, sisters, and daughters are subject to, ". . . her ways are moveable, that thou canst not know them." "For by means of a whorish woman a man is brought to a piece of bread: and the adultress will hunt for the precious life." The same hypothetical young man is urged to make his wife the object of his love: ". . . rejoice with the wife of thy youth. Let her be as the loving hind and pleasant roe; let her breasts satisfy thee at all times; and be thou ravished always with her love." The verse is, I suspect, unique in the literature of the ancient world in its celebration of physical passion between husband and wife and in its ideal of marital fidelity. When women were understood to be, equally with men, the children of a particular and jealous god, the repression of their sexuality was the price of enhanced standing as wives and mothers.

It is certainly expressive of the Hebrew anxiety about uninhibited sexuality, that the prophets, upbraiding Israel for faithlessness, constantly employed the image of the whore and harlot: "Then I said unto her that was old in adulteries [Israel], Will they now commit whoredoms with her, and she with them? . . . Thus will I cause lewdness to cease out of the land, that all women may be taught not to do after your lewdness."

Daughterhood and sonhood are central themes of the Old Testament. In large part, of course, this emphasis is due to the problems of succession. The Hebrews understood that in order to survive they had to keep records. Descent was traced through the female line, and Josephus tells of the scrupulous and arduous keeping of the rolls by the priests for over two thousand years. Throughout the Old Testament Israel is referred to continually as "the daughter of Zion," and her relationship to the Lord is likened to that of the virgin bride to her husband. The image is crucial because it is an image of fidelity, the fidelity of the true marriage to which the husband is to be as

faithful as the bride. When the daughter of Zion strays from the path of righteousness, from faithfulness to her Lord, she is chastised by suffering and desolation. The daughter of Zion must not go whoring after false gods.

The daughters of Zion, on the other hand, are the women of Israel and they, like the men, are called to judgment: "Moreover the LORD saith, Because the daughters of Zion are haughty, and walk with stretched forth necks and wanton eyes, walking and mincing as they go and making a tinkling with their feet: therefore the Lord will smite with a scab the crown of the head of the daughters of Zion, and the LORD will discover their secret parts. In that day the Lord will take away the bravery of their tinkling ornaments about their feet, and their cauls, and their round tires like the moon, the chains, and the bracelets, and the mufflers, the bonnets, and the ornaments of the legs, and the headbands, and the tablets, and the earrings, the rings, and the nose jewels, the changeable suits of apparel, and the mantles, and the wimples, and the crisping pins, the glasses, and the fine linen, and the hoods, and the vails."

And in the day of deliverance ". . . seven women shall take hold of one man, saying, We will eat our own bread, and wear our own apparel: only let us be called by thy name, to take away our reproach. In that day shall the branch of the LORD be beautiful and glorious, and the fruit of the earth shall be excellent and comely for them that are escaped of Israel."

Both in the chronicles of the Old Testament and in the determined efforts of the prophets to impose a moral order on a primitive and unruly people, women figure very prominently in the life of ancient Israel.

That sexuality and worldliness remained critical problems for the Hebrews is indicated by the later development of ascetic Jewish sects such as the Essenes. One of these sects, which rose in the early years of the Roman Empire, followed a prophet from Nazareth. The Christians' most distinctive attribute was that, influenced as they doubtless were by such groups as the Essenes, they nonetheless almost at once transcended the character of a Jewish sect and, disregarding ties of tribe, race, and nation, made claims to universality. In virtually every other way they were thoroughly Jewish and, if the genealogy of the

DAUGHTERS OF THE PROMISED LAND

Old Testament were no longer a pressing concern, its cosmology and its prophetic writings were incorporated into the teachings of Christianity from the beginning. Certainly the early Christian church inherited the Hebrew attitude toward women and toward feminine sexuality.

Christianity proposed a new order for a demoralized world, and it is clear that from the beginning it had a very strong appeal to women who entered the new faith on the same basis as men, confident that they were accepted equally with men as the children of one god, a god as solicitous for their souls as for the souls of their husbands. Christianity thus offered the fragmented, divided woman of specialized function — mother *or* sacred prostitute *or* concubine *or* courtesan *or* mistress — a new wholeness. Christ himself was surrounded by women who played important roles in his life: "And many women were there [at the crucifixion] beholding from afar off which followed Jesus from Galilee, ministering unto him." "And the women also, which came with him from Galilee, followed after, and beheld the sepulchre, and how his body was laid." The most important of these women was Mary Magdalene, the prostitute, next to His mother, the woman closest to Christ: witness at His crucifixion, watcher at His tomb. "It was Mary Magdalene, and Joanna, and Mary, the mother of James, and other women that were with them, which told these things unto the apostles." The two Marys, running to spread the news given them by the angel, were met by Jesus who said to them, "Be not afraid: go tell my brethren that they go into Galilee and there they shall see me."

Christ cured many women ". . . of evil spirits and infirmities, Mary called Magdalene, out of whom went seven devils, and Joanna, the wife of Chuza, Herod's steward, and Susanna, and many others, which ministered to him of their substance." It was to Mary and Martha, sisters of Lazarus, that Christ is accounted to have first declared, "I am the resurrection and the life: he that believeth in me, though he were dead, yet shall he live . . ."

Martha's sister, Mary, took a ". . . pound of ointment of spikenard, very costly, and anointed the feet of Jesus, and wiped His feet with her hair: and the house was filled with the odour of the ointment."

We have in the Gospels different versions of what is apparently the

same symbolic episode, washing the feet of Christ, clearly a potent act of humility and expiation. At the supper before His trial and crucifixion, a woman anointed His head with oil. In Nain, when Christ visited the house of Simon, a Pharisee, a prostitute came with the alabaster box of oil that appears in the accounts of Matthew and Mark ". . . and stood at His feet behind Him weeping, and began to wash His feet with tears, and did wipe them with the hairs of her head, and kissed His feet and anointed them with ointment." When the Pharisee protested at the effrontery of a sinner touching a holy man, Christ took the occasion to deliver a little sermon, ending with the familiar words: "Wherefore I say unto thee, Her sins, which are many, are forgiven: for she loved much . . . and He said unto her, Thy sins are forgiven. . . . Thy faith hath saved thee: go in peace."

If Christianity were to redeem women to their full humanity, it obviously had to deal with feminine sexuality. The honored place of Mary Magdalene, the forgiveness granted at least one other repentant prostitute, the episode of the washing of Christ's feet, all have to do with the theme of redeemed sexuality. Christ's own celibacy is, of course, the supreme symbol of this transcendence. When celibate orders of monks and nuns appeared in the fourth and fifth centuries, there was already a long Christian tradition of mortification of the flesh by desert hermits like Simeon Stylites. The monastic orders represented, among other things, the fact that it was possible to live fruitful and rewarding lives without sexual relations. Indeed, it might be argued that sexuality could only be put in its proper context when it was dramatically demonstrated that the celibate life was not only possible, but that it had a potency of its own and that the sublimation which it represented could be used to the benefit of human society as well as to the glory of God. The effort, of course, was not always successful, and one conspicuous line of Christian thought is morbidly obsessed with sexual fantasies. Saint Jerome spoke of woman as ". . . the gate of the devil, the path of wickedness, the sting of the serpent, in a word a perilous object." The conquest of those more or less indiscriminate sexual appetites which formerly, through fear and desire, had so narrowly defined the position of women in the ancient world was the precondition for the development of Western civilization. The partnership of men and women was based on repression of female sexuality outside of the institution of marriage and the at least nominal acceptance by men of the monogamous marriage as the only proper outlet for sexual energies.

To the Greek *eros,* which was primarily self-love and self-gratification, was added the Christian *agape,* the disinterested, self-sacrificing love of the individual for God and, of course, of God for man. Christ sacrificed His life to redeem a humanity which He loved. It was the *agape* that the nun felt for Christ when she was married to Him in her initiation. Erotic love was, inevitably, mixed with the *agape* and thereby given a new dimension (for instance, it gave the compilers of the New Testament a rationale to describe the Songs of Solomon as songs of *agape* in praise of Christ).

The notion of *agape* entered the Church through the love feasts or communions of the early church where the members of the congregation, men and women without distinction, ate a sacred meal together to symbolize their partnership in the work of redemption. Women held church offices and preached the good news of the new covenant. There is no question that the Christian marriage took on a dignity and importance that marriage had not had in the pagan world. The church, from the beginning, viewed sexual intercourse as being directed exclusively toward procreation. It was not that every sexual union should produce a child but that husband and wife should never lose sight of the fact that their otherwise essentially selfish lovemaking should always bear the possibility and responsibility of producing offspring, children, like themselves, of the Heavenly Father. So while the fathers of the early church inveighed against fornication and adultery, against all sexual relations outside of marriage, they were as much concerned with the character of sexual relations within a Christian marriage and they clearly wished to inhibit them as much as possible, or perhaps better, to subordinate them to God's work in the world. Saint Gregory put the issue in classic Christian terms: "When not the love of producing offspring but pleasure dominates the act of intercourse, married persons have something to mourn over in their intercourse."

Such an attitude may be uncongenial to us today, but it was the basis of the modern family since it placed children at the center of family life. It should also be pointed out that the emphasis of the Church on intercourse for the production of offspring was also a way of encouraging women, by taking control of their bodies, to assert their independence. The monk was a man who took on a celibate life to prove his devotion to Christ by sublimating those aspects of life so highly valued by the nonreligious. The situation was somewhat different with a woman. She had been used, since the fall of matriarchal society, by man to produce his children and serve his erotic needs. To deny men the opportunity to use her for their own purposes and to do this in a context that enhanced her value was a primary act of emancipation.

Saint Paul's injunctions against fornication are often pointed to by modern critics as marking the beginning of a repressive and puritan attitude toward the joyful expression of *eros*. "Flee fornication," Paul wrote to the congregation of Christians at Corinth: "Know ye not that your body is the temple of the Holy Ghost which is in you, which ye have of God, and ye are not your own? . . . It is good for a man not to touch a woman. Nevertheless, to *avoid* fornication let every man have his own wife, and let every woman have her own husband." Husband and wife have power over each other's bodies, not over their own, in the sense that they may not abuse their bodies, or give them to others. Neither should they practice continence within marriage except for prayer and fasting. In Paul's opinion it was better to remain single like himself. But if Christians ". . . cannot contain, let them marry; for it is better to marry than to burn." Paul's attitude toward marriage is best understood in the light of his conviction that "the time is short," the end of the world is near, and all the energy of Christians is needed to prepare themselves, to complete the conversion of the rest of mankind and before the fateful hour. Yet at the same time Paul seems to condone sexual relations between lovers: ". . . if any man think that he behaveth himself uncomely toward his virgin, if she passes the flower of her age, and need so requireth, let him do what he will, he sinneth not: let them marry."

Paul's general anxiety about sex and marriage is in part that of a bachelor, in part that of a prophet who foretells the end of the world, in part that of a man well acquainted with the weaknesses of the flesh and the threat they posed to piety and order in the new faith. The anxiety has certainly remained as a persistent thread through Christian thought, manifesting itself with varying degrees of intensity in different epochs of the Christian era. What Christianity preached was a new harmony of the self — that the body was the dwelling place of the Holy Spirit and was thus not to be abused or profaned, of husband and wife as one flesh, a union not to be violated in the name of simple appetites.

There was little in the latter period of the Empire to encourage any change in attitude on the part of the fathers of the early Church. Public licentiousness was more often the rule than the exception, and we know from the letters of Paul and the writings of the fathers that the Christian community was not immune.

I would not wish to imply that the insistence of Christianity, following the Jewish tradition, in restoring fragmented woman to wholeness solved the problem of feminine sexuality. Saints, monks, Christian mystics, and holy men continued to be obsessed with it and ordinary mortals to struggle with it as best they could.

With the collapse of the Roman Empire, a new social order had to be devised. For a time the Western world was in a chaotic condition; gradually what we refer to as the Middle Ages took form — a highly structured, feudal society, a society of "lions" in Pareto's term, a warrior society which was at least nominally Christian and had to come to terms with Christian dogma on, among other things, the position of women.

Beside the Church itself the two types that dominated medieval society were the monk and the knight. It is hardly necessary to point out that a world of chronic and endemic disorder, of violence and savagery, on the one hand, and monastic austerity on the other was not one congenial to the feminine spirit. By and large we hear only of noble ladies, queens and duchesses and princesses. They "knew well enough that they were not mistresses of their situation, that men regarded them as loot or merchandise, as objects openly and secretly traded among themselves, as prizes sometimes taken by stealth. Lands, men and crowns might flow from such golden booty. In feudal society marriage was an important political and commercial transaction . . ."[1]

Many women escaped from being pawns in dynastic struggles by taking a nun's vows and found in their convents a refuge from the bloody contentions and insatiable appetites of the masculine world.

In the convents able and energetic women found important careers. As one historian has put it:

"No institution of Europe has ever won for the lady the freedom and development that she enjoyed in the convent in the early days. The modern college for women only feebly reproduces it. . . . The lady-abbess . . . was part of the two great social forces of her time, feudalism and the Church. She was treated as an equal by the men of her time. . . . She had the stimulus of competition with men in executive capacity, in scholarship, and in artistic production . . ."[2]

Women with their bent for the practical and specific were at a serious disadvantage in a world where everything was absorbed into the ideal type and individuality had no play. The first important breach in this aggressively and arrogantly masculine world was made by Peter Abelard (1072–1142) who questioned the formal structure of Platonic thought that characterized the intellectual life of medieval Europe. Early in his career he had a love affair with a young girl, niece of a prominent cathedral canon in Paris. The lovers were apprehended and the family reacted with the brutal forthrightness of the age by, as Abelard wrote in his autobiography, "cutting off those parts of my body with which I had done that which was the cause of their sorrow." Héloïse entered a convent and she and Abelard began a remarkable correspondence on Christian life and doctrine. Their romance, perhaps because of its tragic outcome, captured the imagination of medieval Europe and provided, in its Platonic character, a model for all such romances down to Dante's *Divine Comedy*. Their necessarily sublimated love was the perfect background for their intellectual and spiritual affinity. In the new human order which Abelard dimly envisioned, women would be the partners of men, not their creatures.

Ironically, Abelard's remorseless opponent, Bernard of Clairvaux, a theological conservative, also contributed to a more exalted position for women by encouraging the cult of the Virgin. This cult, beginning as a movement to soften some of the rigors of Christian doctrine by offering Mary as an intercessor, ended by virtually taking possession of the Church. Bernard was a pioneer in that arduous journey of the soul through the dark corridors and strange bylaws of man's interior life. If Abelard espoused skeptical reason and in doing so shook the whole stiff but rickety structure of the twelfth-century Church, Bernard, by dramatizing the psychic life and insisting that man held fast to Christ by faith and by emotion, stimulated a tradition of Christian mysticism that included a number of great female mystics and that remains a vital theme in twentieth-century Christianity.

It was primarily to Abelard, however, that we owe the spirit which flowered in the tradition of courtly love. In Heer's words, Abelard presented his contemporaries "with the idea that the type of the New Man was to be found in Woman: hers was a higher form of manhood, refined in soul and spirit, capable of conversing with God the Spirit in the inner kingdom of the soul on terms of intimate friendship."[3] Abelard called attention to the importance of women in the life of Christ and, perhaps most significant of all, he elevated Mary Magdalene as the symbol of redeemed sexuality to a position of first rank among the followers of Christ.

Frederick Heer sees that strange fusion of *eros* and *agape,* of erotic love and Christian asceticism, as culminating in a revolt by the noble ladies of the twelfth century, led by Eleanor of Aquitaine, against ruthless masculine domination. The anxiety of the Church about feminine sexuality as well as the rituals of knighthood had made sodomy (which included most sexual aberrations but more especially homosexuality) the most common vice of the age among members of the courtly class. After Eleanor's separation from her second husband, Henry II of England, she established her court at Poitiers in a thoroughly feminine atmosphere surrounded by like-minded ladies, her daughter Marie among them. Attracting young noblemen, she and her coadjutors set about "ennobling this turbulent, tempestuous crowd of young men by curing them of their uncouth habits and educating them to higher things by example, precept and ideas."[4]

Love was the agent of this reform; not the wilder shores of love, but passion controlled and molded by the lover's mistress. Eleanor charged a young chaplain with the task of drawing up the rules of the game of love and his code, when completed, contained thirty-one articles. The queen and her ladies sat as judges in a grand assize of love where the *arrêts d'amour* involved such questions as whether a man loved his lady as the "law" required. This exotic pageantry spoke most eloquently of the determination of strong-minded women to force from men some acknowledgment of the feminine side of social life. It represented also the endless tension in the nominally Christian world between sacred and profane love. The nobles of Europe were infatuated by the game. Troubadours appeared in every court to compose epics celebrating courtly love. It has been estimated that between 1150 and 1250 there were over a hundred troubadours of whom twenty were women. In these *chansons* and *romans* significant numbers of women for the first time challenged masculine performance in an area of the arts. After all it was, in essence, *their* game. In Huizinga's words, "When . . . unsatisfied desire was placed by the troubadours of Provence in the centre of the poetic conception of love, an important turn in the history of civilization was effected. Love now became the field where all moral and cultural perfection flowered."[5]

The *romans,* the greatest of which was the *Roman de la Rose,* an agonizing refinement of desire, were as formalized as a minuet. A married woman, most typically a queen, and a knight, usually of her husband's court, fell in love because of a potion taken by mistake. They were thus entangled through no fault of their own. But once so desperately involved they could not escape their fate. They suffered agonies at their betrayal of the king, their liege lord. They were pursued by his vengeance. They found help from a sympathetic monk or cleric. They prayed to God for help and they received certain signs and intimations that He was not unsympathetic to their plight and generally, in the end, as in the case of Tristram and Iseult, they died, sometimes with their love unconsummated.

Unfulfilled desire was often the major theme. Dangerous trysts, perilous and hasty meetings, interminable separations — these were the fate of the unhappy lovers. As Heer puts it, "the theme of the great romantic epics is initiation, dedication, metamorphosis and absorption into a higher and fuller life, at once more human and more divine. . . . The remedies prescribed for the man who has strayed a thousand times into the jungle of his immature passions are woman, 'nature,' *mysterium* . . . A woman is always at hand to transform and ennoble a man."[6] One can hardly read these tales, so touching and so naïve, so passionate and so similar, with feeling that they represent classic archetypes, psychodramas by means of which a whole society struggled to assert a higher vision of man's common life and, primarily, of the relationship between men and women. In the search for the Grail we seem to have a representation of the mother symbol that carries us back to the Eastern cults of Cybele, Isis, and Mithras. The two disprized lovers of the *romans* play out, again and again, the theme of sublimated sexual passion. Above all, they are not triflers; they are victims, the antithesis of casual seducers. Their passion is unqualified, heedless of all law or restraint. They are guilty in a formal sense, but innocent in their hearts. Since God understands this, if the world does not, they are often able to withstand ordeals intended to disclose their sin. The selflessness, the self-forgetting, the self-sacrificing nature of this love is, directly or indirectly, derived from the Christian conception of *agape*. Courtly love gives us for the first time in literature the image of the spiritualized woman, the woman as reconciler and channel of grace. In every epic God's presence is felt in ways that are not merely formal but which express the yearning for reconciliation.

The highest expression of courtly love is also the last, Dante's. In the *Divine Comedy* the poet sets out guided by Virgil, in Dante's view the greatest spirit of the ancient world. But his beloved Beatrice accompanies the two men and replaces Virgil in the sacred wood at the end of the ascent of Mount Purgatory to guide him through paradise, explaining to him obscure points of Church doctrine, the Christian view of free will, the nature of divine love, bringing him at last to the snow-white rose of paradise, the end of his journey. Startled by her departure, Dante celebrates her as the one who has brought about his redemption:

> *Of all that I have looked on with these eyes*
> *Thy goodness and thy power have fitted me*
> *The holiness and grace to recognize.*
>
> *Thou has led me, a slave, to liberty,*
> *By every path, and using every means*
> *Which to fulfill this task were granted thee.*
>
> *Keep turned toward me thy munificence*
> *So that my soul which thou hast remedied*
> *May please thee when it quits the bonds of sense.*[7]

The effects of the dream of courtly love on the Western imagination have been incalculable. All modern notions of romantic love stem from that tradition, all inclinations to see women as creatures containing a special spiritual power, as distinguished from the dangerous and often hateful erotic power, owe a considerable debt to that ideal. Fitfully and imperfectly and perhaps unfortunately reconciled with the Christian view of marriage it has also been the foundation of the romantic movements of the eighteenth and nineteenth centuries.

One of the indices of continuing sexual tensions among the lower levels of the population of late Medieval and early Renaissance Europe is doubtless to be found in the records of the witchcraft frenzies which swept over Europe. As Trevor-Roper has pointed out, we are often inclined to think of the period from the Renaissance on to recent times as a period when a more rational order was making itself evident, when darkness and superstition were being enlightened, when a new humanism was making itself felt as the precursor of the modern age. But in the sixteenth and seventeenth century witchcraft broke out like a terrible epidemic. The madness of persecution flaring up early in the fifteen hundreds blazed like a raging fire for the next hundred and fifty years. Witches suddenly began to swarm through all of Europe, burning hayracks, holding witches' Sabbats, consorting with the devil, working mischief and destruction everywhere. The most learned theologians and scholars recorded their comings and goings and affirmed their authenticity. Thousands of old women, lubricating themselves with devil's grease made out of the fat of murdered infants, slid through cracks and keyholes to make their airborne journey to a witches' Sabbat. Specialists in witchcraft located eight hundred meeting places in the province of Lorraine. Twelve thousand witches were believed to have assembled for meeting in southwest France; often they came to such gatherings with their demon-lovers in attendance.

At the gatherings the devil himself appeared, sometimes in the form of a bearded man, sometimes as a goat or a toad. The witches danced to music made from bones and skulls, enjoyed sexual orgies with their demons or ate meals that might consist of boiled children, corpses, bats and other tasty bits. Bizarre and horrible as witchcraft persecutions were it is notable that they were directed primarily at women. Not a few men, priests and civil officials, were charged and burned as witches but the vast majority were women and a very considerable number confessed, without torture, to being members of that dark sisterhood.

It is possible that a relation existed between witch-hunts and the surplus of women over men, between the reconstruction of women's social and occupational roles in the late Middle Ages and the intense anxieties produced by a prolonged and painful transition from the medieval to the modern world. Mass persecutions were not a new phenomenon in the sixteenth century. The witch craze remains inexplicable; but central to its fantasies was the notion of intercourse with the devil, in masculine or feminine form depending on the sex of the witch. It is hard not to see in these hideous illusions the same anxiety about feminine sexuality that gave rise to the earliest taboos. In the poor creatures who confessed themselves witches there was clearly a profound disturbance of their own psychic life, perhaps the consequence of their desperately ambivalent position in a disintegrating society.

The flowering of scholarship in the Renaissance extended to women, many of whom shone as poets and critics. Isotta Nogarola was famous for her literary knowledge. She and others like her won "the highest honors for their sex in every department of science, art, and learning . . ." Cecelia Gonzaga read the Gospels in Greek at the age of seven and contemporaries believed that Cassandra Fidele of Venice deserved to rank with the great Pico della Mirandola. The universities which were opened to them at the end of the Middle Ages gave them doctorates and appointed them to some of their most distinguished faculties. In the words of Jacob Burckhardt "there was not the slightest hesitation among the Italians of the Renaissance in according the same literary and even philosophical instruction to sons and daughters . . . The education of the woman of rank, just as well as that of the man, sought the development of a well-rounded personality in every respect. The same development of mind and heart that perfected the man was necessary for perfecting woman." The Renaissance also produced a number of books on the accomplishments of women throughout history. At the same time much of the sophisticated intellectual life of the age took place in the salons of famous courtesans and in ducal courts, little in the circles presided over by wives.

It is tempting to argue that the seeds of the Protestant Reformation were to be found in the teachings of Peter Abelard, and the emancipation of women in his famous romance with Héloïse. The latter proposition may, in fact, be more defensible than the former. Although the romance of Abelard and Héloïse conformed almost too neatly to the ideal of courtly love, its deeper significance lay, ultimately, in the fact that Abelard treated his beloved as a person of dignity and consequence in her own right, perfectly capable of entering and sustaining an intellectual exchange of considerable sophistication. Almost four hundred years later, Martin Luther, Augustinian monk and priest-professor, formally launched the Reformation by nailing his theses to a church door in Wittenberg. But the finality of his break with Rome was perhaps better symbolized by his marriage to a nun.

The Reformation might thus be said to begin with one of the most important marriages in history. Luther's doctrines of free election, justification by faith, public worship in the vernacular, salvation and grace; his attack on papal authority and the sale of indulgences and his translation of the Bible into German were all acts of profound revolutionary import. They made an opening in the crust of a decadent society through which poured the dammed-up energies of a new age. Luther's marriage was a highly dramatic episode in itself. A classic romance, it stated in effect that the most fruitful life was not to be lived in the seclusion of the monastery or convent but in the world with all its conflicts and complexities. For those who embraced the new faith the carefully maintained forms and orders of the old world fell away, no longer relevant.

The reformers' determination to return to the practices and spirit of the early Church meant discarding a structure built up over fifteen centuries. As far as the status of women was concerned it meant taking on the attitudes of the Pauline age when women were full partners in furthering the Lord's work and when marriage was a covenant the purpose of which was the production of young Christians and the preservation of Christian family life. Included, of course, in Luther's teaching, were the strictures against sexual relations outside of marriage, but omitted was the almost pathological fear and even hatred of women that was sometimes found in the patristic writers of the fourth century, most notably Jerome.

The rejection of the authority of Rome and of the priesthood as the necessary mediator of God's word meant that with the Scriptures available in the common tongue, the family itself became a small congregation with the father assuming the priestly role. Learned ministers expounded Protestant doctrine in interminable sermons but much emphasis was placed on family prayers and Scripture reading. In Protestant countries and in reformed communities and congregations virtually all traditional relationships with institutions and between people were reordered: the attitude of individuals toward contractual obligations, education, the agencies of government, law and theology. Prior to the Reformation, the great majority of Europeans had their position in society fixed for them by their place in some kind of corporate structure or series of structures — church, guild, commune, province. Furthermore they were sustained by an elaborate system of consolation created by the Roman Church which represented the primal aspects of life in a rich and intricate symbolism. All this was stripped away by the Reformation. Residues of course remained, but where they survived they were absorbed or transmuted into the new order.

It is the reordering of family relationships that most interests us here. Many of the functions heretofore performed by the feudal lord, by the church, or by the state fell upon, or were preempted by, the family. The father's priestly function overshadowed his classic role in providing for the perpetuation of the family name and estate through a male heir who, as a reinforcement of the father's ego, had been traditionally, the beneficiary of the best resources that could be mustered by the family; formerly all other aspects of family life had taken second place to the need of the father to provide for his succession. In the radical reordering of family life the priestly father could not prefer one member of his family, or "congregation," over another. All must be equally precious. God was not interested in distinctions of sex and had never suggested that one sex was more precious to him than another. Indeed Abelard had argued as long ago as the twelfth century that, if there was to be a Divine preference, at least so far as Christ himself was concerned, the preference might indeed turn out to be for the woman rather than the man. Dante's

Divine Comedy reiterated the point. No one in Paradise ranked so high as Beatrice except, of course, Mary herself.

The consequence was that Protestant fathers took a direct responsibility for the education of their daughters. They had to be taught to read in order to enjoy the benefits of the Scriptures; when salvation might depend on literacy, education took on a new urgency. Fathers and daughters thus entered into a novel relationship out of which daughters acquired a new sense of personal dignity and worth. They were no longer simply dutiful and self-effacing servants of their masters, fathers or husbands, they were the children of God, precious in his eyes and filled with heretofore undisclosed or barely-hinted-at potential.

In all other societies, in all other cultures, in all other times in history, women, whether courtesans, concubines, wives, domestic slaves, priestesses, prostitutes or mistresses, had been relegated to an essentially feminine sphere. Indeed, we can see today in twentieth-century Italy or India, or Brazil or Iran the same intimate and separate feminine world where the decisive female relationships are with others of her sex, with mothers, grandmothers, and aunts. The Reformation thus revolutionized many of the existing notions of the world and the relation of the individual to it. Nowhere was its effect more radical and decisive than in the position of women within the family and, subsequently, in the wider community.

It is a cliché to say that the Reformation produced a new human type — the aggressive, self-confident, autonomous, inner-directed man, capable of organizing his environment with remarkable skill and energy. But it is less often recognized that this new type of man had his feminine counterpart and that the decisive element in her evolution was her relation as daughter to the priestly father in the reformed family.

Rome produced the noble and exalted mother, the Roman matron. The Hebrews, learning to exist as a people, surviving by means of their common history, overcame the threat of pagan goddesses, "internalized" the sanctions of customary law as a system of morality, and gave "the daughters of Zion" a place of dignity and consequence in Jewish life.

Catholic Christianity "spiritualized" the monogamous marriage by elevating the woman as wife and, in the figure of the Virgin Mary, created a new female archetype, a popular deity, a goddess free of the terrible ambiguity of an Ishtar, Cybele or Isis; the eternal loving and forgiving mother. Reformed Christianity drew forth a new facet of feminine multiformity — the daughter. We thus see woman fully represented — Hebrew woman, Roman mother, Catholic wife, Reformation daughter.

3

Colonial America

We thus come, after what has perhaps been an inordinately lengthy preamble, to the American species of that larger genus, woman. The English men and women who settled the first American colonies were, with the exception of some (but by no means all) of those who established themselves in Lord Baltimore's Maryland, Protestants of one stripe or another. Many were perfectly orthodox members of the Anglican Church, but a critical minority, in most cases the planners and promoters as well as the initial settlers, were radical or left-wing Protestants, most typically Separatists (Plymouth), Congregationalists (Massachusetts), Quakers (Pennsylvania), or Presbyterians.

The principal difference between the Separatists and the Congregationalists was that the Separatists, being for the most part simple people in very modest circumstances, had no stake in the Anglican Church or in the English "establishment" and thus wished to separate themselves from the Church as a corrupted and irredeemable body. The Congregationalists, on the other hand, had in their ranks a number of persons of education and social standing. They wished to reform the Anglican Church and, if their chances of doing so seemed less good with each passing decade, to protect themselves so far as possible from overt persecution by remaining at least nominally within the Church of England. These left-wing agitators against the

forms and doctrines of the English Church were generally denomi-
nated Puritans because of their claim that they wished to purify the
Church of all remaining popish doctrines and rituals. The Puritans
who came to Massachusetts Bay were a comparatively pure strain of
the Reformed Church. Moreover, by starting a new society in the
wilderness, they were able to give effect to Reformation doctrines in
the organization and governing of the new communities to a degree
impossible in England where they remained a persecuted (albeit
mildly) minority and had constantly to compromise with the *status
quo*. It is thus in *New* England that we can observe the working out
of the logic inherent in the teachings of the reformers, especially
Calvinists, for the Puritans traced their theological descent from the
Genevan rather than from Luther.

It is clear that the Puritans who came to America brought with
them the conception of the role of women and the family that we
have already described. In addition, since the early communities were
thoroughly rural, an ideological predisposition to regard women as
people of worth in their own right was reinforced by the need for
their contributions to the farm economy. Since women were in great
demand and short supply as wives and mothers, their value was correspondingly enhanced. A farmer without a wife was, needless to say,
severely handicapped.

An emigrant from Switzerland wrote from South Carolina to his
brother: "We have provided well for our single women, who con-
sisted of 13 persons. They have all been favorably married. In the old
country they would not have had such good fortune . . . poor
females who are of scanty means should come to America if they are
virtuous and sensible. They will get along nicely inasmuch as all can
make their fortune, for here men do not care for money as they do in
Switzerland."[1]

And George Alsop of Maryland declared that "The Women that
go over into this Province as Servants, have the best luck as in any
place of the world besides; for they are no sooner on shoar, but they
are courted into a Copulative Matrimony, which some of them (for
aught I know) had they not come to such a Market with their Vir-
ginity, might have kept it them untill it had been mouldy. . . ."[2]
and Nicholas Cresswell called the same state "a paradise on Earth for
women. . . . That great curiosity, an Old Maid is seldom seen in

this country. They generally marry before they are twenty-two, often before they are sixteen."[3] However, the functioning of the law of supply and demand could not, in itself, have guaranteed status for colonial women. Without an ideological basis, their privileges could not have been initially established or subsequently maintained.

The saints (which is simply to say the believers) of the Massachusetts Bay colony had hardly established their simple settlements when the colony was riven by a bitter theological dispute. Anne Hutchinson was the product of a classic Puritan family. Her father, Francis Marbury, was a vigorously dissenting minister, a man so contentious that his bishop declared in a rage that he was "a verie Asse, an idiot, and a foole." "By my troth," the furious prelate declared, "I thinke he be mad, he careth for no bodie."[4] One of Anne's most recent biographers (of which she has had, it might be said, an uncommon number) describes her relationship with her father as an unusually strong one. The eldest girl in a family of thirteen children, she married a man "of very mild temper and weak parts . . . wholly guided by his wife," who confessed himself to be "more nearly tied to his wife than to the Church."[5] William Hutchinson's "parts" were not so weak but that he was able to sire fifteen children by Anne.

It has been the custom of both male and female advocates of the feminine cause to seize on Anne Hutchinson as a forerunner of the women's rights movement — as a courageous and independent lady, a pioneer in the fight against the rigid and repressive theology and practice of New England Puritanism. There is no doubt that she was a person of unusual force and intelligence. John Winthrop spoke of her as "a woman of ready wit and bold spirit," and more frequently as "fierce." She was, in fact, as rigid and contentious as her opponents and the doctrine she espoused, her antinomianism (anti-law), was related to heresies as old as the Manicheanism of the fourth century and the Cathari of the twelfth. She maintained that only those seized by the Holy Spirit were qualified to preach and, in essence, that she herself was the proper judge of those who were in the covenant of grace. She declared a number of the most prominent and respected ministers of the Puritan community to be under a covenant of works and therefore unqualified to speak the word of God. Moreover, those who were in the covenant of grace were not to be held to the law, hence were antinomian, or anti-law. The surprising thing is not that the Puritan leaders tried to root out a dangerous heresy but that this doctrinaire and intractable woman could muster to her cause a large number of the most important men in the colony, among them a visiting dignitary, Sir Henry Vane, who was elected governor of the colony on what was, essentially, a pro-Hutchinson platform. Equally remarkable was the patience with which the orthodox faction, led by Governor Winthrop, dealt with this contumacious lady.

The episode kept the Bay colony in an uproar for several years, and whatever else it may or may not reveal about the Puritan temper, it offers us a vivid example of the new woman, a woman who was beyond any question a product of the reformed radical Protestant family, of the new relationship between father and daughter with the extraordinary access of feminine energy and initiative that resulted from it. If Anne Hutchinson was neither a liberal innovator nor a precursor of the woman's rights movement, she was an example par excellence of the potency of daughterhood, the first feminine historical figure in the American colonies (if we pass over Virginia Dare), and thus quite rightly cherished by the champions of her sex, if usually for irrelevant or muddled reasons.

In order for Anne Hutchinson to play out her brief but intense drama she had to have a degree of confidence and self-assurance that marked an entirely new stage in the emergence of women. She could only have acquired such confidence from a family in which a priestly father took pains to educate her and in the process to bestow upon her a spirit as fiery and obdurate as his own. Beyond that her mission would have had no chance of success if she had not been addressing herself to a very particular audience, an audience which was not ruled by the familiar notion that a woman's place was in the home. To be sure, her opponents made such a charge but it carried no weight with her masculine adherents who saw nothing untoward in her behavior nor anything inappropriate in being instructed by her and in placing themselves under her leadership.

In considering the Puritan marriage we should not be distracted by what seems to the modern mind a perhaps excessive anxiety about sexuality. I hope it is clear by now that such anxieties are not peculiar to any one culture, religion, or historical era. Whether the problem is dealt with by incorporating it into religious rites or by repression, it

remains. Yet it might be well at this point to take note of Calvin's doctrines in his *Institutes of Christian Religion.* "Since man was created in such a state as not to live a solitary life," he wrote, "but to be united in a help-meet; and moreover since the curse of sin has increased this necessity, the Lord has afforded us ample assistance in this case by the institution of marriage — a connection which he has not only originated by his authority, but also sanctified by his blessing. Whence it appears that every other union, but that of marriage, is cursed in his sight; and that the conjugal union itself is appointed as a remedy for our necessity, that we may not break out into unrestrained licentiousness."[6] Marriage is thus conceived of by Calvin primarily as an antidote to masculine sexuality.

Calvin follows loyally, but with a clear ambiguity, the admonitions of Paul. Continence is indeed the highest state, but it is "a peculiar gift of God" conferred on only a few. It would therefore be presumptuous for the ordinary Christian to aspire to it. No one should aspire to a celibate life who is not confident that he has the strength of will to resist his animal impulses. For those who are by nature incontinent, marriage is the means of "curing their infirmity." On the other hand, marriage is not itself a field of unchecked lust. It "must not be contaminated by libidinous and dissolute intemperance. For if the honour of marriage conceals the shame of incontinence, it ought not on that account to be made an incitement to it." Marriage, like all relations in life, should be "regulated by moderation and modesty and not break out into the vilest lasciviousness."[7]

What is striking about Puritan marriage is the degree of mutuality that characterized it. The preservation of the Puritan community superseded the more traditional concern with male succession; it was God's word which must be perpetuated, not a male succession. Marriages were thus not contracted, and while law required that a suitor obtain the permission of his intended's father, the law was seldom invoked. Piety was more important than property, although the latter undoubtedly remained an important consideration with some of the more materialist saints. For perhaps the first time in history, young men chose their brides and brides their husbands.

The Plymouth colony even had its own Romeo and Juliet. Governor Prence had bitter opponents in the Howland family who attacked his administration and were in turn harassed by the authorities. The governor discovered to his rage that a Howland son was secretly courting his daughter, Elizabeth. Young Arthur was haled into court and fined £5 for "inveigeling" the girl. The young people remained faithful to their love, and seven years later Arthur Howland was again brought to court for having "disorderlie and inrighteously endeavored to obtain the affections of Mistress Elizabeth Prence." Again he was fined and put under court order to desist. Finally the old man yielded and the couple was married.

Since lovers had often to delay their marriages, the Plymouth colony instituted a medieval practice known as pre-contract. Under its terms a couple might appear before two witnesses and declare their intention of marrying. Thus betrothed, they were allowed a remarkable degree of privacy and liberty. Pre-contract was in fact a kind of semi- or trial marriage, and sexual intercourse "in time of contract" was clearly distinguished from fornication.

It is clear enough that most Puritan marriages originated in physical attraction. The frequency of premarital intercourse is astonishing to the modern mind, but the important fact is that by far the majority of such incidents took place under the pre-contract or between couples whose intention it was to marry and who considered themselves betrothed. We have also, through diaries and letters, the records of innumerable Puritan marriages that were true "romances," marriages in which husband and wife experienced a relationship which was, by and large, a new kind of human encounter. They chose each other with a minimum of parental interference and came together as equals. As husband and wife their love often deepened into a passion far stronger than sexuality, although, surely, a strongly disciplined but nonetheless powerful sexuality lay at the center of many married relationships. The extraordinary freedom granted by the Puritan community to its boys and girls undoubtedly had its roots in the sense that they were all bound in a sacred covenant. In most societies young females have been closely confined and jealously guarded for fear that they might, through a love affair, be spoiled for an advantageous marriage, or, only slightly less serious, might marry an inappropriate suitor. The family, especially the father, had a vested interest in a proper marriage which he had no intention of leaving to chance, which is to say to the unpredictable workings of

feminine emotions. Among the saints, however, there were, technically, no undesirable alliances. Assuming, as they must, that a saint was a saint, piety and industry were far more important than family or wealth.

At least in theory. In practice, of course, the Puritans were undoubtedly quite conscious of the difference between advantageous and disadvantageous marriages. And when I speak of the Puritan marriage as involving "a new kind of human encounter" I do not mean to suggest for a moment that there had not been throughout history a very great number of deeply loving marriages, rich in all the particular pleasures of the married state. By the same token there were obviously many bitter and destructive marriages in Puritan communities. But at their best Puritan marriages did reveal heretofore undisclosed potentialities in this classic relationship.

A few specific examples should suffice. Anne Bradstreet was the daughter of Thomas Dudley, one of the leaders of the great Puritan emigration from England to New England who took great pains with her education. She was married at sixteen to Simon Bradstreet and came with him and her father to Massachusetts Bay, settling eventually in North Andover and raising a large family. Between domestic tasks, faithfully performed, she wrote learned poems on subjects popular in her day — the seasons, the four monarchies, Divine love. These were published in England in 1650 under the title *The Tenth Muse Lately Sprung up in America. Or, Severall Poems, compiled with great variety of Wit and Learning, full of delight.* It is, however, in her lyrics that Anne Bradstreet speaks most vividly and touchingly —"Before the Birth of One of her Children"; on the occasion of her house burning down, on her own reflections on her poems and in her charming love lyrics to her husband:

> *If ever two were one, then surely we.*
> *If ever man were loved by wife, then thee.*
> *If ever wife was happy in a man,*
> *Compare with me, ye women, if you can.*
> *I prize thy love more than whole mines of gold,*
> *Or all the riches that the East doth hold.*
> *My love is such that rivers cannot quench,*
> *Nor ought but love from thee give recompense.*

Thy love is such I can no way repay;
The heavens reward thee manifold, I pray.
Then while we will, in love let's so persever,
That when we live no more we may live ever.

In another poem she compares her absent husband to a sun gone from her sky: "My chilled limbs now numbed lie forlorn:/ Return, return, sweet sol, From Capricorn./ In this dead time, alas, what can I more/ Than view those fruits which through thy heat I bore?"

Her lyric poems were published in Boston in 1678 after her death under the title, *Several Poems Compiled . . . By a Gentlewoman in New England*. That poems so sensuous and so intimate were considered suitable for publication was perhaps as significant as the fact that they were written at all. Passionate love poems from a wife to her husband, a wife who bore eight children and, in all the terrible rigors of pioneer life, preserved inviolate her faith and good spirits, were a new phenomenon. Again they tell a great deal about the quality of the Puritan marital relation, for they could only have been composed in a time and a place where romantic love had finally been brought within the confines of marriage. The Puritans were realistic enough to perceive that they could neither banish sexuality (or concupiscence as they called it) nor confine it entirely to the married state. What they could and did do was to surround it with certain taboos and effectively subordinate it in marriage itself. Premarital sex was, in fact, a kind of apprenticeship for marriage. As such it could not damage the social fabric of the community. The true field of erotic love was, plainly enough, marriage. But even in marriage it was an expression of a higher love, not an end in itself.

Jonathan Edwards, America's greatest theologian, was the architect of the remarkable religious outpouring, the Great Awakening, and the source of religious movements as diverse as Unitarianism and evangelistic revivalism. Edwards entered Yale when he was thirteen. Seven years later, after a visit to New Haven, he took note of a young lady of that city "who is beloved of that Great Being, who made and rules the world, and that there are certain seasons in which this Great Being, in some way or other invisible, comes to her and fills her mind with exceeding sweet delight, and that she hardly cares for anything, except to meditate on him — that she expects after a while to be

received up where he is, to be raised up out of the world and caught up into heaven. . . . There she is to dwell with him, and to be ravished with his love and delight forever. . . . She has a strange sweetness in her mind, and singular purity in her affections; is most just and conscientious in all her conduct; and you could not persuade her to do any thing wrong or sinful, if you would give her all the world. . . . She . . . seems to be always full of joy and pleasure; and no one knows for what. She loves to be alone, walking in the fields and groves, and seems to have some one invisible always conversing with her."[8] The description was of his future wife.

Four years later Edwards married Sarah Pierrepont who bore him ten children, eight of them daughters. His wife's capacity for ecstatic religious experience had a strong influence on Edwards's own teachings and beliefs. Although he never attained such states himself, he used her accounts of her ecstatic experiences to defend the extreme emotionalism of the Great Awakening, concealing her identity but otherwise using her own words.

Many similar examples of husband and wife relations could be given. All wives were not poets like Anne Bradstreet or saints with the spiritual gifts of Sarah Edwards, but such marriages seem to have been more often the rule than the exception. Most important, they were a possibility. The marriage of John and Abigail Adams, a life-long romance, is perhaps the best known of such unions. Since both were classic letter writers and since they were frequently separated, we have a treasury of letters between them. We have many such correspondences between husbands and wives in colonial New England which reveal a degree of intimacy, a respect for each other's minds and spirits, and a delight in each other's company that are seldom to be found earlier, and that by the mid-nineteenth century have become rare indeed.

The perfect trust and intimacy, the "mutuality" that characterized so many Puritan marriages, did not sustain itself very far past the era of the American Revolution. American marriage seems to have suffered a drastic loss of morale as the nineteenth century wore on. But daughterhood proved to be a more solid and enduring relationship, resistant to changing styles of life and the increasing pressures on what sociologists call the "nuclear family."

The most notable New England wives were, with few exceptions, the daughters of vigorous and devoted fathers. One has the impression, moreover, that many families were distinguished by an unusual number of bright and energetic girls. Jonathan Edwards, as we have noted, had ten children, eight of them girls. Ezra Stiles, the president of Yale University, had seven children, of whom five were girls. Edwards and his wife took special pains with their daughters' education, and they were bright and able girls. Most of them married ministers, two married college presidents, Timothy Dwight of Yale and Aaron Burr of the College of New Jersey (later Princeton). Another was betrothed to the brilliant young David Brainerd and died a few months after his premature death.

In three generations of feminine descendants of Edwards, the emphasis on daughterhood persisted. Esther Burr, an intelligent and energetic woman, evidently passed on to her son, Aaron, a solicitude for the proper education of daughters. Burr's preoccupation with the training of his remarkable daughter, Theodosia, was almost an obsession. While she was still in her teens, she was known for striking beauty and her intellectual attainments.

Ezra Stiles was keenly interested in the intellectual capacities of women and took special pains over the education of his five daughters. He also recorded in his diary the occasion when he had examined Lucinda, the precocious twelve-year-old daughter of the Reverend John Foot, and given her a certificate testifying to her learning. But for her sex she could have entered the freshman class at Yale. Stiles's own daughters had displayed no marked intellectual gifts but were "accomplished and refin'd." The Otis family produced a number of talented daughters, the most famous being Mercy, daughter of James Otis and wife of James Warren, a delightful letter writer, a mediocre poet and a skillful if contentious historian of the American Revolution. Another Yale president, Thomas Clap, married a girl of fifteen when he himself was twenty-four. She bore him six children in eight years and died before the age of twenty-four. His description of her is a classic recipe for a Puritan wife:

"She was a woman of Such great Prudence and Discretion in the Conduct of Her Self and Affairs, that She Was Scarce ever taxed with taking a wry Step. She was Diligent neat and Saving, and always endeavoured to make the Best of what She had. . . . She Endeavoured to treat Her friends and Al that Came in as Handsome and

Decent . . . as She Could: and was very Kind and Compasionate to the Poor and all In Distress. She was Adorned with great Humility and meekness, and Never Affected anything above Her Degree, or to Appear fine or gay, but Rather Like the Holy women of old who Trusted in god She Put on the ornament of a meek and quiet Spirit which is in the Sight of god a Pearl of great Price. . . . She exceeded all Parsons that ever I Saw in a most Serene Pleasant and Excellent Natural temper. . . ."[9] Of Clap's six children by his first marriage only two, Temperance and Mary, survived. Clap took great pains with their education and both married distinguished men.

Margaret Fuller, one of the most gifted women of the nineteenth century, wrote a classic account of such a father-daughter relationship when she described a certain Miranda (probably Margaret Fuller herself), a woman whose father treated her "as a living mind," rather than a toy. "He called on her for clear judgment, for courage, for honor and fidelity; in short, for such virtues as he knew." Thus nurtured "she took her place easily, not only in the world of organized being, but in the world of mind." At home in the world, she encountered men as equals and was secure in her own self-dependence. Questioned about the grounds of her achievement, Miranda replied, "My good father's early trust gave the first bias, and the rest followed, of course."[10]

When Cotton Mather (1663–1728), that most prolific of New England divines and himself the father of ten children, six of them girls, set out to write a tract for women, he addressed it to the Daughters of Zion. *Ornaments for the Daughters of Zion* which was published in Cambridge in 1692 was a manual for "the female sex . . . in every age and state of their life." Much of it is, as we would expect, a sententious warning against the vanities of the world, but it is emphatic in its insistence on the worth and the capacities of women.

The book opens rather gloomily with a passage from Proverbs: "Favour is deceitful and Beauty is vain; but a Woman that feareth the Lord, She 'tis, that shall be praised." It is the "Brightest Honour" of women that God "when the Fulness of Time was come, . . . sent forth His Son, made of a Woman." As Eve had been the agent of man's undoing, Mary had the glory "of bringing into the

World that Second Adam, who is the Father of all our Happiness."
In pagan times and even among Christian writers, Mather wrote
"The petulant Pens of some Forward and Morose Men, have sometimes treated the Female Sex with great Indignities. . . . Whole
volumes have been written to disgrace that Sex, as if it were, as one of
those unnatural Authors calls it, The meer Confusion of Mankind."
But Mather assures his feminine readers that they are "among The
Excellent in Earth." And if "any men are so wicked (and some Sects
of men have been so) as to deny your being Rational Creatures" they
can be readily refuted. There is abundant evidence of the honorable
position of women of the Bible both as writers of Scripture in the
Songs of Deborah, Hannah, Ruth, and of Bathsheba to "her darling
Solomon" ("Divers women have been the Writers of His Declarative
word"), and as actors in its dramas.

In Greece women were "Tutoresses . . . to the famous old Pro-
fessours of all Philosophy." The daughter of Pythagoras wrote a
commentary on her father's work. Hypatia taught the liberal arts and
"wrote some Treatises of Astrology" and Sarocchia was "Moderatrix
in the Disputations of the Learned men at Rome. The three Corinnae
'equal'd if not Excell'd, the most Celebrated Poets of their Times'
. . ."

And then there were "the ladies of Olympias, or Trota, whose
Physical skill, was the wonder of the Universe," Rosuida "who
compiled the Lives of Holy Men and Paphilia who Penn'd no
Despicable Histories," besides legends of female saints and martyrs.
All of which should make it clear that women were not only precious
to the Lord but reasonable and rational creatures with gifts no less
conspicuous than those of men. "Our Daughters," Mather wrote,
were coworkers in the great task of "the Building of the Temple" of
the Lord. In that divine architecture they were "Gates of Palaces."

Not only were there more women than men in the church, and they
its most loyal supporters, but the channels of redemption were more
readily available to women than to men. A woman may have been,
like Mary Magdalene, "remarkable and notorious for sin" and yet
win forgiveness. In addition they have more time "to Employ in the
more immediate Service" of their own souls.

Wives should be the thrifty, faithful, patient, devoted "help-
meets" of their husbands. In addition to music, language, weaving,

and the domestic arts, they would do well to study "arithmetic, accounting and such business matters" as will enable them to assist their husbands. The wife beater was "a mad wretch, a divil" to be counted not better than "a Murderer of his Father or his Mother."

A consequence of the inherent worth of women was that their lives had meaning beyond childbearing and rearing. Indeed, spinsters, widows, and those wives who were "naturally barren" might find an easier path to "Spiritual Fruitfulness . . . in all good Works of Piety and Charity." Without the responsibilities of a large family and the burden of constant pregnancy, they could devote more of their time to the service of the Lord. The point was a crucial one. For a Christian woman childbearing was not the only proper and honorable function. She was valuable in herself as the handmaid of Jesus Christ. The worth and importance of women *outside* of marriage, or of maternity, had to be established if they were to be properly valued *within* marriage.

The familiar anxieties about feminine sexuality show clearly enough in Mather's rather feverish strictures against those shameless women who indulged in "artificial paintings" of their faces. Beauty was a gift of God and a temptation to vanity. The beautiful woman should be especially careful "lest . . . she deceive Unwary men, into those Amours which bewitching looks and smiles too often betray the Children of men . . . into." (Mather's ideal of feminine beauty was "a good Proportion and Symmetry of the parts and a skin Well Varnished . . . a Good mixture of Blood and Flegm shining through a good Skin.")

"The wicked Harlots of old," he reminded his readers, "Painted their Eyes . . . their Eye-browes and Lids, which they ting'ed with a Preparation of Antimony to Blacken them, and Beautify 'em." Makeup should be avoided because an "Adulterate complexion" may easily become an "Adulterous" one. Perhaps the most telling argument, the practical one, was that makeup would "corrupt, corrode and poison" the face and thereby "hasten Wrinkles and Ruines thereupon." Beauty spots were "Tokens of a Plague of the Soul," and women should be careful not to expose their back and breasts lest they "Enkindle a Foul Fire in the Male."

It was, above all, "Promiscuous Dancing" that was the particular snare of the devil. In dancing where men and women "Leap and

Fling about like Bedlams" all the "Ten Commandments of God" were broken (an assertion which Mather unfortunately failed to explicate). That it should be dancing that seemed to pose such a terrible threat to morality and good order seems to require some explanation. Dancing as a symbol of sexual license could be taken to measure the Puritan's anxiety about "letting go." The strains imposed on the psyche by the arduous task of establishing a new social order were so severe that the faithful had to be treated like soldiers in wartime. Without the bounds set by custom and convention, without specific orders and proscriptions, without systems of consolation, the individual ego carried a staggering load. The Puritan had to keep spiritually "in training," an athlete of the will, a warrior of the Lord. It seems clear that dancing was so terrifying because it began with "abandon," with touch and with movement that might well lead to the toppling of all barriers and restraints. It was associated, in the Puritan imagination, with the bacchanalian orgies of pagan mystery cults.

Cotton Mather's sexual anxieties were rooted in his own experience. He had known all the torments of the flesh. After the death of his first wife, one of the women of his congregation, a lady with a very "aery" reputation, had come to his study and besought "me to make her mine." That Mather was seriously beset is clear enough from his secret diary. His desire for the lady was so great, he confessed, that he was tempted to suicide, to doubt of his vocation, to fear for his soul, and to "self-pollution" and other "indecencies."

In New England a basic index to the status of women might be found in the punishments meted out for breaches of the code governing sexual behavior. It has already been pointed out that in spite of their fulminations against immorality, the Puritans, through such devices as the pre-contract and the popular folk custom of bundling, adopted in fact an extremely practical if not permissive attitude toward sexual irregularities, provided they did not imperil good order in the community.

Formal violations of the code in the records of numerous Puritan churches were so frequent as to make clear that premarital sexual relations were the rule rather than the exception, at least through the middle of the eighteenth century. As early as 1647, William Bradford was complaining of "not only the incontinence between persons unmarried, for which many both men and women have been punished sharply enough, but some married persons also," and a reforming synod meeting at Boston in 1679 took special note of the "hainous breeches of the seventh commandment." The church records of Groton show that of two hundred persons owning the baptismal covenant in a fourteen-year period, sixty-six confessed to fornication. In one three-year period, sixteen couples were admitted to full communion and of these, nine confessed to sexual intercourse prior to marriage.

Punishment was the same for both men and women under church discipline. They were expected to stand up in meeting and confess to their breach of the seventh commandment. If, in the judgment of the congregation, the confession was a genuine act of contrition, the offenders were forgiven. Only the obdurate were punished by excommunication. In Sharon, Massachusetts, everyone confessing to fornication between 1747 and 1766 were continued in full communion, and of the sixty-four members of the congregation in this period, sixteen made such confessions. In Danvers, of one hundred and sixty-four men and women admitted to communion in the last half of the eighteenth century, thirty confessed to fornication. In Deerfield between 1732 and 1780, forty-one couples made such "antenuptial confessions." In the small community of Westfield, Massachusetts, the church, in a period of nine years, dealt with twenty-five persons accused of fornication. This must have included a sizable portion of the unmarried population old enough to have sexual relations. In one congregation violations of the seventh commandment occurred so often that the church had a printed form which the offenders simply filled in: "We, the subscribers, trusting that by the Grace of God we have been brought to see the evil of sin in general and especially of the sins we have committed, do now humbly, we hope and penitently confess the sin of fornication of which we have been guilty; and this we do from a conviction that it is reasonable to bear public and marked testimony against scandalous offenses whereby we may be instrumental in weakening the bonds of society and injuring the cause of religion."

Confessions, of course, came not only prior to marriage. If the bride was not visibly pregnant, the confession might follow the birth of the child; indeed, if the child was born less than seven months after the marriage, the presumption was that it was conceived prior to wedlock, and confession was required. Such lapses were not confined to Puritans of lesser rank. Among the confessed fornicators in Plymouth were Isaac Robinson, grandson of the famous Leyden preacher who launched the migration; Peregrine White, the first child born in New England and the stepson of Governor Winslow; Thomas Cushman, son of Elder Brewster's successor, and the two sons of Assistant Governor James Cudworth. In the early days of the Plymouth colony, fornication outside of the pre-contract was a felony under law punishable by the stocks, the lash, three days in jail, and a £10 fine. Sexual relations with Negro slaves or Indians were not infrequent. Goodwife Mendame of Duxbury was sentenced "to be whipt at a cart's tayle through the town's streets, and to weare a badge with the capital letters AD cut in cloth upon her left sleeve. . . . And if shee shall be found without it abroad, then to be burned in the face with a hott iron."[11]

Adultery was a far more serious matter, of course, since it might more readily weaken the bonds of society. It struck at the stability and health of the family and fortunately was much less frequent. The real threat was promiscuity on the part primarily of women. The woman who made herself an object of overt sexual attraction to men aroused understandable anxieties.

Even in Puritan towns there were women who "walked disorderly." Most were simply girls of an accommodating disposition. They, too, were called before the congregation. Sarah Westcott of Marblehead was charged by her mother with violations of five commandments, the seventh among them. She had additionally abused the church, threatened her mother's life, and attempted suicide. Sarah refused to appear to answer the charges against her and was suspended. Two years later, after hearing that she had given birth to her third illegitimate child, she was called to account again and once more refused to heed the summons. For three days the minister visited her to try to explain the seriousness of excommunication. Finally she showed up at meeting unrepentant, to declare that she had been "hunted like a partridge upon the mountains as David was by Saul," and to denounce the church as not of Christ but of St. Paul, whose injunctions against sexual relations outside of marriage were obviously repugnant to her. When the minister undertook to summarize her heresies, she interrupted to dispute him and then left the church in the midst of excommunication proceedings.[12]

Prudence Parker, who was charged with "walking disorderly" in Falmouth, was borne with for several years because she was judged to be of an unsound mind. She disappeared before the congregation could decide on appropriate action; twenty years later she appeared in meeting to confess her ancient sins and was restored to full communion.[13]

That the churches were often long-suffering with sinners is suggested by the case of Lydie Foster of Haverhill. Suspended in 1732 for having her second illegitimate child, she proceeded to have a third for which she gave "a very penitent" confession which was received with some skepticism. The arrival of a fourth baby resulted in her excommunication, "And after all this, Having this winter, again been delivered of *another* Bastard Child," the record reads "twas voted unanimously that She is worthy of a *Solemn Censure of Excommunication.*" Six years later, Lydie, now Mrs. Dowe, made a confession and was accepted back into communion.[14]

It should be said that there were few cases of prostitution. A twelve-year-old Boston boy was reprimanded in 1653 for patronizing a bawdy house, but it was well into the eighteenth century before Boston was troubled by professional whores.

In colonial New England divorce required an act by the legislature of the colony, the Court of Assistants. But divorces were granted to men and women upon petition where the dissolution of a marriage seemed the only reasonable course. In Massachusetts the records mention forty divorces granted in the years between 1639 and 1692. Annulment was easier, and marriages were most often annulled because of the sexual inadequacy of husband or wife. Impotence and willful abstention from intercourse were typical grounds for annulment, but we have a secondhand report of a case where a wife sought annulment on the grounds that her husband's member was of insufficient size.

A classic example of Puritan practicality was demonstrated in the case of a charge of adultery brought against a wife and her lover. When the case came to trial the wife argued that her husband was delinquent in his duties. He spent so much time hunting and fishing that her unsatisfied needs had driven her to adultery. The court accepted her argument and sentenced the husband, as well as the wife and lover, to pay a fine and sit in the stocks.

It was not until the end of the colonial era that the idea of a "suitable" or "proper" sphere of feminine activities began to emerge. Women were thought of primarily as wives or mothers and their functions defined positively in terms of these basic roles. There were, in the early years, very few negative definitions — that this or that activity was unsuitable or inappropriate for a woman to engage in. In consequence colonial women moved freely into most occupations in response to particular needs and opportunities rather than abstract theories of what was proper. Most frequently they took over a dead husband's or father's business, and we find them acting as shop-keepers (in very considerable numbers), teachers, blacksmiths, hunters, lawyers, innkeepers, silversmiths, tinworkers, shoemakers, shipwrights, tanners, gunsmiths, barbers, and butchers. Eleven women ran printing presses, and ten of these published newspapers in America before 1776.

That women were active in business and in crafts is suggested by a notice in a New York paper in 1733: "We, widows of this city, have had a meeting as our case is something deplorable, we beg you will give it place in your Weekly Journal, that we may be relieved, it is as follows. We are house keepers, pay our taxes, carry on trade and most of us are she merchants, and as we in some measure contribute to the support of the government, we ought to be entitled to some of the sweets of it."

Nor was it only in the towns of the Northeast that women played a man's part. William Byrd, surveying the Virginia–North Carolina boundary line, encountered "a very civil woman" who showed "nothing of ruggedness or immodesty in her carriage, yet she will carry a gun in the woods and kill deer, turkeys, etc., and shoot down wild cattle, catch and tye hogs, knock down beeves with an axe and perform the most manful exercises as well as most men in these parts."[15]

Women had no formal political rights in the colonies but they not infrequently mixed in public affairs. In Virginia women were active in Bacon's rebellion, and in Maryland Mistress Margaret Brent was "one of the most prominent personages in the colony" whose business and public activities "fill many pages of court records and suggest a career which the most ambitious of modern feminists might envy."[16] She was the executrix of Governor Leonard Calvert, and as executrix she quieted a rebellious contingent of Virginia soldiers and saved the colony from what might very well have been civil war.

In addition to acting as midwives, women had been allowed unlimited freedom in practicing "physick" and even "chirurgery." As late as 1785, the *Independent Journal* of New York (September 30) announced the arrival of a Mrs. Malcolm from Edinburgh "where she studied and practised Midwifery for a considerable number of years, and had the honour of attending several Ladies of the first rank in that City. She has recommendations from most of the principal professors of that art in Scotland, with a Diploma from the late Dr. Thomas Young, Professor of Midwifery in the University of Edinburgh." The course of study at Edinburgh was evidently an arduous one. A Mrs. Monroe, coming to America in 1796, stated that she had studied midwifery at the university for six years.

Rachel Bunker of Nantucket, in addition to leaving a hundred and thirteen grandchildren and ninety-eight great-grandchildren on her death in 1796, had assisted at 2,994 births, among whom were thirty-one pairs of twins. Mrs. Lucretia Lester of Southold, Long Island, who practiced from 1745 to 1779, was described as "justly respected as nurse and doctress to the pains and infirmities incident to her fellow mortals, especially to her own sex. . . . She was during thirty years, conspicuous as an angel of mercy; a woman whose price was above rubies. It is said that she attended at the birth of 1300 children, and of that number, lost but two."[17]

Judith Corey advertised in the *New England Palladium* as late as 1808 (March 4) that "she follows the Midwife and Doctress business; that she cures Burns, Salt Rheum, Canker, Scald-head, Fever Sores, Rheumatism, & the Piles."

When doctors began to crowd out midwives, they were attacked as awkward and brutal practitioners. An indignant newspaper editor wrote that the familiarities taken by men in attending pregnant women and those in labor were "sufficient to taint the Purity and sully the Chastity of any Woman breathing."

In the period of colonial American history from 1620 to the 1750's or '60's, Puritan women were figures of unquestioned worth and importance, partners with their husbands in the economy of the farm and in the redemption of Christendom. Even in the very different slaveholding society of the South, women enjoyed unusual prestige.* Where theoretical or more properly theological support was needed, it was found in the position of women in the New Testament and in the early Christian Church. The new human relationship between father and daughter was responsible in large part for the confidence and sense of worth possessed by Puritan women.

The seventh commandment states "thou shalt not commit adultery"; adultery is sexual relations of a husband or wife with someone to whom they are not married. The seventh commandment does not say "thou shalt not commit fornication," which is sexual relations between unmarried men and women. Premarital lovemaking was common in Puritan New England. Where it existed outside of the precontract and was discovered, it was punished but it was, nonetheless, accepted as a fact of life and a fact with its own practical utility. For a couple *destined to get married* to encounter each other in a direct physical way seems to have resulted in marriages in which the sensual aspect was of considerable if not primary importance. There was about Puritan society, in consequence, a directness, a practicality, a lack of hypocrisy and subterfuge, an absence of prudery in matters that affected sexual relations and the functions of the body that is unique, certainly, in American history. Much could be tolerated as long as the *social nature* of marriage was generally acknowledged.

Moreover, in a simple frontier society without any very clearly defined notions of the "role" of women, able and enterprising females moved quite easily and naturally into a wide variety of jobs.

By the end of the eighteenth century, however, this openness of American life had changed beyond recognition.

* When Dr. Alexander Hamilton, a Maryland physician, visited in Philadelphia in 1744, he commented on the "free and affable as well as pretty" women. "I saw not one prude while I was there." In the earlier history of the Virginia colony, the same kind of candor in language, in subject and in behavior was apparent. Talk was still "Anglo-Saxon" and often bawdy, and courtship was not yet surrounded by the intricate rituals and absurd formalities that later characterized upper-class relations between betrothed couples. Betsy Hansford was ardently courted by a young man whom she rejected. The rejected suitor begged the minister to intervene in his favor. When the Reverend John Camm pressed Miss Hansford, she told him she was in love with another man although she refused to tell his name. Urged by the Reverend Camm, she gave him a Scriptural passage — Samuel xii, 7. When the minister looked up the verse, he read "thou art the man." He married Miss Hansford.

4

The Great Repression

Into the Puritan Garden of Eden came the serpent of social distinction, of class and fashion. As colonial society became more urban in character, sharper class differentiations appeared, the prosperous middle class began to imitate English models and English styles. The essays of Addison and Steele provided a mirror in which the socially ambitious colonial hostess yearned to see herself reflected. The insidious notion of the fashionable woman migrated across the Atlantic and infected the emerging middle class in cities like Boston, New York, Philadelphia, and Baltimore.

Dress and etiquette rapidly became major preoccupations of the newly rich bourgeoisie. The importance of women diminished correspondingly.

When young James Wilson, who later played an important role in the framing of the Federal Constitution and was appointed to the Supreme Court, began a column with his friend, Billy White, in the *Pennsylvania Chronicle* early in 1768, he and White modeled their essays after the *Spectator Papers*. Their composite picture of the Visitant, their collective nom de plume, was that of a man of the world at home in any circle but "happiest in small companies; and those, I think, are the best when they are composed of near and equal number of both sexes." Indeed, the Visitant was particularly concerned with the fair sex and prided himself on his preference for "the conversation of a fine woman to that of a philosopher." Middle-class colonial America became much preoccupied with the character of cultivated life, with good manners, and social graces. Books of etiquette instructed young men and women on proper deportment. Most of these were infused with moral precepts as well as instructions on how to enter a living room or greet the hostess, how to sit and what to do with one's hands, appropriate topics of conversation, and so on. In the creation of a middle-class, essentially urban style of life, women who early had shared in the direction of farms and the rigors of pioneer existence, were expected to preside gracefully over drawing rooms. The Visitant, for example, boasted of frequenting "the company of the Fair Sex" and thus becoming somewhat of an expert on their "foibles" and "excellencies." "I have acquired a general acquaintance among the Ladies," he declared, "and the veneration I always discover for them encourages my fair companions to express their sentiments more freely."[1] It was, unfortunately, in tones such as these that much of the discussion of the position and role of women would be carried on for the next hundred years or so.

Yet the Visitant was a notably enlightened and liberal spirit. He insisted that the qualities of the feminine mind were all too seldom appreciated and that women were often treated as mere adornments and playthings for male vanity, their real merit concealed by fripperies and fashionable poses adopted to please callow men. The ladies of Philadelphia responded gratefully in verse.

> *Hail candid, gen'rous man, who'er thou art;*
> *Thy sentiments bespeak a noble heart. . . .*
> *Thee, who canst give to virtue praises due,*
> *We safely trust to lash our errors too.*
> *No keen reproach from satire's pen we fear,*
> *Of little minds, or painted toys to hear.*
> *You, Sir, with better sense, will justly fix*
> *Our faults on* education, *not on* sex.[2]

While most urban women capitulated to their diminished role, an older and more radical tradition prevailed in rural towns. John Adams, teaching in Worcester after his graduation from Harvard, was dismayed to find that two citizens of the community, Dolittle and

Baldwin, who were "great Readers of Deistical Books, and very great Talkers," were also "great Sticklers for Equality" between the sexes as well as between all members of society. Another "eccentric Character" of Worcester was Joseph Dyer who "carried his Doctrine of Equality, to a greater Extremity, or at least as great as any of the wild Men of the French Revolution. A perfect Equality of Suffrage was essential to Liberty," in Dyer's opinion. Adams asked if he would include the suffrages "of Women, of Children, of Ideots, of Madmen, of Criminals, or Prisoners for Debt or for Crimes."[3] This from the husband of Abigail Adams.

Toward the end of the eighteenth century, we find numerous lamentations about the decline in morals and the general tone of social life. Vanity, luxury, and display are taking the place of the older virtues of selflessness, simplicity, and piety. A contributor to the *Lady's Magazine* wrote, significantly, "If women would recover that empire which they seem in a great measure *to have lost* [italics mine] . . . they must change their present fashionable mode of living, and do what their grandmothers did before them, go often to church, and be well acquainted with their own houses."[4]

Young John Quincy Adams returned to New England in 1790 from three years in France to find that the girls of his native land were, variously, "superficial," "affected," and "simpering," with little interest in anything but dancing and talking scandal, in which, he wrote his mother, "they have attained great perfection." Indeed, he was moved to write a bit of doggerel on the young ladies:

> *The eye half shut, the dimpled cheek*
> *And languid look are cuts too weak*
> *To win the heart of any youth*
> *Who loves simplicity and truth.*

There was no doubt they were handsome enough, if all rather of one piece. There was in fact a kind of glut of pretty girls but too many of them were to young John Quincy "like a beautiful apple that is insipid or disgusting to the taste," as he wrote his mother. Abigail replied tartly that it was the fault of their education and of masculine expectations. Women were, by and large, what men wished them to be, and if American girls were giddy, frivolous, and affected, it was because American men apparently liked them that way.[5]

Even so liberal and enlightened a spirit as Benjamin Rush wrote to a young friend on the eve of her marriage warning her that "you will be well received in all companies only in proportion as you are inoffensive, polite, and agreeable to everybody. . . . Don't be offended when I add that from the day you marry you must have no will of your own. The subordination of your sex to ours is enforced by nature, by reason, and by revelation. . . . In no situation whatever, let the words 'I will' or 'I won't' fall from your lips till you have first found out your husband's inclinations in a matter that interests you both. The happiest marriages I have known have been those when the subordination I have recommended has been most complete. . . ." The ideal wife is "kind, obsequious, uncontradicting."[6]

Along with much freedom, Moreau de St. Méry observed among upper-class girls in Philadelphia a quite un-French prudishness, a "ridiculous . . . aversion to hearing certain words pronounced" and a bashfulness about bodily functions.

"American women," he wrote, "divide their whole body in two parts; from the top to the waist is stomach; from there to the foot is ankles." They were too modest to let a doctor touch their bodies and they could not even bring themselves, in some instances, to describe an ailment, like one young mother with an ulcerated breast who, too prudish to speak frankly to her doctor, described her condition as a pain in her stomach. At the same time, he was caustic about what he considered the "frigidity" of American girls and their lack of affection.[7]

The uneasiness about the use of basic Anglo-Saxon words is susceptible of two interpretations. If we assume that this squeamishness was missing in early Puritanism, we would then read the primness of the latter part of the eighteenth century as evidence of an increasingly restrictive attitude toward sex, the body, and bodily functions; as part of the effort to create an order of middle-class respectability, an effort which culminates in so-called Victorian morality. This reading would see the rise of taboo words as a by-product of the movement already described; part of an effort to suppress sexuality as constituting a threat to the emerging commercial and urban elite. What evidence there is, largely in the form of court records and letters, suggests that there was widespread use of such an explicit vocabulary among the lower orders of society and the same may well have been true in the period of which St. Méry writes.* There seems no question that the prudishness about bodily functions of which St. Méry speaks was not characteristic of the early period. The evidence, scanty as it is, does suggest a very decided change in attitude which we might expect to see reflected in the language. Certainly one of the ways in which a class defines itself is by developing an "appropriate" language which distinguishes it from other levels of society.

Julia Spruill, in her work on Southern women, noticed the same constriction in the role of women and in the way in which they themselves think of their role. "A comparison of petitions," she writes, "presented by the undaunted dames of the first years of the colonies with the requests of the more modest ladies of the next century reveals a consciousness of sex and an unnatural prudishness in the latter not observable in their pioneer grandmothers."[8]

The pairing off of boys and girls at an early age, which we have already commented upon meant inevitably an emphasis on youth unknown since classical times. This emphasis and the remarkable freedom allowed under the pre-contract survived as residues long after the specific circumstances under which they had developed had changed radically, to a time when they were, in a sense, thoroughly incompatible with the general mores of society.

The pattern of courtship and marriage which distinguished the classic Puritan community was dependent on a highly disciplined will and a remarkable degree of social cohesiveness. When the rigid and carefully articulated theological and social framework which supported these practices began to disintegrate, no effective substitutes were developed. In short, every other society has surrounded this

---

* Another possible explanation lies in what might be called the "sacramental" character of language for the Reformers. The Word, especially in the form of the sermon, was the channel of redemption. All the saints were enjoined to decent and seemly carriage and speech. A faithful man sought to talk with piety, eschewing blasphemy and coarse language. Much of Luther's own language was "anal," as Erikson and others have pointed out, and coarse and vigorous metaphors were not absent from Puritan sermons. But they were used calculatedly, not casually or blasphemously. Sweet speech and pious utterance — that was the language proper for one who walked with the Lord. Thus the classic four-letter words came under the same ban as all gross language, and when the religious taboos weakened they were undoubtedly superseded by social constraints, the basis of which was the sexual repressiveness of the new commercial and professional classes.

crucial episode (feminine puberty) with what were, at least from society's point of view, essential safeguards, safeguards designed to make the marriage subordinate to the larger purposes of the community. Whom a boy or girl married was never considered a purely private matter until the later years of the nineteenth century. It was certainly not so considered by American Protestants.

Freedom in the choice of a mate and in the courtship pattern was only allowable because the ultimate aims were universally agreed upon and the necessary social disciplines thoroughly internalized and vigorously enforced by the community. The consequence was that when marriage became an essentially private matter, of concern only to the parties involved, the institution was stripped of all the social supports and constraints which both enhanced and stabilized it. When a young man and a young woman entered into matrimony in the seventeenth century, they did so with the sense that they were serving a vital social and, indeed, religious purpose. They were enlisting in the service of Christ with the responsibility of producing more faithful Christians to carry on His work and with an almost equally important if mundane function in the community. The choice of a mate was personal but the marriage was notably public.

The diminution of the Protestant passion into the Protestant "ethic" meant in time that the marriage became as "personal" a matter as the choice of a toothpaste, and thus what was, at best, a complex and precarious union was deprived of the forms, orders, and social imperatives that had formerly helped to sustain it. For the first time in history the full weight of this inherently difficult relationship fell on the overburdened egos of husbands and wives. The effect of this radical change was felt perhaps more keenly by the woman than by the man.

In traditional societies the woman had the help of the society or at least of her family in securing a mate. She had a dowry which, if she was abused or abandoned, would, in most societies, be withdrawn from her mate. She had the protection of a father and often of brothers determined to defend the honor of the family in her person. She often had specific laws to safeguard her in her function as wife and mother. If she was homely or lumpy, she might still, by the payment of a larger dowry, secure a husband who was not, in any event, particularly concerned about her appearance; he did not look on her primarily as a sexual partner or as an object of romantic interest but as the mother of an heir. Such a girl was thus freed of a considerable burden of anxiety. She was, at least in theory, free to grow as she might wish to. Of course, there was a training appropriate to her function, but as long as she had mastered the modest domestic arts expected of a wife, she was under little pressure to devise strategies for attracting a husband. The problem was that her role was so severely circumscribed that she had little opportunity to develop her potentialities. However, within the limits of her role, she could achieve a genuine individuality.

The Reformation, then, had placed courtship and marriage on a new basis. The reformers considered it debasing to treat women like a commodity to be traded away. The new relations between men and women were successful because they were supported by powerful sanctions. But when these withered away, women were left to secure husbands *on their own*. This meant that they were, for virtually the first time in history, in the position of adapting themselves to the prevailing masculine notion of what constituted desirability in a woman. There was, as a consequence, a new possibility for romantic love in marriage, but also the woman, as prospective wife, was at the mercy of the man's quite arbitrary stereotype of the desirable female. This turned out to constitute for many middle-class women the severest kind of inhibition, and it resulted in that trivializing of women that St. Méry and other foreign visitors commented on as characteristic of a certain type of American girl. It meant for the woman a preoccupation with courtship that distorted other values and aims. The irony of the situation was that at the same time that the girl was left to attract and secure a man by her own devices she was forbidden by the mores of American middle-class society to employ any overt sexual allurements. The ancient division between the woman as mother on the one hand and the woman as object of sexual passion reappeared as a prominent aspect of the urban middle and upper class. St. Méry noted in 1795 that Philadelphia had many houses of pleasure as well as free-lancing procuresses who arranged assignations, according to St. Méry's informants, with certain socially prominent young women who were generally known as models of propriety.

An additional pressure to suppress feminine sexuality came from the "spirit of capitalism." As de Tocqueville observed, "religious communities and trading nations entertain peculiarly serious notions of marriage . . . as the highest security for the order and prosperity of the household."[9] Paul Achard, another French visitor a hundred and fifty years later, noted that the American male profited from this "standardization of feminine fidelity, enforced by law." He was thus able to pursue money free from worry about his wife's chastity. In the East men had locked their women in harems to protect them. In America, for the same purpose, they were given "full liberty," but around them was "woven the barbed network of the law."[10] Capitalism required predictable behavior and an increasingly complex level of social organization. All passions were thus suspect because passions interfered with orderly procedures, with planning and with organization.* A considerable part of the Protestant will that in the seventeenth and early eighteenth centuries devoted itself passionately to God, now devoted itself passionately to money.

On the other hand, Puritanism had always stressed seriousness, decorousness, a restrained and austere demeanor. Laughing immoderately, speaking too loudly, being demonstrative, were all failings warned against by Puritan ministers. Such an attitude was tolerable when it was balanced by the directness and practicality of rural life, the warmth of large and affectionate families, and the support of the community. Transposed to a metropolitan setting and fused with an aggressive, expansionist capitalism, its repressive aspects undoubtedly did serious psychic damage to many Americans.

One of the consequences of the new middle-class moralism was an extended period of courtship which, among other things, enabled a girl to assure herself that no better husband was available. As repression came more and more to characterize the sexual aspect of the relationship between men and women, the extended courtship became a kind of test and a token of the purity of the love of the suitor although, in practical fact, it undoubtedly led, in many instances, to young men taking mistresses or finding an outlet for sexual urgencies with prostitutes or amiable serving girls.

---

* At the end of the eighteenth century, it was not considered unmanly for a man to weep openly (and of course in many societies it is not considered unseemly today), but by the end of the nineteenth century it was considered most inappropriate for an Anglo-American male to display extreme emotion, especially to weep.

We also find, increasingly, that young men and women were urged to choose sensible and agreeable mates of the same social and economic standing. Charles Carroll advised his son to select a wife "virtuous, sensible, good-natured, complaisant, neat, and cheerful in disposition; of good size, well proportioned, and free from hereditary disorders; and the same social rank and religion as he."[11] The wealth of prospective wives was almost as much a matter of concern to the groom as the prosperity of the husband to the wife. Governor Nicholson of Virginia believed that the decrease in the number of men of ability coming from England to America was due, at least in part, to the fact that while "formerly, there was good convenient land which were encouragement for men of good parts to come but now all or most of these lands are taken up and if there be any widows or maids of any fortune the natives for the most part get them."[12]

The number of cases where young men married wives in their sixties, seventies and, on several occasions, their eighties, suggests how little romance and how much material considerations had come to prevail by the end of the eighteenth century.

Captain Marryat, observing this aspect of American marriages, wrote that he considered it "on the whole . . . very fortunate that in American marriages there is, generally speaking, more prudence than love on both sides, for from the peculiar habits and customs of the country, a woman who loved without prudence would not feel very happy as a wife." That marriage was considered "a business or, I should say, a duty," seemed evident to him by the comparative ease with which engagements were broken off.[13] It may well have been that the captain was right, and it is clear that in certain segments of American society from the end of the eighteenth century to the present day, calculation rather than love has been the major element in marriage. In a society in which class lines have a low degree of visibility and in which a woman's social and even domestic situation is determined almost entirely by the man whom she marries, women with any instinct for self-preservation are apt to be somewhat calculating. They cannot afford to give themselves with heedless ardor to some well-set-up young man for fear a more promising one may come along tomorrow. Since they are all enthusiastic apostles of romantic love, they have to believe that every attraction is a consuming devotion while at the same time they realize very well that it is not.

Although the evidence seems to be clear enough that the relationship between the suitor and his fiancée and husband and his wife underwent considerable change, most of it unfavorable to the women, the father-daughter relationship remained a remarkably stable one, and there is considerable evidence that it was the principal source of much of the energy and ambition that American women displayed, especially in the late eighteenth and nineteenth centuries.

Coincident, as I have suggested, with the diminution of the status of women, came increasing discussion about their proper roles. What had once been taken largely for granted now became the subject of argument and debate, of essays, books, and poems, and, indeed, of legislation, as men withdrew from women legal rights which they had earlier enjoyed. Thus, if the argument offered here can be accepted, American women, more particularly middle-class city dwellers (who were, to be sure, a small minority of the population), at the same time that they found courtship and marriage considerably less satisfying than they had been earlier, suffered an erosion of their position and their power in almost every other area.

As late as the American Revolution, there is much evidence that the marriages of most of the revolutionary leaders (and these are simply the marriages about which we know most because a large body of correspondence has been preserved) were notably happy and successful and, more important perhaps, were characterized by a respect on the part of the husband for the concern of the wife with political and social problems, an attitude that is, for the most part, missing from the correspondence between husbands and wives three-quarters of a century later at the time of another great national crisis, the Civil War.

By the end of the eighteenth century, the Protestant passion had, to be sure, dwindled to the Protestant ethic, at least in the more cultivated seacoast towns and cities, but the marriages of the leaders of the revolution had been made several decades before the outbreak of the war; the war, moreover, had heightened the political consciousness of those women whose husbands were caught up in the conflict. The talk of rights and freedom set at least a few ladies to reflections on the rights of their own sex. Many of them raised money for the Continental Army by soliciting from door to door, and others sewed shirts for the soldiers (and often embroidered their initials thereon).

Chastelleux was shown a room with two thousand two hundred soldiers' shirts made by the ladies of Philadelphia. To husbands campaigning in the Carolinas or moving from one congressional meeting place to another, wives provided a flow of intelligence from the home front.

Again, the classic example is to be found in the letters of Abigail Adams to her so-often-absent husband. But there were hundreds of other Abigails up to their necks in the political and military events of the conflict. Abigail Adams was not the only one to remind a husband that his rhetoric about the rights of the American colonists, and sometimes about the rights of man, was silent on the rights of women. When he and his fellows took up the question of freedom from Great Britain, Abigail teased John, might they not, quite properly, consider the independence of women? A new code of laws should not put "such unlimited power into the hands of husbands." Since all men "would be tyrants if they could," particular care and attention should be paid to the rights of ladies who might otherwise "foment a rebellion, and . . . not hold ourselves bound by any laws in which we have no voice or representation."

The teasing was prophetic, but Adams's reply was not encouraging. "I cannot but laugh," he wrote. "We have been told that our struggle has loosened the bonds of government everywhere; that children and apprentices were disobedient; that schools and colleges were grown turbulent, that Indians slighted their guardians, and Negroes grew insolent to their masters. But your letter is the first intimation that another tribe, more numerous and powerful than all the rest, were grown discontented." Adams's defense was that, although the men might nominally hold the power, Abigail knew very well that "We are obliged to go fair and softly, and, in practice, you know we are the subjects. We have only the name of masters, and rather than give up this, which would completely subject us to the despotism of the petticoat, I hope General Washington and all our brave heroes would fight."[14]

John Adams corresponded frequently with Mercy Warren in regard to her projected history of the revolution (when it appeared it enraged him by its accusations of monarchial sympathies on his part) and in matters of political theory. "The Ladies," he wrote incautiously, as the case would prove, "I think are the greatest Politicians that I have the Honour to be acquainted with, not only because they act upon the Sublimest of all Principles of Policy, viz, that Honesty is the best Policy, but because they considered Questions more coolly than those who are heated with Party Zeal and inflamed with the bitter Contentions of active public Life."[15]

It was as though the woman as sexual object having been incorporated in the woman as wife, the woman as woman (or, in Mary Wollstonecraft's words, the woman as human creature) was evaded by being made into a fashionable object. The triumph of the Reformation in restoring women to a position of worth seemed to be imperiled by a society which left the woman more vulnerable than she had been in societies which made no pretension to giving any recognition to her sex. It could at least be argued that Greek or Roman women within their particular "classification" — wife, courtesan, mistress, concubine — had a chance to achieve more personal satisfaction and a fuller and deeper kind of development than the upper-class urban women of England and America in the late eighteenth and the nineteenth centuries.

Men, having diminished the role and often the character of women to that of fragile, delicate creatures and having, thereby, repressed middle-class feminine sexuality, reverted to a polarized conception of sexuality versus motherhood akin to that of Greece and the Roman republic. However, conscious acknowledgment of such a bifurcation was obviously impossible. It ran counter to all the teachings of the Church, primitive, Catholic, or Protestant. Extramarital sexual encounters and arrangements must be clandestine.

By the late eighteenth century it was apparently not uncommon for men who could afford to to have mistresses and for those who could not to have recourse to prostitutes, or, in the case of Southern men, to the more readily available slave women. Since the strictest social sanctions were invoked against such relationships, and they were, when discovered, buried as quietly and discreetly as possible, we must base our judgment on the few cases that actually became public, assuming them to be representative rather than entirely eccentric; and, perhaps more important, on the prominence of the theme of what might be called sacred and profane love in nineteenth-century popular novels.

Increasingly for young unmarried males and married males of the middle and lower middle "socio-economic" brackets, prostitutes were the most practical and cheapest sexual outlets. In the larger cities they were notorious. George Templeton Strong speaks of the efforts of the mayor of New York to try to curtail "the scandal and offence of the peripatetic whorearchy" while admitting that nothing could be done to suppress the brothels. Keeping a mistress was a more dignified and humane solution, although not without its emotional trials. The most famous piece of eighteenth-century scatology was Benjamin Franklin's advice to a young man on choosing a mistress. While declaring that a mistress should only be acquired if a man could not contain his appetites and that marriage was "the proper remedy" for "violent natural inclinations," Franklin recommended an old mistress as being more discreet, experienced, and accommodating. Moreover, in "every animal that walks upright" the upper portions age more rapidly and more visibly than the lower, "so that covering all above with a basket, and regarding only what is below the girdle, it is impossible of two women to tell an old one from a young one." Therefore, "the pleasure of corporal enjoyment with an old woman is at least equal, and frequently superior; every knack being, by practice, capable of improvement." (This, of course, is what Kinsey says, too.) In addition, Franklin points out, "having made a young girl miserable may give you frequent bitter reflection; none of which can attend the making an old woman happy. . . . and lastly, they are so grateful!!"

When the philosopher recommended old women as mistresses "because there is no hazard of children," he spoke with some experience since he had fathered at least one illegitimate child of his own. The fact is Franklin was much preoccupied with "concupiscence" and inclined to a rather clinical approach. The *Advice* was undoubtedly written with tongue in cheek, and yet not entirely. Franklin was invariably more concerned with practical arrangements than moral subtleties; how the carnal affections might be "managed" rather than with any notion of romantic love.

The point of the transformation in sex attitudes can perhaps best be made by citing two episodes in a single family, episodes separated by some sixty years. When John Adams began to court Abigail Smith, there were, from the beginning of the relationship, frequent references to mutual physical attraction. Addressing Abigail as "Miss Adorable," Adams brought her a "draft" for "as many Kisses, and as many Hours of your Company after 9 o'Clock" as he might demand, on the grounds that he had "given two or three Millions [kisses] at least, when one has been received, and of Consequence the Account between us is immensely in favour of yours, John Adams."[16]

When a storm prevented Adams from traveling to Weymouth to be with Abigail, he wrote: "Accidents are often more Friendly to us, than our own Prudence. . . . Cruel, Yet perhaps blessed storm! Cruel for detaining me . . . and perhaps blessed to you, or me or both, for keeping me at *my Distance*. For every experimental Phyloso-pher knows, that the steel and the Magnet or the Glass and feather will not fly together with more Celerity, than somebody and some-body, when brought within striking Distance — and, Itches, Aches, Agues, and Repentance might be the Consequences of a Contact in present Circumstances."[17]

And again he wrote: "Patience my Dear! Learn to conquer your Appetites and Passions . . . the Government of ones own soul requires greater Parts and Virtues than the Management of King-doms. . . ."[18] Taking the lengthy and tedious cure for smallpox John Adams wrote his fiancée of his "vomits" and threatened "a minute History of Close stools and Chamber Potts."[19]

There is no way, of course, of knowing whether in a courtship extending over more than two years, John Adams and Abigail Smith had premarital sexual relations (though, as we have seen, they would not have been exceptional if they had), but it is plain enough that they made ardent and explicitly physical love and that they spoke and wrote to each other without prudishness.

Charles Francis Adams was a favorite grandson of John Adams. In 1827, when he was twenty, he began to pay court to a proper Boston heiress, Abigail Brooks. His assessment of her, committed to his diary, is hardly that of an infatuated youth. "She has," he noted, "many faults, arising as much from the education she has received as from her natural disposition. She seems to have been looked upon by the family as a darling and her feelings have always atoned for her hasty errors." She displayed an engaging frankness, and while not handsome had an expressive face. "On the whole," he concluded, "I think her calculated to make a person happy, provided he is aware of the duties which fall upon him."[20] Hardly the words of a young man swept away by romantic ardor.

Three months later Charles Francis wrote: "I do love this girl as I think a woman ought to be loved. Sincerely, fervently and yet with purity and respect. I can think of her in no other light. Other women have acted upon me in a voluptuous manner, to which I am unfortunately peculiarly susceptible, but I have never known one who has produced any respect before."[21]

Four months after he had first met Abigail Brooks and more than two months after he had asked her father's consent to their marriage, Charles Francis Adams wrote: "In the evening I went through one of those disagreeable scenes which occur sometimes in life. No man of sense will ever keep a Mistress. For if she is valuable, the separation when it comes is terrible, and if she is not, she is more plague than profit. Ever since my engagement, I have been preparing for a close of my licentious intrigues, and this evening I cut the last cord which bound me. What a pity that experience is *always to be learnt over and over by each successive generation*"[22] (italics mine).

The diary entries are, plainly, an epitome of the upper middle-class male's attitude toward sex and marriage in the nineteenth century. Charles Francis Adams was a New Englander, the son and grandson of two Presidents. He was educated at Harvard and was a devout and practicing Christian. The most striking fact about the final passage quoted is its matter-of-factness. Taking mistresses is something young men do, unwisely, to be sure, but most commonly. Discarding a mistress to marry a fine, pure-minded young lady who, reassuringly, arouses no voluptuous feelings, is always awkward and sometimes tragic.

John Adams might have had sexual liaisons with neighbors' daughters (though he was at some pains to deny that he ever had), but the notion of keeping a woman simply for the purposes of sexual satisfaction would not have occurred to him because in Adams's day women had not yet been divided into sexual partners on the one hand and wives-mothers on the other. By the time that Charles Francis Adams made his candid diary entries, it was clear that they had. The grandfather's marriage was based on mutual sexual as well as intellectual attraction between John and Abigail Adams; the grandson's most evidently not. Moreover, Charles Francis Adams took pride in the fact that sexual attraction was not involved; this indicated an entirely proper alliance.

The division of women into the two major categories, good and bad, is also represented in the popular novels of the nineteenth century. In many, if not most, of these the heroine was fair, chaste, docile, loyal, and uncomplaining. Pitted against her was a dark, voluptuous woman, a figure of sexual potency, full of depraved attractions. The heroine's lover was a tormented figure, torn between his animal appetites and his yearning for higher, purer things, represented by the fair one. The heroine of such novels was sternly opposed to anything with the vaguest tinge of "woman's rights." In the words of one heroine, women were "secondary objects of creation. . . . Nor have we any right to require of superior men an example of the virtue to which he would train us. . . . Our state of society is a dependent one, and it is ours to be good and amiable, whatever may be the conduct of the men to whom we are subjected." Helen Wells, in the *Step-Mother,* endorsed the axiom that the man was *"lord* and *master,* from whose *will* there is no appeal." The unmarried woman was an object of amusement or derision. Often, as in *Constantia Neville,* a "tall meagre female . . . a virago disappointed in the accomplishment of her favorite wish."

The perfect heroine was delicate as a flower, "fair," accomplished, but not vain or ostentatious about her talents, melancholy, much given to weeping, especially over the work of the "graveyard" school of poets; undefiled by any sensual impulse, of a charming innocence.

"The house of mourning, my dear Mary, is instructive," one such lady confided to a friend. "I would not exchange my present melancholy sensations, this sweet pensiveness which is far from being unpleasing, for all the giddy mirth I ever experience." Dr. Gregory's popular *Father's Legacy* warned females that "the possession of even an average share of vitality and animal spirits was something less than fashionable and more than feminine."

Isaac Mitchell in his best-selling book, *The Asylum,* touched the bottom of this preoccupation with decay. Contemplating the death of a young girl, the hero asked himself, "Must that heavenly frame putrify, moulder, and crumble into dust: Must the loathesome spider nestle on her lily bosom? The odious reptile riot on her delicate limbs! The worm revel amidst the roses of her cheek . . . and bask in the lustre of her eyes! Great God! What a thought! Alas!"

Beneath all this lurked, of course, a disguised but unmistakable sexuality. And as the pale and languishing heroine took the center of the stage, the dark lady of passion, of dangerous vitality, intrigue and wild desire hovered in the wings. Lilith, the temptress, the wanton, reappeared to menace the soft gentility of the home, to torment with her dark designs the chaste and delicate heroine, and in so doing to reveal the inexhaustible nobility of her character even to accepting as her own the offspring of husband and mistress.

The "lord and master" appeared most often in the character of a wayward child in matters of the heart. It was assumed that for all his innate superiority, he would err and stray, would follow the lure of profane love. The injured wife saw her straying husband less the offender than the victim. She wielded the terrible weapon of forgiveness with a soft implacability.

But the main point of all this was to confirm the notion that the world was made up of the good girls and the bad girls. The bad girls represented sexuality, the good girls purity of mind and spirit, unclouded by the shadow of any gross or vulgar thought. Outside of sentimental novels, the largest collection of "bad girls" were the prostitutes who collected in such alarming numbers in the larger cities. They posed a persistent and shattering dilemma for the good girls, especially those who wrote on the subject of women's place in society. "Fallen women" lay like a vast collective sin on the "Victorian" conscience. They mocked its most sacred pretensions and raised serious questions about the female sex itself. The general line taken by the advocates of woman's rights was that prostitution was the consequence of destitution.

Prostitutes were, in effect, women without means of making a living. Seen in this light they became ammunition in the battle for equality between the sexes. But it was clear that for some women, at least, the problem was not so simple. Beneath much of the writing on the subject by women is an evident uneasiness. They could never entirely suppress the suspicion that there were some women perfectly capable of making a decent living as domestic or factory workers or something better who simply preferred a life of sin. Certainly many wives needed no special wit to deduce that among the clients of these abandoned women were somebody's husbands, perhaps, on occasion, their own.

The knowledge of such intrigues was not, of course, as immediate and inescapable as it was to the wives of Southern slave owners. But that the only partly buried consciousness was there is indicated by the obsession of the popular novelists with the theme of masculine sexuality. The novels undoubtedly provided an essential solace for many of their women readers. They made endurable what otherwise might have been quite unendurable. By representing feminine sexuality as dangerous and evil (and chastity as blessed and honored), they reinforced respectable young women and anxious wives in their moral code. Chastity and virtue always triumphed if only through the generosity and acceptance shown by the wronged ladies to their erring men. The denouement of these works was often a scene in which a repentant husband or lover, kneeling in tears, confessed his weakness and folly and implored forgiveness from the angelic creature whom he adored with a refined and spiritual ardor untainted by any sensual desire. All this must have been as bad for the psyche of the husband as of the wife.

One American literary figure penetrated to the heart of this strange moral double-dealing, a world in which nothing was ever quite what it appeared to be, a world covered with dense layers of pretense. Flawed as it is, Melville's *Pierre* is one of the rare American novels in the nineteenth century that comes to grips with the problem. Pierre cannot cope with or understand his own emotions. Believing in and trying to follow the highest imperatives of his class and his society, he produces nothing but disaster and, finally, tragedy. He lives in such a tangle of conventionalized emotions he cannot tell fiancée, sister, or mother one from another. His mother's artful play is unconsciously seductive; his sister's importunings arouse in him feelings he cannot face; his fiancée's misery only deepens his confusion. The message of *Pierre* is that with falsity and sentimentality, the most honorable motives are simply paths to destruction. But *Pierre* stood alone. Few had read it, and those who did failed to understand it. It was *cri de coeur* unheeded in the cloying and overheated corridors of the century.

In summary it can be said that the adherence of the urban middle class to a stricter code of morality and the postponement of the age of marriage worked to the disadvantage of women. If it is the primary

concern of a girl to secure a decent mate, the permissiveness of the pre-contract gave her the best opportunity to attract a young man and place him under an obligation that the community would see to it that he made good on. She did not have to compete, as she did later, with women who had a specialized sexual function servicing the needs of young unmarried men, who, while waiting to marry "nice," i.e., sexually restrained girls, found relief from sexual pressures with accommodating and less inhibited girls of a lower social class or, where necessary, with prostitutes. There was little adultery and less prostitution in colonial America because the sexual drives of young men and women were met quite directly. Also it can be assumed, I think, that marriages to which sexual union was the prelude rather than the consequence were apt to be, as we say today, more compatible. The simple and rather novel fact seems to be that the Puritans, from whose sexual prudery we think ourselves in revolt, actually attained a healthier balance in sexual matters than Americans have achieved since.

If the fall from matriarchal society to masculine society was the first fall for women, an almost equally serious fall for American women, at least, may have been the fall from the uninhibited directness and practicality of Puritan sexual attitudes to the more sophisticated theories and repressive practices of their urban middle-class descendants.

A people who have a great task to perform have to be mustered up like an army; they must subject themselves to a rigorous discipline. This is the discipline of "thou shalt not" which has to be balanced by the imperative "thou shalt" of the enterprise itself. When the energy of the original mission is spent — the passionate "thou shalt"— the negative injunctions are left —"thou shalt not," and these become more onerous the further we move from the spirit of the founders, obsessed by the "thou shalt." This was the story of the Puritans. Convinced that God had commissioned them to redeem the world, they cheerfully submitted to the same cruel discipline that had enabled the children of Israel to become a people and conquer the land of Canaan. But the "thou shalt not" came, in time, to devour the "thou shalt." That is part of the story of the Great Repression and the revolt against it. People who have it in their power to live at ease in Zion are not inclined to accept a quasi-military discipline.

DAUGHTERS OF THE PROMISED LAND

The original passion of the Puritans had suffused life and all its relationships with its own severe beauty and remarkable power. The passion receded or, more properly, took new forms, and piety was replaced by moralism. That moralism served the social and economic needs of the rising middle class. Its effects on the psyche of Americans, men and women alike, were profound.

5

Some Attributes of American Women:
Foreign Perspectives

From the 1770's on foreign travelers viewed the American woman as they came later to view the Grand Canyon or the falls of Niagara, a phenomenon of the New World, a wonder of the age. They devoted pages of description and analysis to this novel creature. No memoir of an odyssey through the United States was considered complete without some particular attention to "the other sex." The ubiquitousness of such reflections seemed to a British journalist in 1908 to indicate "a vein of unusual significance, or at the very least of unusual conspicuousness." Observers had written numerous accounts of other nations and peoples with no more than a passing reference to women. "The European visitor to the United States *has* to write about American women, . . . because they seem essentially so prominent a feature of American life, because their *relative* importance and interest impress him as greater than those of women in the lands of the Old World, because they seem to him to embody in so eminent a measure that intangible quality of Americanism, the existence, or indeed the possibility, of which is so hotly denied by some Americans."[1]

As we read the accounts by foreign visitors a kind of composite portrait of American women emerges which must, I think, be given great weight. Undoubtedly certain clichés or stereotypes emerged quite early. Subsequent travelers, aware of the stereotypes, looked for them and found them. The earliest accounts, however, were written before the American woman had been identified and described. They preceded the stereotype and, indeed, established it. People like the Marquis de Chastellux, Brissot de Warville, and Moreau de St. Méry were practical men, sympathetic and intelligent observers. There is no reason not to take their accounts seriously. Among the subsequent visitors were a number of novelists and professional journalists — individuals like Harriet Martineau, Mrs. Trollope, Alexis de Tocqueville who were perfectly capable of penetrating existing stereotypes. Thus when we discover a remarkable degree of unanimity among a wide variety of visitors from different countries in different periods of American history, from the mid-eighteenth century to the mid-twentieth, it would seem to be a rather sophisticated form of naïveté to believe that they were not, generally speaking, coming as close as fallible human beings are able to come to the reality. In any event this chapter is concerned with the characteristics of American women (her character is something rather different) and our principal witnesses are foreign travelers.

All our foreign travelers agreed that American women were favored and flattered by American men, their needs dutifully attended to, their whims taken as law. But one traveler, Captain Frederick Marryat observed that intelligent women did not "consider themselves flattered by a species of homage which is paying no compliment to their good sense" but rather emphasizing their weak and delicate nature. "When men *respect* women," Marryat wrote, "they do not attempt to make fools of them, but treat them as rational and immortal beings and this general adulation is cheating them with the shadow, while they withhold from them the substance."[2] The caustic Harriet Martineau had similar reflections. "Indulgence," she observed, "is given [the American woman] as a substitute for justice." To Miss Martineau the situation of the woman in the United States was comparable to that of the Negro slave. The principal difference was that the indulgence of the slave was "petty and capricious" while hers was "large and universal." "While woman's intellect is confined, her morals crushed, her health ruined, her weaknesses encouraged, and her strength punished, she is told that her lot is cast in the paradise of women . . . Her husband's hair stands on end at the idea of her working, and he toils to indulge her with money." Frances Wright, the English reformer, agreed with her country-women. She noted the "delicate attentions" paid by the American husband to "the idol of his fancy," but deplored the constricted life that this pampered lady led.

A positive side of "the universal deference and civility" shown was the fact that they could "travel without protection all over the United States without the least chance of annoyance or insult. This deference . . . exists from one end of the Union to the other; indeed, in the Southern and more lawless states, it is even more chivalric than in the more settled. Let a female be ever so indifferently clad, whatever her appearance may be, still it is sufficient that she is a female; she has the first accommodation, and until she has it, no man will think of himself."[3]

Alexis de Tocqueville differed sharply from Marryat. The French-man did not agree that the attitude of American men toward women trivialized them, or represented an essentially patronizing attitude. While men seldom complimented a woman they gave daily evidence of esteem and "constantly display an entire confidence in the under-standing of a wife and a profound respect for her freedom; they have decided that her mind is just as fitted as that of a man to discover the plain truth, and her heart as firm to embrace it; and they have never sought to place her virtue, any more than his, under the shelter of prejudice, ignorance, and fear." In France, by contrast, women were treated as "seductive but imperfect beings." Yet even de Tocqueville noted that "the women of the United States are confined within the narrow circle of domestic life, and their situation is in some respects one of extreme dependence . . ." He added, however, that they nowhere occupied "a loftier position." If, he wrote, he were asked "to what the singular prosperity and growing strength of that people ought mainly to be attributed," he would reply, "To the superiority of their women."[4]

De Tocqueville considered the Americans the first people to apply the "great principles of political economy" to the relations between the sexes. Following the practice of specialization of labor which was to prove so important in the emergence of industrial capitalism, Americans saw to it that women did not intrude into the man's sphere. "In no country," de Tocqueville observed, "has such constant care been taken as in America to trace two clearly distinct lines of action for the two sexes and to make them keep pace one with the other, but in two pathways that are always different." "American women," he wrote approvingly, "never manage the outward concerns of the family or conduct a business or take part in political life." On the other hand one never saw them laboring in the fields or doing the kind of rough work so often done by French and English women of the lower classes. Despite having often "the hearts and minds of men," "manly energy," and "a masculine strength of understanding," they were at great pains to appear feminine in manner and dress.[5]

By the beginning of the twentieth century the status of American women had of course changed dramatically. If they had seemed to foreign travelers a hundred years earlier to have, to a remarkable degree, the deference and admiration of men, they had by 1900 converted this masculine regard into a thousand practical and specific achievements. It was not that women exercised political power — the power was still firmly in the hands of men with merely token concessions — but it was rather that their influence was felt in every area of American life and virtually all male bastions had fallen to their assault.

To James Fullerton Muirhead in 1908 the importance of American women lay beyond "politics and publicity." America had "meant opportunity for women even more than in some ways for men . . . The average American woman is distinctly more different from her average English sister than is the case with their respective brothers . . . The American woman has never learned to play second fiddle." Muirhead agreed with Henry James that the American girl was "either (and usually) a most charming success or (and exceptionally) a most disastrous failure." While the American man was making money with terrible dedication, his wife "has been sacrificing on the altar of the graces. Hence the wider culture and more liberal views are often found in the sex from which the European does not expect them; hence the woman of New York and other American cities is often conspicuously superior to her husband in looks, manners, and general intelligence."[6] Lord James Bryce also noted the superior "literary taste and influence" of American women, an influence much higher than that exercised by women in any other modern nation: "In a country where men are incessantly occupied at their business or profession, the function of keeping up the level of culture devolves upon women. It is safe in their hands."

Muirhead felt that "among the most searching tests of the state of civilization reached by any country are the character of its roads, its minimizing of noise and the position of its women."[7] If the United States did not rank very high by the first two standards, "its name," Muirhead wrote, "assuredly leads all the rest in the third. In no other country is the legal status of women so high or so well secured, or their rights to follow an independent career so fully recognized by society at large." Muirhead noted that there were eighty women doctors in Boston alone and twenty-five women lawyers in the city of Chicago. There were also numerous women dentists, barbers, and livery stablekeepers. One of the steamboats on Lake Champlain was "steered by a pilot in petticoats."[8]

James Bryce was also impressed by the prominence of the weaker sex. He decided that the American man, "perceiving in women an intelligence and will, which, if never equal to that of the very strongest men, yet makes the average woman the equal for most purposes of the average man, inasmuch as she gains in quickness and delicacy of perception what she loses in force and endurance . . . have found no reason why women should not share the labours, duties, and privileges of man."[9]

Like Muirhead, Bryce agreed that "nothing in the country is more characteristic of the peculiar type [American] civilization has taken" than the position of its women. Women had been, by 1910, placed "in an equality with men as respects all private rights . . . taking one thing with another, it is easier for women to find a career, to obtain remunerative work either of literary or of a commercial or mechanical kind, than in any part of Europe. Popular sentiment is entirely in favour of giving them every chance, as witness the Constitutions of those Western States . . . which expressly provide that they shall be equally admissible to all professions or employments. . . . Their services in dealing with pauperism, charities, and reformatory institutions have been inestimable . . ."[10]

Beatrice Forbes-Robertson Hale echoed Bryce: "There can be no question whatever that the general estimation in which women are held by men is higher in America than in England . . . In America girl-infants are not hailed into the world with parental regrets for their sex. From their first breath to their last, their opportunities march more nearly with those of their brothers than in England."[11]

When Paul Achard, the French journalist, visited America in the 1930's, the balance, at least in his opinion, had swung decisively in the direction of feminine influence in American life. Twenty years earlier Bryce felt that he detected a predominance on the female side. Perhaps the most marked difference was a vast improvement in the physical health of American women. They had been liberated from their crippling clothes and lured out of their overheated parlors. By the 1930's, moreover, they represented a racial amalgam which had been in the making for three hundred years, with aesthetically impressive results. It was clear to Achard that "woman has become a queen in America." She was marvelously free before marriage and when she married she gave up none of her freedom but her husband gave up most of his; "he cannot go out with his friends unless madam approves." It seemed to Achard that whether married or single, the American woman was "supported by the entire American social organization."[12]

Her aim was to reign over men and for this purpose she had at her disposal two weapons — marriage and divorce — "the combination of these permits her to live the life that pleases her." Achard rhapsodized over "this beautiful creature, vigorously but harmoniously built, with clear eyes, thick hair, well cut, mobile nostrils, nervous hands, long muscular legs . . . incomparable brilliance, due as much to the mixture of races she represents as to the intelligent indulgence in exercise and hygiene that regulates her life." The subjugation of men was accomplished by her determination "to marry, divorce, and cause divorce . . . In spite of the danger of generalization one can affirm that the American woman is the most successful creature in the world."[13]

In spite of the increasingly constricted role of women from later colonial times on, American girls, by common agreement, continued to enjoy a freedom that was, by European standards, astonishing. From fifteen or sixteen, Moreau de St. Méry observed, they "become their own mistresses, and can go walking alone and have suitors." Even more surprising to St. Méry was the fact that girls made their own choice of a suitor "and the parents raise no objection because that's the custom of the country." The suitor "comes into the house when he wishes; goes on walks with his loved one whenever he desires." On Sundays he might drive her out in his carriage and bring her back in the evening "without anyone wanting to know where they went."[14] Frances Wright wrote that young men and women mixed freely: "they dance, sing, walk, and 'run in sleighs' together, by sunshine and moonshine, without the occurrence or even the apprehension of any impropriety. In this bountiful country, marriages are seldom dreaded as imprudent, and therefore no care is taken to prevent the contracting of early engagements."[15]

Marryat also spoke of the unlimited liberty which American girls enjoyed, and de Tocqueville was equally impressed, observing that "In the United States the doctrines of Protestantism [are] combined with great political liberty and a most democratic state of society, and nowhere are young women surrendered so early or so completely to their own guidance." The American woman has scarcely passed childhood "when she already thinks for herself, speaks with freedom, and acts on her own impulse. The great scene of the world is constantly open to her view; far from seeking to conceal it from her, it is everyday disclosed more completely and she is taught to survey it with a firm and calm gaze. Thus the vices and dangers of society are early revealed to her; as she sees them clearly, she views them without illusion and braves them without fear, for she is full of reliance on her own strength, and her confidence seems shared by all around her."

American girls seldom showed "that virginal softness . . . or that innocent and ingenuous grace" so characteristic of European women in the transition from girlhood to womanhood. On the other hand, they rarely displayed the "childish timidity or ignorance" that often marked their European counterparts. To de Tocqueville, American girls had a shrewd practicality, however chaste its possessor might be, that was far removed from innocence. In France, de Tocqueville felt, girls were sheltered and protected and society generally undertook to guard them from the effect of "the most vehement passions of the human heart." The consequence was that after a protected childhood, French girls were abandoned "without a guide and without assistance in the midst of all the irregularities inseparable from democratic society." In America, on the other hand, the effort was to develop the will and moral stamina of a girl from an early age in order "to enhance her confidence in her own strength of character. As it is neither possible nor desirable to keep a young woman in perpetual and complete ignorance, they hasten to give her a precocious knowledge on all subjects. Far from hiding the corruptions of the world from her, they prefer that she should see them at once and train herself to shun them . . ."[16] The results of such a training were not, by any means, all positive. It tended to produce "cold and virtuous women instead of affectionate wives and agreeable companions to man." Society was thus better regulated but domestic life had fewer graces.

De Tocqueville was convinced that the openness of American society where any girl might in effect marry any man helped to discourage premarital sexual relations. A young man could not, very convincingly, make passionate, romantic love to a girl and not propose marriage since he could not plead differences in their social position which made the union unsuitable or impossible. "No girl then believes that she cannot become the wife of the man who loves her, and this renders all breaches of morality before marriage very uncommon; for, whatever be the credulity of the passions, a woman will hardly be able to persuade herself that she is beloved when her lover is perfectly free to marry her and does not."[17] Bryce, writing almost a century later, was sure that, "In no country are women, and especially young women, so much made of. The world is at their feet. Society seems organized for the purpose of providing enjoyment for them . . ."[18] It was the attention to public education for girls as well as boys, Bryce thought, which accounted for "much of the influence which women exert . . . They feel more independent, they have a fuller consciousness of their place in the world of thought as well as the world of action. . . . In the rural districts, and generally all over the West, young men and girls are permitted to walk together, drive together, go out to parties, and even to public entertainments together, without the presence of any third person, who can be supposed to be looking after or taking charge of the girl."[19]

Frenchmen were often misled by the openness and affability of American girls which they initially interpreted as sexual looseness. The Marquis de Chastellux, landing in Rhode Island, met "a most beautiful girl" who had "like all American women, a very becoming, even serious bearing; she had no objection to being looked at, having her beauty commended, or even receiving a few caresses, provided it was without any appearance of familiarity or wantonness." The Frenchman was surprised to find that in America "conversation with young women leads no further [whereas in France, by implication, it usually led to bed], and that freedom itself bears a character of modesty unknown to our affected bashfulness and false reserve."[20] In 1895 Madame Blanc, a French novelist, noted that some American girls were not as robust as British girls — there was "too much fragility, too much thinness" and that their "shoulders and breasts were not so well formed as those of French women," but added "the Americans are as quick-witted, and as graceful as any women in the world."[21]

Fifty years later, Paul Achard was dismayed to find that the only way to make love to a woman in America was to marry her. To follow a woman on the street or to speak to her in a public place could result in arrest.

American girls still behaved with a casualness, almost an abandon, which plainly bewildered the Frenchman, suggesting as it did a quite different character from that of the respectability that, it became quite clear if one presumed, lay behind it. "They may," Achard noted, "without reserve display their arms and shoulders — and such perfect legs. After a few hours in the United States legs become part of the landscape for you. No matter where you go you will see feminine American legs, beautiful, arresting, and free!" And on these beautiful legs, "she dances and dances and dances."[22] (The mania of American girls for dancing was one of the earliest traits noted by foreign visitors. Frances Wright noted that they loved to dress in the French fashion — but more modestly — and that, gathered at balls and parties, they danced "with much lightness, grace, and gay-heartedness" and far outshone the men "in general ease of manner and address.")

According to James Muirhead, traveling in the United States in 1908, what struck Europeans about the American girl was "her candour, her frankness, her hail-fellow-well-met-edness, her apparent absence of consciousness of self or of sex, her spontaneity, her vivacity, her fearlessness." He was charmed by "the sprightliness, the variety, the fearless individuality . . . by her power of repartee, by the quaint appositeness of her expressions, by the variety of her interests, by the absence of undue deference to his masculine dignity." In England, Muirhead wrote, women belonged to types and classes: "The English girl is first the squire's daughter, second a good churchwoman, third an English subject, and fourthly a woman" but in America "every new girl is a new sensation." The American girl's absence of any consciousness of social distinctions ("unless she belongs to a very narrow coterie") "endues her, at her best, with a sweet and subtle fragrance of humanity that is, perhaps, unique . . . she combines in a strangely attractive way the charms of eternal womanliness with the latest aroma of a progressive century."

Much the same point was made by two French visitors in the 1890's; M. Bourget wrote of the incomparable delicacy of American girls and Paul Blouet found "in the American woman a quality which, I fear, is beginning to disappear in Paris and is almost unknown in London — a kind of spiritualized politeness, a tender solicitude for other people, combined with strong individuality."[23]

The freedom which American girls enjoyed was, as has been suggested earlier, a survival from colonial days. It was maintained in the face of an increasingly repressive society, in part because of a rather cold-blooded calculation on the part of the most candid and agreeable girls and because of what we today would call the "internalization" of conventional moral values. Above all, it was a practical manifestation of the very special character of "daughterhood" in American life. Girls who were permitted what was, by European standards, such remarkable freedom, had their freedom primarily because of their special status as daughters.

The beauty and early maturity of American girls was another characteristic that almost invariably impressed foreign travelers. The Marquis de Chastellux, while exclaiming over the number of handsome girls had some shrewd comments to make upon the differences between the physical beauty of American and French women. He observed that American girls matured much more rapidly. Those of twelve or thirteen showed "roundness of form . . . united with freshness of complexion and with that more perfect regularity that features have when they have not yet been modified by passions and habits." In France it was quite different. Girls were very pretty up to the age of seven or eight. But as they approached puberty their appearance changed markedly and it is not until the age of twenty to twenty-five that a French woman's "features develop and declare themselves and Nature completes her work . . ." On the other hand, French women retained their beauty much longer. "Nature, helped rather than hindered by Art, is not surrendered to the indulgence of domestic life, nor lavished on unrestrained fecundity."[24] To Chastellux the beauty of French women "though less precocious and less perfect, is more bewitching and more lasting . . . though others may be better models for the painter, they are better to behold; and that, in short, though they are not always those who are most admired, they are certainly the most- and the longest-loved."

What is of special interest, of course, is Chastellux's judgment that American girls ripened, in a manner of speaking, far earlier than their French sisters, and that the former paid the price of precocious maturity by failing to develop into rewarding and richly individual women.

Moreau de St. Méry was much struck in the decade of the 1790's by the comeliness of American women. In Philadelphia, he wrote, one could see on "any fine winter day on the north sidewalk of Market Street between Third and Fifth Street . . . four hundred young persons, each of whom would certainly be followed on any Paris promenade." But, like Chastellux, St. Méry noted that "they soon grow pale," and suffer "almost universally" from a loss of "freshness and youth . . . and all the little details which adorn beauty, or rather which join to create it, soon fail most of them. In short, while charming and adorable at fifteen, they are faded at twenty-three, old at thirty-five, decrepit at forty or forty-five." By eighteen "their breasts, never large, already have vanished."[25]

Captain Marryat observed that American women, while "very delicate and very pretty" reminded him "of roses which have budded fairly, but which a check in the season has not permitted to bloom. Up to sixteen or seventeen, they promise perfection; at that age their advance appears to be checked. Their teeth were bad and their skin blemished. This Marryat attributed to the climate which kept them indoors and prevented exercise, and their bad complexions to "the universal use of close stoves." It was primarily in the East that these deficiencies in the feminine face and form were noted. In Cincinnati for example, "you will find . . . not only good teeth, but as deep-bosomed maids as you will in England; so will you in Virginia, Kentucky, Missouri, and Wisconsin." This proved to Marryat that the fault was in the climate. England's was much more healthy "than the exciting and changeable atmosphere" of America. When Captain Marryat called American women "the *prettiest* in the world" he was at pains to explain that as was appropriate in the land of equality, there was a generous distribution of good looks but few real beauties. "I think that the portion of the time which elapses between the period of a young girl leaving school and being married is the happiest of her existence."[26]

If American girls were allowed extraordinary freedom before marriage, the situation changed dramatically once they had entered into matrimony. Like virtually all other commentators on the American scene, de Tocqueville noted that "the independence of woman is irrecoverably lost in the bonds of matrimony. If an unmarried woman is less constrained there than elsewhere, a wife is subjected to stricter obligations. The former makes her father's house an abode of freedom and pleasure; the latter lives in the home of her husband as if it were a cloister."[27] The last sentence contains an epitome of the main thesis of this work: that is to say, as a daughter in her father's house, an American girl had a status and a freedom never before experienced by her sex; as a wife she led a singularly cramped and constricted existence. In that tension is to be discerned a major part of the life experience of women in American history.

Considering the "unlimited liberty" which young women enjoyed, St. Méry was surprised by "their universal eagerness to be married, to become wives who will for the most part be nothing but housekeepers of their husbands' homes." To the Frenchman such an attitude could only be accounted for on the ground that failing to get a husband would subject a girl to ridicule. The girls whom he observed in Philadelphia society were just such girls as John Quincy Adams was so critical of. To St. Méry they were distinguished by calculation and "self-love," and he went so far as to accuse them of widespread auto-eroticism and lesbianism, evidences to him of their unhealthy narcissism, though it is not at all clear how he could have gotten such information.*

* "These women . . . give themselves up to the enjoyment of themselves and . . . seek unnatural pleasures with persons of their own sex."

Marryat thought the married state in America a rather dreary one. Men were busy; their whole time was "engrossed by their accumulation of money." They had an early breakfast, left for work and did not even return for lunch, or what was worse, for tea. Grinding away all day at whatever sordid occupation was necessary for money-making, they ended the day fagged out and in need of recreation. Since "the recreations of most Americans are politics and news, besides the chance of doing a little more business," American males repaired, after work, for the nearest bar and after a few drinks then "come home late, tired, and go to bed; early the next morning they are off to their business again."

Wives, in consequence, had little of their husbands' time; "their husbands are not their companions," and even if they could be they were, for the most part, too poorly educated to be very good company. They acquire "a great deal of practical knowledge useful for making money, but for little else." Women, on the other hand, are more generally educated and, "during the long days and evenings, during which they wait for the return of their husbands, they have time to finish, I may say, their own educations and improve their minds by reading." As a result they were much more cultivated than their husbands who, in addition to being hopelessly engrossed in making money, lessened their social attractiveness in most instances by drinking and smoking. There were, of course, exceptions and Marryat extended one to a whole profession — that of the law. Lawyers were much better educated than the common run of American businessmen, and much better company.

It is perhaps worth including a quotation from Marryat which has nothing to do directly with women but rather with their mates. When Marryat first arrived in America and walked down Broadway, "it appeared strange to me that there should be such a remarkable family likeness among the people. Every man I met seemed to me by his features to be a brother or a connection of the last man who had passed me; I could not at first comprehend this, but the mystery was soon revealed. It was that they were all intent and engrossed with the same object; all were, as they passed, calculating and reflecting; this produced a similar contraction of the brow, knitting of the eyebrows, and compression of the lips — a similarity of feeling had produced a similarity of expression, from the same muscles being called into action. Even their hurried walk assisted the error; it is a saying in the United States 'that a New York merchant always walks as if he had a good dinner before him, and a bailiff behind him,' and the metaphor is not inapt."[28]

American middle-class urban wives and even children were thus sacrificed to their husbands' obsession with making money. But it could not very well have been otherwise for making money was the way in which American society arranged itself. To have a successful or prosperous husband was as important to the wife as to her partner. In the absence of a formal class structure, a man was defined by what he did and how well he did it. According to Max Weber, the Protestant ethic indeed claimed that there was a clear connection between a man's material success and his state of grace. Those who were rich were those most favored by the Almighty.

So after her golden girlhood, the American woman entered the constricted world of the home. She was expected to be a self-effacing dutiful wife, to give up the carefree social life, the gaiety and the freedom which she had enjoyed as a girl. In the opinion of Frances Trollope, American women "are tender and attentive in the nursery, bustling and busy in the kitchen, unwearying at the needle, and beautiful in the ballroom; but in the drawing-room — they are naught . . . They marry very early; once married, they seem to drop out of sight or of court, out of all competition with the blooming race that are following them."[29]

James Stirling, touring America in the 1850's, knew of "no people with stronger domestic affections. The American marries young; he loves his wife and children . . . the American pioneer carries his family with him . . . the American bagman scours the country in company with his wife . . . an American's wife is the peg on which he hangs out his fortune; he dresses her up that men may see his wealth; she is a walking advertisement of his importance. The Englishman loves his house and decks it out when he makes money; the American loves his wife and decks her out for want of a house."[30] Stirling's point is perhaps worth dwelling on. For the American man, a wife has always been a status symbol. He has encouraged her preoccupation with dress which was the means by which she attracted him in the first place and because he wishes her to bear testimony to his material success.

"The Americans," Marryat noted, "have reason to be proud of their women, for they are really good wives — much *too good* for them." Americans, since they were obliged to earn money, could hardly be blamed for the neglect of their wives. But they were to blame on one point "which is that they do not properly appreciate or value their wives, who have not one half the influence which wives have in England, or one quarter that legitimate influence to which they are entitled. That they are proud of them, flatter them, and are kind to them after their own fashion, I grant, but female influence extends no farther . . . The women are more moral, more educated, and more refined than the men, and yet have at present no influence whatever in society."[31]

In addition few of them were permitted any control over family finances. Money was ladled out to them grudgingly; Mary Chesnut complained that it "ought not to be asked for, or given to a man's wife as gift. Something must be due her, and that she should have, and with no growling and grumblings nor warnings against waste and extravagance, nor hints as to the need of economy, nor amazement that the last supply has given out already. What a proud woman suffers under all this, who can tell?"[32]

De Tocqueville noted that "the American woman is subject to the same tyranny of public opinion as the men." She thus is "not slow to perceive that she cannot depart for an instant from the established usages of her contemporaries without putting in jeopardy her peace of mind, her honor, nay, even her social existence; and she finds the energy required for such an act of submission in the firmness of her understanding and the virile habits which her education has given her. It may be said that she has learned by the use of her independence to surrender it without a struggle . . ." De Tocqueville speaks also of "that cold and stern reasoning power" of the American woman which gives her the capacity to follow "the only road that can lead to domestic happiness." To de Tocqueville, this same spirit enabled wives to withstand the shock of a husband's financial misfortune, so frequent in America, or endure the hardships of the frontier.[33]

From independence to dependence — that was the path trod by the American girl. That her husband expected unimpeachable virtue was without question. For a wife to talk to, flirt with, or be seen with a man other than her husband was, as de Tocqueville suggested, to invite gossip and imperil her good name. Yet the husband, preoccupied with making money, offered little company. Social occasions, such as they were, were thoroughly segregated.

Mrs. Trollope attended a number of parties at which men and women dined separately and when they were together they were awkward and ill-at-ease: "The fair creatures . . . sat down on a row of chairs placed round the walls, and each making a table of her knees, began eating her sweet, but sad and sulky repast." It seemed to her as though "all the enjoyments of the men are to be found in the absence of women. They dine, they play cards, they have musical meetings, they have suppers, all in large parties, but all without women. . . . The two sexes can hardly mix for the greater part of a day without great restraint and ennui; it is quite contrary to their general habits . . ."[34]

Almost a hundred years later, in 1914, another Englishwoman, Beatrice Forbes-Robertson Hale, had very similar observations. "Just as there is less companionship between the sexes before marriage in England," she wrote, "so there is more afterwards. The English girl has socially less freedom, the English wife more . . . In America the segregation of the sexes after marriage appears to foreigners one of the most singular and unfortunate developments of social life . . . In the cities it is almost complete."[35] There was clearly truth in Mrs. Trollope's comment that American men were attentive if not passionate suitors and considerate husbands, "but of women as women they had little understanding and no desire to improve what they had."[36]

What it came to was this: American men accorded their women more deference, lavished more money on them, regarded them with more respect than was accorded the women of any other country. But they did not particularly like them. They did not enjoy their company; they did not find them interesting or rewarding as people and as women in themselves. They valued them as wives and mothers; they sentimentalized over them; they congratulated themselves on their enlightened attitude toward them. *But they did not (and they do not) particularly like them.* However, the regard of American men for women was also the agency by means of which women have been able to vastly alter their situation in American life. The deep and profoundly American feeling that, in the vernacular, "Nothing is too good for the little woman," made it possible for women to emerge from their state of dependence.

But not without a bitter struggle.

6

The Theoreticians:

Mary Wollstonecraft and Hannah More

The original theoretician of what in time came to be called the woman's rights movement was Mary Wollstonecraft, an Englishwoman. Her *Vindication of the Rights of Women* stands in much the same relation to the so-called emancipation of women as Karl Marx's *Das Kapital* does to international communism. Published in 1792, the *Vindication* was at least a century ahead of its time. Much too radical for its contemporaries, the book was an inspiration to every worker in the woman's rights movement, in England and America, for the next hundred years. Its rhetoric, its images, its arguments recur with almost monotonous regularity in the writings of those women devoted to reform. Mary Wollstonecraft's basic argument was that no healthy society was possible that was not based on genuine equality among those groups that constituted it. It was, in the long run, for the good of men themselves that women should have a position of equality. Very few masculine institutions escaped her condemnation — armies, navies, kings, parliaments. The measure, for her, of the unhappy relations between the sexes was the homosexual tendencies promoted by English boarding schools and the lesbian attachments of girls forced to keep each other company. Women were expected to be the ivy clinging to the oak (man). "But, alas! husbands . . . are often only overgrown children . . ."[1]

To Mary Wollstonecraft, "queens and fashionable ladies" were the enemy as much as men, although, to be sure, they existed in response to the wishes of men. She agreed with Edmund Burke's scorn for the homage offered women as sublime and beautiful creatures "because such homage vitiates them, prevents their endeavoring to obtain solid personal merit; and, in short, makes those beings vain inconsiderate dolls, who ought to be prudent mothers and useful members of society."[2] She was determined to persuade men to regard women "in the grand light of human creatures" who, in common with men, are placed on this earth to unfold their faculties rather than accumulations of conventionalized traits. To praise woman for her "elegancy of mind, exquisite sensibility, and sweet docility of manners," was simply a masculine tactic to keep her in "slavish dependence." Women, in Mary Wollstonecraft's view, were generally trained like overgrown children, pampered and petted and admired and guided in everything.

"The weak, enervated women who particularly catch the attention of libertines are unfit to be mothers . . . so that the rich sensualist, who has rioted among women, spreading depravity and misery, when he wishes to perpetuate his name, receives from his wife only a half-formed being that inherits both its father's and mother's weaknesses." Modern man "by his promiscuous amours produces a most destructive barrenness and contagious flagitiousness of manners."

Women should study politics and seek careers in business, as physicians, running farms or managing shops. Marriage can never realize its potential until women become "enlightened citizens, till they become free by being enabled to earn their own subsistence, independent of men. . . . Nay, marriage will never be held sacred till women, by being brought up with men, are prepared to be their companions rather than their mistresses. . . ."

Mary Wollstonecraft indignantly dismissed the notion that mental and physical exercise would unsex women: "I am of a very different opinion for I think that, on the contrary, we should then see dignified beauty, and true grace."[3]

Her *bête noir* was Dr. Gregory's *Legacy to Daughters,* a popular work filled with saccharine pieties, and admonitions to young ladies to be chaste, dutiful, diffident and ever attendant upon the needs and desires of their masters. Given such stuff to muse upon it is hardly

surprising that Mary Wollstonecraft came to see monogamous marriage as the real impediment to equality of women. She discerned what others preferred to ignore — that the marriage which had seemed for a time to offer a new worth and dignity to her sex had become a consumingly selfish and very often positively degrading relationship. She saw clearly what history has subsequently and most dramatically confirmed — that it cannot be left to a dominant group, however enlightened and well-intentioned, to decide what is proper and desirable for a dependent group. Human egoism is too profound and the limits of imagination too narrow to make this possible. Equality cannot be given conditionally or in terms defined by the grantees. In a certain sense men did the best they knew; it simply was not very good. The Western society that began to take shape in the early years of the Industrial Revolution was exploitive; women were among those exploited. There was truth in Mary Wollstonecraft's charge that men wished passive, malleable wives. On the other hand it is more than a little doubtful that the abolition of marriage in favor of what came to be called "free alliance" was a solution. "I love man, as my fellow," Mary Wollstonecraft wrote in one of her most eloquent passages, "but his sceptre, real or usurped, extends not to me, unless the reason of an individual demands my homage; and even then the submission is to reason, and not to man."[4]

Women had "been stripped of the virtues that should clothe humanity" and in their place "decked with artificial graces that enable them to exercise a short-lived tyranny." Passionate love was transitory; it could not serve as the basis for a life-long association between two people. One of her main lines of argument was directed against the limits placed on women's *physical activities,* the notion that as refined and delicate creatures they should do nothing active: "the limbs and faculties are cramped with worse than Chinese bands . . . confined in close rooms till their muscles are relaxed, and their powers of digestion destroyed." Mary Wollstonecraft was right. To the modern mind nothing seems quite so extraordinary as the ability of a considerable number of men and a great many women of the eighteenth and nineteenth centuries to convince themselves of the weakness and frailty of women. Any man familiar with the often terrifying energy displayed by a wife, mother or daughter will be astonished to consider how this particular swindle was maintained. Its practical effect on the psychic as well as the physical health of women was, in fact, hardly short of disastrous.

Love as a physical passion, Mary Wollstonecraft regarded with some uneasiness. It too easily degenerated into licentiousness or vanished completely, leaving husband and wife trapped in a sterile relationship. The emphasis on romantic love was the first step in the enslavement; the second was the marriage that consummated such love. Indeed sexual love was so selfish and devouring that it was, in her opinion, incompatible with friendship. A match founded on esteem rather than passion was much more likely to be a happy union: "The vain fears and fond jealousies . . . of love . . . are both incompatible with the tender confidence and sincere respect of friendship."[5]

Mary Wollstonecraft's solution to the problem of sexuality in marriage was to divorce the two. Passionate attachments should only last so long as the fire blazed. Marriage should take place only between "friends," individuals of congenial interests, well suited by training and education to cultivate each other's reasonable propensities. To mix love and marriage was to mix basically incompatible elements thereby perverting love and debasing marriage.

In Mary Wollstonecraft's view it was "time to effect a revolution in female manners — time to restore to them their lost dignity — and make them, as a part of the human species, labour by reforming themselves to reform the world."[6]

Mary Wollstonecraft's own life reads like one of Dickens's grimmer novels. Her father was a master weaver who tried to ape the manners of a country gentleman, frittered away a modest inheritance, drank immoderately and bullied his submissive wife and six children. When she was nineteen Mary took a position as companion to a widow and two years later went to nurse her sister Eliza who had just had a child and who was losing her mind because of brutal treatment by her husband. To save her sister's sanity, Mary took her away from her home, leaving the infant child behind.

Gradually she found her way into the radical intellectual circles of the day: the Reverend Richard Price, Joseph Priestly, William Godwin, John Horne Tooke, and William Blake. She herself enjoyed a modest success as an author and journalist. After a passionate affair with Henry Fuseli, a prominent painter, she went to Paris and met and became the mistress of Gilbert Imlay. Pregnant by Imlay, she was abandoned soon after the birth of her daughter, Fanny, and tried to commit suicide. Imlay prevented her but a few months later when she heard that Imlay was living with an actress she went to his apartment and in a passion burst in on them. When Imlay turned her out she tried to commit suicide by leaping into the Thames, but was rescued by two boatmen.

She then met William Godwin, a member of her publisher's literary circle, and she became his mistress. When she found that she was pregnant, she and Godwin were married although they continued to live in separate houses. She died in 1797 at the age of thirty-eight from complications following the birth of her daughter Mary.

The events of her life following the publication of *A Vindication* give the book an added poignancy just as the circumstances of her childhood and youth help to explain the bitterness of feeling so evident in it. For Mary Wollstonecraft marriage was, as we have noted, a trap for women. At the same time she saw men as lecherous brutes and despoilers of women as well as their exploiters. If her resentment against men seems pathological we must remember the facts of her own early life. The picture of insatiable sexual appetites that we get from the diaries of individuals like William Byrd and James Boswell suggests that her indictment did not fall entirely short of the mark. However, it is certain that such behavior was far less characteristic of America than of England and, by her own admission, applied primarily to the British upper classes. What did apply equally well to both countries was a trivialization of women which was not so much due to masculine sensuality as to the nature of the eighteenth-century society. The sexual excesses which so obsessed Mary Wollstonecraft had to be, and, in short order, were brought under control, at least to the degree that they became covert rather than overt.

In her basic insight Mary Wollstonecraft was correct. Women were enslaved and had to be liberated. This liberation was, ultimately, as much in man's interest as woman's. He could not achieve a fuller humanity until the woman did also. A husband's petty tyranny corrupted him as surely as it debased his wife.

If the terms of her argument are misconceived and her insistence on woman's *reason* misses the real issue, much of the book, wicked and perverse as it seemed to eighteenth-century readers, was wonderfully perceptive and acute. Her sometimes strident insistence on "equality" was also necessary. Equality in the context in which she used it did not mean "the same." To say that men and women were equal, or should be equal, or would be equal (if they were educated equally and women were freed from the burden of masculine sexuality) was not to say that they were the same. It was to say that they should approach each other as *equals* rather than as a superior and an inferior being. And that only by approaching each other as equals could their relationship be an honest and fulfilling one for the husband as well as for the wife. There could furthermore be no such thing as separate but equal education for men and women. Separate meant unequal, she insisted.

Mary Wollstonecraft's most noted antagonist was another English-woman, Hannah More, whose *Strictures on the Modern System of Female Education* was an amiable codification of most of the existing middle-class prejudices about "a woman's place." It was, in consequence, enormously popular and became a kind of manual for proper young ladies and, perhaps more significantly, for the establishment of female academies for proper young ladies. For Hannah More "the chief end to be proposed in cultivating the understanding of women," was "to qualify them for the practical purposes of life. Their knowledge is not often like the learning of men, to be reproduced in some literary composition, nor ever in any learned profession; but it is to come out in conduct." She shared Mary Wollstonecraft's scorn for the frivolous, merely fashionable woman, but she also proposed an education that would "put an end to those petty cavils and contentions for equality which female smatterers so anxiously maintain." Hannah More warned against the "new philosophy" that children should learn through playing: "Do what we will we cannot *cheat* children into learning or *play* them into knowledge, according to the smoothness of the modern creed. . . . There is no idle way to any acquisitions which really deserve the name. . . . The tree of knowledge, as punishment, perhaps, for its having been at first unfairly tasted, cannot now be climbed without difficulty." Education was man's and woman's introduction "to that state of toil and labour to which we are born. . . ."[7]

Her female readers were advised to avoid novels whose authors use "a metaphysical sophistry" which "debauches the heart of woman" by casting doubt on the value of chastity. German and French literature were special sources of corruption. "Religious knowledge" and "practical industry" were the best recourse for women who wished to serve their Maker. The wild talk about *"rights"* was no better than "impious defiance of the natural order." Each sex had "its proper excellencies, which would be lost were they melted down into the common character by the fusion of the new philosophy." Her readers were advised to be excellent women rather than indifferent men; to follow the "plain path which Providence has obviously marked out to the sex . . . rather than . . . stray awkwardly, unbecomingly, and unsuccessfully, in a forbidden road."[8]

There was much good sense in Hannah More, far more, in truth, than in Mary Wollstonecraft. But common sense does not rule history. The tiny band who followed the siren song of Mary Wollstonecraft were to shape the history of Anglo-American women in the nineteenth century.

But Hannah More remains important for all that. Not only did she express the sentiment of the overwhelming majority of men and women alike, she made herself the spokesman of that great body of women who insisted that the Christian family was the foundation of all social order. If the American reformers adopted many of Mary Wollstonecraft's arguments, they placed them solidly in the framework of the family. Only a handful dared to carry forward their heroine's assault on the monogamous marriage.

The Genesis
of Women's Rights

The Protestant passion did not everywhere dwindle to the Protestant ethic. It remained alive in many small-town, rural and frontier churches, in revivals and awakenings that rekindled year after year the ardor of the early congregations of New England. The torch was passed on to a succession of new sects, each marked by an evangelical enthusiasm missing from the older denominations — Methodists, first; then Baptists, Reformed Presbyterians, Millerites, Predestinarians, and on and on. And moving with the frontier were the old denominations, most conspicuously the Presbyterians, Congregationalists, and Quakers, kept young by their constant exposure to the demanding life of the West.

The passion also animated the secular reformers of New England and the Middle West. Many of them, Quakers, many more Unitarians, they combined a liberal theology with a radical attack on the defects of American society. In both these groups women constituted a majority. If there is any reliable generalization to be made about the "female character" it is that it is on the whole more responsive to suffering and inhumanity than its masculine counterpart. Women were in the majority in the radically orthodox new denominations and sects that flourished in the American hinterland throughout the nineteenth century; they had always been better represented in the religious life of the communities in which they lived. They were in a majority in the reform movements which began to burgeon by the end of the eighteenth century, perhaps because their emotions were more readily touched by instances of human suffering and injustice.

For the purpose of this narrative, the most important involvement of American women in the years between the American Revolution and the outbreak of the Civil War was in the antislavery movement. The woman's rights movement was indeed an offshoot of the agitation against slavery, a campaign most of whose foot soldiers and many of whose officers were women.

There is not space here to retrace in detail the first steps of the antislavery movement. One of its guiding spirits was Lucretia Mott, (1793–1880) a young Quaker minister, a gifted speaker, the mother of six children, who was an encouraging friend to two sisters from South Carolina, Sarah and Angelina Grimké. The Grimkés, as Southern women who knew at firsthand the horrors of slavery, came to play leading roles in the antislavery movement. Sarah, born in 1792 and thirteen years the elder, had had a conventional Southern upbringing and acquired the "different branches of polite education for ladies." From these she went on to study mathematics, geography, the history of the world, Greek, natural science and botany. Her father was much interested in her education and their relationship was an unusually close one.

One of the stories of Sarah's childhood was that at the age of four she had seen a slave whipped, and had run from the house, sobbing. She later recalled her childhood as a happy one but added, "Slavery was a millstone about my neck, and marred my comfort from the time I can remember myself." She taught Bible classes to the slave children every Sunday afternoon and although there was a large fine for anyone "who shall teach any slave to write," she undertook to teach her own slave-girl to read and write. "The light was put out," she wrote in reminiscences of her childhood, "the keyhole screened, and flat on our stomachs, before the fire, with the spelling-book under our eyes, we defied the laws of South Carolina."

In her late teens, Sarah often visited a friend and neighbor who was known as a devout churchgoer, a generous and charitable lady. On one visit she recalled seeing a run-away mulatto woman who had been brutally whipped, have a heavy iron collar with three long prongs attached to it placed around her neck, and one of her front teeth extracted as punishment. Sarah Grimké wrote that the slave "could lie in no position but on her back which was sore from scourging. . . . This slave, who was the seamstress of the family was continually in her mistress' presence, sitting in her chamber to sew, or engaged in other household work, with her lacerated and bleeding back, her mutilated mouth, and heavy iron collar, without, so far as appeared, exciting any feelings of compassion."[1]

Some years later, returning to Charleston from a long visit in Pennsylvania, Sarah Grimké wrote that "it seemed as if the sight of their condition was unsupportable, it burst on my mind with renewed horror . . . deprived of ability to modify their situation, I was as one in bonds looking on their sufferings I could not soothe or lessen. . . . Events had made this world look like a wilderness. I saw nothing in it but desolation and suffering. . . ." She felt that her whole emotional life had dried up: "I was tempted to commit some great crime, thinking I could repent and thus restore my lost sensibility."[2]

Angelina, brought up by Sarah as much as by her mother, was, if anything, more resolute than her sister. She had to go frequently to the workhouse in Charleston where slaves were sent to be punished by masters too squeamish to inflict punishment themselves. There, women as well as men were whipped for a price. The most dreadful torment was "the treadmill" with broad steps which revolved rapidly. The slave's arms were secured to a beam above it. When a slave could no longer keep up with the revolving steps that went faster and faster, he hung from his arms while the heavy steps struck his back and legs. Meanwhile a "driver" would lash him with a heavy whip. "No one," she wrote, "can imagine my feelings walking down that street. It seemed as though I was walking on the very confines of hell. This winter being obliged to pass by it to pay a visit to a friend, I suffered so much that I could not get over it for days and wondered how any real Christian could live near such a place."[3]

The Grimké sisters became Quakers and moved to Philadelphia, where, except for the support of individual Quakers like Lucretia Mott, they did not find much sympathy for their views among the Society of Friends. The path they followed in their own feelings about the slavery issue was characteristic of the movement of radical antislavery sentiment. The traditional position of those who were opposed to the institution of slavery which included, prior to the 1830's, a great many Southerners themselves, was African colonization. Slaves were to be gradually freed and shipped back to Africa to form a colony of ex-slaves. The plan was based primarily on the assumption that freed slaves could not live as equals in a white society. Liberia is the consequence of this plan which had many prominent supporters and did, in fact, manage to resettle several thousand freedmen. But the more zealous and more practical reformers soon realized that the scheme was more effective as a poultice for the white American conscience than as a solution to the problem of slavery. They advocated "Immediate, not Gradual Abolition" (the title of an influential pamphlet written by a British Quaker, Elizabeth Heyrich, and published in 1824), the improvement of the lot of the Negro by education, and an end to race prejudice.

The doctrine of immediate abolition was considered highly subversive by the great majority of those who called themselves antislavery men and women. Nonetheless, it had the supreme virtue of cutting the Gordian knot on the slavery issue. The imaginations of the best-intentioned Americans had not been able to confront directly the fact that the slaves must be freed and must be accommodated by the white American society. This was an idea so alien, so farfetched, so counter to the deepest feelings of white men and women that it remained for generations unspeakable. The "immediate" abolitionists, encouraged by their English allies like Frances Wright, by the manumission of slaves in all the possessions of Great Britain in 1833, and by the resistance of the freed Negroes themselves to all schemes of colonization, had the wit and courage to declare that the nettle of emancipation must be grasped *at once*. Furthermore, the abolition society itself must be interracial, including free Negroes as full members.

Sarah Grimké insisted that it was "the duty of abolitionists to identify themselves with these oppressed Americans by sitting with them in places of worship, by appearing with them in our streets, by giving them our countenance in steamboats and stages, by visiting them at their homes and encouraging them to visit us, receiving them as we do our white fellow citizens."[4] This was a good deal further than most abolitionists, however strong their theoretical distaste for slavery, were willing to go.

The Reverend Charles Grandison Finney was of this extreme persuasion and embodied that combination of religious fundamentalism and social radicalism that was characteristic of the early period of reform. He frightened his listeners with sulphurous word pictures of hellfire and then warned them that the only sure path to salvation was through good works, which included the temperance and peace movements and antislavery. The Lane Theological Seminary in Cincinnati was an indirect outcome of Finney's evangelizing. Arthur and Lewis Tappan, wealthy New York reformers, hired young Theodore Weld, a Finney convert, to help start the seminary, and the Reverend Lyman Beecher was chosen as its head. Weld enrolled to pursue theological studies and as a student arranged a series of debates on the slavery issue. The debates lasted for eighteen nights and resulted in the conversion of most of the students and some of the faculty from colonization to abolition. The new converts, espousing direct action, organized Bible classes, an employment agency and social services in the community of free Negroes to prove by practical example that the abolitionists' hope of raising the intellectual and economic levels of free Negroes was a realistic one. The trustees, appalled at such extremism, outlawed the society and forbade its activities. Beecher supported the trustees and Weld and a number of other students resigned.

Angelina Grimké and Theodore Weld met and fell in love. The story of their mutual discovery of this astonishing fact is a charming one. Angelina, like most of the women in the antislavery and woman's rights movement who married, went through a long struggle with her conscience. She wondered if her love was selfish or idolatrous. Why was not the love of Christ sufficient for her? "I am a mystery to myself," she wrote Weld, "Why must I have *human love?* . . . Why do I feel in my inmost soul that you, *only you,* fill up the deep void there is. . . . Why do I so anxiously desire to hear from you, to see you?"[5]

Angelina doubted that she could make her fiancé happy as a wife, cataloged her faults, worried over the effect of marriage on her mission, fretted about the sexual aspect of their future relationship as husband and wife. She wrote to say that she was willing to give him up rather than hamper his work and he replied warmly: "Talk not to me of giving you up. . . . God sparing me, come what will, I'll marry you in spite of earth or hell." That was the kind of talk even a reforming woman wished to hear. Weld continued: "We marry, Angelina, not *merely* nor *mainly* nor *at all comparatively* TO EN-JOY, but together to do and dare, together to toil and testify and suffer . . . to keep ourselves and each other unspotted from the world, to live a life of faith . . . rejoicing always to bear one another's burden, looking not each on his own things but each on the things of the other, in honor preferring one another and happy beyond expression."

Angelina Grimké and Theodore Weld were married soon after her triumphant appearance before the Massachusetts legislature. A Negro baker baked the cake and only used "free sugar." At the wedding itself, the bride and groom spoke no religious formularies but only "such words as the Lord gave them at the moment." Weld reprobated the unjust laws which gave the husband control over his wife's property and Angelina responded by promising to honor him and love him. A Negro minister prayed and then a white minister.[6]

The Grimké sisters' mentor Lucretia Mott was the daughter of a retired Quaker sea captain who, as she put it, "had a desire to make his daughters useful." She was sent to a Quaker boarding school for girls in New York State. Later she taught school, married James Mott at the age of eighteen, worked for her father, after his death "engaged in the dry goods business," and then took charge of a school. "My sympathy," she wrote, "was early enlisted for the poor slave, by the class-books read in our schools, and pictures of the slave-ship. . . . The unequal condition of women in society also early impressed my mind. . . . I early resolved to claim for my sex all that an impartial Creator had bestowed." The causes of peace and temperance also enlisted her efforts and she finally took "the ultra non-resistance ground" — that no sincere Christian could "actively engage in and support a government based on the sword, or relying on that as an ultimate resort." The oppression of the working classes by monopolies, the low wage rates, the inequities of a society in which the rich grew richer and the poor poorer, all these issues concerned her deeply. But slavery was her first concern: "the millions of down-trodden slaves in our land being the greatest sufferers, the most oppressed class, I have felt bound to plead their cause, in season and out of season, to endeavor to put my soul in their souls' stead, and to aid, all in my power, in every right effort for their immediate emancipation."[7] The duty was essentially a religious one. Its roots lay deep in the Protestant passion.

I have quoted extensively from the Grimké sisters and Lucretia Mott because I wish to make clear three points: (1) the antislavery emotions of women were directly related to the *suffering* of slaves; (2) they drew their support from the wellspring of Protestant theology; and, finally, (3) these emotions were directly related to the status of women in America.

Lucretia Mott, who, incidentally, had read and digested Mary Wollstonecraft's *Vindication of the Rights of Women* was a kind of godmother to the women of the antislavery and woman's rights movements. The Grimké sisters were encouraged and guided by her. Elizabeth Cady Stanton, who encountered "the lovely Quakeress" in London, was fascinated by her and wrote, "She was the first liberal-minded woman I had ever met, and nothing in all Europe interested me as she did." Like Mrs. Mott, Elizabeth Cady had read the standard works of the day on the role of women, "But," she wrote, "I had never heard a woman talk of things that, as a Scotch Presbyterian, I had scarcely dared to think." When she heard Mrs. Mott preach in a Unitarian church, it seemed to the New York girl "like the realization of an oft-repeated happy dream." One of six children, five of them daughters, Elizabeth Cady (1815–1902) was the daughter of a prosperous New York judge. Again, like the father of the Grimké sisters and of Lucretia Mott herself, Elizabeth Cady's father took a great interest in her education. To Elizabeth he was "truly great and good — an ideal judge," who, "to his sober, taciturn, and majestic bearing," added "the tenderness, purity, and refinement of a true woman." Her mother's "stern military rule" was modified by the father's "great sense of justice."

In a scene almost too pat, Elizabeth Cady told how upon the death of her brother whom her father adored, she climbed into his lap, a child of ten, to comfort him. He said, " 'O my daughter, I wish you were a boy!' *'Then I will be a boy,'* said I, 'and I will do all that my brother did.' "[8]

The two things she settled upon to make good her promise to her father were mastering Greek and "managing a horse." She learned Greek from her minister, entered the academy, won first prize in

Greek, rushed home with her spoils to tell her father "aching to have him say something which would show that he recognized the equality of the daughter with the son." He kissed her, "appeared to be pleased . . . and exclaimed with a sigh, 'Ah, you should have been a boy!' "9 The judge thereby qualified himself as one of the principal founders of the woman's rights movement in the United States.

At the Johnston Academy, Elizabeth Cady excelled at sports as well as studies. She hoped on graduation to go to Union College at Schenectady but this was too much for the Judge. He sent her instead to Mrs. Willard's Female Seminary in Troy, one of the first colleges for women in the country, and there she spent "the dreariest years" of her life. Glad to be graduated and at home she spent half her time taming horses and the other half studying law with her father's active encouragement. Gerrit Smith, who was one of the great reformers of the day, involved in the temperance, peace and antislavery movements, was a cousin, and visiting him at his Peterboro home, Elizabeth Cady met a vigorous young antislavery orator, Henry Stanton, fell in love, and in 1840 married him. The marriage turned out to be an unhappy one, and was thereby distinguished from most of the marriages of the reforming ladies of the woman's rights and antislavery movements.

In 1833 the American Anti-Slavery Society was formed in Philadelphia, combining the streams of radical abolitionist sentiment: William Lloyd Garrison's Massachusetts Anti-Slavery Society, the New York Anti-Slavery Society, and the Western antislavery movement. Yet even at the moment of its formation, it served to emphasize the absurd position of women. It was not thought proper by the reforming males who were leaders of the movement that the sexes should be mixed in any social organization and the Female Anti-Slavery Society was formed as a feminine counterpart of the masculine organization.

Even so, women continued to be conspicuous among the antislavery leaders. When Frances Wright, who ran a school for freed Negroes in the South, lectured in Pittsburgh the Quaker journal, *The Friend,* spoke of the dogmas of "this fallen and degraded fair one" as being such as "produce the destruction of religion, morals, law and equity, and result in savage anarchy and confusion."10

The work of the antislavery forces resulted in doubling the number of abolition societies in a period of two years. In 1837 there were 1006 societies with a combined membership of more than 100,000, of which women made up more than half. One important tactic developed by the societies was the use of petitions. They had, of course, earlier been presented to Congress on a variety of issues, but the abolitionists developed the petition as perhaps their most effective instrument of propaganda. The collection of signatures became a major part of the work of women abolitionists. They had more time than men; they were less apt to be rudely rebuffed (although many certainly were); they could appeal more readily to other women.

When Southern congressmen persuaded their colleagues to refuse to accept any more petitions, they only served to stimulate a flood, many from signers to whom the issue was one of free speech more than of slavery. In April of 1838 the abolition petitions received and tabled filled a room 20 by 30 by 14 feet, an estimated half million signatures.

The antislavery movement was, then, the means of entry into American political life of a vast number of women who organized, attended and chaired meetings, prepared agenda, made motions, debated issues, circulated petitions and did all of this in the face of passive and often active resistance from most men, from virtually all the "media," and from the great majority of their sisters. It was a new phenomenon in the world. James Bryce put it: "Many of the most zealous and helpful workers in the Abolition movement were women. They showed as much courage in facing obloquy and even danger in what they deemed a sacred cause as Garrison or Lovejoy. They filled the Abolition societies and flocked to the Abolitionist conventions. . . . In an aggressive movement, as in a revolution, those who go farthest are apt to fare best. The advocates of women's claims were the bolder spirits who retained the direction of the Anti-Slavery movement."[11]

The point at which the antislavery movement turned into the woman's rights movement came in 1840 at the World Anti-Slavery Convention where several dozen American women, among them Lucretia Mott and Elizabeth Cady Stanton, who had traveled across three thousand miles of ocean to attend were refused seating because of their sex. Wendell Phillips argued eloquently in their behalf (his wife was one of the women delegates) and William Lloyd Garrison in protest refused to present his credentials or take any part in the proceedings. The indignant women returned to the United States determined to assert their rights as well as those of the Negro slave.

Theodore Weld became the center of the antislavery movement in the West and rallied around him a group of followers who helped to found Oberlin College, which from its beginning in 1850 accepted Negro students, and a year or so later permitted girls to enroll. One of the early women students at Oberlin was Lucy Stone (1818–1893) a small, energetic girl who worked her way through the college and formed a close friendship there with another student, Antoinette Brown (1825–1921). Nette Brown had decided as a child to be a preacher when she grew up. Nette and Lucy would sit, as Nette later recalled, with their arms around each other "at the sunset hour and talk and talk of our friends and our homes and of ten thousand subjects of mutual interest till both our hearts felt warmer and lighter for the pure communication of spirit."[12] After graduating from Oberlin, Nette taught for several years and then decided to get a degree in theology so that she could become a minister. Lucy Stone, who was already launched in a career as a lecturer on abolition and woman's rights, did all she could to persuade Nette that she was embarking on a dangerous and frustrating course. The rigorous and highly orthodox training at Oberlin would cramp Nette's style and inhibit her thought. Nette, for her part, insisted that her theological training simply had the effect of making her a more disciplined person without being any less "of a free thinker or independent actor."[13]

With Nette back at Oberlin, the two girls corresponded regularly about education, slavery, the woman's rights movement and marriage. The latter was a major preoccupation and Lucy Stone was convinced that it meant, inevitably, the enslavement of the wife. Nette, thinking of her own happy family was convinced that there was "no bondage in real marriage."

Daunted by the prospect of the long fight before her Nette wrote Lucy: "What hard work it is to stand alone! I am forever wanting to lean on somebody but nobody will support me, and I think seriously of swallowing the yardstick or putting on a buckram corset, so as to get a little assistance somehow, for I am determined to maintain the perpendicular position."[14]

In their discussion about marriage, the two girls came finally to the same conclusion. "Well, Lucy," Nette wrote, "so you think more than ever you must not get married. I am glad of it for so do I too. Let us stand alone in the great moral battlefield with none but God for support. There will be a lesson of truth to be learned for our very position. . . . Let them see that woman can take care of herself and act independently without the encouragement and sympathy of her 'lord and master'. . . . Oh no don't let us get married. I have no wish to I am sure."[15]

The year of the first Woman's Rights Convention, 1848, was promoted most assiduously by Elizabeth Cady Stanton and held in her hometown, Seneca Falls, New York. Lucretia Mott, "the Benjamin Franklin of the woman's rights movement," was "the ruling spirit." The convention's Declaration of Independence, drafted by Mrs. Stanton, began with the statement "We hold these truths to be self-evident; that all men and women are created equal. . . . The history of mankind," the declaration continued, "is a history of repeated injuries and usurpations on the part of man toward woman, having in direct object the establishment of tyranny over her." Then followed a list of specific grievances, ending with the charge that man "has endeavored, in every way that he could, to destroy [woman's] confidence in her own powers, to lessen her self-respect and to make her willing to lead a dependent and abject life."

So much was by now familiar rhetoric of the movement. But Mrs. Stanton wished to go further; she introduced, over the objections of Lucretia Mottt and most of the other leaders at the convention, a resolution declaring "it is the duty of the women of this country to secure to themselves their sacred right to the elective franchise." The idea was so novel that Judge Cady feared his daughter had lost her mind and traveled to Seneca Falls to determine for himself whether she was still rational. He concluded that she was and was reported to have said, "My child, I wish you had waited until I was under the sod, before you had done this foolish thing!"[16] The reaction of the country to the convention and more especially to the suffrage resolution was one of mockery and derision.

Lucy Stone and Nette Brown were fired by the Seneca Falls convention to give their energies increasingly to the cause of woman's rights. Nette Brown preached wherever she could find a pulpit or a platform, and Lucy Stone was soon one of the most popular lecturers on abolition and female emancipation in the country.

In 1850 Susan B. Anthony (1820–1906) came to the woman's rights movement through temperance reform. She had grown up in New York State, the daughter of a Quaker cotton manufacturer who took a strong interest in her education, encouraged her to work in his factory and organized a school in his own house which she attended until she was seventeen. She taught school for the next fifteen years and finally was recruited to the woman's movement by Elizabeth Cady Stanton. The two women came to be the closest of friends and associates. Susan Anthony, convinced that she could never appeal to a man because of a cast in one eye, became the drillmaster of the little company of soldiers in the war for female equality. She warned them against men, and when they fell in love she warned them against marriage and when they married she warned them against having children and when they had children, warned them against having more. Almost from the first there was tension between Mrs. Stanton and Susan Anthony, on the one hand, and Lucy Stone, Nette Brown and the New England contingent on the other. The New Englanders resented what seemed to them New York parochialism and a tendency for Mrs. Stanton to play the great lady.

In addition, the movement was often riddled by dissension, by contentions over strategy, and by petty bickerings. Nette, writing to Lucy about the Rochester convention in 1852, observed, a little dryly: "Some things were good and glorious but they quarreled a good deal of course. Douglass and Remond grew painfully personal. . . ."[17]

On another occasion Nette Brown broke out against "these womanish jealousies. . . . It seems as necessary to keep away from Conventions altogether if one is not to be contaminated as it is to keep out of politics for the same reason."[18] Even Lucy and Nette fell out briefly because Nette wore artificial flowers in her hat and Lucy, thinking them a sign of vanity and frivolity, burst into tears.

Lucy was dismayed at indications that there might soon be a number of woman's rights groups with differing programs and aims. The movement must be organized upon "true grounds" not a "narrow minded partial affair of some stamp that will shame the cause and retard its progress. . . . We may have a dozen ephemeral

Woman's Rights organizations like successive crops of mushrooms springing up and dying one after the other as the temperance parties have done," she wrote Nette, adding, "I am sick to death of this running forward blindfolded without even asking where we are going to."[19] The cause needed a William Lloyd Garrison.

Nette Brown was ordained minister in the Congregational Church of South Butler, New York, in 1853, the first woman to be ordained as a minister in the United States, and she invited Lucy to visit and hear her preach. Nette must have a difficult enough time, Lucy wrote back, without having her life complicated by the arrival of so controversial a friend. Nette reassured Lucy promptly: "You are the biggest little goose and granny fuss that I ever did see." The congregation knew Lucy wore bloomers and was an "infidel" but they were still prepared to welcome her. Two girls in the church wore bloomers and all believed in free speech. As for Nette she assured her friend that she was "still more of a woman than a minister." She had even attracted some suitors but she considered them a bother and added, "Now I hate love letters and pity lovers."[20]

Both women lectured constantly on woman's rights and abolition, traveling all over New England on speaking engagements. In addition, the number of conventions that they were expected to attend multiplied alarmingly. There were local, state, and national conventions of abolitionists, temperance reformers, peace advocates, and fighters for woman's rights. All four women — Elizabeth Cady Stanton, Susan B. Anthony, Lucy Stone and Antoinette Brown — were much in demand, Susan Anthony for her managerial and organizing talents, the others as speakers. Where Nette at first wrote to Lucy Stone of "sermonizing" and talking to her heart's content, she came before long to speak of the need "to fill these miserable engagements" as "a stern duty."

In their reform work Lucy and Nette met the Blackwell family. The Blackwell clan was the English counterpart of the Lyman Beecher family, obsessed with the same Protestant passion to improve the world. Samuel and Hannah Blackwell produced seven children, five of them girls. Of the girls, two became doctors, Elizabeth the first woman in the United States to get a medical degree. The sons, Samuel and Henry, were active in the antislavery movement and Samuel soon found himself under the spell of pretty and vivacious

Nette Brown who did her best to discourage him. Fond of him as she was, she could never be more to him than "a friend — a sister." She had a great mission which she could not compromise by marriage. Her attitude had in it nothing personal, she assured Sam; it rose "from my peculiar public position."

But Sam persisted and Nette was soon taking a different view of the matter. Marry she might but she could not bear to give up her causes. "This lecturing," she wrote Sam, "is a grand field and must be improved in the future; it brings me into competition with the best speakers of the day and has a stimulus in it exceedingly valuable." She and Sam could, she felt, "be self-sovereigns . . . we can bend everything within and without to our wills and our wills to our intellects. You asked me one day if it seemed like giving up much for your sake. Only leave me *free,* as free as you are and as everyone ought to be and it is giving up nothing. Relations will be changed but more gained probably than lost. It will not be so very bad to have a dear quiet . . . home, with one's husband to love and be loved by, with his big heart full of sympathy and an active spirit ready to cooperate in everything good."

She suggested a period of probation so that they might both be sure of their course, for she recognized that the marriage would, in fact, represent a far greater sacrifice on his part than on hers. She was asking him to give up all the traditional rights of a husband over his wife. Like Angelina Grimké and Theodore Weld, she would "reverence" her husband but not promise to "obey" him. They discussed at length how they would handle their property: "We own *together.* The *whole* is *ours* — not yours or mine. Each earns, not for himself, but for both. . . . So you see, darling, I won't have that hard earned 'paltry gold' of yours and let it ever get a chance to vex me."

Nette, abandoned to her love, wrote poignantly: "Well Sam there was a strong waif once who belonged to no one. She believed nothing and loved nobody. Then by some strange process her good genius came and joined the poor lost wanderer closely to another soul till she grew there as a kind of parasite on his sympathies. For good or ill they seemed to have grown together. Their destiny was one and the weary little outcast felt more and more ready to nestle quietly into his heart and rest there, at least until her tired spirit had grown strong again."

Even though she had fallen in love with Sam and longed to come to him as a bride and lover "her evil genius kept her toiling on in rough by-places and he pulled her haps and mishaps about her ears in hopes to crush her courage." But "a silent voice in her soul," whispered to her "to be bravehearted still." The voice was Sam's and hearing it she knew "that this fellow spirit that has been so woven into hers that nothing could quite tear them asunder."[21] She found new strength in work and in the sense that it would be a partnership.

Nette Brown and Sam Blackwell tried to keep their plans to marry a secret but rumors circulated in the little band of reformers. Lucy was being courted by Sam's brother Henry, but her friends believed her to be proof against any weak romantic notions. The word spread that Sam Blackwell was to be married but the name of the bride was unknown and Susan Anthony, knowing Nette was fond of Sam, was so innocent as to ask her if she was disturbed at the news that Sam was planning to marry. Nette, suppressing her laughter, kept her secret, and when Susan inquired as to whether Lucy Stone was engaged, Nette assured her that she was not, adding, "I believe she never will be married to H. B. Blackwell and I know she will not be to the brother." Both Lucy and Nette were aware that the views of the New Yorkers on the matter of marriage were very mixed ones. While they upheld the institution as the basis of society, they also looked on it, as it existed, as an unhappy form of bondage; above all, they would be dismayed at the prospect of losing two of the movement's most effective workers.

The day before her marriage Nette, writing to inform Susan and to apologize for not inviting her to the wedding, added, placatingly, "Susan, darling, I love you a little better than ever." She would, she promised, continue to write and lecture for the cause.[22]

Lucy Stone, who had a series of dreadful headaches for the week prior to her marriage, married Henry Blackwell not long after Nette's marriage to Sam. Again the marriage was preceded by an explicit agreement between Lucy and her fiancé on her status and rights as a wife. Lucy, indeed, went further than Nette. She must continue to keep her maiden name of Stone and be known by it and not as Mrs. Blackwell. It was a courageous if quixotic gesture. It subjected Lucy Stone, and her husband as well, to ridicule all their lives. But it was perhaps the most dramatic representation of the new relationship between husband and wife that the reformers envisioned. Elizabeth Cady had retained her maiden name of Cady as part of her married name and Antoinette Brown had done likewise. Lucy Stone carried the matter a step further and in so doing demonstrated as perhaps nothing else could have done quite so well that one woman at least was determined to make the point in a way that could not be over-looked, even if it could be, and was, misunderstood. It was, more-over, the kind of gesture that need only be done once. Lucy Stone did it for her sex but it cannot be said that they were grateful.

Nette Brown Blackwell produced a baby girl scarcely a year after her marriage and Lucy Stone had a daughter a few months later. The births seemed to confirm Susan Anthony's anxieties about the effects of domestic life on these two stalwarts of the cause. When Nette had her second child, another girl, Susan left her off the program of the woman's rights convention on the grounds that her domestic respon-sibilities would probably keep her away. Nette wrote indignantly to Susan that "the public has nothing to do with my babies or my home affairs. It may take care of its own personal interests as best it may. I will do the same."[23] But Susan Anthony could not forbear to lecture her younger friend: "Now, Nette, *not another baby,* is my *peremp-tory command, two* will solve the *problem* whether a *woman can* be anything *more* than a *wife* and *mother* better than a half dozen or *ten even.*"

Susan Anthony sent word to Nette from Lizy Stanton. If Nette intended to have a large family she should get on with it and "finish it up at once, as she has done." Lizy had, she reminded Nette, "de-voted *18* years out of the very heart of existence here to the great work. But *I say stop now,* once and for all. Your life work will be arduous enough with *two.*"[24]

Even Elizabeth Cady Stanton let Susan down. After being cited to Nette as an example of a reformer who had had her children early in order to leave her career unhampered by the care of infants, Elizabeth Cady, in her early forties became pregnant once again. "For a *mo-ment's pleasure* to herself or her husband," Susan B. Anthony wrote despairingly to Nette, Elizabeth had greatly increased "the *load* of *cares* under which she already groans."

Henry Stanton, an impractical man who pursued, in Susan An-thony's scathing phrase, "Political Air Castles" did nothing to help his wife engage in the work of the movement. Susan Anthony had a bad back and Mrs. Stanton had suffered more intensely in childbirth than ever before. "Ah me!! ah me!!! alas!! alas!!!!" Susan wrote Nette, "*Mrs. Stanton!!* is embarked on the rolling sea — three long months of terrible nausea . . . behind and what the future has in mind — the *deep* only knows."[25] She was equally provoked with Lucy "just to think that she would attempt to speak" on a program with outstanding male lecturers and "as her special preparation, take upon herself . . . *baby cares,* quite too absorbing for careful close and continued intellectual effort" in addition to "the entire work of her house. A woman who *is* and *must* of necessity continue for the present at least, as the representative woman, has no right to disqualify herself for such a *representative occasion.*"[26] As a *"baby tender"* and *"maid of all work"* Lucy was letting down the movement. Lucy was, at least for the moment, too entranced with "the radiant little face" of her daughter, and too concerned with being a good wife to be responsive to Susan Anthony's admonitions. "I never feel her little cheek beside of mine . . . never hear her sweet baby voice," she wrote her husband, absent on a business trip, "without the earnest purpose to gather to myself more symmetry of being — sustain all my relations better." She was trying her best to be a good wife and mother. "But," she wrote, "I *have* tried before, and my miserable failures hitherto make me silent now. But if I have conquered myself, or gained anything in all these weary weeks, you will find it in my actions — I hope to be more to you and better when you come to me."[27] Susan's barrage of letters to her "chieftans" warning of the hazards of bearing children finally brought a smug response from Nette Brown, blissfully happy in her married state. Susan should "get a good husband — that's all, dear."[28] Despite Susan Anthony's admonitions, Nette and Sam Blackwell had five daughters, two of whom became doctors.

The reformers were, in many ways, like a great family, or, if we consider the division between the New Yorkers and the New Englanders, like two great families bound together by common ties, and even, as in the case of Nette Brown and Lucy Stone, by marriage. Living in enemy territory, their public and private life was spent very largely in each other's company. When they were not together, they wrote voluminous letters to each other. Their children grew up together and, in time, their grandchildren. A century-long struggle lay ahead of them.

Henceforth suffrage reform would be carried along on the momentum generated by the little band of reformers who had taken up the cause in the two decades preceding the Civil War. In the antislavery agitation, women had, for the first time in history, shared the leadership of a profoundly important social movement. For those who participated it was an intoxicating experience. Born out of a simple moral indignation, fueled by the Protestant passion, it ran against all the tides of national complacency and spiritual obtuseness. The outcries against the woman reformers were continuous and generally hysterical. The editor of the *Albany Register* commenting on the New York Woman's Rights State Convention, wrote: "People are beginning to inquire how far public sentiment should sanction or tolerate these unsexed women, who make a scoff of religion, who repudiate the Bible and blaspheme God: who would step out from the true sphere of the mother, the wife, and the daughter, and taking upon themselves the duties and business of men, stalk into the public gaze, and by engaging in the politics, the rough controversies, and the trafficking of the world, upheave existing institutions and overturn all the social relations of life." That is, of course, what they had set out to do —"to upheave existing institutions and overturn all the social relations of life"— and what in fact they did.

It is impossible to say what course the abolition movement and the emancipation of the Negro slave might have followed without the support of the hundreds of thousands of women. But one can say with assurance that it would have been a very different course and it is also questionable whether the woman's rights movement would have made such substantial progress without the cadres formed in the antislavery struggle. It was, quite literally, the opening chapter in the struggle that brought women into world history in a new role and with a heretofore unimagined potency. The women drew their power from their relationship with their fathers. The daughters of Zion, treated in their families as persons of worth and consequence, were armored thereby for an assault on the strongholds of masculine arrogance and prejudice. They spoke in public, they wrote, they harangued, they *appeared,* suddenly and dramatically visible. Assumed, taken-for-granted, feared or adored, they found a voice and a cause.

Thousands of people of both sexes came, like visitors to a zoo, simply to *see* a woman stand on a platform and talk like a man about politics and social injustice and a better human order, and, above all, about a new kind of relationship between men and women.

Along with a certain self-righteousness and some hyperbole there was a large measure of truth in the introduction to the *History of Woman Suffrage:* Women, the editor wrote, had been victims of the "same principle of selfishness and love of power in man that has thus far dominated weaker nations and classes." This impulse to domination was encouraged by "the slavish instinct of an oppressed class. . . . She has long been bought and sold, caressed and crucified at the will and pleasure of her master."[29]

The leaders of the woman's suffrage movement had been women "of superior mental and physical organization, of good social standing and education, remarkably alike for their domestic virtues, knowledge of public affairs, and rare executive ability; good speakers and writers, inspiring and conducting the genuine reforms of the day; everywhere exerting themselves to promote the best interests of society."[30]

8

Speaking the Word

Something must be said about what was perhaps the most remarkable phenomenon of the antislavery–woman's rights movement — the speaking of women to large and responsive audiences. Hearing a woman speak in public in the early years of the nineteenth century was at once a shocking and exciting novelty.

How can the success of women lecturers in the first half of the nineteenth century be explained? It must be said first of all that women were speaking of the two most fundamental of all human relationships — those between the sexes and those between races — and they were preaching a revolutionary doctrine with evangelical fervor. Many of them were attractive women, and most of them had an eloquence that was the consequence of passionate conviction. Moreover, the advocates of woman's rights were giving practical demonstrations of the principles they espoused. It was a primary article of faith that women were unsuitable for public life, that their "powers of reasoning were radically deficient," that they were too frail and delicate to endure the rough give-and-take of politics, that physically, mentally, and in their emotional and nervous constitutions they could not possibly find their way in a man's world. So they were engaged in acting out a drama which gave the lie to all the accepted formularies about their sex. Their remarkable energies were directed to conversion and they themselves were aware of their significance as revolutionists, as the first women in history to break out of the confines of the harem, the seraglio, the court or the home. They were like engineers who had discovered and released into society a vast new source of energy.*

Angelina Grimké became one of the first great orators of the anti-slavery cause. Wendell Phillips, considered the most gifted of all reform lecturers, spoke of her Odeon lectures as "eloquence such as never then had been heard from a woman. Her own hard experience, the long, lonely, intellectual and moral struggle from which she came out conqueror, had ripened her power and her wondrous faculty for laying bare her own heart to reach the heart of others shown forth, till she carried us all captive."[1]

In 1837–38 Angelina and Sarah Grimké went on a nine-month speaking tour during the course of which they spoke at eighty meetings in sixty-seven towns and cities to an estimated 40,000 people. Most of these communities had never heard a woman speaker before and the Grimkés were often bitterly attacked and ridiculed in the press. As the climax of the tour Angelina appeared before the Massachusetts State Legislature to speak in behalf of abolition. She came armed with the signatures of 20,000 Massachusetts women protesting the institution of slavery and spoke to a hall packed to bursting with friends of the cause and spectators come out of curiosity to hear a lady orator.

She began by recalling the story of Queen Esther pleading before King Ahasuerus for her people: "Mr. Chairman, it is my privilege to stand before you on a similar mission of life and love." She came as representative of the women of Massachusetts, "And because it is a political subject, it has often tauntingly been said, that women had nothing to do with it. Are we aliens, because we are women? Are we bereft of citizenship because we are mothers, wives and daughters of

---

* Again the analogy with the Negro rebellion of the 1960's is irresistible and instructive. The twentieth-century Negro, like the nineteenth-century woman, has suddenly become dramatically visible. No longer the invisible man, he is suddenly seen to be a powerful and threatening figure, full of destructive potentialities, someone who has defied his "place" and his "betters," the ruling white class, the "establishment." He appears dangerously problematical, ready as women were in the early nineteenth century to "upheave existing institutions, and overturn all the social relations of life."

a mighty people? Have women *no* country — *no* interests staked in public weal — no liabilities in common peril — no partnership in a nation's guilt and shame? . . . I hold, Mr. Chairman, that American women have to do with this subject, not only because it is moral and religious, but because it is *political,* inasmuch as we are citizens of this republic and as such our honor, happiness and well-being are bound up in its politics, government and laws."[2]

She ended with a moving *mea culpa:* "I stand before you as a southerner, exiled from the land of my birth, by the sound of the lash and the piteous cry of the slave. I stand before you as a repentant slaveholder. I stand before you as a moral being endowed with precious and inalienable rights, which are correlative with solemn duties and high responsibilities; and as a moral being I feel that I owe it to the suffering slave, and to the deluded master, to my country and the world, to do all that I can to overturn a system of complicated crimes, built up upon the broken hearts and prostrate bodies of my countrymen in chains, and cemented by the blood, sweat and tears of my sisters in bonds."[3]

The Grimké sisters were joined by others: Lucretia Mott (already well-known as a speaker), Abby Kelley, Anna Dickinson, Amelia Bloomer, Susan Anthony and Mrs. Stanton; Lucy Stone and Nette Brown of course; Caroline Severance, the exotic Ernestine Rose, a beautiful Polish, Jewish girl, and many more. Invariably they made their way against masculine resistance. After Abby Kelley was granted permission to speak at a meeting of the Connecticut Anti-Slavery Society in 1840, the chairman of the meeting resigned his post, declaring "I will not sit in a chair where women bear rule. I vacate this chair. No woman shall speak or vote where I am moderator. I will not countenance such an outrage on decency. I will not consent to have women lord it over men in public assemblies. It is enough for women to rule at home. It is woman's business to take care of children in the nursery. She has no business to come into this meeting, and by speaking and voting lord it over men. Where women's enticing eloquence is heard men are incapable of right and efficient action. She beguiles and blinds men by her smiles and her bland and winning voice . . . *I have had enough of woman's control in the nursery. Now I am a man, I will not submit to it.*"[4]

Perhaps the most spectacular woman speaker for the abolitionist cause was a young Quaker girl, Anna Dickinson, who won the title of the American Joan of Arc for her impassioned eloquence. In 1862 at the age of twenty she began a lecture tour on behalf of Republican candidates for Congress. When she visited Connecticut to support the "Loyalist" Buckingham, "the halls where she spoke were so densely packed that Republicans stayed away to make room for Democrats, and women were shut out to give place to those who could vote." From Connecticut she went on to give an address at Cooper Institute in New York, and we are told in the somewhat perfervid prose of an historian of her own sex: "There never was such excitement over any meeting in New York. . . . There were clergymen, generals, admirals, judges, lawyers, editors, the literati, and leaders of fashion, and all alike ready to do homage to this simple girl, who moved them alternately to laughter and tears, to bursts of applause and the most profound silence." In July, 1862, she addressed the first regiment of Negro troops recruited to fight in the Northern army and again: "As she stood there uttering words of warning and prophecy, it seemed as if her lips had been touched with a live coal from the altar of heaven."[5]

Since the woman's rights movement came directly out of the anti-slavery agitation — indeed, the advocates of both causes were the same women and they often combined the causes in the same speech — it was inevitable that their rhetoric on the matter of woman's rights should be suffused with images of slavery and bondage. Women were the slaves of selfish and tyrannical husbands. Even the kindest of husbands, like the kindest of slaveholders, were corrupted by the absolute power that they held over their womenfolk. Women, like slaves, had to receive as concessions the rights to which they were entitled as human beings. As one woman put it, "Slave deceives master, and master deceives slave. So in the marriage relation in thousands of instances."[6]

The woman orators soon developed professional attitudes and techniques as well as their own particular themes. Since two or three often spoke on the same program there was a problem of timing. It was no novelty in the history of oratory that the ladies were apt to be carried away and talk too long. Thirty minutes was adjudged to be generally an appropriate length for a talk when three or more women shared the same platform. It was Susan B. Anthony's command that

the members of her troupe "must condense"; it seemed to her sometimes "as if every woman who spoke felt she must tell all she knew on every subject." Different orators had different gifts, their own "thing"; they must develop that. Nette Brown Blackwell, as a new wife, was inclined to "try to reduce great principles to *details* of everyday life, as the sewing machine turning . . ." But this, Susan warned her, was not her forte. No one elucidated "great fundamental principles better than Antoinette Brown, with grand illustrations of life." Lucy Stone did best the homely little parables from everyday life.[7]

Having won a place on the antislavery platform and gone on from there to espouse woman's rights, feminine reformers were determined to establish themselves as temperance speakers. Since drunkenness was almost exclusively a masculine failing, there was strong resistance to having women speak on the subject. In some instances where women became active in temperance organizations they were either forced to establish their own societies or the men simply withdrew to form associations exclusively male.

To the argument that temperance was no business of a woman, Amelia Bloomer replied with some vehemence. In the first place, she declared, "Home is said to be woman's sphere; herein, at least, she should forbid the intoxicating cup to enter. . . . Woman has also retarded the cause of temperance by using intoxicating drinks for culinary purposes. Such a one voluntarily yields up her children to the Moloch of intemperance. . . . None of woman's business, when she is subject to poverty and degradation and made an outcast from respectable society! None of woman's business, when her starving naked babes are compelled to suffer the horrors of the winter's blast! . . . In the name of all that is sacred, what is woman's business if this be no concern of hers? (Great applause.) None of woman's business! What is woman? Is she a slave? Is she a mere toy? Is she formed, like a piece of fine porcelain, to be placed upon the shelf to be looked at? Is she a responsible being? or has she no soul? . . . She must not wait for man to help her; this is her business as much as his. Let her show to the world that she possesses somewhat of the spirit and blood of the daughters of the Revolution! Such thoughts as these may be thought unladylike; but if they are so, they are not unwomanly. (Applause.)"[8]

This was stemwinding oratory in the best American tradition. It is easy to understand its appeal to a feminine audience, urged to rebel against male domination. Not only did women win a prominent place for themselves in the temperance movement, they virtually took it over, and the issue in many associations founded by women came to whether men should be admitted. This same question plagued the woman's rights movement. Just as present-day black power advocates exclude white liberals from their organizations, the more militant female reformers wished to exclude men from their organizations while the moderates insisted on admitting them and welcomed their support. Without such support women could in fact never win the equality they sought.

If anything, temperance was a more popular lecture topic than slavery or woman's rights. When in 1853 Amelia Bloomer went to New York to give three temperance lectures with Susan Anthony and Nette Brown, she addressed packed houses with audiences estimated at between 3,000 and 5,000 persons. That they were not universally admired is indicated by an entry in George Templeton Strong's diary: "Great shindy between Bloomers and anti-Bloomers, at the Temperance Convention in session here. As for the 'Rev.' Antoinette Brown & Co., I should be glad to see them respectfully jumped upon by a crowd of self-appointed conservators of manners and morals, though perhaps they have womanhood enough left in spite of themselves to be worthy of better usage. The strumpets of Leonard and Church streets are not *much* further below the ideal of womanhood than these loathsome dealers in clack, who seek to change women into garrulous men without virility. I'm glad I'm too stolid tonight for full realization of their folly. It would surely lead to a sick headache tomorrow. Womanhood is still reverenced in this irreverent age and country, as every omnibus and railroad car can testify. Destroy its claim to concession and protection and courtesy by putting it on an equality in everything but physical strength with manhood, and manhood is gone, too . . ."[9] And the *New York Herald* editorialized: "These women would not be guilty of such vulgarity as to live with their husbands . . . infidelity and socialism . . . have distorted their silly heads. . . . How funny it would sound in the newspapers that Lucy Stone pleading a cause took suddenly ill in the pains of parturition, and perhaps gave birth to a fine boy in court!"

SPEAKING THE WORD

In the contrast to musty official rhetoric of the era, women speakers had a force and vividness that enthralled their audiences. They illustrated their points with stories, anecdotes, "homely" metaphors; they each found a style adapted to their particular talents and background. Their passion gave them eloquence. The word, never uttered before in public by women, came from their lips with a peculiar power. They spoke to crowded halls, listeners packed in every corner. Men came to scoff and stayed to applaud. For more than a generation women speakers in the abolition, temperance, and woman's rights movements made up a disproportionate number of the most popular public speakers in the country. In the aggregate they addressed millions of listeners.

The life that the lady warriors of woman's rights laid out for themselves was an exhilarating but often frightening one. For males their doctrines doubtless were less unnerving than the sight of these theoretically delicate and fragile women barnstorming around the country, enduring the classic difficulties and discomforts of primitive transportation, giving speech after speech, often several in a day, facing down hostile crowds, enduring the often obscene jibes of men and the venomous attacks of newspaper editorialists. It was an astonishing spectacle and for those willing to reflect upon its significance it demonstrated, as no amount of logical disputation could have done, how remarkably wide of the mark were the accepted notions of the nature of women.

It was, above all, the *speaking* that was potent, that gave both the speakers and the listeners the sense of a new power loose in American society. Women had broken the sound barrier. Because these women, like the Negroes of present-day America, spoke with passion, they *had* to be heard. They changed the way people thought, but even more the way they *felt*. And that was the basic transformation; everything else followed from it.

The Delicate and Ailing

There is substantial evidence that the vast majority of American marriages, at least in the larger cities of the East and Middle West in the nineteenth century, were minor disasters. Women who were treated as objects of reverence, too pure and refined for the world, given to vapors and fainting spells, to sick headaches and bad backs, and a multitude of nervous disorders, who blushed at the mention of a leg or chemise, could not have been very rewarding sexual partners. Nor, it may be assumed, can the harassed male, his thoughts constantly focused on the problem of making a living, have been a very ardent suitor. He had, nonetheless, certain appetites common to the species, even if perhaps fortunately of diminished vigor, and the satisfaction of these in the bed of his wife could well result in pregnancy.

For the nineteenth-century woman, with her nerves, her delicate constitution and her hopeless prudery, pregnancy was far more threatening than to her grandmother. If she was too modest even to tell a doctor what portion of her anatomy pained or reveal any part of it to his professional examination, pregnancy must certainly have been something to avoid, if possible, once the obligation to produce a respectable number of offspring had been fulfilled. It seems clear enough that many wives, consciously or unconsciously, developed elaborate strategies for limiting the occasions of sexual intercourse with their husbands, and thus limiting their families. The most obvious strategy, of course, was ill health. Since it was a sign of being ladylike to be in delicate health, there was the greater incentive. In addition, as one traveler after another noted, American wives led confined and unhealthy lives.

The ills of Americans, men and women alike, but more notably women, centered on "the nerves." Nervous exhaustion, nervous prostration and, more recently, nervous breakdown were medically vague descriptions of simple inability to cope with life. These states were marked by symptoms that today are readily recognized as various forms of neurosis, of hysteria, of crippling anxiety — headaches, frequent nausea, dizziness, fainting spells, backaches, partial paralysis, "lassitude," and so on. Moreau de St. Méry was one of the first foreign travelers to comment on the tendency of American women "to nervous illness . . . which is extremely frequent." Brissot de Warville had noted a few years earlier that American wives were very susceptible to consumption and laid this to "the submission to which they are accustomed, or rather condemned, [and] acts on them like chains which compress their limbs, gnaw at their flesh, cause obstructions, deaden their vitality, and impede circulation. The gradual depression of the soul results in a weakening of the body."[1]

Captain Marryat likewise observed that the principal American disorder was that of the nerves. Menstruation was also a basic source of women's ill health; it was surrounded by such a hopeless crust of superstition and prudery that a proper understanding of it was impossible. It was taken to be a sign of woman's inferior health and vitality, a kind of hereditary disease which was part of the "curse" that women must bear for the sins of Eve. It was thus surrounded by all the accompaniments of actual illness — weakness, headaches, "fevers," rest, bland food, medicine. Every month a woman had "spells," or vapors, or indispositions, all delicate euphemisms for her menstrual period, which reminded her ceaselessly that she was a fragile creature diseased in some strange and terrible fashion. Today it is almost impossible to imagine how large this unspoken matter loomed in the imaginations of women and men alike in the nineteenth century. One of the principal contributions of women doctors when they broke into the medical profession was to spread the news that "the seasonal disturbance of the woman's physique is a perfectly normal function which, if rightly understood, need not detract from her full healthfulness and efficiency."[2]

The contrast between the freedom of a daughter and the confinement of a wife undoubtedly contributed to the woman's willingness to employ such a strategy. The most enterprising and independent threw themselves (and in many instances drew their husbands with them, or chose mates sympathetic to such involvements) into reform activities of every kind, the great majority found solace in church work, and most of them doubtless discovered a welcome avenue of escape in "ailing." Ailing wives created a new profession — the running of sanitariums and health resorts which catered specifically to their needs.

In the state of submissiveness and dependence which characterized most marriages, it was difficult, if not impossible, for a wife to keep a husband at bay even if she was "poorly." The foreign doctor offering the newest nostrum in his health resort provided a welcome refuge. Hydrotherapy had a great vogue and was preceded and followed by a variety of restorative diets, purges, colonic treatments (as the therapy grew more sophisticated) and God knows what remedies. Since the ill health was often genuine as well as psychosomatic, many cures were perfectly sensible ones involving the wearing of loose clothing, the taking of invigorating baths, long walks and regular exercise.

If we add to the unhealthy physical confinement of women — their stays, corsets, constricting garments, tight shoes and lack of exercise, their intellectual confinement and the repression of their sexuality, we have quite enough to explain the almost endemic bad health.

Catharine Beecher, sister of Harriet Beecher Stowe and Henry Ward, and daughter of Lyman, became so obsessed with the question of the health of American women that she spent forty years trying to discover why chronic illness was the lot of "the women of this generation." Her travels through most of the states had convinced her that "there was a terrible decay of female health all over the land." She herself had suffered from "extreme prostration of the overworked brain and nerves" to the point where she could not walk without crutches, and she had exhausted all the popular remedies of the day. She had tried rhubarb, iron and camphor and been twice bled for "nervous excitement." In an effort to regain her health, she had experimented with food cures, water cures, electric cures, sulphur baths, vapor baths, Russian baths, chemical baths, Turkish baths, sun baths, the Grape Cure, the Lifting Cure for "internal displacements," various "breathing cures" and finally, and most successfully, the Swedish cure consisting of fresh air and exercise. She conducted a crude kind of poll by writing to friends and acquaintances in every town she had visited asking them to report on the health of the ten women in their community that they knew best. Her respondents were given a scale that ranged from "perfectly healthy" through "feeble" and "delicate" to "sickly."

In the vast majority of cases that Catharine Beecher knew of at first hand, wives and mothers were partially incapacitated and thus their effectiveness vastly reduced. The family was the heart of any vigorous society. If its wives and mothers were the victims of neurosis and a variety of physical disabilities, it had no prospects but decay and dissolution. Why, above all, she asked, did she find so many "comfortably situated" wives, "united to the most congenial and devoted husbands expressing the hope that their daughters would never marry."[3]

In Milwaukee her informant gave Catharine Beecher a depressing inventory of the health of the ladies she knew in that frontier metropolis. Their ailments ranged from "headaches," "very feeble," "well, except chills," to "consumption," "pelvic displacements," and "coughs." "I do not know," her correspondent wrote, "one healthy woman in the place."

So it ran from Milwaukee, Wisconsin, to Essex, Vermont, and Peru, New York (which counted three "healthy" and two "pretty well," out of ten). In Oberlin, of the ten wives best known to the respondent, none was healthy. In Wilmington, one of ten was healthy, and in New Bedford her respondent could think "of but one perfectly healthy woman in the place." In other towns and cities throughout the country, the "habitual invalids" and "delicate or diseased" outnumbered the "strong and healthy" from four to one to ten to one. Catharine Beecher wrote that of her nine married sisters and sisters-in-law "all of them [were] either delicate or invalids, except two." She had fourteen married female cousins "and no one of them but is either delicate, often ailing or an invalid . . ." In over two hundred towns only two had a majority of healthy women among the ten sampled. And in Boston, from her wide acquaintance, Catharine Beecher knew of only one married woman who was "perfectly healthy." Indeed, she professed herself unable to recall in her "immense circle of friends and acquaintances all over the Union, so many as ten married ladies born in this century and country, who are perfectly sound, healthy, and vigorous." She was convinced that the same appalling statistics applied to the "industrial classes."

Everywhere she went mothers appealed to her! "What shall I do? As soon as my little girl begins school she has the headache." She was convinced that the remedies were "Light, Air, Sleep, Food and Clothing." This was a doctrine, as urgent as that of salvation, which must be preached in every city and town in the land. Doctors were so inept, Catharine Beecher argued, that it was especially important that women be trained as "health keepers" as well as "housekeepers."[4]

Catharine Beecher blamed, quite properly, the clothes women wore, their confinement to poorly ventilated houses, and their lack of exercise and fresh air. She became in consequence the first active advocate of physical education or training for women. But important as such reforms were, the problem lay even deeper. How much deeper is suggested by the experience of Catharine's own marvelous sister, Harriet.

Harriet had neurotic symptoms in abundance. Father Lyman Beecher was full of the Protestant passion and passed on large portions of it to his six minister sons and his three remarkable daughters. We might propose the elder Beecher as the very model of the nineteenth-century father. Although he was an orthodox Calvinist who preached fiery sermons on the horrors of hellfire, and who hated liquor and Catholicism equally, he was a loving and devoted father whose relations with his daughters were especially close ones. He infused them with his own passionate desire to reform mankind, starting of course with wayward Americans. As children, Catharine and Harriet Beecher had often listened to their father recite in the accents of the pulpit orator, Cowper's *Task*. All their lives in memory's ear they could hear him read to their mother in exulting tones the poet's version of this millennial consummation, which in

Catharine's words "was the inspiring vision of his lifelong labors — a consummation to which all their children were consecrated, and to which some of them may possibly live to belong."

With such goals before her, Harriet often felt herself hopelessly inadequate. At the age of sixteen, ten years younger than her sister, she confided to Catharine, "I don't know as I am fit for anything and I have thought that I could wish to die young and let the remembrance of me and my faults perish in the grave rather than live, as I fear I do, a trouble to everyone. Sometimes I could not sleep and have groaned and cried till midnight . . . I felt as though I should be distracted."[5] Nine years later, in 1836, having assisted Catharine in a girls' school that she had opened in Cincinnati, Harriet married Professor Calvin Stowe, a classics professor at the seminary over which her father presided.

Calvin Stowe was a typical nineteenth-century husband, fussy, tyrannical, tormented by piles, a depressive who "cultivated indigo," suffered "nervous irritability" and treated his wife like a serving-woman. Even after his shrewish mother came to live with them, Harriet stuck it out through three children and ten exhausting years. Then, her right side mysteriously paralyzed, she went off to Brattleboro, Vermont, to take a "water cure" recommended by Catharine, loyally writing every day or so to her husband marooned with his mother, the children and several incompetent servants.

The professor, unable to refrain from dabbling in speculative ventures and unwilling to live on his modest professorial salary, was perpetually despairing over his failure to achieve "an easy situation." This did not, Harriet assured him, trouble her. She wished only to know and do the will of God. Were her health equal to it, she would in fact prefer privations to ease; in her view the fortunate ones were those who suffered for Christ's sake.

As Harriet's days at the Brattleboro sanitarium stretched into weeks and months, she gave poor Calvin a course in the duties and responsibilities of a husband. She confessed that she longed to be "a wife and mother" once more but that her right hand was still partially paralyzed and she was too weak to do more than walk four or five miles a day — sometimes up to seven — in the Vermont countryside for therapy. The blessed peace was balm to her: "Not for years have I enjoyed life as I have here. . . . I could tell you worlds of

God's nearness and goodness to me — of heaven begun on earth as I walk through these beautiful mountains."[6]

"I trust," she wrote in another of the flood of letters written or dictated, "you have almost entirely obtained the mastery of yourself in the most difficult point of all." What this "point" is, the writer does not say. It is, in essence, surrender to God's will. But what God's will is and how Stowe has resisted it is not revealed unless it is by his demanding and dictatorial attitude and his impatience at her deficiencies as a housekeeper. It may equally be his fits of depression, or, possibly, his sexual desires. Certainly she is quite frank to speak of the years of their marriage as "years of pain, confusion, anxiety, disappointment and suffering." She had finally learned the bitter lesson that God did not wish her to make her family "my chief good and portion." Both she and Calvin were "morbidly sensitive and acute": the "one hasty and impulsive — the other sensitive and brooding — one the very personification of exactive and routine and the other to whom everything of the kind was an irksome effort." She had gone from the happy and loving disorder of her father's huge family to the petty cavils of a domestic martinet. Though she could never love again "with the blind and unwise love with which I married, I love as truly tho far more wisely," she assured her distant husband. He, too, was a better man with only a "few more traces of the earthly to be burned away in the fires of affliction." She herself was, she wrote, "a shattered broken invalid just able to creep along by great care." But she did after all walk five miles a day!

She had done her best to arrange things for his comfort and convenience only to have him exclaim: "Things *never* are regular." If he could only admit sometimes that he himself had been hasty or unjust. It was hard to confess her own shortcomings under "hasty and irritated censure." Her year of change and rest had restored her only partially. She would be for the rest of her life "at best an amended invalid . . . obliged to walk softly and carefully," to take up "a life of entire quiet without any undertaking or responsibility of any kind." These warnings were sweetened by assurances that she longed to put her arms around him and comfort him; that she dreamed constantly of him and was impatient to be home.[7]

Stowe must have been at his wit's end after months of such treatment and ready to make any concessions to entice back a wife whom he loved and on whom he had a childish dependence. Whatever Harriet's deficiencies may have been, she was certainly better than no wife at all. He evidently promised to "master himself in the most difficult point of all," and by bathing his feet in warm water and taking sitz baths, he at least moderated his "nervous irritability."

Harriet persuaded Stowe to take a position at Bowdoin College in Maine and the family was finally reunited. If her situation as a favored daughter and a tyrannized wife was typical of American middle-class women of the last century, the strategy by which she produced in her husband a more reasonable and compliant attitude was equally typical.

In New Brunswick Harriet began *Uncle Tom's Cabin*. She felt that the novel was in essence a story of the disruption of family life. Uncle Tom is a kind of father to Eva as well as to Eliza. The cruelty of slavery lies in the fact that it destroys the family. Uncle Tom is separated from his wife; Eva in turn is separated from her father and Uncle Tom by death and Eliza forced to flee with her infant child, leaving her husband George behind. Mary Chesnut felt that Mrs. Stowe missed the essential evil of slavery — slaveholders who dishonored their marital beds by their sexual indulgences with Negro women. A sense of the loss of family was at the very center of her own despair. In this sense *Uncle Tom's Cabin* was a story about the death of that consoling love peculiar to families, and especially to her own.

Uncle Tom's Cabin was, beyond measure, the most popular and important book written by an American in the nineteenth century. It may well, in its direct social and political consequences, have been the most important literary work in our history. It formed a national conscience on the issue of slavery where before only lonely voices had been heard. Not a great literary work, it was not, on the other hand, a collection of stiff and stereotyped figures. The sentimental passion that suffused the book derived from the anguish of the author's own disastrous marriage forced through the characters and events of the novel. Harriet's paralysis was related to the failure of her marriage. *Uncle Tom's Cabin* followed her own "dark night of the soul" in Brattleboro, Vermont. The episode of her "cure" gives us an insight into the tactics of many nineteenth-century wives. Their ill health was as much as anything else a birth control measure. We find a constant

litany running through the writings of the more daring spokesmen of
the woman's movement: women must gain control of their own
bodies; marriage is a form of legalized prostitution because the husband may lay claim to sexual intercourse *at his own will.*

An elaborate mythology about man's animal nature circulated in
the feminine underground. It was believed that "the least appearance
of coldness or withdrawal for whatever cause, in the wife is wicked,
because liable to turn her husband's thoughts to illicit indulgence; for
a man was so constituted that he must indulge his passions or die!
. . . A great part of women look upon men as a kind of wild beast,
but 'suppose they are all alike'; the unmarried are assured by the
married that 'if they knew men as they do,' that is, by being married
to them, 'they would not expect continence or self-government from
them.' " Such attitudes, widely disseminated and widely believed,
helped to make the nineteenth-century middle-class marriage a
shambles.

10

The Sexual Rights
of Women

As with every major war in America's history, the Civil War saw great advances in the status and opportunities of women. With the outbreak of the conflict, the issue of emancipation suddenly acquired a new urgency and respectability.

Susan B. Anthony and Mrs. Stanton took the lead in organizing the Women's Loyal National League to support the war effort and create pressure for immediate emancipation. In 1863 the league began a campaign to secure one million signatures in favor of emancipation, urging it "as an enterprise most honorable to the sex which conceived and completed it." "There must be a law abolishing slavery," Mrs. Stanton declared. "We have undertaken to canvass the nation for freedom. . . . Go to the rich, the poor, the high, the low, the soldier, the civilian, the white, the black — gather up the names of all who hate slavery — all who love liberty . . . and lay them at the feet of Congress. . . ."[1]

The fact that women had been among the leaders in the antislavery movement inevitably enhanced their prestige. Lincoln met Harriet Beecher Stowe and is supposed to have said, "So this is the little lady that caused the great war." And if Harriet Beecher Stowe's famous book helped to harden Northern sentiment against slavery and Anna Dickinson was the most famous Republican and orator, Julia Ward

Howe wrote the "Battle Hymn of the Republic" and Clara Barton organized a volunteer nurse corps for wounded and disabled soldiers.

Women were the moving spirits in putting on mammoth sanitary fairs held in New York and Philadelphia, the first of which raised a million and the second a million two hundred thousand dollars, by far the largest private philanthropic ventures recorded up to that time. The money was used primarily to outfit and maintain military hospitals. When the war was over and the emancipation of the slaves a fact, thousands of young women went south to staff the schools for the education of Negro children that were being established by Northern philanthropists as well as by the Freedman's Bureau.

It seemed to the reformers that the next order of business was votes for the free Negro and for the women who had done so much to bring that freedom about. One group felt strongly that women should receive the vote *before* the freed slave; the other wished to devote all its energies to securing the vote for the Negro. The split was primarily regional. Elizabeth Cady Stanton and her faction were determined to give priority to women; Lucy Stone and the New Englanders, whose involvement with the abolitionists was far deeper, were content to see the Negro given priority. When the Fifteenth Amendment was proposed, Lucy Stone wrote "woman has an ocean of wrong too deep for any plummet . . . and the Negro too has an ocean of wrong that cannot be fathomed. But I thank God for the Fifteenth Amendment, and hope it will be adopted in every state. I will be thankful in my soul if anybody can get out of the terrible pit. . . ." And Julia Ward Howe was quoted by Frederick Douglass as saying, "I am willing that the Negro shall get the ballot before me," adding, "I cannot see how anyone can pretend that there is the same urgency in giving the ballot to women as to the Negro."[2]

Negro men who had been among the leaders of the abolition movement proved to be not very different from white men in their attitudes toward woman's suffrage. Men like Frederick Douglass did not hesitate to denounce those women who wished to push the vote for their own sex before the vote for the Negro or even to associate the two causes.

One of the most poignant moments in the struggle for woman's rights came when Sojourner Truth, the ancient Negro abolitionist and loyal worker for the cause of women, spoke her mind on the subject of suffrage: "There is a great stir about colored men getting their rights, but not a word about the colored women theirs, you see the colored men will be masters over the women, and it will be just as bad as it was before. So I am for keeping the thing going while things are stirring; because if we wait till it is still, it will take a great while to get it going again. White women are a great deal smarter, and know more than colored women, while colored women do not know scarcely anything. They go out washing, which is about as high as a colored woman gets, and their men go about idle, strutting up and down; and when the women come home, they ask for their money and take it all, and then scold because there is no food. I want you to consider on that, chil'n. I call you chil'n; you are somebody's chil'n, and I am old enough to be the mother of all that is here. I want women to have their rights. . . . I have been forty years a slave and forty years free, and would be here forty years more to have equal rights for all. . . ."[3]

There were other issues in addition to suffrage that divided the movement. One was divorce, on which the New Yorkers were liberal, the New Englanders conservative. Then there was the greenback issue and, finally, free love. The free love question never, of course, defined itself as exactly that. It presented itself in the more enticing and more ambiguous form of the Claflin sisters, Victoria and Tennessee (or Tennie C. as she called herself for a time) Claflin. Before the episode of the Claflin sisters was over, the woman's rights movement which, after the Civil War changed its name to the woman's suffrage movement, was in complete disarray. The New Yorkers founded the National Woman's Suffrage Association in May, 1869, and Julia Ward Howe, Lucy Stone and Nette Blackwell the American Woman's Suffrage Association shortly after.

It is the Claflin sisters who must get the credit (or the blame) for projecting the issue of sex into the woman's suffrage movement. Mary Wollstonecraft had been the most explicit explicator of this theme. As the reader will recall, Mrs. Wollstonecraft had argued that sexual passion was transient. When a man and a woman no longer felt strong physical attraction for each other, their relationship should be dissolved; it could only become exploitive and embittering if perpetuated. Since virtually all the women reformers for the next hundred years read her *Vindication,* they were certainly aware of her arguments in regard to love and marriage. With mutual love dead, a woman ran the risk of simply being a means of release for her husband's sexual needs with little pleasure to herself (since she much more than her mate needed to be warmed by a constant love transcending the mere sexual act), and with the danger of pregnancy from this unrewarding union. These issues could not, in the atmosphere of the nineteenth century, be discussed by the most militant champion of woman's rights. But as we have seen, the strategies devised worked to the end of securing for women control over the sexual encounter without directly challenging the notion that they were "a lesser order of creation" with no other role than to fulfill a husband's needs. The compliance of the "compliant wife" thus stopped short of passive acquiescence in the frequency if not the nature of sexual unions.

But the issue was too central to be entirely suppressed. It surfaced in the late 1860's when Victoria Woodhull publicly advocated free love and proposed herself as candidate for President of the United States on a platform that endorsed the principle.

Victoria and her sister got Commodore Vanderbilt into their clutches and with his backing set themselves up as Woodhull Claflin & Company, Wall Street Brokers, where an enthralled press hung on their every word. Improbably enough, the sisters soon took up the cause of woman's rights. Victoria fell under the influence of Stephen Pearl Andrews, the archetype of the eccentric homemade philosopher who had embraced every nostrum of the age — spiritualism, free love, communism and health foods. He had had an honorable career before the war as an abolitionist and now attempted to establish a "Universal Science" and a common language (in the process he developed shorthand). Andrews learned Chinese and wrote a book in the language, married a woman physician and, to be congenial, took a medical degree at the New York Medical College. He studied the teachings of the Englishman, Robert Dale Owen, and Josiah Warren, a radical Yankee reformer. Andrews lived for awhile at Modern Times, a Long Island community whose guiding principles were communism and free love, and became the grand panjandrum of a group of radical intellectuals who called themselves the Pantarchy and espoused a kind of state socialism in which free alliance was an important element. Andrews's huge tome entitled *The Basic Outline of Universology* converted Victoria and her sister, who had some practical experience with free love, to the "philosophical" doctrine. Like spiritualism, to which it was closely related, free love stressed the sovereignty of the individual. He was free, untrammeled, autonomous. The laws and conventions of society were irrelevant to the superior person. In America the doctrine was as old as Anne Hutchinson.

Victoria Woodhull told Stephen Pearl Andrews that she had had a conversation with Demosthenes in which he foretold that she would live in a great city surrounded by ships (New York) and become the ruler of her country (i.e., the President of the United States). With Andrews's encouragement she announced herself a candidate. The next step was a newspaper to advance the doctrines of Victoria and her candidacy. With the backing of Vanderbilt, *Woodhull & Claflin's Weekly* was established. It was to be "primarily devoted to the vital interests of the people and will treat of all matters freely and without reservation. It will support Victoria C. Woodhull with its whole strength; otherwise it will be untrammeled by party or personal considerations, free from all affiliation with political or social creeds, and will advocate Suffrage without distinction of sex."

When the American woman became truly emancipated, Victoria suggested, "she will consider superior offspring a necessity and be apt to procreate only with superior men. Her intercourse with others will be limited, and the proper means will be taken to render it unprolific. . . ." Rebuffed initially by Susan B. Anthony, Victoria arranged to go to Washington and at the moment that the National Woman's Suffrage Association was to begin its yearly convention in January 1871 she appeared before the Judiciary Committee of the House of Representatives to present a memorial asking for the enactment of such laws as were necessary to secure the vote for women.

It was a great coup. Disconcerted, the leaders of the National Woman's Suffrage Association, Susan Anthony and Isabella Beecher Hooker, postponed the opening of the convention and went to hear Victoria present her memorial. Like the congressmen, they were charmed by the beautiful woman with the mellifluous voice, and that night when the convention opened Victoria sat on the speakers' platform, was introduced by Mrs. Hooker and read her memorial once more. Many supporters of woman's suffrage, men and women, were dismayed at the news that a woman with Victoria's lurid reputation had been featured at a suffrage gathering. The episode helped to deepen the rift between the New York and Boston wings of the movement. But Elizabeth Cady Stanton, who was entirely won by "the Woodhull," as Victoria was called, wrote to Lucretia Mott defending the action of the national association which was in effect her action and that of a rather reluctant Susan Anthony. Mrs. Stanton felt "it is a great impertinence for any of us to pry into her private affairs. . . . This woman stands before us today as an able speaker and writer. Her face, manners and conversation, all indicate the triumph of the moral, intellectual and spiritual." And Susan B. Anthony, with an unusual tolerance but typical asperity, declared that Victoria Woodhull's character, however flawed, was certainly as good as that of most congressmen, which was doubtless true but which, it may be presumed, failed to win congressional support for woman's suffrage. Miss Anthony went on a tour giving lectures based on Victoria's memorial and wrote her young protégé: "Go ahead doing, bright, glorious, young and strong spirit, and believe in the best love and hope and faith of S. B. Anthony."

At the suffrage anniversary held at the Apollo Hall in New York in May of 1872, Victoria Woodhull stole the show with her Great Secession speech. The talk marked the high point of inflammatory female rhetoric: "If the very next Congress refuses women all the legitimate results of citizenship," she declared, "we shall proceed to call another convention expressly to frame a new constitution and to erect a new government. . . . We mean treason; we mean secession, and on a thousand times grander scale than was that of the South. We are plotting revolution; we will overthrow this bogus Republic and plant a government of righteousness in its stead. . . ."

A few days later Roxy Claflin, the sisters' raddled old mother, started a suit against Colonel John Harvey Blood, Victoria's "husband," and it was brought out in court that her former husband, Canning Woodhull, was living in their remarkable ménage, along with a younger sister, Polly, and children by several marriages, among them an afflicted son, Byron, and a daughter named Zulu Maude. To attacks on her morals Victoria replied in the pages of the *Weekly,* "Mrs. Woodhull will always appear when justice calls, even if it be in the police court. . . . She is a life-long spiritualist and

owes all she is to the education and constant guidance of spirit influence. . . . She also believes in and advocates free love in the high,
the best sense . . . as the only cure for the immorality, lewdness,
and licentiousness which may corrode the holy institution of the
Sexual Relation."[4]

With that preliminary she went on to blow the lid off the most
sensational scandal of the century by accusing the great Henry Ward
Beecher, brother to Harriet, Catharine and Bella, of adultery with the
wife of his dramatic young aide, Theodore Tilden. That extraordinary story which proceeded to a court case that dragged out over
some five months and kept the newspapers supplied with a daily fare
of lurid testimony, cannot be told here, but Victoria, undaunted, went
on to espouse the cause of labor and form section twelve of the
International Workingman's Association known as the Woodhull-
Claflin section. She issued a manifesto in the name of the section
which advocated woman suffrage, sexual freedom and a universal
language. This was too much for the International Workingman's
Association. The central committee was reorganized in order to expel
section twelve. The one delegate to the London council who voted to
retain section twelve was expelled by an indignant Karl Marx. Marx
was a family man.

Victoria Woodhull's doctrines on free love were an amplification
of the views of Mary Wollstonecraft. It is difficult at this point to
estimate how many Americans accepted the idea of so-called free
alliance. It was a central tenet of John Humphrey Noyes's Perfectionist communities and a number of other communist societies founded
in the same era. Its advocates saw in it a solution to a sexual competition as deadly in its own way as the economic competition that, in
their view, was rapidly destroying the promise of American life. Free
love often accompanied spiritualism and it was estimated that at the
height of spiritualism's vogue four million Americans subscribed to
its principles. A judge from the "burnt-over district" of New York
State founded a town in Ohio in the 1870's dedicated to spiritualism,
democracy and free love, and dozens of similar communities were
founded in the decade of the seventies.

Women were the principal promoters and, it may be suspected,
made up the greater portion of the adherents of spiritualism. The Fox
sisters with their tappings and rappings started an infatuation with

spiritualism that began in 1850 and lasted almost to the turn of the century. George Templeton Strong called its popularity "one of the most astounding facts of this age . . . very conscientious, educated, intelligent people belong to it," and two years later he noted again: "It [spiritualism] is surely one of the most startling events that have occurred for centuries and one of the most significant. A new Revelation, hostile to that of the Church and the Bible, finding acceptance on the authority of knocking ghosts and oscillating tables, is a momentous fact in history as throwing light on the intellectual calibre and moral tone of the age in which multitudes adopt it."[5]

Most of the practitioners were women whose extrasensory powers and intuitions were presumed to make them best suited for communication with the spirit world. As the century wore on, spiritualism formed at least temporary alliances with most of the other panaceas of the age. Its alliance with free love was one such.

The argument of the free love advocates was that the improvement of the race called for unions between men and women based on the best scientific principles. "Mothers of humanity!" Tennie C. Claflin wrote, "yours is a fearful duty, and one which should in its importance lift you entirely above the modern customs of society, its frivolities, superficialities and deformities, and make you realize that to you is committed the divine work of perfecting humanity." This commission made marriage "a thousand times more sacred than you or any other has ever regarded it. So fearfully sacred should it be that it should never be consummated until the researches of science and the teaching of wisdom are exhausted in the effort to prove that it will be a benefit to humanity." It was for these reasons that the sisters denounced "the present marriage systems."[6]

It was the home and marriage that attracted the particular attention of Tennie C. The home was growing increasingly arid because husband and wife were not companions. The home could not hold the husband who formed masculine enclaves for his games, his drinking and even for his furtive lecheries. Women, in turn, were forced to imitate the men with their own exclusively feminine circles for tea, cards and gossip. "Thus the distance between man and woman, as the husband and wife, is gradually widening, and the home of the family every year becomes less and less the central point of attraction for all concerned. This . . . indicates a revolution in domestic life, such as the world has never known. Does woman comprehend whither she is floating? Does she realize that as a sex she is becoming estranged from man? Does she understand what estrangement of the sexes means for her?" It means a diminution of her own individuality and power and, with every loss, less and less chance of becoming her husband's companion. The reason for the withdrawal was "the growing aversion on the part of women to bearing children," the unmentionable fact "shut out from sight and consideration." And here it is the women who are at fault. "The means they resort to for their prevention is sufficient to disgust every natural man, and to cause him to seek the companionship of those who have no fear in this regard." Women should realize the inevitable result of such a strategy, in brief, "that it must induce conditions unfavorable to her continuance as the sufficient attraction for the man who has chosen her from among the whole. . . . Man does not wander from home, wife, and perhaps, children, for no cause."[7]

On the other hand, it was the men who drove women to such strategies. "So long as women are the mere slaves of men," Tennie C. wrote, "forced by the laws of marriage to submit their bodies to them, whenever and wherever they may so determine, and by thus being subjected are still further and more barbarously forced to become the unwilling mothers of unwished-for children, so long will the millennium days be delayed." It was the private prostitution of marriage that must be abolished as much as the public prostitution. At least a man had to pay for the body of a prostitute and she was free to withhold it if she chose; his wife's he could command.

It was on this specific issue that "the main part of the Woman Question" rested. The resistance of men to woman's suffrage had little to do with the vote as such, but much to do with masculine prerogatives in general. "Men under the new *regime* will become the companions of women instead, and will receive it as a special favor if so permitted to be."[8]

"Woman, as a whole," Tennie C. Claflin insisted, "is possessed of a healthful, saving, purifying power that is needed everywhere. The basest sensualist bows and worships in the presence of a pure and holy woman, and loses the power to think of such a being falling to his level. And this is the saving element that is required by the body politic, to arrest its present tendencies to complete corruption."

It was her conviction that "If the millennium ever come — and we have the most perfect faith that it will — it must come through the mothers of humanity." If women were granted full equality with men the "drinking-saloons, gambling-halls, houses of prostitution" would soon disappear.[9]

It was, in fact, for the good of children themselves that conventional marriage should be repressed. Children must be so reared as to make them "better citizens, and better men and women"; to do this may require abandoning "all old forms, all present customs, all supposed interests." The real question to be faced is "What is for the best interests of children, not merely as children, but principally as the basis of future society . . . he belongs to humanity." Virtually everything presently done was worthy only of "the severest condemnation." If necessary, children should be withdrawn from the care of their parents and placed "in the proper kind of industrial institutions." The implication, which Tennie C. nowhere specifically states, seems to be that ideal men and women will produce children that will be scientifically reared by the state. Thus the monogamous marriage may be replaced by temporary alliances whose purpose is not personal indulgence but the production of superior offspring. It is society which, in the last resort, is "responsible to children for the condition in which they are admitted to it as constituent members of itself."[10]

Tennie C. and Victoria constantly compared "The Woman Question" with the "Negro Question": "The Negro Question vitalized the Republican Party, because there was a principle involved in it; so, too, will the Woman Question vitalize the party that shall become its champion. If the Republican Party did a great service to the cause of general civilization, the party that shall lift the banner of female freedom and equality will do it a much greater service. The Woman Question involves hundreds of millions scattered all over the face of the earth. It is meet that the country which was almost the last to abjure slavery should be the first to enfranchise woman. We lost much prestige by clinging to slavery; let us gain what we lost by boldly meeting and settling this newer, greater, and graver question, which other nations have scarcely begun to talk about. . . ."[11]

In Tennie C. Claflin's words, everyone who advocates "more and better freedom for woman" was accused of being for "Free Love." "If to advocate freedom is 'free love' as contra indicated from *forced love,* then by all means do we accept the application. If there is one foul, damning blot upon woman's nature and capacities, it is this system that compels her to manifest and act a love that is forced; this kind of love is all the prostitution there is in the world. None of the acts that may be suggested by a genuine love can be held to be the prostitution of the power or capacity exhibited." Free love, Tennie C. Claflin insisted, meant for a woman to be free to love and not coerced by a brutish husband in an unhappy marriage. The marriage of "two pure, trusting, loving equal souls" was the only true marriage. She and her sister had no desire to "reduce the relations of the sexes to common looseness." What they wished to make clear were "the realities of marriage."[12]

It must be said that these "apostles of licentiousness" were virtually alone in identifying the institution of American marriage as it existed as intolerable for women. While Catharine Beecher and her sister Harriet sought to remedy the unhappy state of the family by better ventilation and exercise, those other and far more exotic sisters, Victoria Woodhull and Tennie C. Claflin, were trying with little success to persuade women to look at their situation realistically and to refuse to be taken in by the angelic woman syndrome.

The differences between the old-line reformers and the Claflin sisters were in part differences in class. Victoria and Tennie C. were among the ten children of Roxy and Buck Claflin; the mother a fortune-teller, the father an improvident ne'er-do-well. But if the emotional and intellectual world of the daughters of Buck Claflin was as remote from that of the daughters of Lyman Beecher as the earth from the moon, the Claflin girls, fighting their way out of the lowest level of society, emerged free of those inhibitions which characterized their middle-class sisters. That simple fact was the source of their power as well as the root of their vulnerability. They had a kind of genius made up, most conspicuously, of energy, physical beauty and adaptability. They certainly used the woman's suffrage movement, but they also believed in it. They had the instinct or good fortune to realize that its rhetoric fitted their own situation and that by appropriating it they could raise the rather sordid facts of their own lives to the level of universal drama. In this enterprise they had the backing of Commodore Vanderbilt, one of the shrewdest and most unscrupulous tycoons of the age, and Stephen Pearl Andrews, one of its most selfless and eccentric visionaries.

The combination was the strangest of its kind in American history. The two men were fascinated by the sisters for quite different reasons. Vanderbilt was charmed by Tennie C., and she was in all probability his mistress. He took a malicious pleasure in using "the Lady Brokers" to scandalize the proper financial circles of New York. For Andrews they were irresistible agents of his utopian schemes. But they were never simply tools; they were too tough and resourceful to allow themselves to be exploited without clear gains to themselves. They were both ambitious and more than slightly mad, but they knew instinctively how to use their rich experience of the seamier side of American life to vitalize the genteel doctrines of the Susan B. Anthonys and the Lucy Stones. The Claflins could at the same time see more clearly and articulate more compellingly the situation of a great number of American women.

In 1872 Victoria gave a talk entitled "The Scare-crows of Sexual Freedom" at Vineland, a town in upper New York State. The legal safeguards placed around the family, she told her small-town audience, made it "a community of hot little hells." She developed the argument that a loveless and indissoluble marriage was simply legalized prostitution. "They say I have come to break up the family," she declared; "I say amen to that with all my heart. . . . In a perfected sexuality shall continuous life be found." The vision was apocalyptic: "So also shall life not come to an end when its springs shall not cease to send forth the vitalized waters of life, that earth's otherwise weary children may drink and live. . . . Then shall they, who have in ages past, cast off their mortal coils be able to come again and resume them at will; and thus also shall a spiritualized humanity be able at will to throw off and take on its material clothing, and the two worlds shall be once more and forever united. Such to me, my brothers and sisters, is the sublime mission of Spiritualism, to be outwrought through the sexual emancipation of woman, and her return to self-ownership, and to individualized existence. . . ." And at a meeting of the American Association of Spiritualists when questioned by someone in the audience about her virtue, she declared defiantly "If I want sexual intercourse with one hundred men I shall have it . . . and this sexual intercourse business may as well be discussed now, and discussed until you are so familiar with your sexual organs that a reference to them will no longer make the blush mount to your face any more than a reference to any other part of your body. . . ." This was strong talk even for spiritualists. To it she added a lesson on the right of women to experience orgasm, declaring that "men shall not, either from ignorance or selfish desire, carry [a woman's] impulse forward only to cast it backward with its mission unfulfilled to prostrate the impelling power and breed nervous debility or irritability and sexual demoralization. . . . This involves a whole science and a fine art, hardly yet broached to human thought, now criminally repressed and defeated by the prejudices of mankind. . . ."[13]

It was this power of uninhibited thought and speech in Victoria Woodhull which made her so compelling a figure to Mrs. Stanton, who hailed her as "a deliverer." Listening to Victoria had been a revelation: "I have worked thirty years for woman suffrage," Elizabeth Cady wrote, "and I now feel that suffrage is but the vestibule of woman's emancipation. . . ." And even more alarmingly, she declared: "The men and women who are dabbling with the suffrage movement for women should be at once . . . and emphatically warned that what they mean logically if not consciously in all they say is next social equality and next Freedom or in a word Free Love, and, if they wish to get out of the boat, they should for safety get out now, for delays are dangerous."[14]

Gradually Victoria Woodhull changed her tune. She had a revelation in which Christ appeared to her and told her that her mission was to exalt motherhood. Subsequently she carried a Bible when she lectured and read copiously from Scripture. No more was heard of free love. She turned on her old friends and lovers and attacked them mercilessly. She denied that she had ever espoused free love and began a remarkable campaign to try to wipe from the record every trace of her former views. Victoria, it seemed, wished above everything in the world to marry a solid, prosperous, respectable man. She discovered what other women have discovered; that free love is exciting at twenty, possible at thirty, a drag at forty and a nightmare at fifty. The wild disorder of her life was suddenly insupportable. She continued to announce herself as candidate for President of the United States, to plan her campaign, solicit support, issue statements on current problems, but now she ran on the motherhood platform.

A beautiful woman, however mad or blemished, can always find some rich and respectable booby to marry her. Victoria found herself such a husband and one for Tennie C. as well. Victoria Woodhull became Mrs. John Biddulph Martin, wife of a rich young Englishman, and constructed for herself a classic Victorian nest in London. A visitor to the Martin mansion at 17 Hyde Park Gate entered a hall featuring marble busts of Aphrodite and Hermes and a blue and gold ceiling. Upstairs in the drawing room the parquetry floor was covered with bearskin rugs. The Venetian wood chandelier was carved into little cupids. An inlaid table had around its edges mosaic medallions of the great musicians, and most stunning of all, in an artistic nook against a background of dark velvet, stood a silver statue of the goddess Nike. The room was filled with a profusion of knickknacks, bric-a-brac, whatnots, a tastefully adorned and canopied love seat and, conspicuously displayed, a copy of Herbert Spencer's *Synthetic Philosophy*.

Tennie C. met a rich widower named Francis Cook, an Indian importer, and told him that his wife had sent her a message from the spirit world advising that they marry. He did so and Tennie C. established herself at Doughty House overlooking the Thames. Francis Cook had a splendid art gallery and a famous collection of rings and Oriental rugs. In addition to his London residence, he had a feudal estate in Portugal; the King of Portugal gave him the title of Visconde de Montserratel; he endowed an artist's home in London and was made a baronet. Tennessee called herself Lady Cook.

Not satisfied with all the trappings of wealth and respectability, Victoria Woodhull Martin spent years trying to "vindicate my good name," which turned out to be a task as futile as bailing the ocean. However, she did publish in London in 1890 a collection of lectures "delivered throughout America and England," under the title *The Human Body the Temple of God or the Philosophy of Sociology*. She had not discarded all the articles of her old faith. The essay from which the book took its title argued that the Garden of Eden was not a geographical place but in fact the human body. Jesus had said "The Kingdom of God is within you." "Suppose . . ." she wrote, "it should after all turn out that the long-lost Garden of Eden is the human body; that these three, the Kingdom of God, the Temple of God, and the Garden of Eden, are synonymous terms and mean the same thing — are the human body? Suppose this, I say. What then? Would not the people be likely to regard it with a little more reverence than they do now? — and to treat it with a little more care? Would they not modify their pretences that, in their natural condition, any of the parts of the body can be vulgar and impure, and unfit to be discussed either in the public press or the public rostrum? . . . I am well aware that there must be a great change in the present thoughts and ideas about the body before it can be expected that there will be any considerable difference in its general treatment. But a great change has to come, and will come. Certain parts of the body — indeed, its most important parts — are held to be so vulgar and indecent that they have been made the subject of penal laws. Nobody can speak about them without somebody imagining himself or herself to be shocked. Now, all this is very absurd, foolish, and ridiculous, since, do you not know, that this vulgarity and obscenity are not in the body, but in the associated ideas in the minds of the people who make the pretence. . . . The despised parts of the body are to become what Jesus was, the Savior conceived at Nazareth. The despised body, and not the honoured soul, must be the stone cut out of the mountain that shall be the head of the corner, though now rejected by the builders."

The arguments, again, were supported by Scripture and, surprisingly, it was Pauline: "And base things of the world, and things which are despised, hath God chosen . . ." "And those members of the body, which we think to be less honourable, upon these we bestow more abundant honour."

Genesis told in allegorical form the story of the body, "cursed by the acts of primitive man (male and female), through which acts they became ashamed and covered themselves, because they had done evil to the parts that they desired to hide." Revelation refers to the body saved and from Genesis to Revelation "the human body is the chief subject that is considered — is the temple of God, which through long ages He has been creating to become, finally, His abiding place, when men and women shall come to love Him as He has commanded that they should; and this important thing is the basis of all revelation and all prophecy."[15]

Much of the essay is devoted to the problem of menstruation. Victoria Woodhull saw it as the wasting of the "blood of life," a curse on women because of the misuse of sexuality. It is, in her image, the river Euphrates, the fruitful stream perverted, and in the day of the New Jerusalem ("which is the purified woman"), women will cease to menstruate and the river of waste will become again "a pure river of the water of life proceeding out of the throne of God." That Victoria Woodhull expended so much eloquence on the transformation of the dark and poisoned stream into the clear stream of life is the plainest evidence of the centrality of menstruation in the minds of nineteenth-century women. It was a wound that would, in some better day, be healed.

In that millennial age all men and women will understand that "their sexual organs, being the means by which His crowning work is created, ought never to be defiled by an unholy touch or thought, or ever made the instruments of selfish gratification merely. . . . Let the sexual act become the holiest act of life, and then the world will begin to be regenerated, and not before." Sexual intercourse should be preceded by the reading of the Bible and by prayer and worship. Let us become "consistent at least and in the most important act of life ask God's blessing to rest upon it. Selfish lust and inordinate lasciviousness" should be eschewed. Christians have misinterpreted the Holy Scriptures and given "all their attention to saving the soul hereafter, when this salvation depends entirely upon saving the body here and now."[16]

The essay ends with the last two chapters of the Revelation of St. John the Divine, the seal of the new human order based on the liberation of the body, the temple of God.

What is one to say of this extraordinary lady? If she repented of her free love doctrines, she remained true to her experience of her own body. The desire for comfort and order was not so strong that she was tempted to make peace with Victorian respectability at the price of her convictions. In a sense she was truly a medium, a voice through which was released the repressed sexuality of the age, albeit briefly. Men and women by the tens of thousands went to hear her and undoubtedly got a vision of a "free life" with all the hope and terror that the word suggested. Victoria Woodhull acted out what was probably the most remarkable psychodrama of the nineteenth century. Before it was over it involved, directly or indirectly, almost every important figure in the reform movements of the day. She gave that sturdy warhorse of the woman's rights movement, Elizabeth Cady Stanton, a new conception of the emancipation of women. And even Susan B. quite lost her head. The attraction was, in part, her beauty, but it was obviously much more than that. It was her ability to speak the unspeakable. To stand before a mixed audience and speak of the tyranny of sexual attitudes, the dismal fruits of repression, and of the prospect of a new relation between men and women, to talk quite specifically of sex organs and ovaries, of menstruation, and of venereal disease without being struck down by a bolt from heaven. There was just a chance that what she said might be true — and she said it so thrillingly!

But she could not sustain the moment. Brash, assertive, irrepressible, emancipated as she seemed, she wished for the home she had never had, the marriage she had scorned, the respectability she had so dramatically flouted, the husband whose tyranny she had inveighed against. She certainly was entitled to all of them, and one can only be pleased she got them and sorry that as a comfortable English matron she wasted so much time and energy trying to rewrite the history of her spectacular years in America.

As for the reformers, they read her out of their noble company. The name of the woman whom Mrs. Stanton had called a "deliverer," whom Theodore Tilton had acclaimed as the prophetess of a Golden Age, to whom spinsterish Susan B. Anthony had pledged her "best hope, love and faith," was expunged from all the voluminous memorial histories and retrospective accounts of the movement. She and Tennie C., or Tennessee, existed in American history as a footnote, a colorful and titillating episode mentioned most often in relation to the Beecher-Tilton scandal, and illustrating . . . well, one hardly knows what. With all the absurdity there is as well a terrible poignance. In a sense, she *was* a heroine; she *did* suffer on the cross of Victorian morality; she *did* make a small opening in the wall of silence that surrounded everything that had to do with her beloved body.

As Victoria Woodhull Martin had had a predecessor in Mary Wollstonecraft, she had a successor to whom history has been gentler. Margaret Higgins (1883–1966), was one of eleven children. Her father was an improvident stonecutter and sometime sculptor, a social radical and follower of Henry George, a figure reminiscent of Thomas Wolfe's father in *Look Homeward, Angel.* He lived to be eighty. Her mother, a Catholic, died at forty-eight worn out by child-bearing and housework.

Margaret Higgins was a slight girl with fresh Irish features and a dreamy, emotional nature. Guided by her father she read the litera-ture of reform and embraced radical causes, most passionately the complete emancipation of women. She early decided that a woman must make herself "absolute mistress of her own body," have "the absolute right to dispose of herself, to withhold herself, to procreate or suppress the germ of life."[17]

Inspired by such notions she had a passionate romance with a young architect, William Sanger, and married him when she was four months pregnant. At almost the same time, she found out she had incipient TB. Her husband packed her off to a sanitarium at Lake Saranac. When labor began neither her doctor nor his assistant could be located, and a young general practitioner was hastily summoned. The labor was a desperately difficult one. The doctor was little help. After the baby, a boy whom she named Stuart, was born, Margaret Sanger suffered from severe postpartum depression, and a return of the TB symptoms. She spent almost a year in an Adirondack sanitar-ium before she could return home. Years later when she was on a lecture tour in Los Angeles the doctor who had attended her wrote: "Someday I want to hear from your own lips just what bearing my lack of knowledge of obstetrics may have had upon the profound movement that is essentially yours. It was a hard night for both of us." In Margaret Sanger's words, "something in that note affected me like a shot. . . . I had to leave my work and go home. All that night I suffered with pains in the back and had all the symptoms of labor pains! And this, twenty-five years after my son was born! . . . I am not a hysterical person, yet it was all I could do to pull myself together for the next two days. The memory of that agonizing birth kept me in mental torture, and I felt again the physical pangs of those lingering hours."[18]

Spiritualism, Rosicrucianism and extrasensory perception had a strong attraction for Margaret Sanger. She read, rested, and picked up her interrupted life as mother to her adored son, "l'infant," and as wife to her hardpressed husband. After her second son, Grant, Margaret became preoccupied with having a daughter. Unwilling to go through such agony again, she made plans to adopt an infant girl. The Sangers had started adoption proceedings when Margaret discovered that she was pregnant again.

About this time, too, William Sanger had designed and supervised the building of a house for Margaret and the two boys. The day before they were to move in, it caught fire and was burned virtually to the ground. The mother of two young children and pregnant with a third, Margaret Sanger recalled later: "I stood there amazed, but I was certain of a relief, of a burden lifted, a spirit set free. It was as if a chapter of my life had been brought to a close." The fire taught her "the absurdity of placing all one's hopes, all one's efforts, involving as they do heartaches, debts and worries in the creation of something external that could perish irretrievably in the course of a few moments. . . . My scale of suburban values had been consumed by the flames." Peggy, the third child, an exquisite, frail creature with fair hair and blue eyes, was born twenty months after Grant.[19]

In the years immediately following Peggy's birth, Margaret Sanger became more and more preoccupied with the issue of birth control. She decided to visit Europe to learn at firsthand what was being done in the modern clinics of England and Holland. Abandoning William and the children, she set off. In London she met Havelock Ellis. She had read his articles on the psychology of sex and they had seemed like revelation. To Margaret, the English sex reformer was "a godsent liberator." He invited her to tea, she found him "a veritable god," and, predictably, fell in love. Ellis was fifty-five and Margaret twenty-four. Ellis's wife, Edith, was away on a lecture tour and Margaret and Havelock entered on an affair which, in Margaret Sanger's words, "succeeded in avoiding the blind volcano of passion," whatever that meant. The cultivated "the peaceful and consoling and inspiring elements of love — and tried to escape the other."[20]

Poor Edith, when she returned, failed to react like an emancipated woman. "Havelock darling," she wrote, "I feel that the foundations of the deep have gone if you are merged with someone else. . . ."[21] Ellis tried to explain that it was just a temporary merger, a modern love affair that had avoided "disorderly passions," but his wife was not consoled. She tried to commit suicide; she and her husband were reunited and went off to live in the country. She had the old-fashioned notion that Havelock should divorce her and marry Margaret (who still had a husband in Hackensack). But the romance was broken off and Margaret Sanger went on to Holland and France to pursue her researches in birth control. In Europe she collected a suitcase full of birth control devices, pamphlets and recipes for contraception, many of which had been passed on by French women to their daughters and granddaughters for generations.

The "movement" became an obsession. William Sanger was left at home to manage the children as best he could while Margaret toured and lectured and wrote on the emancipation of women through birth control.

When she was in Europe on a tour, her adored Peggy fell ill with pneumonia. Margaret Sanger rushed back to be with her sick child. Peggy was unconscious and opened her eyes only once to say to her mother, "Are you back? Are you back from London?" Mrs. Sanger reported that she saw her daughter's spirit leave her body and float in a dazzling white cloud before it left the room. The child died on the sixth of November, and six became a magical number to Margaret Sanger. Desolated, and filled with guilt, she "went out to find the answer — where was Peggy?" The search led her to Theosophists, to Annie Besant, to Oriental mysticism, to seances where she felt she established contact with her dead daughter. "Deep in the hidden realm of my unconscious," she wrote years later, "Peggy has never died . . . and in that strange, mysterious place where reality and imagination meet, my little girl has grown up to womanhood."[22]

She threw herself into all of the radical causes of the day. She met and had a love affair with Big Bill Hayward, the leader of the International Workers of the World, then America's only truly radical labor movement, and became a kind of a convert to communism, or syndicalism or anarchism — she was never apparently quite sure which. Hayward, arrested for his opposition to America's involvement in world war, wrote her an exultant letter from Leavenworth: "You remember what I said at the subway station about 'it coming,' Margaret, all my dreams are coming true. My work is being fulfilled, millions of workers are seeing the light, Russia, Poland, Germany, France, Great Britain, Australia, South America, we have lived to see the breaking of the glorious Red Dawn . . . The world revolution is born, the change is here, We will of course not live to see it in its perfection, But it is good to have been living at this period."[23]

She also wrote articles for the *Blast,* a journal edited by Alexander Berkman, "designed to arouse all the rebel elements in the country, especially labor." She had a romance with Berkman — "Sasha," who wrote about the progress of the revolution and ended, "I hold you close and kiss your dear face."[24]

In 1920 Margaret Sanger published a book entitled *Women and the New Race.* It contained as much "new philosophy" as birth control information, and its essential message had nothing to do with the limiting of population. Contraception was, to be sure, a means for impoverished wives to control the size of their families, and this was a problem for which Margaret Sanger felt genuine sympathy and concern, but far more important to the author was the "sexual emancipation" afforded middle-class women who were thereby freed from the drudgery of a monogamous marriage. Thus liberated there emerged for women of the new race "a deep, transcendental belief in her own destiny, in her own role as the voice of motherhood, which had created in her the overwhelmingly urgent mission to unloose the force of love throughout the world, and in doing so, to cleanse and regenerate it."[25]

A hundred and thirty years had passed since Mary Wollstonecraft's *Vindication* and thirty since Victoria Woodhull's essay on *The Human Body, The Temple of God* but the accents were the same; a millennium, ushered in by women who would teach the world the joys of erotic love.

When Margaret Sanger visited London in the 1920's, Victoria Woodhull was a handsome old lady living at Bredon Norton, a beautiful country manor, and dispensing largesse to villagers in classic style.

From Woman's Rights to Feminism

After the Civil War, the woman's rights movement directed its attention to the vote. As we have seen there was a brief period from the end of the war to the early 1870's when the vote for women seemed in the air, the next important step in the liberalization of American democracy.

The rift between the New York and the New England wings of the woman's suffrage movement had its roots in the differences in temperament and personality of the women who were the leaders in the two factions, and those differences were in part regional differences and in part an expression of the relations of the two sets of leaders to men. Elizabeth Cady Stanton had a difficult marriage, Susan Anthony was a spinster. The New England ladies were happily married. The marital situation of the Stanton-Anthony faction on the one hand and the Brown-Stone-Howe group on the other determined their respective attitudes toward divorce and "free alliance" as well.

As late as 1853 Lucy Stone and Mrs. Stanton were in agreement that reform of the divorce laws was necessary and that "the right idea of marriage was at the foundation of all reforms." Liberalized divorce laws were essential for the protection of women, and we find in the correspondence of the two ladies the familiar assertion that women must win control over their own bodies. Divorce laws must provide recourse for the wife whose husband's lusts force her into "legalized prostitution." Lucy Stone wrote Mrs. Stanton about a "noble woman [who] told me how she fled from her husband to the *Shakers,* because he gave her no peace." "I *very much* wish," she wrote again several years later, "that a wife's right to her own body should be pushed at our next convention."[1] But it was 1860 before the issue was raised at the annual woman's rights convention in New York.

Mrs. Stanton introduced the question and proposed to the delegates ten resolutions looking toward the reform of the divorce laws. The reaction was immediate and surprisingly strong. Nette Brown was vigorously opposed and Wendell Phillips moved that the resolutions be excluded from the record of the convention. While the delegates were unwilling to go so far, they refused to endorse Mrs. Stanton's proposals for reform, and her insistence on pressing the issue, supported by Susan B. Anthony, was one of the causes of the eventual split in the woman's movement. The rift was widened in the years immediately following the war by Susan Anthony's and Mrs. Stanton's alliance with George Train, an Irishman, a Democrat, and a self-confessed communist who espoused such radical causes as paper money and the eight-hour day and underwrote a campaign to persuade the voters of the new state of Kansas to give the suffrage to both women and Negroes. Garrison called him a "ranting egotist and low blackguard," and Lucy Stone wrote to a friend deploring "the spectacle Miss Anthony is making of the woman's cause by parading through the country with a man such as Train. It seems to me she can hardly be less crazy than he."[2]

As the *Revolution,* a reforming paper supported by George Train and run by Mrs. Stanton and Miss Anthony, bore down on the divorce issue, the New Englanders grew increasingly uneasy at the public reaction to the crusade, a crusade which, however justified in the state of New York, was in their opinion alienating the more conservative supporters of the rights movement itself. Mrs. Stanton's marriage, despite (or because of) six children, was not a happy one (it may well be that Mr. Stanton insisted on his husbandly prerogatives). Mrs. Stanton's principal ally was Susan Anthony, and we are already aware of her uneasiness about marriage and children. Both women, in any event, displayed a rancor toward men that was largely

missing in the rhetoric and in writings of the New England reformers. It is hard not to believe that Elizabeth Cady's experience with her
father, the judge, did not leave her with a lifelong resentment of that
masculinity which her father, devoted as he was to her, nonetheless
clearly preferred to his adoring daughter's femininity. It is perhaps
worth noting also that both Mrs. Stanton and Miss Anthony had a
touching susceptibility to dynamic men or women.

Henry Blackwell, Lucy Stone's husband, tried to undo some of the
damage caused to the movement by Elizabeth Cady Stanton's increasingly radical statements about marriage. "As friends of Woman
Suffrage," he wrote, "we protest against being compromised in this
matter by the ultraism of a few individuals. Ninety-nine out of every
one hundred of the active workers in our movement are happy husbands and wives, who believe in marriage as a noble and life-long
partnership of equals, and who believe in political equality because
men and women should go hand in hand as mutual friends and
helpers."[3]

The more secular-minded reformers professed to believe in the
perfectability of man (and woman) through a reform of repressive
institutions misshapen by superstition and bigotry; the religiously
motivated reformers for the most part concentrated on bringing about
specific reforms as desirable *per se.* They were more cautious about
extravagant claims although their language was certainly not free of
the millennial expectation. The difference was, in part, that between a
utopia and a millennium. The utopia was much more a secular vision,
an immediate reordering of human institutions to produce a heaven
on earth. The millennial dream was apocalyptic. Only the virtuous
could be saved or would enter the new and purified company of the
faithful.

But the *Revolution* refused to abandon the cause. "The ballot," it
declared, "is not even half a loaf; it is only a crust — a crumb." The
question of the nature of marriage was much more important than
"any such superficial and fragmentary question" as woman's suffrage.[4]
The difference between the factions was strikingly similar to that
between the present-day advocates of nonviolence and integration on
the one hand and the champions of violence and black power on the
other. The differences were also regional and historical. New England
had a long tradition of relatively liberal divorce laws. It may be

suspected, moreover, that it had a tradition of happy marriages since it was better armored than other regions against the dislocations that the industrial revolution produced in family life and had, in consequence, preserved better the status and standing of its women.

But the *Revolution,* for reasons perhaps no more profound than Elizabeth Cady Stanton's unsatisfactory marriage, or the profound, if transitory, influence of Victoria Woodhull, had the deeper insight. The ballot was indeed "a crumb"; the real issues lay much deeper and they lay exactly where the editors of the *Revolution* said they lay — in the "administration" of marriage. And Mrs. Stanton, still under the influence of Victoria Woodhull, noted that the opponents of divorce were declaring that the liberalization of the divorce laws would inevitably mean "freedom to institute at the option of the parties new amatory relationships" and that the reformers were thus, in effect, espousing free love. "Well, yes," Mrs. Stanton replied, "that is what I mean. We are all free lovers at heart though we may not have thought so."⁵

Negro suffrage, Victoria Woodhull and free love, George Train, greenbacks and divorce split the woman's suffrage movement into two rival factions. It was to be fifteen years and more before the breach was healed. In 1886 Elizabeth Cady Stanton made a conciliatory gesture by writing Nette Brown to try to arrange a meeting between the four now elderly ladies who had waged such splendid battles together — Susan B., Lucy Stone, Nette and Mrs. Stanton herself, "once more, to have it seem like the old days; before we all go forward 'to work or rest' "; the four of them together, "with all the remembrances not desirable buried; and judgment left where it belongs."⁶ The wounds were healed or patched over and when Elizabeth Cady Stanton's autobiography came out three years later, Nette wrote to Lucy: "It is spicy and readable enough at any rate, but occasionally it says what one fancies it was not intended to put altogether so clearly between the lines. But Mrs. Stanton is bright, broad and delightfully self-possessed. I do like a woman who can both know and speak her own mind and stand on her own feet. With some quickening of conscience and a sense of concrete practical justice she would be magnificent."⁷

On the question of who was to be the first president of the united suffrage movement, some of the bitterness of old wrangles showed itself. Susan B. Anthony had been proposed for the honor, but Nette felt that "under the circumstances she has no right to be first union President, and I shall tell *her* so and why. Of course she will be President soon," she added, "and probably ought to be. As a spinster she has given all her time."[8]

The union of the two associations was to be celebrated by a mammoth parade in New York. Alice Stone Blackwell, Lucy's only daughter, went, and Nette's children, Agnes and Tom, and little Ethel dressed as a butterfly. The day was bitterly cold, and Nette took the one hundred and ten dollars in bills that she had brought to contribute to the cause and stuffed them under her blouse to protect her chest. Elizabeth Blackwell, now professor of gynecology at the Women's Medical College in London, was in England, but a banner with her name was carried in the procession.

Despite the disruption of the woman's rights movement by the split into two organizations, there was every reason in 1870 to anticipate the rapid passage of an amendment which, it was hoped, would give the franchise to women. And yet it was to be fifty years and another war before the women were enfranchised. What happened?

The fact of the matter was that the woman's rights movement lost many of its most devoted supporters when it concentrated its efforts on the suffrage. American women were, for a fact, not particularly interested in voting. Even Elizabeth Cady Stanton who had first dared to introduce the idea of women voting declared it to be "a crumb" beside the profounder issue of sexual emancipation.

Catharine Beecher was typical of those women who had been enthusiastic supporters of woman's rights but who rejected the notion that women should vote. She was, moreover, one of the most formidable female opponents of woman's suffrage. In 1871 her book, *Woman Suffrage and Woman's Profession,* took issue with the suffragettes.

"This *woman movement,*" she wrote testily, "is one which is uniting by co-operating influences, all the antagonisms that are warring on the family state. Spiritualism, free love, free divorce, the vicious indulgences consequent on regulated civilization, the worldliness which tempts men and women to avoid *large* families, often by sinful methods, thus making the ignorant masses the chief supply of the future ruling majorities." At the heart of all these ills is "the feeble constitution and poor health of women" which threatened the health of "the rising generation."[9]

It was absurd to talk about women voting and playing a part in political life when the vast majority of them were too "ailing" to run their own households properly. Women, in Catharine Beecher's opinion, should have "equal advantages" with men in living happy and fruitful lives and these they clearly had not had. Women had suffered "multiplied wrongs and sufferings" but the lack of the franchise was not one of them. It was the duty of all women to "employ the power of organization and agitation, in order to gain those advantages which are given to the one sex, and unjustly withheld from the other." If women got the vote, they would also have the responsibility of framing "wise laws to regulate finance, war, agriculture, commerce, mining, manufacturing, and all the many fields of man's outdoor labor." And even more of a threat would be the votes of those "vast masses of ignorant women whose consciences and votes would be controlled by a foreign and domestic priesthood"— the Irish. If this should happen, the stupid and idle would "lavish wealth on useless schemes, and vote away the property of the industrious to support the insolent and vicious." This trend was already observable in some of the larger cities of America. Women needed a "profession" and one that they should be trained for scientifically. The profession, of course, was that of housewife and mother.[10]

Due to the loss of life during the Civil War and the westward movement which carried away tens of thousands of young men, many women would never be able to find husbands, and it was this fact which was "the chief moral problem of our age." The central issue vis-à-vis the suffrage movement was that women were intended by the Almighty to be the redeemers of a fallen world. It was their patient, self-sacrificing love which nurtured the rising generation, supported religion, and preserved the bonds of society. In restoring the dignity and importance of the family "every cultivated woman who dignifies domestic labor by living in such a style as enables her to work herself, and to train her sons and daughters to work with her is a co-labourer in the beneficent enterprise" of "calling attention to the honors and duties of the family state." The Christian family should take in orphans, the aged indigent and "vicious" to retrain and rehabilitate them.

Catharine Beecher was in favor of woman's universities in which "every girl shall secure as good a literary training as her brothers, and then be trained to some profession adapted to her taste and capacity, by which she can establish a home of her own, and secure an independent income — *this* is what every woman may justly claim and labor for, as the shortest, surest and safest mode of securing her own highest usefulness and happiness and that of her sex."[11] It is the "fair and rosy daughters" of America, properly trained in the "highest intellectual culture" and the "highest practical skill" who will enforce a "Pink and White Tyranny," make men *their* slaves, and work with them "from early dawn to dark night under the Great Taskmaster, the Lord of love and happiness, until everyone on earth shall fear him . . . and then do justly, love mercy, and walk kindly with God, as the whole end and perfection of man."[12]

It was undoubtedly "the depressed and suffering condition" of women which had given birth to the fight for the elective franchise. But the cause had mistaken the cure. The vote had become a distracting and attractive symbol of ills that lay far deeper.

The defection of Catharine Beecher was a straw in the wind. In the next fifty years there were to be many able and articulate women reformers, devoted to the cause of full equality for women, who did not care a fig for the suffrage issue. In 1911 Ida Tarbell, the famous woman journalist and exposer of the Standard Oil Company, wrote the introduction to *The Book of Woman's Power*. In it she claimed that the woman's suffrage movement had only succeeded in the "vulgarizing of the woman it sought to dignify." Woman's most basic function as mother had been denigrated and the "fine and subtle qualities which differentiate her from the man" obscured.[13] Throughout the little volume ran a current of hostility toward feminists and suffragettes. There was nothing in modern life, the editor wrote, "more poignantly interesting than the restlessness of women. There is something half amusing, wholly pathetic, about the woman who honestly feels cramped, who believes that the home does not offer scope for her energies — while she remains equally ignorant of the nutritive values of food and of preventive medicine." The impulse of certain modern women to compete with men seemed to one contributor most alarming. She saw "peril in the rapid desire for riches . . . ; peril in the hard, loveless sensuality abounding in it; peril even in the offences to good taste perpetuated by it; peril in the feminine cry for political voice and place. The same desires in womanhood which abhor privacy and domesticity lead on the one hand to the suffragist, and on the other to Faustina and all her infamous sisterhood."[14]

To have suffragettes paired off with prostitutes by a leading woman reformer suggested some of the problems of the movement. As the suffrage issue became thoroughly respectable, many "advanced" ladies concentrated their attention on the sexual emancipation of women. The suffrage question thus passed into the hands of such groups as the Populists — whose ranks included many able women, the most famous being Mary Lease, a vivid speaker who urged farmers to raise more hell and less wheat; the Prohibition Party; and into the preserve of the woman's clubs such as the W.C.T.U. While it thereby gained important support, it became identified with other causes and lost its broad national base.

Furthermore, woman's suffrage was undoubtedly set back by the tide of immigration and the growth of racist attitudes in the United States. The influx of immigrants from central and southern Europe aroused the profoundest anxieties among native Americans.

Women themselves were demoralized by the racial issue. The "failure" of the Fifteenth Amendment to materially improve the situation of the freed Negro in the South was disconcerting, and many suffragettes went to some pains to disassociate the cause of "refined, well-educated females of Christian character" with the hordes of unwashed immigrants. Thus Frances Cobbe, an American suffragette, introducing a collection of essays, spoke of the problem of "the place which ought to be assigned under each constitutional government to alien races of men . . . the sudden admission of aliens in large numbers to a share in the working of our own machinery, are experiments fraught with difficulty and danger." Greeks, Italians, French, Spanish and Irish were all aliens unfit by training and character to take their places in an advanced democratic society. It was thus, Mrs. Cobbe argued, quite natural that statesmen, showing a "patriotic anxiety lest the introduction of a new force should disturb the working of the machine of State," should oppose the vote for women. They must be taught that while the influx of an "illiterate rabble" undermined the morals and order of the nation, "the enfranchisement of women will tend to the stability and prosperity of the State, and to the maintenance of social order and religion." There was a vast difference between admitting "the dregs of a population to the franchise, and to admit the mothers, daughters and sisters of the men who already exercise it."[15]

The campaign for women's rights attracted some masculine support that was based on simple nativism. Dio Lewis confessed that his "hopes of the future rest upon the girls . . . I believe America's future pivots on this great woman revolution." While not himself a Yankee, Lewis confessed: "I believe in Yankees. This first great success in self-government, is a success, because guided by Yankee brains. I tremble lest the rudder should fall to hands, which, in other lands, have been found utterly incompetent. The Yankee brain has realized the brightest hopes of the political seer."[16] What unnerved both masculine and feminine champions of woman suffrage was the fear that if woman were enfranchised Catholic priests would march battalions of Irish, and later in the century Italian immigrant girls, to the polls and see that they voted according to the dictates of the Pope, who was still not entirely dissociated in Protestant imaginations with the Anti-Christ. It was a cruel dilemma. To grant the suffrage to the fine if misguided ladies who in every state of the Union were fighting so eloquently under the banner of the Christian religion was one thing. It would mean, in effect, doubling the vote and, presumably, the power of the splendid Anglo-Saxons; it was apparent enough that female Celts (Greeks, Spanish, Italians and French as well) were politically passive, but there were always those ubiquitous priests taking their orders from the Holy Father in Rome. It was a nice question. Contemplating it, some reformers lost their zeal for enfranchising women.

In view of the ambiguities associated with woman's suffrage, feminism came to be the more appealing slogan. It was general enough to include any reform designed to improve the status of women, and while most feminists were strong advocates of woman suffrage, they need not be. Vaguer but more exciting horizons beckoned.

Most basic was the simple fact that the great majority of American women cared very little for the vote. In Massachusetts there were more than six hundred thousand qualified women voters, but only some twenty thousand of them bothered to go to the polls in state elections. James Bryce found less interest in woman's suffrage in America than in England. Of the women to whom he talked, "the enormous majority expressed themselves hostile." The hostility was related to the view that politics was a dirty business and that women who became engaged in it would inevitably be coarsened. The increasing sordidness of American national and municipal politics after the Civil War strengthened the feeling that it was not a proper arena for women. Bryce was unable in 1910 to tell whether the tide of public sentiment in regard to woman's suffrage was rising or falling. In any event, if suffrage came he judged that it would fulfill the prophecies neither of those who saw in it the salvation of the republic or those who anticipated a precipitous decline in moral standards. In the view of the reformers, women who were opposed to feminism were either "clinging, coquettish, privileged, jealous, idle or luxurious," or "the narrow ultra-conservative type . . . born temperamental reactionaries."[17] Charlotte Perkins Gilman was, if anything, more caustic: they were "innumerable weak and little women, with the aspirations of an affectionate guinea pig."[18]

In any event such women viewed the duties and responsibilities of their sex in much the same light as Hannah More. The despair of the reformers, they were, one hopes, the delight of their husbands and children. Yet not entirely. From the woman's rights movement to woman's suffrage to feminism, it is possible to trace very clearly the shifting aims and aspirations of those women who wished to reform the condition of their sex. The great age was the pre-Civil War era, roughly the twenty-year period from 1840 to 1860. It was then that a few enterprising and courageous women, drawn to the antislavery cause, went on to break the crust of a conventional and repressive society. They wished to assert the fact that women as human beings had certain "rights." It was an exciting and romantic time, analogous, in many ways, to the first phase of the present-day civil rights movement. The second period, from the end of the war to the late 1880's, was a time of some confusion and disarray within the movement itself. The immediate practical goal of the franchise proved strangely elusive. Factions and divisions appeared. The old guard saw the issue in terms of conventional kinds of power (more especially the vote), integration with a male-dominated society, jobs and professional careers for women. The younger radicals saw the problem as less integration than as the assertion of true feminism, whatever that was, and the reform of the inner spirit, the psyche of a sick society.

Although little or nothing was accomplished on the national level, at state level woman's suffrage made some notable gains, especially in the West. In 1869 the legislature of the Wyoming Territory gave suffrage to women, and when Wyoming became a state in 1890, women's suffrage was written into the state constitution. In Colorado, the ascendancy of the Populist Party in 1893 brought suffrage for women. In Washington Territory it was declared in 1883, declared invalid by the courts in 1887, was re-enacted immediately and again declared invalid by the courts. When Washington became a state in 1889, women's suffrage was defeated in a popular vote two to one, but in 1910 it carried on an initiative vote with little discussion. Thus by the end of the first decade of the twentieth century, five states had granted women the right to vote. In addition, twenty-two women occupied school offices without restriction. In fact, one of the interesting aspects of the extension of the suffrage in the United States was that, with few exceptions, when women were given the vote it was assumed that they could also be candidates for any elective public offices. In many countries where women were given the vote, they were specifically denied the right to hold office.

In Kansas in 1886 and in Michigan in 1893, women received the suffrage in all municipal elections. The enemies of women's suffrage pointed to the fact that comparatively few women exercised their right in those states or territories in which it had been granted and that the social and political life of such states had shown none of the improvement which the champions of women's suffrage had argued would accompany the extension of the franchise.

The liberal spirit of Kansas, born in the antislavery struggles of the fifties, was expressed in the occasional election of women to virtually all municipal offices from the mayoralty to judgeships. In Colorado a number of women served as county superintendents of school, and between 1893 and 1909 eleven women were elected to the state house of representatives. It took another war, World War I, in which once again women were most actively involved, as nurses and Red Cross workers, money raisers and factory hands, to produce, as a smashing anticlimax, the Nineteenth Amendment giving women at very long last the right to vote in national as well as state elections. The more visionary advocates of woman's suffrage hailed it as the dawn of the millennial age wherein the influence of women would wash away the impurities of American society. The prediction of Lord Bryce has proved more accurate.

12

The Protestant Passion

Throughout this book I speak of "the Protestant passion" in preference to the Protestant ethic. The Protestant ethic of "thrift, piety and hard work" really explains very little about the development of America. These virtues have, after all, characterized peasant societies for more than a thousand years. For better or worse, America is a great nation and, in Hegel's words, "nothing great is accomplished without passion." The Protestant passion was to redeem the world for and in the name of Jesus Christ and this passion was the spur of every one of the innumerable reforms of the nineteenth and the early twentieth centuries. Gradually its force was spent; by the 1930's the secular spirit had superseded it.

If the Protestant passion was the driving force of American reform, this was most particularly the case in those reform movements dominated by women or in which women were most heavily involved. The meetings of the feminine branches of the antislavery, temperance, peace and woman's rights movements were, in effect, religious services. They featured prayer, they included hymns and, in some instances, special liturgies. At the meeting of the World Conference of Women in 1895 the conference was opened by a lengthy service with a processional, hymn-singing, plainsong, a religious meditation by Helen Solomon Levy of the National Council of Jewish Women, a litany of thanksgiving and remembrance: "For the women who have gone before us, seers of visions and doers of deeds, pioneers of freedom and pathfinders of humanity, leaders of a great cause, builders of a better world,

We praise Thee, O God

For their vision of the wrong of all distinction because of color, creed, or sex, their righteous anger against all oppression of the weak and exploitation of the helpless, their stern struggle against all injustice and hardness of heart,

We praise Thee, O God. . . ."

Then the litany of dedication:

"O God, who art Life, and Light, and Truth, and Love, help us to see into the meaning of the way by which women have been led. . . .

We dedicate ourselves,

To the dream of the glorious Golden City, where all may live their lives in comfort, unafraid; a city of justice where none shall prey on others; a city of plenty where vice and poverty shall cease to fester; a city of brotherhood where all success shall be founded on service; a city of peace where order shall not rest on force, but on the love of all for the city, the great mother of the common life and weal,

We dedicate ourselves,

To the breaking down of barriers, that cleansed from class antagonisms, national hatreds, race prejudices and religious intolerance, all men may stand side by side in mutual worth, mutual appreciation and true fellowship . . ."

Margaret Fuller who wrote the first important woman's rights tract in America published initially as a lengthy essay in the *Boston Dial* under the title "The Great Lawsuit — Man *versus* Men; Woman *versus* Women" and later as a book entitled *Woman in the Nineteenth Century,* saw the campaign for feminine equality as a divinely ordained fight to exalt the race. "We would have every path laid open," she wrote, "to Woman as freely as to Man. Were this done, and a slight temporary fermentation allowed to subside, we should see crystallizations more pure and of more various beauty. . . . The divine energy would pervade nature to a degree unknown in the history of former ages, and . . . a ravishing harmony of the spheres, would ensue. . . . Since the sliding and backsliding men of the

world, no less than the mystics, declare that, as through Woman
Man was lost, so through Woman must Man be redeemed, the time
must be at hand. . . . I wish Woman to live, *first* for God's sake.
Then she will not make an imperfect man her god, and thus sink to
idolatry. . . . Then, if she finds what she needs in Man embodied,
she will know how to love, and be worthy of being loved."[1]

Every aspect of the woman's movement was related to the will of
God. Clothes should be made healthier and more practical, houses
should be better ventilated and food less greasy in the name of Christian principles. When the Protestant reformers rejected the structure
and dogmas of the Roman Church and espoused "the priesthood of
all believers" they probably made inevitable the domination of the
American Protestant churches in the nineteenth century by women.

Not only was the Protestant passion the wellspring of feminine
reformism, the church dominated the social and intellectual life of
middle-class women who had no interest in reform. Frances Trollope
noted that the clergy were the most sought-after group of males in
America. "Where equality of rank is affectedly acknowledged by the
rich," Mrs. Trollope noted caustically, "and clamorously claimed by
the poor, distinction and pre-eminence are allowed to the clergy
only. . . . I think . . . that it is from the clergy only that the
women of America receive that sort of attention which is so dearly
valued by every feminine heart throughout the world. With the
priests of America, the women hold that degree of influential importance which, in the countries of Europe, is allowed them throughout
all orders and ranks of society, except, perhaps, the very lowest; and
in return for this they seem to give their hearts and souls into their
keeping. I never saw, or read, of any country where religion had so
strong a hold upon the women, or a slighter hold upon the men."[2]

In all the new sects and denominations such as the Methodists and
Baptists, women played a very prominent role. Barbara Heck established Methodism in America in 1760. While she did not preach
herself she was responsible for organizing the first Methodist meetings and for the erection of the first church in America. In the words
of Julia Spruill, "the Reverend Francis Asbury found here many
'heroines for Christ,' who opened their houses for preaching, enter-
tained itinerant ministers, gave testimonies at love feasts, and, as class

leaders, traveled about the country conducting prayer meetings and teaching and exhorting members of their own sex."[3]

Lyman Beecher was an orthodox Calvinist, and his daughters at first followed dutifully in his doctrinal footsteps, but when Catharine Beecher's adored fiancé, an avowed agnostic, died at sea, she revolted against her father's strict faith. She would not accept the dogma that because her beloved had died without accepting the faith he was doomed to eternal damnation. She knew him as a kind and gentle man, a Christian in everything but name. She argued the case with her father and her minister brothers and found support in her sisters. To relieve her own black despair she wrote a book offering what was, in effect, a doctrine of universal salvation. She was thus a representative of that temper in Protestant women which, impatient with dogmas that seemed harsh and unfair, created great moral pressure for a more liberal Christianity.

Not only was the church the center of the social and emotional life of nineteenth-century women, but women made up the vast majority of the active members of the churches — indeed to such a degree that it is not putting the case too strongly to say that on the level of the practical daily life of the faithful, the Protestant churches became thoroughly feminized. The overwhelming majority of ministers were men (although Nette Brown had a number of well-known successors) and the vestries, elders, deacons, and governing bodies of the churches remained securely in masculine hands, but the work of the church was carried on very largely by women and its spirit inevitably affected by the simple weight of their numbers.

In the 1830's Alexis de Tocqueville reflected that pantheism, the notion that the universe as a whole is God, would have particular attractions for a democratic people. "When the conditions of society are becoming more equal," he wrote, "and each individual man becomes more like all the rest, more weak and insignificant, a habit grows up of ceasing to notice the citizens and considering only the people, of overlooking individuals to think only of their kind. At such times the human mind seeks to embrace a multitude of different objects at once, and it constantly strives to connect a variety of consequences with a single cause. The idea of unity so possesses man and is sought by him so generally that if he thinks he has found it, he readily yields himself to repose in that belief. Not content with the discovery that there is nothing in the world but a creation and a Creator, he is still embarrassed by this primary division of things and seeks to expand and simplify his conception by including God and the universe in one great whole."

The citizen of a democratic state is most susceptible to "a philosophical system which teaches that all things material and immaterial, visible and invisible . . . are to be considered only as the several parts of an immense Being." Such a scheme "although it destroys the individuality of man, or rather because it destroys that individuality, will have secret charms," de Tocqueville predicted, "for men living in democracies."[4]

The various sects that appeared in the United States after the Civil War were a fulfillment of the Frenchman's prophecy. There were, of course, many permutations of pantheism. Spiritualism was an early form, the originators and high priestesses of which were the Fox sisters. The Claflin sisters, as we have noted, got their start as spiritualists and hundreds and thousands of women and men as well were drawn to this strange mystery cult. There were attendant fantasies such as mesmerism and phrenology and finally the various forms of what Donald Meyer has called "mind cure" which became a major force in American religious experience. "Scientific psychology" was directed to quieting the nerves of Americans of both sexes. Essentially, mind cure, the by-product of the new psychology, held that ills of the flesh as well as endemic nervousness, despair and anxiety were in the mind. There was no real illness, just wrong thoughts, a disharmony with the Divine Mind of which the individual was a part. Reality was not in the world but in that all-encompassing Mind. The unhappy, frustrated person had only to place himself in alignment with the universal consciousness and peace and success would flow inward to him or her. One had only to let go of that austere and implacable will, that will with its attendant guilts and anxieties and all the power of the world to pierce and pain could be neutralized. Even the insatiable beast of sex could be appeased. "You must become mentally so translucent," one mind cure prophet wrote, "that you see men and women as sexless beings — which they are in the spiritual consciousness."[5] Mind cure, like the utopias, like the Church of the Latter Day Saints, was a touching effort to escape from the disintegrative effect of American life, from the efficiency, the organization, the competitiveness and the sexual tensions that were so destructive to the nervous systems of men and women alike.

But it was women who responded most readily to the tenets of mind cure. As Donald Meyer puts it: "the most obvious evangel of mind cure was the ubiquity of women. Not only was its most famous exponent a woman [Mary Baker Eddy]; scores of its lesser exponents were women, as founders, writers, preachers, teachers, healers. Mind cure gave jobs to women by hundreds and thousands. The clear majority of Christian Science practitioners were women. The majority of preachers in the proliferating Unity churches were to be women."[6]

While it might be competition that the man found especially corrosive, it was the ambiguity of her role that was undoubtedly most unsettling to a woman and here again, it was about her role as sexual partner that she felt her greatest anxiety. Mind cure was a technique for dissolving this and other anxieties. These sects drew more women and offered more opportunities to them, in part because religion always does and in part because as new religions they had no existing masculine-dominated organization to resist them. Moreover, pantheism or mind cure was, in its mildly asexual character, disinclined to make any distinction between male and female psyches or spheres; after all, men and women were to become "sexless beings" in some happier world.

In that vast release of energy that characterized their emergence, women might well have constituted a majority in many fields if it had not been for the resistance of entrenched males. Women flowed, almost as readily as water, into those occupations and areas of American society where they encountered the least masculine opposition. Religion, new and old, was one of these. If then, American Protestantism produced the "character-set," self-reliant, aggressive, individualistic, that made possible American capitalism, it produced also, as a kind of counterirritant, that eternally renewed hope of purifying and redeeming the world, a hope the particular custodians of which came to be American Protestant women, a tireless tribe armed with the knowledge that they labored for the Lord and that Christian service was the highest good in life. And on every crucial social issue they represented the best and most liberal spirit of the witnessing church.

13

Raising Up the Heathen

One of the most important outlets for the Protestant passion in nineteenth-century America was the foreign and domestic mission field. Starting with a trickle of hardy spirits in the early years of the century, by the end it had swelled to a flood of Christian workers, the great majority of them women. Like every reform movement of the age, women were in the forefront. The mission field was, in fact, the first area of American life where women achieved a more or less equal professional status with men. From the beginning missionary activity had a strong appeal to able and energetic females who did not wish to marry or who were unable to find husbands sympathetic to their notions of a proper role for women. It thus attracted women who, with few exceptions, were deeply committed to the cause of woman's rights. Such women accompanying their husbands to foreign countries found, inevitably, that they enjoyed more freedom and far wider outlets for their energies than they could have in America. Even with a domineering husband a wife could usually mark out her own sphere of work, most often organizing and teaching in a school for girls.

The basic notion of redeeming the heathen had a particular attraction for women. With the ministry in effect closed, those who wished to render a special service to the Lord were drawn in large numbers to the mission field. Service and self-sacrifice, caring for and raising up those who lived in misery and ignorance — such prospects were irresistible to thousands of American women in the hundred years from 1820 to 1920.

In 1801 a group of Congregational women started the Boston Female Society for Propagating the Diffusion of Christian Knowledge, and a year later the first Female Cent Society was founded, the members of which contributed a cent a week to the work of missions. Eight years later a group of young men, students at Williams College who wished to become Christian evangelists in foreign countries, prevailed on the Congregational Church to form the American Board of Commissioners for Foreign Missions. Encouraged by the reported success of English missionaries in India, the church issued a statement of purpose at its annual meeting at Worcester, Massachusetts in 1811: "The Eastern world . . . presents most extensive fields for missionary labors: fields which appear to be fast whitening for the harvest. All . . . are full of people sitting in darkness and in the region and shadow of death, and by experiments already made it has been abundantly evinced that it is by no means . . . vain . . . to attempt to spread the Gospel of salvation among them . . ." In another statement the newly formed board announced, "Prophecy, history and the present state of the world seem to unite in declaring that the great pillars of the papal and Mohammedan impostures are now tottering to their fall." The time was clearly ripe for the conversion of vast numbers of heathens and the redemption of innumerable souls. The board decided to direct its activities to four fields: "(1) peoples of Ancient civilizations (2) peoples of primitive cultures (3) peoples of ancient Christian churches (4) peoples of Islamic faith."

A mission was established in Bombay for the Marathi state in 1813; one in Ceylon for the Tamil people three years later; in the Sandwich Islands in 1820; with fifteen American Indian tribes in the period between 1817 and 1883, starting with the Cherokees, Chickasaws, Choctaws, and Dakotas. The Guinea Coast northwest of Palmas was added in 1833; Sumatra and Borneo a year later and the Zulus of South Africa in 1835. Then came Siam, Madura, Singapore, Madras, Amoy, Foochow (in 1847); Shanghai and Peking seven years later, and Japan following Perry's voyage, in 1869.

On November 14, 1815, the Female Charitable Society was organized in South Salem, New York, dedicated to the proposition that "the gospel is the only effectual means of civilizing the heathen and of preventing the most barbarous and cruel superstitions . . . we feel it to be both a duty and privilege to contribute our mite to send the word of life and the ambassador of God to those perishing for lack of vision."

Missionaries were sent to the Christians of the Ottoman Empire — the Armenians, Greeks, Bulgarians, Syrians — starting in 1820, and the same year a few brave souls carried mission activity to the Turkish, Arab, and Persian Muslims. The latter was to become one of the most active though least fruitful areas of Protestant mission work. The missionaries, men and women alike, went out to countries where conditions were often primitive in the extreme and always strange and unfamiliar. The hardships they endured are perhaps best suggested by the fact that in the early years of the missions, especially in India and the Middle East, missionaries died faster than they could be replaced. For a time the life expectancy of a missionary was less than five years. Since most of them went out as comparatively young men and women the mortality rate is impressive testimony to the rigors of missionary work.

Everywhere, even in ancient civilizations of great sophistication such as Persia, India, and China, the sanitary conditions were appallingly bad by American standards. Without immunity, without drugs or doctors, Americans were struck down by every sort of illness and disease. Indeed, the earliest call for medical missionaries was less to attend natives than to keep American missionaries alive in alien environments.

Adoniram Judson, a leader in the band of Williams students who formed the American Board, and one of the first American missionaries in India, described the hazards of missionary life quite accurately in writing to request the hand of Ann, the daughter of Deacon John Hazeltine. "I have now to ask whether you can consent to part with your daughter early next spring, to see her no more in this world? Whether you can consent to her departure to a heathen land, and her subjection to the hardships and sufferings of a missionary life? whether you can consent to her exposure to the dangers of the ocean; to the fatal influence of the southern climate of India; to every kind of want and distress; to degradation, insults, persecution, and perhaps a violent death? Can you consent to all this for the sake of Him who left His heavenly home and died for her and for you . . . for the sake of Zion and the glory of God?"[1] Judson married Ann, famous as a beauty; within a year she had died, and three years later he was dead himself.

Armed with the conviction that "even under difficult political circumstances, the Gospel could transform men and society," American men and women ventured into every corner of the globe. Missionaries have gotten such a bad press of late — depicted as grim, thin-lipped fanatics, putting muumuus on unself-conscious women and filling happy natives with Western inhibitions — that it is important to emphasize that the great majority of them were men and women of far more than ordinary intelligence, patience, understanding and compassion, as well as exceptional hardihood. In 1819 the American board issued instructions to missionaries dispatched to the Sandwich Islands. "Your views," the board declared, "are not to be limited to a low or narrow scale; but you are to open your hearts wide, and set your mark high. You are to aim at nothing short of covering those Islands with fruitful fields and pleasant dwellings and schools and churches; of raising up the whole people to an elevated state of civilization." An historian of the board was not far off the mark when he wrote: "By and large it was discovered that friendliness expressed through loving concern for the poor and the sick, eagerness to learn and listen, patient endeavors to satisfy human curiosity, unwillingness to take offense, calmness under provocation and persecution and a disposition to be content with what seemed at first meager results — these characteristics of the missionary were in demand among Oriental peoples."[2]

Certainly there were misfits and psychotics among the missionaries but after reading many missionary journals and letters it seems clear to me that they were, if anything, to be found in fewer number proportionately than in most other professional fields. Education was the initial, if not the primary concern of the missionaries. Before they could preach the Gospel they had to learn the native language, they had to teach their charges to read and write, and often they translated the Bible into the native tongue. Schools were thus the first step and these were almost invariably in the hands of women. Gradually education became a more and more important part of the missionary venture. Many missionaries in the field were convinced that elementary and some secondary education was not enough. There must be colleges and even theological seminaries.* The most serious split between the American board and the missionaries in the field came, in fact, over the issue of education. The board had become increasingly uneasy over the strong emphasis in Ceylon on schools and teaching. A minimum of education was necessary: enough to make it possible to read the Bible in English or, where possible, in the native tongue. Any education beyond this level represented a drain on time and money that should be spent for direct evangelizing. It was also apparent to the commissioners that while many were educated, comparatively few were converted. And even those converted as well as educated rather than becoming themselves ministers of the word and missionaries among their own people, showed an alarming tendency to take material rather than spiritual advantage of their new learning by seeking jobs in the colonial administration or entering business and professional careers.

Missionaries had to be reminded, from time to time, "that the establishment and instruction of schools, and other labors directly aimed at the amelioration of society, should always be kept strictly subordinate to preaching the Gospel."[3] The problem was twofold: it was, generally speaking, easier to educate than to convert. Many missionaries, especially in the early years, undoubtedly went out with visions of mass conversions where eager natives flocked to hear the message of salvation. The indifference of the natives, the hostility of their leaders, the frequent opposition of colonial administrators must have been a shocking disillusion to the missionaries. There was far less resistance to education than to conversion; the missionaries, being human, and of course being themselves, in most instances, educated men and women followed the line, if not of least resistance, at least of tangible results. The board meanwhile fretted over the discouragingly slow progress of the missions in developing a native ministry

---

* While the American board was perhaps the most active and successful of all the denominational mission groups, its work was paralleled by other religious organizations, by the Presbyterians, Methodists, Episcopalians, and Baptists, as well as, later, by the Church of Christ, the Seventh Day Adventists and the Disciples of Christ. Southern Baptist women raised over a million dollars in a single year for missionary work at home and abroad and the Woman's Missionary Union had a budget in 1931 of $2,530,000.

and was alarmed to see the greater part of its resources, human and material, diverted into what was, from its point of view, a secondary enterprise. The more doctrinaire commissioners insisted that it was much more economical to convert the natives first and then to educate them, rather than educate in the hope of conversions which were by no means certain: "the teaching of schools is alone valuable," a spokesman for the conservatives wrote, "when applied to cultivate the understanding of those whose wills are already converted."[4]

In 1823 the plan of the Ceylon missionaries for a Mission College which would teach Sanskrit, Hebrew, Latin, and Greek brought the issue to a head. "When those who are engaged in meliorating the condition of their fellow men have knowledge of the means of disseminating knowledge," the Ceylon group argued, "they have the power of doing good . . . Man is an intelligent and religious being; and under the combined influence of pure science and true religion, of these only, he attains the real dignity of his nature."[5] "Pure science and true religion" reinforced each other; there could be no conflict between them. They were the means of redemption. The board took a less enlightened view; or a more practical one. After thirty years of debate, it came out officially in 1860 for "the vernacular theory of education," in essence the minimum of education to prepare the native for conversion. The edict was bitterly resisted by many missionaries and some resigned from their posts in protest. Another thirty-five years later and the board finally accepted the principle that "higher education was essential to the permanent success of the foreign missionary enterprise." By this time a number of colleges had in fact been established. As the historian of the board has put it: "the social center, the clinic or hospital, the school [became] *officially* as important as the witness of preachment and word . . . Simple remedies to fight the fever, better houses to afford greater security, tools and seed for finer crops, simple books to record their language and make reading possible, songs and music . . . schools where children learned both letters and manners — all these and many other avenues led into the hearts and minds of the multitude."[6]

In all educational efforts women played, as we have said, the primary role. Those in foreign lands labored as teachers, as unofficial preachers of the word, and, finally, as doctors and administrators. The first important benefaction to the American board was a bequest of

$27,527 given by a Salem lady in 1811, the year of the board's organization. A more modest but more touching donation was $500, the carefully hoarded savings of a domestic servant in Cornish, New York. It will be recalled that even before the establishment of the board, the Female Cent Society was collecting money for missions. In 1814 The Female Foreign Mission Society was started to solicit money, and four years later it was estimated that there were over two hundred fifty local missionary associations in which women played the most prominent part. By 1838 there were six hundred eighty "ladies' associations" with more than three thousand "local agents" collecting funds for foreign missions. From the beginning of the missionary enterprise most men who went out were married to women who had chosen to share their husband's labors. Judith Chace was the first single woman appointed by the board. In 1818 the board appointed her a schoolmistress to the Cherokees. Five years later Betsy Stockton of Princeton, New Jersey, a Negro woman, was sent to the Sandwich Islands, the first unmarried woman sent overseas. She was called a "domestic assistant" but she soon became a full-time teacher.

In 1827 Cynthia Farrar of Marlboro, New Hampshire, went to Bombay as "Superintendent of Female Schools," schools started by the wives of missionaries in Marathi state. Soon the trickle became a tide. The gathering momentum of the woman's rights movement persuaded more and more women to look for careers; the shift from evangelizing to social work provided them with increased opportunities. It was also evident that it did little good to educate and convert men who then had no choice but to marry ignorant and superstitious wives. Native women must be educated as well as men. There is a good deal of evidence to suggest that native women were more easily educated and far more often converted. Many of them became what were called "Bible women," in effect itinerant lay preachers who accompanied missionaries on preaching and evangelizing trips and preached specifically to women who were often inaccessible to the missionary himself. It seems evident that Bible women were, in fact, more effective and certainly more numerous than Christianized native men, and the Bible women were, virtually without exception, trained in missionary schools run by American women.

One of the strongest appeals to women to enter missionary work was to be found in their conviction that foreign women or, more specifically, non-Christian women lived lives of hopeless degradation. Reading their letters and journals one finds that they were obsessed by the harem and seraglio; purdah, odalisques, bound feet, concubines, and male prostitution dismayed them. They stood down enraged Zulu fathers whose daughters had fled to mission schools to find refuge from detested marriages. In India they found wife-killing a common practice. Indians who would not kill a cat or a dog or a sacred cow did not hesitate "on the slightest quarrel" to hack their wives to death. They were perfectly aware of incidents such as that described by Sir Charles Napier where a seventeen-year-old girl was suspected of being unfaithful to her thirteen-year-old husband. "Her father led her to the front of his house . . . twisted her long hair in his hands, and holds her on tiptoe while her brother hacks off her head! This was all done openly," Sir Charles noted. Unwanted daughters in many Eastern societies were killed. The Ameers of India gave their mistresses potions to cause miscarriages and if that failed "they chop up the child with a sword . . . In Clutch they kill daughters who do not marry quickly." In Todas, near Goa, "infant daughters were drowned in milk or trampled to death by water buffaloes and among the Belochis the girls were killed with opium."[7]

The effect of such incidents on women already acutely sensitive to the position of females was excruciating. They felt an immediate identity with natives of their sex and longed to emancipate them. Certainly, to many native women, the victims of barbarous practices, missionary women came as genuine deliverers. For American women, as well as for their native students, education and conversion to Christianity had a very special meaning, a social as well as a spiritual redemption. The attitude of missionary women is perhaps best suggested by a member of that band who wrote that she felt that the greatest single argument for Christianity would be its attitude "toward women and children as over against the attitude of every other religion of the world toward women and little children." The preoccupation of missionary women with social reform is symbolized for me by a case in the library of Pilgrim Place, a retirement home of missionaries, ministers, and Christian workers. Amid books on foreign lands, travel, history, and theology there is a beautiful Chinese gown and arranged around it half a dozen pairs of miniature shoes for bound feet. American and English women were leaders in the fight to have foot-binding outlawed in China. Moreover, the fact that so many non-Christian women were treated primarily as sexual objects was certainly not lost on missionary women; they were doubtless aware that foot-binding itself was a powerfully erotic deformation.

In 1868 the Woman's Board of Missions was started to take direct charge of the work of female missionaries. The American board, exclusively male, had with the best of intentions, little understanding of the particular problems and concerns of women. The woman's board estimated that one hundred and forty single women had served since 1840 under the board alone. Forty-three were in the mission service in that year, nineteen in various parts of the Turkish empire, three in Syria, four in Persia, four in Madura, three in North China, and three in the Sandwich Islands.

The various woman's boards cranked out a great tide of literature written by women advising, guiding, admonishing, encouraging women missionaries. Journals, books, magazines, pamphlets — *The Helping Hand; The Gospel in All Lands; Missionary Link; The Missionary Herald; Life and Light; The Foreign Missionary; Woman's Work for Women* — all designed to help bear "the burden of lost souls to the throne of grace."

The mission field had a special appeal to the graduates of women's colleges who, in the years after the Civil War, were being turned out in a rapidly increasing number. These institutions were themselves suffused with the Protestant passion and with a devotion to woman's rights. The great majority of the students went to these colleges to prepare themselves for professional careers. Quite typically Isabel Trowbridge Merrill of the Vassar class of 1900 addressed herself to "The College Girls of America," assuring them that "the life of a missionary is the happiest, most joyous, most satisfying one I know . . . A college girl's whole training is toward activity and what else can give her so great pleasure and satisfaction as to be in an environment that calls out all her powers, and gives her a chance to live a vital life and a life that tells? Oh, girls, it pays so many times over. And if *we* do not take Christ to the women and girls in Turkey, *who will?*"

The woman's board of the Congregational Church had been preceded by the Woman's Union Missionary Society of New York, a coalition of female missionary groups, which declared that it had organized "in view of the increasing demand for labor which could only be performed on missionary ground by single women." It boasted that it employed twenty women "in eight stations," as well as eighty Bible women, and that it had opened twenty-five schools for girls. The woman's board encouraged the organization of the "Daughters of the Covenant" who pledged: "I gladly enter into this covenant of obedience, that I will not cease to make offerings of Prayer, Time, and Money to the end that the daughters of sorrow in all Christless lands may know the love of Jesus," and considered "the establishment and support of girls' boarding schools as of primary importance."[8] Besides supporting its own activities the woman's board contributed between forty and fifty percent of the costs of the American Board of Commissioners; fifty years after the founding of the woman's board it had contributed over ten million dollars to mission work. When the woman's board joined with the American board in 1926 it had, over a period of some sixty years, supported more than nine hundred single women missionaries, hundreds of day and boarding schools, and nine hospitals and dispensaries. The American board itself (Congregationalist) has sent out over 4800 men and women, in approximately even numbers, in thirty-four mission fields. The girls' school at Jaffna in Ceylon, one of the earliest mission schools for girls, took children from six to ten from different castes and kept and trained them until they married. If the girls married a husband approved by their teachers, they were given $25. Other denominations followed in the footsteps of the Congregationalists.

The Methodists had their own extensive missionary venture. In 1847 Methodist women founded the Ladies' China Missionary Society of Baltimore and soon after began a major effort in India. "If we do any great and good work among the women of India," a Methodist leader wrote, "we must show them the superiority of Christian womanhood . . ." Increasingly, with all denominations, the emphasis, which had shifted earlier from evangelizing to educating native peoples, moved on to medical missionary work and again women were prominent as doctors, as the founders of nursing schools, and as administrators.

In India by 1932 the Methodists had established fifty hospitals which treated over 700,000 outpatients; they had 5913 Sunday schools with over 200,000 scholars; and 43,306 young Indians were enrolled in 942 Youth Societies. Such figures would have to be multiplied by three or four to reflect the total American missionary activity. It should, of course, be remembered that a number of European countries sent out many Protestant missionaries, with England ranking next to the United States in the mission field. However, since the United States was not a significant imperial power until the end of the nineteenth century, American missionary activity was largely free from any imperial taint. Mission schools, in many instances founded by women and with women making up the great majority of teachers up to college level, were the most pedagogically advanced in the world. The women who established girls' schools had been trained in excellent institutions themselves — Oberlin, Antioch, Frances Willard's Female Academy, and, later, Smith College, Mt. Holyoke, and literally dozens of small denominational colleges with high educational standards. In India, or China or Africa they were free to introduce the most modern educational notions without battling conservative school boards, suspicious parents, or hidebound principals. We often find such subjects as psychology and sociology taught in mission schools decades before they made their way into American curriculums. It would then not be too much to argue that the best free elementary or secondary education in the world in, let us say, 1910, was probably to be found in a girls' school in Beirut, Bombay, or Foochow run by a bright graduate of Smith College.

The American Presbyterian Mission in Syria was a typically vigorous one. It ran fourteen Bible classes for women in Beirut in 1890, "conducted by ladies of the American, English, and Native Syrian communities." It listed in its directory ten Christian educational institutions ranging from the Theological Seminary of the American Mission, to the British Syrian Schools for Blind Men and Women and including the Prussian Deaconesses' Orphan House and Boarding School for Girls. The Syrian Protestant College had forty-two medical students in 1890, fifty-seven in the Collegiate Department and a hundred and one in the Preparatory Department. Of forty American missionaries, twenty-four were women, sixteen, men. They were responsible for eighty-six "outstations," thirty churches and five thousand members of the Syrian Protestant Community related to the

American Presbyterian Mission. They ran two boys' boarding schools with a combined enrollment of 156 and three "female seminaries" with 167 pupils. Altogether they counted 6346 pupils in elementary and secondary schools, college and seminary, of whom approximately one-third were girls, probably a better ratio than the United States could boast in the same year. The mission printed 76,000 volumes in 1890, a third of them Syrian Bibles.

The curriculum of a girls' school in Sido, Syria, was not atypical. There were "two American ladies in charge" and assisting them six Syrian teachers. Catharine Beecher's *Domestic Science* was an honored text and physical education was emphasized. The girls learned to "sweep and dust, wash and cook, sew and mend." The instruction was in Arabic. Bible studies were given preeminence and a visitor noted that the studies compared favorably with that of any school in the United States. Although the school had been established to educate the daughters of Protestant Syrians, its boarding pupils included girls from twenty villages, and from Greek Catholics, Orthodox Greeks, and Maronite faiths, while the day students included Protestants, Moslems, Jews, and "nominal Christians."

In 1863 there were ninety-three married and single Methodist missionary women in China but by 1887 the number had declined to seventy. However, by 1902 the number had increased to 783 in China, and in the entire Methodist missionary field, to 1500. Missionary women founded seven orphanages and five anti-foot-binding associations before 1900. (The first Anti-Foot Binding Society was founded in 1874 in Amoy and soon had a membership of over a thousand.) By 1898 there were Protestant missions in China representing fifty-four denominations. Twenty-three of these missions were American, seventeen British, and ten European. . . . The Americans had 276 ordained ministers; the British 174. There were 310 American missionaries' wives and 256 unmarried women in China in 1898 as compared to 166 and 183 respectively for the British. The Americans thus had 566 women workers as opposed to 402 men. Of 111 physicians among the American contingent, forty-three were women. Out of sixty-two British physicians twelve were women. The Methodists ran 474 day schools with a combined enrollment of over 6000 students, and the American mission schools counted 16,000 pupils and all Protestant missions together 30,000. In higher education Americans ran seventy-four colleges with 3819 students.

Missionary women going out to China were reminded that China was an ancient civilization when the Israelites crossed the Red Sea, and had existed for fifteen centuries when Isaiah prophesied of her future conversion. They were highly educated and "the knowledge of the classics is so widely diffused that it is said were they all destroyed there are a million men in China who could reproduce them from memory." Yet prayer was never offered for female children. Their birth was generally viewed as a calamity and many were simply drowned like unwanted kittens.

Elmira College, a co-educational institution founded in 1855, sent forty-seven of its graduates to the mission field, many to China and Turkey. Dr. Mary Miles, a member of the class of '75, established a school for the blind in China and translated a book on obstetrics into Chinese.

The editor of the *Missionary Review* spoke perhaps more truly than she knew when she wrote: "That today oriental women are taking a great part in the revolutions of life and thought that are transforming Asia, is due primarily to the faith and effort of unknown and unappreciated women missionaries. It was these women who gathered together little groups of untaught girls, and in spite of the opposition of fathers and husbands, yes and even of the missionary men themselves, taught them to read."

The Kiangsi Women's Conference Report of 1919 urged the delegates to keep in mind "the host of children of school age, 95,000,000 of them, not in any school at all, growing up without any education, utterly unprepared for citizenship in China and to be the mothers and fathers of the future generation of this great land." Only two percent of the women of China could read. "We are going to try to reach the many women for whom we alone are responsible," the report read, "and TEACH them."

The women of Foochow Conference of 1913 took heart from the students of the Kude Day School. "Even the little ones are learning to read, learning the Catechism, Scripture, hymns, and kindergarten songs, and also learning to play — an instinct seemingly dead in many of our village girls. And then the older ones are getting

glimpses of the great outside world through their studies and their teacher, and best of all slowly learning the true way of life."*

By the early twentieth century, missionaries themselves were aware that the expectations of the mission work had not been fulfilled and the legacy of almost a hundred years of devoted labors was an ambiguous one. In 1911 a Board of Missionary Preparation was established and at its third annual meeting in January, 1914, gave a sober report on the problems faced by mission workers in the Far East. The contact between East and West, rather than bringing about the conversion of the East to Christianity had, in fact, created an explosive situation but the board renewed the old assurances that "only Christian education of the highest type can counteract the forces of evil liberated by the impact of the West and East." And the key to this conflict lay in turn in the "vital relation of the condition of women to the strength of the Christian church of the future." Important as intellectual attainments were, they were no substitute for a deep and abiding faith. A college education was necessary for missionary women; they must cultivate "the scholarly habit" but knowledge of the Bible remained of supreme importance. They must, in addition, acquire "a general view of the growth and spread of Christianity and of modern missionary movements in their relation to world progress." Sociology was highly recommended to prospective missionaries to give them an insight into "the social problems which are perplexing the Orient. Many of these," the report continued, "Western civilization has created and most of them Christianity is able to solve." If the missionary considers the natives among whom she is sent to work "as barbarians or inferiors, as objects of pity, or 'natives' or 'converts' she can never hope to be a successful missionary." They would serve God best by creating "a beautiful home of gracious hospitality, good manners, refined culture, comfort, sanitation and taste . . ."[9]

As we have said, the number of "heathen" converts was always

* Miss Martha Wylie, a resident of Pilgrim Place recalls that at the first public dinner she attended in Foochow, given by officials of the city for the staff of the missionary school, she, as the only woman, was seated with the concubines. As soon as she realized the situation, she rose and demanded to be seated elsewhere. She had not come all the way from the state of Washington, she told her astonished Chinese hosts, to be insulted, and she would return at once if she was to be treated in such fashion. She was promptly moved.

disappointing, but the number of educated Zulus, Guineans, Indians, Turks, Persians, Arabs, Chinese, or, for that matter, Brazilians, can probably be counted a pure gain for the human race. In any event, it is clear enough that new Western-trained if not always Western-oriented elites were created in virtually all the countries where extensive missionary activity was carried on. Native women were, of course, essential parts of those elites. As the Christian partner of a native leader who might himself have never been converted or who might have lapsed, native women played an essential part in the Westernizing process. Christianity might be for the man a political or social encumbrance. For the woman it was her lifeline, a passport to at least a degree of emancipation. But men and women alike received in most instances their initial and usually principal nurture from American women missionaries. They learned English, and through the Bible and the personal style and influence of their teachers, they absorbed the fundaments of Western culture and the framework of Western ideals and values. Whether Sun Yat-sen or Chiang Kai-shek, whether Nkrumah or Gandhi or Nehru, the leaders of the non-Western peoples were prepared to cope with the problems of the modern world in missionary schools. It is, I suspect, no exaggeration to estimate that in Africa ninety percent of present-day leadership was educated in institutions established and run by missionaries. The percentage would vary, of course, from country to country, but I think that we could nowhere find an "emerging" nation in which at least seventy percent of its leadership has not been the product, directly or indirectly, of missionary education.

By 1910 there were ten thousand women, divided almost equally between married and unmarried, in seventeen mission fields; three hundred and thirty-two were physicians. Behind the statistics lies the fact of the social transformation of non-Western societies, conspicuously the change in the status of women, which one might say is one of the preconditions of modernization. About the effects of Westernization on non-Western societies one may, I realize, argue, and people obviously do. Western ideas have destroyed indigenous cultures, brought exploitation and the disorganization of simple, essentially rural economies by the intrusion of the methods and techniques of industrial capitalism. Nonetheless, whether we call missionaries "the running dogs of white colonialism" or some other equally opprobrious epithet, the fact is that the relative improvement in the position of women in the non-Western world, unsatisfactory as it may still be in many quarters, is, one presumes, an undisputable and unclouded gain. And it was the great accomplishment of missionaries, the majority of them women fired with a holy passion for the emancipation of their sex in every tribe and in every society.

Ultimately the story is that of individual women taking up one of the most arduous tasks in the history of the race. The labors of the vast majority of these valiant ladies are lost to posterity; the travails of a few must speak for all their unnamed sisters.

A typical Syrian missionary story was that of a New England girl, Loanza Goulding, who married a minister named Benton, a young man with a missionary calling. Her older sister was a missionary to the Choctaw Indians and Loanza herself wished to be a missionary to "the Indians of our Western wilds," but her husband's calling was to the Middle East. After a long and trying voyage, the Bentons reached Beirut early in 1847 and from there began their journey to the mission station at B'Hamderin.

For Loanza, who had never been on a horse before, it was a strenuous journey "up, up, up those steep and rugged mountain sides." "We passed," she wrote, "through so many villages and groves of tall pine trees and fields of cactus and olive and mulberry trees, the acacia trees with their fragrant blossoms like little soft balls of gold." When her horse fell from the narrow mountain trail to its death far below, Loanza slipped off its back and escaped by the narrowest of margins.

At B'Hamderin, a mountain village, Loanza labored for the conversion of the Syrians, and committed her thoughts and reflections to a classic New England diary in which she kept a daily audit of her own state of grace. She felt full of imperfection and wondered if she was a fit instrument of the Lord. Had she, she asked, "a greater loathing of sin and a stronger desire after holiness? Has Heaven more attractions and earth fewer charms?" Struggling with "her sinful deceitful heart" she feared she loved her husband more than her Savior. "I sometimes tremble lest I am making him my idol," she wrote.

At the beginning of a new year (1848) she took inventory of her soul's progress and was dismayed to find that she was still "vile and guilty." Yearning for her beloved New England in the cruel mountains of Syria, her heart cried out: "How beautiful is an American forest . . . I fancy I hear the reaper's songs and see the loads of golden grain."

The day before Thanksgiving, 1874, she wrote: "What a busy day is this in New England, everyone preparing for tomorrow. How many sweet unbroken family gatherings will take place." And when she went with her husband to visit Aleppo she noted in the diary "O, how different everything is from our dear New England!"

The Syrian women were "a poor ignorant and oppressed race of beings" who "regard it as a disgrace to learn to read their language, and manners are crude in the extreme." Yet their condition was certainly not their fault. "Who made us to differ?" she asked. "If we had been brought up and lived in a like state we should have been like them." She was especially dismayed at the contempt of Syrians for female children. They did not treat them as well as their animals and an Arab who wished to divorce his wife simply sent her away, or, if she demurred, in some cases, killed her. In the terrible Druse uprising she watched men shooting small boys out of trees like crows.

Filled as it is with nostalgia for home and with gloomy reflections on her own depravity, her diary is also rich in accounts of Syrian life and the Syrian landscape. She looked on fascinated as Arab boys fed a pet chameleon, offering it small leaves on a stick. The little creature seized flies with its tongue "catching them as they flew past him or lighted on a leaf." Traveling to Beirut for the annual missionary meeting, the Bentons passed shepherds with their crooks and lunch bags filled with bread, raisins, and olives, calling "taal, taal, taal" to their sheep who left their fold and followed them up the hillside. She watched the shepherds take three or four leaves and roll them in kurseni, put the ball-shaped mass into a sheep's mouth, take hold of the animal's jaws "and make the sheep eat and help him too." Shepherds did this for twelve or sixteen hours at a stretch to make the poor animals fat.

Loanza's first child, Willie, was born within a year after the Bentons' arrival in Syria. He was a great comfort to his mother, "a very good little boy and obeys us very quick," she wrote in her diary, adding dutifully, "but I know his little heart is depraved and sinful."[10]

Sickness was always a threat and during a dangerous illness of her husband twenty leeches were applied to the side of his head to relieve his pain and fever. When Willie died an agonizing death after a long illness, it seemed to Loanza more than she could bear. She realized that even the most rudimentary medical attention was desperately needed and, arming herself with a few simple remedies, she became, in fact, a medical missionary.

Loanza Benton had six children besides Willie, five or whom survived. In addition to looking after her growing family she established and ran a mission school for girls that grew year by year and into which, as the symbol of her devoted service to the Lord, she poured her time and energy unstintingly. When her husband died of a heart attack in 1874, Loanza Benton returned to the United States and helped to put the three boys through Yale and the girls through the University of Minnesota, largely from the proceeds of public lectures that she gave with the younger children dressed in Syrian costumes and singing Syrian songs. Her son Charles, who spoke six languages and could read and write fifteen, became professor of Semitic Languages at the University of Minnesota and founded a mission for local Syrians. Mary Benton got her Ph.D. at the University of Minnesota and taught at Smith College and Carleton; Hattie married a professor of Latin at the university.

The Benton School at B'Hamderin which Loanza had started and been forced to abandon after the death of her husband was reestablished by Raheel Saleeby, one of Loanza's "Syrian daughters." The school is still in existence and when a friend of one of Loanza's grandsons, William Benton, son of Charles, founder of the advertising agency of Benton and Bowles and Assistant Secretary of State under Truman, visited it after World War II, the children sang three verses of "My Country 'Tis of Thee" in English and the principal told her visitor: "We teach our children the name of Benton as we teach them to eat bread . . . The memory of the Signora's life lingers like a sweet perfume on the mountains of Lebanon."[11]

Like Loanza Benton, Seraphina Haynes was a New England girl who married a young minister, Joel Sumner Everett, and accompanied him to a missionary post in Turkey. She wrote her parents the first

Sunday at sea: "We were able to have our season of devotion in the cabin, and found it good to commune with God in this our floating chapel. But did not our thoughts lead us back over the dark waters to the paternal roof . . . Our hearts ascended in gratitude that we, although so unworthy, are called to be messengers of the Cross to those who sit in darkness."[12]

On the voyage, seasick, miserable, and "wicked" as she was, she so far forgot herself and her mission as "to wish for a moment she could see the cheering kind faces wont to gather around the fireside and wish for a little rest beneath the parental roof." But she quickly repented these weak and foolish thoughts. Seraphina, ill almost from the time of her arrival in Turkey, died in 1856 and was buried in the Protestant graveyard in Istanbul.

Katherine Pearce, a graduate of Smith College and a missionary teacher in Constantinople was dismayed by "the dirt and disorder" and startled to see men kissing each other and wearing beads. "This is country," she wrote her parents, "in which one learns or loses patience." When the famous evangelist, Sherwood Eddy, came on a tour of Christian missions in the Middle East, he told the men and women, among them Katherine Pearce, who gathered to hear him that what was needed in mission work was "character built foursquare on a solid foundation to save the world." His cornerstones were "honesty, purity, unselfishness, and righteousness."[13] Rebecca Toy Lore who went with her husband to Argentina to establish a mission of the Methodist Church in that country wrote in her journal: "Thoughts of *home* crowd upon my mind very often, and awaken all the tenderest feelings of my nature and I scarcely ever sleep but I dream of *home,* but never for a moment have I regretted the decision made after prayerful deliberation, to become a missionary."[14]

In 1934 a student at Mt. Holyoke College, one of the great producers of woman missionaries, wrote a poem about the college's indomitable missionary band:

> *Abigail Moore went out to India*
> *A century ago, and Susan Waite*
> *To China, and Fidelia Fiske embarked*
> *For Persian cities, from South Hadley Town.*
> *(South Hadley Town, where fertile seed was sown.)*

DAUGHTERS OF THE PROMISED LAND

And all across the world to desolate lands,
And lands most desolate with humanity,
They took their sisterhood, from northern ports
Up the earth's slope to sea-surrounded reefs,
Down the earth's curve to wave-embattled capes,
To Egypt and Japan and Labrador,
Hawaii, Turkey, and Columbia —
Yearly they went, not yearly to return —
And not all to return at any time.

Why did you go, Theresa, Abigail?
God knows! Had you not faith? He knew indeed
Who sent you, why a fire was in your hearts
Burning for all the anguish of mankind,
A torture and a light, until you took
The cross upon your shoulders and went out
To weep, and solace weeping and hunger; to feed
Your thousands by the sea; forget your dreams
And learn the truth of God, and finally
To die worn out with fever, or dispatched
With one neat flashing of a Chinese sword —
So death was conquered and you might go home.

But do not come home to South Hadley Town.
No one's remembrance here will make you live;
You built your monuments outlasting bronze,
Somber and high, written with all your names —
But no one reads them to release your souls.
Abigail, Susan, look out to the west;
There are the hills whereto from Burmese swamps
You lifted up your eyes. There is the snow,
Folded not differently about the pines.
Look to the east, Fidelia, see the streams
Dishevelled on the hills — the waterbrooks
Your spirit panted for beyond Bagdad
Look north, look south — only look never down.

·   ·   ·

They will sleep warm with blankets to their chins.
Blot out the names, and let the ghosts go free,
Sighing across the mountains to their graves
Where spirits rest and fear no further change.

RAISING UP THE HEATHEN

One generation passeth — let it pass
Unhampered in its dying. We also,
After a century, will find no place
For phantoms in our children's home, though we
Should give our lives also for cornerstones.[15]

If Americans think of missionaries at all they usually think of them as resembling the minister in *Rain,* hot-eyed, tight-faced fanatics. How were traditional non-Western societies transformed? By colonial exploitation, by the rape of native populations, by capitalist enterprise. But colonialism in and of itself never taught a single native woman to read, founded a school or started a college or a hospital. A worldwide missionary effort on a remarkable scale, the major portion of which was borne by American missionaries was the real means by which this transformation was accomplished. Education more than conversion was the agency of change and in this venture American women played a major role, if not *the* major role. In doing so they acquired training in public speaking, in organizing, in raising and allocating money, in managing an enterprise of international proportions. They wrote books, started printing presses and founded colleges, kindergartens, training schools, hospitals, and orphanages. They became, moreover, part of a genuine international community of missionary workers. They visited each other and intermarried both with other nationals and with converted native Christians, especially in China and the Middle East. Their children became missionaries, doctors, politicians, and, in very considerable numbers, college professors. Yet as far as academic history is concerned it is as if all of this had never happened. American historians have ignored this whole extraordinary episode, presumably because it happened outside the geographical limits of the United States. But if it is not part of American history, it is certainly a crucial part of world history.

14

Home and Mother

In the nineteenth century the American "home" was a clouded image. Foreign visitors commented on the fact that Americans had little or no feeling for "home"— that ancient, magic word — as a *place*. A home, traditionally, is an accretion of sounds, sights, experiences, textures; it is a kind of stage, a particular recognizable setting, against which the principal dramas of ordinary life are played out. But American homes were mobile long before they were put on wheels. Home is not a castle, a refuge, a bower, an ancestral manor — it is "where you hang your hat." You hang it here today and there tomorrow. "You can't go home again," not simply because home is no longer there psychologically, as in the case of Thomas Wolfe; it is not even there physically.

If the residential hotel in which families lived was a French invention, it was adapted to the American scene very promptly and became, in time, the ubiquitous apartment house. I quoted earlier the English traveler who commented on the fact that American men viewed their wives as Englishmen viewed their homes, that is, as visible symbols of success. They adorned their wives instead of their homes; they expected to have their wives much longer than their homes which, indeed, they planned to change next month, moving to a better location. Foreign visitors frequently commented on the fact that many

Americans, especially newly married couples, lived in hotels. At the Adelphi Hotel in Albany, Frances Trollope was surprised at "the un-English arrangement" whereby a mother and her married daughter with two small children boarded at the hotel on a permanent basis. "Where the husbands were, or whether they were dead or alive," Mrs. Trollope added, "I do not know." The family "breakfasted, dined, and supped at the *table d'hôte,* with from twenty to a hundred people, as accident might decide; dressed very smart, played on the piano, in the public sitting room, and assured me they were particularly comfortable and well accommodated. What a life!"[1]

Mrs. Trollope encountered such arrangements at many other hotels and Captain Marryat had similar observations. He was told in 1830, that married couples stayed in hotels because it was "cheaper to live in a large hotel than to keep a house of your own; another is the difficulty of obtaining servants and, perhaps, the unwillingness of the women to have the fatigue and annoyance which is really occasioned by an establishment in the country — added to which is the want of society, arising from their husbands being from morning to night plodding at their various avocations. . . . In the evening, especially in the large western cities, they have balls almost every night; indeed, it is a life of idleness and vacuity, of outward pretence, but of no real good feeling."[2]

American homes had other serious drawbacks beside their impermanence. Domestic cookery was by all accounts atrocious, the food swimming in grease and overdone; houses were poorly designed, invariably overheated and poorly ventilated since fresh air was thought to be full of deadly miasmas and a terrible menace to good health. It was commonly observed that the anxious and overworked husband was seldom home. He rose in the morning, gulped down a hasty breakfast and dashed off to his office. Moreover, especially to the astonishment of the French visitors, he did not even return for lunch but came home exhausted at dinner time, ate an indigestible meal, and went to bed. The wife, though a devoted and self-sacrificing mother, soon went to seed and was, as we have seen, constantly ailing. Often husband and wife, not surprisingly, both suffered from "Americanitis" — chronic nervousness.

This was the American home in the nineteenth century and indeed certain aspects of it are all too familiar today. As described by our travelers it was a bleak enough environment. But their accounts do not tell the whole story. The self-indulgence of unmarried girls, their preoccupation with clothes and fashion, the fact that an increasing number of them took "jobs" prior to marriage, when combined with their parents' mobility which dragged them from one dreary box-like structure to another meant that, however conscientious, they were, by and large, very indifferent housekeepers. Housekeeping was an art that few American wives mastered.

Further complicating the picture was the constant stream of immigrant families. In Ireland, for example, and in Italy housekeeping was a traditional function which was closely related to the character of domestic architecture and supported by centuries-old ways of doing things in a rural peasant economy, an intricate ritual handed down from mother to daughter. Everything had a "place"; the physical order of the household was ordained, so to speak. Life had accommodated itself to a particular space and that space had been explored and mapped to its tiniest interstices. Halls, kitchens, pantries, bedrooms, sheds and barns were part of an order that was almost like the order of nature herself.

When these women were plopped down in urban tenements (where most of them settled) they often became thoroughly demoralized. They were like workmen assigned to an unfamiliar workshop with tools they had never seen before. A great many of them were unable to cope with their new environments. They lived despairingly alienated in noisome dens and thus contributed their bit to the unhappy picture of the American home.

The home, however, was no more immune to the reforming zeal of women than the institution of slavery or habits of intemperance. Catharine Beecher and her sister Harriet made the reform of the home their special mission. We have already seen that Catharine Beecher's principal objection to woman suffrage was that since American women were doing such a miserable job in the home they assuredly had no time for politics. In a series of books she set the requirements for the reconstruction of the American home on scientific principles, the first of course being to improve the health of the wives and mothers who inhabited it. Catharine Beecher produced the first popular cookbook, and she and Harriet joined forces to write the classic nineteenth-century manual on housekeeping — *The American*

DAUGHTERS OF THE PROMISED LAND

Woman's Home or Principles of Domestic Science Being a Guide to the Formation and Maintenance of Economical, Healthful, and Christian Homes. Published in 1869 it was certainly one of the most influential books of the age. The work was "affectionately dedicated" to "THE WOMEN OF AMERICA in whose hands rest the real destinies of the Republic, as moulded by the early training and preserved amid the maturer influences of home." The determinative word in the title was "Christian." Happy, airy, clean, economical, well-ordered households were, above all, Christian households. To run a house properly was to bear witness to God of one's love and faithful service. Résumés of the first two chapters will perhaps suffice to make the point:

"Chapter I — THE CHRISTIAN FAMILY: Object of the Family State — Duty of the elder and stronger to raise the younger, weaker, and more ignorant to an equality of advantages — Discipline of the Family — The example of Christ one of self-sacrifice as man's elder brother — His assumption of a low estate — His manual labor — His trade — Woman the chief minister of the family estate — Man the outdoor laborer and provider — Labor and self-denial in the mutual relations of home-life, honorable, healthful, economical, enjoyable, and Christian."

"Chapter II — A CHRISTIAN HOUSE: True wisdom in building a home — Necessity of economizing time, labor, and expense, by the close packing of conveniences — Plan of a model cottage — Proportions — Piazzas — Entry — Stairs and landings — Large room — Movable screens — Convenient bedsteads — A good mattress — A cheap and convenient ottoman — Kitchen and stove-room — The stove-room and its arrangements — Second or attic story — Closets, corner dressing tables, windows, balconies, water and earth-closets, shoe-bag, piece-bag — Basement — Conservatories — Average estimate of cost." (For a comfortable house $1600 was a reasonable estimate.)

From "Scientific domestic ventilation" to "Health of mind," "Care of infants" and thence to "Care of the Homeless, the Helpless and the Vicious," illustrated with floor plans, diagrams, and pictures of the latest stoves, most tasteful curtains, and most efficient commodes, with engravings of the lungs and heart to show the benefits to health of proper ventilation. And all of this related to the great Christian work of universal redemption. Many of the "poor, ignorant and neglected ones" were perishing at that very moment "for want of such Christian example and influence."

The woman who raised children and "trained them for heaven" had a noble mission, but much more the woman who earned "her own independence that she may train the neglected children of her Lord and Savior. . . . And a day is coming when Protestant women will be *trained* for this their highest ministry and profession as they never yet have been."[3]

Catharine Beecher's missionary efforts to reform the home and improve the health of American women had far-reaching effects. Under her prodding the American Women's Educational Association resolved: "That the science of domestic economy should be made a study in all institutions for girls. . . ."

Courses in "home economics" gradually penetrated the curriculum of high schools, women's colleges, and the state universities. A generation of devoted women, inspired by Catharine Beecher's teaching, founded home economics colleges across the country. Similarly her concern with women's health was a major factor in the spread of physical education as part of the required curriculum in public institutions at all levels.

When Madame Blanc visited America in the 1890's she noted, as her predecessors had, that American girls were lacking in the gentler graces of domestic life, but she also observed that efforts were being made to repair their more glaring deficiencies by courses labeled "domestic science," taught in the public schools and by the "Christian Associations." The Frenchwoman attributed the domestic shortcomings of American women to "the facilities offered by boardinghouses, clubs, and restaurants" which had "utterly destroyed in many of them those qualities which we are in the habit of regarding as pre-eminently those of their sex." Cooking schools were a new fad but Madame Blanc, observing "independent" wives dining with friends at a restaurant and calling for the bill of fare "as naturally as if they were bachelors," felt little optimism about the future of the culinary arts in America.[4]

One of the most important changes in the quality of middle-class family life has to do with the disappearance of servants. It is hard to overemphasize the effect on the relations of members of a family with each other, on the character of privacy or the absence of it, on the minor constraints and formalities which the presence of domestic servants imposed. Servants meant a kind of psychic distance between the various members of a family that is hard to imagine today when families live in almost suffocating intimacy. While certain strains undoubtedly existed as a result of "outsiders" in the household, others were avoided. There are few inhibiters as effective as an audience, "this observing and repeating army lodged in the very bosom of the family," as Charlotte Perkins Gilman termed it.[5]

The character of the home in nineteenth-century America is important to this story because the home is the particular province of the woman. If it was indeed a dreary place, ugly, constricted, improperly ventilated, in a word, graceless, it is hardly to be wondered that many women wished to get out of it, and many men took their time returning to it, preferring to linger in masculine preserves — from the local saloon to the Pacific Union Club.

The missionary work of Catharine Beecher has borne fruit. While it would be a mistake to argue that the image of the home is today an entirely unambiguous one, or that the vast improvement in the average middle-class home as a place to live is primarily the consequence of courses in home economics and of numerous magazines full of advice (much of it reasonable enough) about how to make the home a pleasanter place to live in, there is little question that the home is a better environment. Lacking individuality, jerry-built in many instances, decorated with the most appalling ticky-tacky, they are nonetheless probably more habitable than their predecessors, pleasanter, brighter, cleaner, more healthful, and more attractive. The food served in them is more palatable and more digestible. The wives who preside over them are more independent, healthier, better looking, more sensibly dressed, and more efficient than their grandmothers. But these differences, important as they are, are, after all, superficial. It is in apparently just such better homes and gardens that the quality of life is most distressing.

If the nineteenth-century woman was on uncertain ground as wife, she was universally acclaimed as mother. As we have seen, virtually every visitor praised her conscientiousness and devotion although there was less agreement as to whether her influence was wholly desirable. One of the facts of American life that made the mother

loom so large was that the urban business and professional father was so seldom home; the raising of children thus fell to the mother's lot by default. It was commonly observed that American children were badly spoiled and indulged. Captain Marryat agreed with the historian, John Sanderson, that "there is no country in which maternal care is so assiduous; but there is also none in which examples of injudicious tenderness are so frequent." Mothers, unsupported by their husbands, spoiled their children. The consequence, according to Marryat, was a "self-will arising from this fundamental error" and manifesting itself throughout the whole career of the American's existence, making the United States "a self-willed nation *par excellence.*"[6] Marryat offered a typical dialogue between parents and child:

> " 'Johnny, my dear, come here,' says his mamma.
> 'I won't,' cries Johnny.
> 'You must, my love, you are all wet, and
>   you'll catch cold.'
> 'I won't,' replies Johnny.
> 'Come, my sweet, and I've something for you.' "

The father is appealed to. He tries, " 'Come in, Johnny,' . . . 'I won't'. . . . 'A sturdy republican, sir,' says his father . . . smiling at the boy's resolute disobedience." The real cause of such lax discipline in Marryat's opinion was "the total neglect of the children by the father, and his absence in his professional pursuits."[7]

Instructions and advice on the duties and functions of the mother were included in most books about the behavior of women from Cotton Mather's *Ornaments for the Daughters of Zion* onward. The precepts were, for the most part, quite "modern." A patient and gentle discipline, lots of love and affection, firm and consistent punishment, seldom if ever corporal, the encouragement of the freedom and independence of children. The wise mother should be at pains to secure the *"respect, confidence and love"* of her children. Mothers were warned that the first years of a child's life were perhaps the most impressionable, and the love and care they gave their infants in this period might shape their future lives.

The basis of all proper education, such manuals agreed, was "the Christian scheme" which "recognizing the child's inherent depravity, his accountability, his immortality, the necessity of his spiritual renewal, and the means by which that end is to be attained," aimed to "educate him at once for earth and heaven."[8]

The advantage of such a view of the child was that the parent was not surprised at any evidence of sinfulness, rather, expected it and set about, with love and patience, to correct it. The mother should preside over a happy but an orderly kingdom. The doctrine that children should be "reasoned into obedience and subjection" was usually rejected. It imposed too great a strain on parents and children alike and replaced obedience with disputation. Children should obey their parents because they believed them to be reasonable, loving, and just. Mothers were advised to be tolerant of the mirth and noise of children, of their exuberant animal spirits —"How delightful to all young creatures is freedom!"— and to try to enter sympathetically into the child's own world, a world of fantasy and make-believe where fact and fiction were often quite mixed up in youthful imaginations.

In this spirit "much must be left to the spontaneous impulses of the child's nature — to his natural love of achievement and of self-reliance and self-approbation, to his conscious bravery, his instinct of self-preservation, and the teachings of experience. Much also must be left to the *providence of God*."[9]

As the women's rights movement entered its early feminist phase, the figure of the mother loomed larger and larger. Some of the Claflin sisters' most passionate statements had to do with the sacred duty of mother to produce a better race by selecting their mates "scientifically," and by being free to escape from marriages to brutes who were not fit through drunkenness, licentiousness and disease to have offspring.

The nineteenth century had two major (and sometimes overlapping) ways of neutralizing woman. One was to elevate her to the angelic creature, fragile and ethereal; the other was to deify her as The Mother, "the key figure in civilization, holy being of total virtue, calm and elevated substance, and perfect comprehension of her children."[10] If the first alternative was proclaimed at the beginning of the century, the second was advanced at the end.

Interestingly enough, no theory developed to embody the most persistent reality which was daughterhood. When the mother role came to be featured, it was almost invariably the mother in relation to her son. The end of the century indeed witnessed a remarkable apotheosis of mother. Dozens of tycoons and other culture heroes came forward to extol their mothers.

The nineteenth-century works on child rearing and the duties of motherhood tell us a good deal about the quality of family life, at least as it related to the rearing of children by mothers. But so far as one can judge, the maternal was kept in balance with the paternal side of the family through the early decades of the century. Certainly this was true so long as the father, with his prayers and Bible reading, appeared as priest in the family. Where the father, as he surely did from the middle of the nineteenth century on, withdrew into business and professional concerns, the moral nurture of the family devolved more and more on the mother. At the same time, in those urban societies which grew in size and importance with each decade, the mother suffered a severe loss of personal power and authority as the consequence of her diminished role. There thus seems to be some evidence that for the successful urban-bred man the relationship with the father remained the dominant and important one, because the father was most often the figure of "power." I think it is clear, on the other hand, that the small town, after its initial period of settlement when it was dominated by the "town-founder" type of male, passed rapidly, at the level of its practical life and psychological atmosphere, under the domination of the women of the community, and it seems to be most often the men bred in small towns who praise their mothers in sentimental terms. "All I am I owe to my mother" is a thus rather late proclamation of filial devotion.

To push these speculations a bit further; the urban mother, deprived of the company of her husband by his devoted pursuit of money and success, focused her attentions and her affections on her children, more particularly her son. The small-town mother, married to a man of diminished power and potency, took over the role and responsibilities of the father. The difference is subtle but important. A mother generally could assume the paternal role with much less danger to the son's psyche than if she overplayed the mother role and tried to use the son as a substitute for an absent or inattentive husband. The average urban woman was apt to be dependent, powerless and trivialized, especially in the period from the late eighteenth to the late nineteenth century. The influence of such a woman on a son was not, at least in theory, inclined to be a healthy one. In such a situation the energetic and ambitious son would naturally gravitate to the father. He was a strong figure, even if he was a rather remote one. In the town, if we are to believe our literature, the father was often an inept and defeated dreamer, the mother the strong and successful figure (much as in the Negro community), and the ambitious son had, perforce, to draw his spiritual nourishment primarily from his mother.

Such a mother was a natural target for the caustic pen of Charlotte Perkins Gilman. She attacked "modern mother-worship" with gusto. After scornfully describing the mother cult —"the dying soldier on the battlefield thinks of his mother, longs for her, not for his father. The traveler and exile dreams of his mother's care, his mother's doughnuts"— she declared that "human motherhood is more pathological than any other, more morbid, defective, irregular, diseased." As a consequence, "human childhood is similarly pathological." Mothers were untrained and uninformed about their duties: "The human mother does less for her young, both absolutely and proportionately, than any other kind of mother on earth."[11] She had too little knowledge of the world, of hygiene — of, in fact, anything — to be an adequate teacher of the young: "It is considered indelicate to give this consecrated functionary any previous knowledge of her sacred duties." It would be far better to turn infants over each day to trained experts who would guide them with professional skill: "Direct, concentrated, unvarying personal love is too hot an atmosphere for a young soul."

Such care would free mothers to work and "the woman who works is usually a better reproducer than the woman who does not." The revered and sentimentalized mother was, in fact "erratic and pathological."[12]

Ellen Keyes, a Swedish writer and lecturer whose writings were widely read in America, was a prophet of the new motherhood. "Modern women," she wrote, "with their capacity for psychic analysis, with their physical and psychical refinement, are often repelled by the crudeness, the ignorance, or the importunities of man's nature." Thus they have lost the maternal instinct. It is this instinct, above all others, which Miss Keyes celebrates — a new, healthy, vigorous motherhood is to redeem the race. Anything which distracts or discourages, which diminishes or attenuates this motherhood must be attacked relentlessly. Under the new dispensation it will be "regarded as a crime for a young wife voluntarily to ill-treat her person, either by excessive study, or excessive attention to sports, by tight-lacing, or consumption of sweets, by smoking or the use of stimulants, by sitting up at night, excessive work, or by all the thousands of other ways by which these attractive simpletons sin against nature. . . ."[13]

To be sure, woman had to express an "egoistic self-assertion" in order to make the point that she was not "solely a sexual being" but having done so she should give up the game for her true role — motherhood. Indeed the apotheosis of motherhood had proceeded so far by the second decade of the twentieth century that Beatrice Forbes-Robertson Hale sounded a warning note: "the insistence upon motherhood and child-care in the writings and speeches of leading feminists is sometimes so intense as almost to endanger the claims of husband and father. . . . It is safe to say that there has never been a time in which the child has received more than a fraction of the earnest care of mind and body bestowed on him by the educated mothers of this generation." There was, it seemed to Mrs. Hale, an almost excessive emphasis on child care, as well as on motherhood: "The college-bred mother flies from her old faith in instinct to an extreme belief in science, and the baby that used to play in the mud now has his toys sterilized."[14]

Why such an exaltation of motherhood should have taken place at the end of the nineteenth century is not easy to explain. Of course it fits in with the sentimentality that characterized the period, and it was clearly related to a general impulse to deify woman. Perhaps as the larger society seemed to become more unjust, brutal and intolerable, there was a tendency to fall back on the family as the ultimate source of sanctification, the true means of grace. Works such as those of the Beecher sisters undoubtedly paved the way for the apotheosis. By the end of the century, Protestantism was running out of steam and becoming in essence sentimental piety, shorn of any intellectual or theological severity. Also it was increasingly clear that, in a certain sense, American men were, as foreign travelers so frequently charged, a failure. Paradoxically, while creating the most revolutionary society in the modern world, performing astonishing and unprecedented feats of skill and imagination, they had recklessly expended a precious inner vitality. Sacrificing some of their essential manhood on the altar of that revolution, they had grown more nervous and irritable, more powerful and at the same time more impotent.

Remarkable as were the energies of the American man, they were not inexhaustible. The attrition of the effective life of the American male, especially in his role as father of a son (much less, I would maintain, as father of a daughter) created a kind of emotional vacuum filled by the figure of Mother who became, in a more cynical age, that monstrous caricature — omnivorous, insatiable, merciless Mom.

South and West

The reader hardly needs to be reminded that the women about whom I have been talking are primarily urban middle-class women of the North. I have had little to say about Southern women or about frontier women, the women of the great westward migration. My excuse for concentrating on middle-class urban women is that they were the principal agents of female emancipation; they were the "creative minority" who led the battle for woman's rights and articulated the ideals and aspirations of their sex.

The women of the South lived in an authoritarian society. In any fight to assert their rights they could count on no masculine allies. Like the Negro slaves, they occupied a rigidly defined role in a society where everyone had a "place" and was expected to stay in it. While they too suffered from the Great Repression, from a constant narrowing of their freedom and a constriction of their personal lives, they were relatively isolated on farms and plantations and were thus denied the stimulus of frequent association with others of their sex in an environment where they might have gained the strength to speak out. Above all, slavery, which most of them hated, led to the development of the strange feudal ethos of the South, where men were knights and women ladies surrounded by the mystique of medieval chivalry. Because slavery must at all costs be defended, it followed that no one could speak out on any subject without arousing an increasingly paranoid fear and hostility.

As mistress of her plantation the Southern lady enjoyed the position and prestige that any woman of an aristocratic class receives by virtue of her membership in that class. On her plantation she was a person of considerable power and importance. Moreover, while her life was in large part patterned after that of a delicately nurtured English lady, she inevitably partook of some of the freedom and enhanced status vis-à-vis the internal society of the Southern aristocracy that characterized her Northern sister. She was often an active partner in the running of the plantation. A large corps of household servants were under her command and, frequently, on the death of her husband, she proved herself equal to the complex and demanding job of running tobacco, rice, and cotton plantations.

Eliza Lucas Pinckney while she was still in her teens assumed the management of three plantations near Charleston. "I have a little library," she wrote a friend, "well furnished (for my Papa has left me most of his books) in which I spend part of my time. My Musick and the Garden of which I am very fond take up the rest that is not imployed in business, of which my father has left me a pretty good share. . . . I have the business of three plantations to transact, which requires much writing and more business and fatigue of other sorts than you can image." But she is "glad I can be useful to so good a father." She read Virgil, studied law and French, planned to grow and dry figs for export and planted a grove of oaks to endow a charity.[1]

From quite early in the history of the plantation system, Southern masters indulged their sexual desires with their female slaves. A succession of travelers and diarists in the South from the end of the seventeenth century on comment on the practice. Josiah Quincy wrote: "The enjoyment of a negro or mulatto woman is spoken of as quite a common thing; no reluctance, delicacy or shame is made about the matter. It is far from uncommon to see a gentleman at dinner and his reputed offspring a slave to the master of the table. I myself saw two instances of this, and the company very facetiously would trace the lines, lineaments and features of the father and mother in the child, and very accurately point out the characteristic resemblance.

The fathers neither of them blushed or seemed disconcerted. They were called men of worth, politeness and humanity."[2]

Mrs. Chesnut reports in her diary a classic conversation with a group of Confederate ladies who had read *Uncle Tom's Cabin* and were discussing its verisimilitude or lack of it. "I hate slavery," one of the women, perhaps Mrs. Chesnut, says. "You say there are no more fallen women on a plantation than in London in proportion to numbers; but what do you say to this? A magnate who runs a hideous black harem with its consequences under the same roof with his lovely white wife, and his beautiful and accomplished daughters? He holds his head as high and poses as the model of all human virtues to these poor women whom God and the laws have given him. From the height of his awful majesty, he scolds and thunders at them, as if he never did wrong in his life. . . . You see, Mrs. Stowe did not hit the sorest spot. She makes Legree a bachelor."

Another woman protested that such things only happened in the past. Women of the present generation wouldn't stand for that sort of thing. But the implication is clear enough that most Southern wives accepted such a degrading situation and pretended to respect their husbands.[3]

Since slaves were considered sub-human, for a Southern woman to have her husband prefer the bed of a slave woman must have been a particularly bitter humiliation. Mary Chesnut wrote revealingly in her diary: "There will never be an interesting book with a Negro heroine down here. We know them too well. They are not picturesque. Only in fiction do they shine. Those beastly Negress beauties are only animals." Mary Chesnut's mother, grandmother, and mother-in-law spent most of their waking hours contending with "a swarm of blacks about them like children under their care, not as Mrs. Stowe's fancy painted them, and they hate slavery worse than Mrs. Stowe does." All the money made by slavery found its way North. "The slave owners," she wrote, "when they are good men and women, are the martyrs. I hate slavery. . . . I have before me a letter I wrote to Mr. Chesnut while he was on our plantation in Mississippi in 1842. It is the most fervid abolition document I have ever read. . . . How I envy those saintly Yankee women, in their clean cool New England homes, writing books to make their fortunes and to shame us." As Mary

Chesnut looked out of the window of her own lovely, airy room she could see the far-stretching lawn and what was once a deer park filled with huge old trees. "In the spring," she wrote, "the air is laden with perfumes, violets, jasmine, crabapple blossoms, roses. Araby the blest was never sweeter in perfume. And yet there hangs here as on every Southern landscape the saddest pall."[4]

Jefferson himself was accused of having a Negro mistress after the death of his wife, a charge which he never deigned to deny. The slave was Sally Hemings, known to be the daughter of a neighboring plantation owner, an unusually attractive and intelligent girl who at the age of thirteen was given the responsibility of bringing Jefferson's daughter from Virginia to France.

A characteristic of feudal societies is a particular masculine "set" strong in such classic male qualities as the martial or "hunting" spirit; a chivalric code of honor and a hyperactive and aggressive sexuality closely involved with a man's honor. (Such attitudes are conspicuous in many Latin countries today.) The pattern of aristocratic life with rich food, and considerable leisure is designed to accentuate the erotic. When William Byrd visited England as a man in his forties he kept a mistress to whom he paid two guineas, picked up women on the streets, frequented brothels, lay on the grass of St. James's Park with a trollop, made love to his mistress's maid while he waited for her to appear and after a rendezvous with her returned home "about eleven and said my prayers. I kissed the maid 'till my seed ran from me.' "[5] We might think Byrd a sport if the secret diaries of Pepys, of James Boswell, and other eighteenth-century figures did not give a similar picture of sexual hyperactivity. It may well have been that the "radical insatiability" of the Southern male was a burden to his wife. William Byrd, who "rogered" his wife with what seems at times like monotonous regularity, also had intercourse with slave women on his plantation. His wife, who was often ailing and who died young, may well have been relieved to be spared his persistent attentions.

The effect of such arrangements was not a happy one for white Southerners of either sex. Since women were the victims they survived with less psychic damage than men, the exploiters, whose truculent arrogance may not be unrelated to their role as sexual exploiters.

In the plantation system marriages came to be in a sense dynastic.

Since the law of primogeniture prevailed, by which the great estates usually passed entail to the eldest male heir there were, inevitably, "arrangements." There were strong pressures on young men and women to marry in their class and to make marriages that would increase and consolidate landholdings.

The Marquis de Chastellux noted that "women have little share in the amusements of the men; beauty here serves only to find husbands . . . and it is in general the young ladies' faces that determine their fortunes. The consequence of this is that they are often coquettish and prudish before marriage, and dull and tiresome afterwards."[6]

The attitude of Southern fathers toward the marriage of their daughters is suggested by William Byrd's letter to an unacceptable suitor. "I am informed upon very good evidence," he wrote, "that you have for some time taken the trouble to follow Amasia (a code name for Byrd's daughter) with your addresses. . . . What success these worthy steps have met in the girl, I do not know; but they shall never meet with any in the father. I fear your circumstances are not flourishing enough to maintain a wife in such splendor. . . . You are deluded if you believe any part of my estate is settled upon her, or that she has anything independent of my pleasure. . . . I . . . assure you beforehand that her portion will be extremely small if she bestows herself upon so clandestine a lover. I have made my will since I heard of your good intention towards me, and have bequeathed my daughter a splendid shilling if she marries any man that tempts her to disobedience."[7]

I suppose it could be laid down as a general rule that in any society based primarily on large-scale entailed landholding, marriages will be, to a degree, arranged. An arranged marriage was more often a loveless one, or at least a passionless one. Since in a society where marriages are manipulated it is important, as we have seen, to protect the value of the merchandise, which is to say the daughter; she must be severely restricted in her premarital activities, watched, guarded, and chaperoned. Thus the natural premarital relations of the betrothed New England couple were forbidden to their Southern counterparts. Most young Southern men doubtless had their initial experience with a compliant slave girl. It was not unnatural that many of them should continue to indulge themselves after their marriages. In addition there was undoubtedly the attraction of the perverse, of the taboo, the association of darkness with pleasant wickedness, the absence of any danger to the sexual exploiter however unwelcome his attentions may have been. Moreover, there was tradition of Negro sensuality which may well have worked to make the white wife a more restrained sexual partner, since to be passionate in love was to be like "one of those savage little nigger girls." Thus, when the Southern male looked to slave women for his basic sexual satisfactions, he increasingly found them there. Since there seems to be in masculine sexuality a measure of aggressiveness and even sadism, passivity and defenselessness seem often to enhance the desirability of the sexual object which was what the Negro woman was for her white master. Human relations can seldom be compartmentalized, however, and in many instances a genuine and tragic love developed between a white man and his black mistress. What we know in fact of these relationships, as opposed to rumor and innuendo, is slight but it is enough to suggest that they were by no means uncommon.

George Wythe was the law teacher of Thomas Jefferson, who called him "one of the greatest men of the age"; he was the leader of the Virginia bar, a signer of the Declaration of Independence, a man of unquestioned integrity, widely esteemed and honored. He had been taught Greek and Latin by his mother, the granddaughter of a famous Quaker preacher, who helped to make him the best classical scholar in Virginia. Wythe's housekeeper Lydia Broadnax was a handsome Negro woman of above-average intelligence. She had a son, Michael Brown, in whom Wythe took a special interest, teaching him Latin and Greek, providing in his will that he should be freed and dividing his bank stock between the boy and Wythe's grand-nephew, George Wythe Sweeney. Sweeney, jealous of the Brown boy, put arsenic in the coffee, poisoning Wythe, the Negro boy, and Lydia Broadnax. Lydia Broadnax was the only one of the three to survive. The terms of Wythe's will gave Lydia Broadnax her freedom, a treasured miniature of himself, and the income from the rent of his property. The murder of Wythe, which Jefferson spoke of as "such an instance of depravity [as] has been known to us only in the fables of the poets," went unpunished, apparently because the Virginia bar feared that the prosecution of Sweeney would bring out the fact that Michael Brown was the natural son of the state's most distinguished jurist.

Miscegenation then was an ever-present fact of the "peculiar system of the South." It symbolized the subordinate and artificial life of the Southern lady; mistress and slave were linked together by a common degradation. Like the slaves, the Southern women developed their own strategies to survive. They grew adept at the arts of manipulation, since women will exercise power covertly if they cannot do so overtly. Tough-fibered and resilient, they became in time as recognizable and famous a type as their reforming sisters of New England. Bearing the anguish and misery of slavery with remarkable stoicism, they were, like the blacks, liberated by the Civil War, and when the war was over it was primarily the women who picked up the pieces and helped to reconstruct Southern society. In addition, they preserved an ideal of femininity which if often vulgarized and sentimentalized nonetheless contained an important measure of the authentic.

The conservatism of the South in regard to the position of women may be indicated by the fact that it was the 1920's before the University of North Carolina, the most liberal and advanced of Southern universities, admitted its first girls. They were accompanied to their classes by chaperones, were required to sit in a group in the rear of the rooms and had to wait until the boys had left before they were allowed to depart. They were also required to wear gloves and hats; they were not allowed to participate in the graduation ceremonies but had to wait outside the hall and their pictures were not published in the yearbook. When it was proposed to build a residence hall for women, the editor of the student paper was horrified. "The University," he wrote, "has always been a college of, by and for men, which largely accounts for its strength of character." To provide housing for women would be a "dreadful mistake." The University, he predicted, "will be overrun with girls . . . an effeminate influence of sentimentality will become paramount, which is so distasteful to men students. . . . Chapel Hill is a place inherently for men, and men who desire no women around . . . women would only prove a distracting influence, could do no possible good, and would turn the grand old institution into a semi-effeminate college." Put to the vote, it was 937 students against women, 173 for.

In the more remote regions of the Southern frontier men and women lived in the crudest and most primitive circumstances. When the Anglican minister, Charles Woodmason, traveled in the Carolina backcountry he was astounded at the conditions he encountered. Going to Flat Creek to preach he found a "Body of People assembled — Such a Medley! such a mixed Multitude of all Classes and Complexions I never saw. . . . Most of these People had never before seen a Minister or heard the Lords Prayer, Service or Sermon in their Days. . . . After Service they went to Revelling Drinking Singing Dancing and Whoring — and most of the Company were drunk before I quitted the Spot — They were as rude in their Manners as the Common Savages, and hardly a degree removed from them. Their Dresses almost as loose and Naked as the Indians, and differing in Nothing save Complexion. . . ."[8] Poor Woodmason had little success imposing any civilization on his unruly charges. "Wild as the very Deer" they roamed around freely, virtually naked, while he tried to conduct services. "The females (many very pretty) come to Service," he wrote, "in their Shifts and a short petticoat only, barefooted and Bare legged . . . Quite in a State of Nature for Nakedness is counted as Nothing — as they sleep together in Common in one Room. . . ." The women were shared as the concubines of the men, and marriage was virtually unknown. The young women had a habit that Woodmason could not break them of, of drawing "their Shift as tight as possible to the Body, and pin it close, to shew the roundness of their Breasts, and slender Waists (for they are generally finely shaped) and draw their Petticoat close to their Hips to shew the fineness of their Limbs — so that they might as well be in Puri Naturalibus . . . they expose themselves often quite Naked, without Ceremony — Rubbing themselves and their Hair with Bears Oil and tying it up behind in a Bunch like the Indians. . . ."[9] Woodmason's picture may be overdrawn but there is little question that on many frontier regions where religion had not penetrated or had died, people lived lives not far removed from those described by the Anglican missionary. And in such places the condition of women was worse than that of savages because they were without the conventions and taboos which gave order and discipline to tribal life.

The pioneer woman is such a classic figure that it is easy to lose the sight of the reality behind the stereotype. On the American frontier women preserved the status that they had enjoyed in colonial New England. Strictly speaking, the urban male did not need a wife; he

could get along with a housekeeper and a mistress. But the frontier farmer was as dependent on his mate as she on him. De Tocqueville noted that most of the settlers on the frontier, "who rush so boldly onwards in pursuit of wealth," were already in comfortable circumstances. "They take their wives along with them and make them share the countless perils and privations that always attend the commencement of the expeditions." He had often met on the "verge of the wilderness" young women who had been gently reared "amid all the comforts of the large towns of New England," and who had passed from a prosperous parental home "to a comfortless hovel in a forest." But "fever, solitude, and a tedious life had not broken the springs of their courage. Their features were impaired and faded, but their looks were firm, they appeared to be at once sad and resolute."[10]

Such women, who were legion, were the shock-troops of Western migration. Clinging to a few treasured heirlooms as reminders of a kinder life, they accompanied their husbands across the continent, suffering the most desperate physical hardships as well as a desolating sense of loneliness. More place-bound than men, more dependent on the company of other women, on the forms of settled social life, they grew old and died before their time, on the trail, in a sod hut or a rude cabin pierced by icy winds. Some of the best representations of this breed are to be found in the historical novels of Conrad Richter, in the figures of Sayward Luckett, her mother, Jary, dead early of consumption and homesickness, Sulie, Granny MacWhirter, Rosa and the rest.

When the Lucketts came over the mountain crest to see the Ohio Valley below them, "Sayward saw his mother's eyes search with the hope of finding some settlement or leastwise a settler's clearing. But over that vasty solitude no wisp of smoke arose." It was a scene with a hundred thousand reincarnations — challenge and opportunity for the man, desolation for the woman. Miss Martha Wylie recalls her mother's accounts of a similar scene on the Western edge of the continent several generations later when her parents stood on the rim of the Yakima Valley, the father exulting in its wild fertility, the mother weeping at its loneliness and isolation. When Mrs. Wylie met the wife of the only other settler in the valley the two women threw their arms around each other and cried for joy.

It is, to be sure, an incredible story. When Eastern ladies were fainting at a coarse word or vulgar sight their Western sisters fought off Indians, ran cattle, made homes and raised children in the wilderness. It was in the West, in consequence, that women had the greatest status. Appropriately enough, Wyoming Territory granted women the vote in 1869 and Colorado followed suit twenty-four years later. But that is only a small part of the story. In countless Western communities women participated actively in the social and political life of their towns.

When Amelia Bloomer moved to Council Bluffs, Nebraska, she found herself a celebrity, invited everywhere to speak to "promiscuous" audiences of men and women. She lectured at the Methodist Church on Woman Suffrage and was invited by twenty-five members of the Nebraska legislature to go to Omaha to repeat her lecture in the State House of Representatives. There she was escorted to the platform by General William Larimer, one of the leading figures in the state, and spoke to a large and responsive assembly. The legislature requested the text of Mrs. Bloomer's address so that it might be published, and a few days later a bill in favor of woman suffrage passed the lower house and was sent to the senate where it died.[11]

Perhaps, ultimately, it was in the area of higher education that the difference between Eastern and Western attitudes toward women were most dramatically revealed. Not only did Antioch admit women (and Negroes) soon after it was founded (the first woman graduated in 1841), but most Midwestern and Western state universities opened their doors as coeducational institutions. The University of Michigan had one of the first law schools to admit women. Madame Blanc was most impressed with the coeducational colleges she visited "almost exclusively in the West." At Knox College in Galesburg the French visitor was charmed by the intelligence of the female students and the open and informal atmosphere combined with intellectual seriousness. When two of the students spoke of going to Paris to complete their education, Madame Blanc did not dare tell them that "they will hardly find as many resources there as in Galesburg." The more "Europeanized" East was far from this fresh and robust spirit which the West so engagingly displayed. The longer Madame Blanc stayed at Galesburg, the more it reminded her of "some little German university town. There is the same simplicity, the same worship of learning and its representatives, the same patriarchal customs."[12] She

was struck also by how many harmonious and happy marriages had their origins in coeducational colleges.

Not only did boys and girls in the Western parts of the United States associate freely in private and on social occasions in the last decades of the nineteenth century, it was not uncommon for parties of boys and girls to go off camping together "in a fraternal way for weeks or months" with no older person to chaperone them. However, Bryce noted that "in the Atlantic cities . . . a conventional etiquette like that of the Old World" was rapidly replacing "the innocent simplicity of the older time."[13]

At the International Council of Women in 1888, one delegate declared that the Western United States, led by Michigan University, was the hope of the woman's movement, extolling "those bright, enthusiastic, large-brained and big-hearted young women of the West. . . . In the Mississippi Valley there is growing up another society — a society that will have a new type of manhood and of womanhood, because it is co-educational. Young men and women are learning to have mutual respect for each other intellectually and morally."[14] All of which perfervid as it was, was rather close to the truth. The West did, in fact, produce a "new woman," and for male and female fellow students to marry became a familiar pattern in the Western part of the United States by the end of the nineteenth century.

Rape, Prostitution and Birth Control

Rape, prostitution, and, to a somewhat lesser degree, birth control were primary obsessions of reform-minded women in the nineteenth century. Rape was the sexual expression of the inferior and dependent position of woman. The response of respectable women to the threat of intercourse is perhaps best suggested by the reputed advice of an English mother to her daughter for her wedding night: "Lie still, dear, and think of the British Empire." It was generally agreed that men had inordinate sexual appetites; they were all rapists at heart. Wives were the victims of the desires of their husbands "whose employment of force is encouraged by church and state . . ."[1]

One unhappy instance of masculine lust was the practice of some husbands of having intercourse with their pregnant wives. This was a time when prospective mothers should be free from any carnal acts or thoughts. There were suggestions that intercourse during pregnancy would produce children with abnormal sexual appetites and one reformer wrote despairingly "of the millions of pregnant women in the world, bowed down under the burdens of manual toil, and yet compelled to satisfy the demands of lust, intensified by drink and by tobacco." (One of the basic anxieties of the temperance movement was the conviction that drinking made men less able to contain their lusts and thus subjected wives to rape by inebriated husbands.) At the International Council of Women in 1888, the champions of "social purity" offered Catharine Beecher's proposal for "mothergartens" where pregnant wives could go to protect themselves against "the lustful, selfish propensities in force and fury" of their husbands.[2]

Prostitution was the overriding "social evil" of the century. It was estimated that there were 20,000 prostitutes in New York City in the 1860's. London counted 50,000 and Paris 30,000. We have already noted the anxiety of middle-class women about prostitution. The unspoken danger of venereal disease cast a shadow over many homes. Dr. Elizabeth Blackwell, sister to the Blackwell brothers, Henry and Sam, and sister-in-law to Nette Brown Blackwell and Lucy Stone, was one of the first women to write specifically on the social evil, informing women "of the hideous danger to themselves and their children."

Sex, she pointed out, had actually been made into a commodity: "shrewdness, large capital, business enterprise, are all enlisted in the lawless stimulation of this mighty instinct of sex." While "immense provision is made for facilitating fornication" very little was done to encourage chastity. Grave as were the dangers of disease in contacts with prostitutes, the falsification of one's relationship with others was more serious. A man's respect for himself and for women generally was lessened once "he has tasted the physical delights of sex, separated from its more exquisite spiritual joys," and he may thus become an addict. For young men, so tempted, Dr. Blackwell prescribed "hard exercise in the open air" as "in most cases, an efficient remedy against vicious propensities."

The old Victorian bugaboos were inevitably presented. Those who indulged their appetites might become "sexual drunkards" or "insane" or, if young, "strain an immature power." At the same time Dr. Blackwell had valid insights. She realized that "the attraction of sex does not cease [in women] with the physical inability to bear children: the soul of passion does not perish with physical decay."[3]

One of the issues Elizabeth Blackwell addressed herself to was the argument that men were more highly sexed than women and thus could not be expected to observe the same moral code. The fact was that "in the attraction of one sex to the other, the young woman is unconsciously impelled, under the inexorable law of race perpetuation, towards the accomplishment of her special race-work, by a force out of proportion to her intellectual development or her worldly experience. She is led in the direction of this great mission of motherhood, not by the conscious craving of any abnormal appetite, but by the far stronger and more irresistible might of creative energy working through her. This energy renders her tremblingly susceptible to those influences which tend toward the accomplishment of her special work. This race instinct over-rides individuality to a degree . . ." Motherhood supported by a "strong and reliable attachment" frees the woman from her "undue burden of sexual instinct so that she may develop harmoniously as an individual."[4]

Horace Greeley was one of the most eloquent defenders of the rights of women. He supported the opening of jobs to women on the same grounds that Catharine Beecher proposed gathering families together out of "the poor and vicious," namely that it was "the tendency of all civilizations, of close settlements and overcrowding populations . . . to make the female sex largely in excess of the male." This was already true in New England and "in the cities of our Atlantic civilization" and it would soon be true throughout all the Eastern states. "Accepting marriage as the duty of all men and women," the editorialist continued, "we find that, after answering this duty we have a large female surplus, who must either support themselves or be supported by others." If "this large female surplus" is not trained to support itself by useful labor it will turn to prostitution ("Our civilization, we blush to say it, has thrown up a class more infamous even than the unnumbered wives of Turkish lords, and infinitely more profitless than the life of the cloister").

Was there no way, Greeley asked, to solve this problem? Must America go on from century to century, "growing richer, happier, wiser every day, advancing morally, socially, politically, improving the whole economy of life and yet dragging with us a class whose life is infamy? This is the ulcer that makes our purest civilization offensive." To the woman who wishes to practice medicine or become a lawyer, man, with his "vulgar prejudice," replies: "No, go to a brothel, and fester in crime; or to a factory and die of consumption; or work sixteen hours a day, sewing shirts at ten cents apiece. You may have intellect, scholarship, judgment; you can know as much or more than we; you can check a fever, or stay consumption, or control the cholera as effectually as any Sawbone . . . but it matters not. You are a woman — so hence to a brothel, or a factory, or a garret!"[5]

Beatrice Forbes-Robertson Hale was convinced that "the knowledge of [disease], with its terrible base in commercialized vice, has contributed more recruits to the suffrage cause than any other except industrialism . . . because [women] are no longer willing to leave their fate in the hands of a sex who have signally failed to protect their most vital needs." To one reformer it was the "burden of prostitution, which saps the life of women in every class, taking hideous toll of their young daughters, their unborn children, their health, happiness and pride . . ."6

Through prostitution men transmitted "scrofula, cancer, consumption, and every hideous disease from thousands of centuries of . . . syphilitic poisons." Men had "sowed the wind in ignorance" and were "reaping the whirlwind in divorces, rape, murder, entailed upon children conceived in lust and gestated with [prostitution's] poison in every vein." So spoke Elizabeth Lisle Saxon to the delegates of the International Council of Women. For twelve years, she told her feminine audience, she had been preaching this doctrine to men and women without distinction. At the end of her lectures to men, they would, she declared, storm the platform "and, with tears running down their faces, say, 'Thank God, that woman has at last realized that we are agonizing as she agonizes.' "7

From the early years of the century American women reformers characterized the dependent marriage as legalized prostitution. In illegal prostitution men had to buy the bodies of their sexual partners, in marriage they simply commandeered them. The same lusts that the male vented on his wife led him to the beds of prostitutes. The real point at issue was that men must be taught to sublimate these lusts. If they practiced restraint in marriage, they would learn to contain themselves out of it and prostitution would vanish.

To many women one of the most infuriating aspects of prostitution was that the women involved were treated like criminals while the men who purchased their favors went free. In Elizabeth Blackwell's judgment the laws in regard to sexual offenses must be made equal: "If we punish the seduction of girls, we must also punish the seduction of lads . . . those who wait to solicit and those who wait to be solicited, must be subjected to the same regime."8

Prostitution was a symbol of the double standard as well as of the failure of the sexual aspect of marriage. Some feminists went so far as to declare that if man's sexual appetites could only be accommodated by free love, if, in other words, free love were the only alternative to prostitution, they would unhesitatingly espouse free love. To Ralcy Bell "Prostitution is a necessity, a regular occupation, an economic livelihood in the capitalist market, a mode of life which millions of women are forced to adopt. . . . When men and women generally realize the immorality of sexual relations unsanctified by a high mutual desire, the closed marriage relations will adjust themselves to the open relations between marriage and society, and prostitution as it now exists will be no more."[9]

As long as men continued to divide women into two classes, Beatrice Hale wrote, one as the object of his affections, the other of his desires, so long would the "social evil," and so long would the unhappy marriage continue. "The new man, whatever his temperament, is no longer willing to gratify it at the expense of any woman or class of women." He may "permit himself — as his fathers have done before him — more sexual experience than the church or law allows him," but at least it will not be in the arms of a prostitute.[10]

Against all movements to have city or state regulation of prostitution, women put up the most determined fight. Regulation meant a kind of official sanction or at least the acceptance of something which for most women was simply unacceptable. Another concern of reforming women was the "white slave traffic": the procuring of young girls and women for purposes of prostitution. Since women were unwilling, for the most part, to accept the notion that others of their sex would undertake prostitution except through force or as an alternative to starvation, they devoted much time and energy to protecting girls from a life of vice. One important result of their labors was the Mann Act which forbade the taking of girls under the age of consent across state lines for sexual purposes. Another and perhaps more important reform was to raise the "age of consent" in sexual relations. In some states the age of consent was ten (in Delaware, it was seven). The reformers wished to raise the age to eighteen (some pushed for twenty-one). Kansas led them by adopting eighteen as the age of consent and eighteen became in time the uniform age in all states.

Birth control was closely related to the issue of marital rape (or "legalized prostitution" in marriage). The reformers insisted with increasing emphasis that women must have, as Margaret Sanger put it, "control over their own bodies." Implicit in this notion from the first was that they should be able to limit the frequency of their pregnancies. As we have already suggested, many women, perhaps the majority of middle-class urban wives, limited their pregnancies by ill health, by going away for "cures" for extended periods of time, and in other ways rebuffing the advances of importunate husbands. But other birth control techniques were available. (Indeed only the most naïve modernist would believe that the Pill marked the beginning of effective birth control. In every society and in every era of history individuals or groups have controlled the rate of birth when it was imperative or desirable — or even merely fashionable — to do so.)

Certainly birth control techniques were not lacking for those who wished to use them. Before the Great Repression the technique probably most commonly used was *coitus interruptus,* stopping the act of intercourse prior to or at the instant of male orgasm. While this method does not appeal to modern sensibilities as a very desirable one, it has been widely and successfully used throughout history. Thought of as a kind of short-circuiting of the climax of intercourse and thus taxing to the nerves of man and woman alike, it certainly required a considerable degree of self-control and discipline in the sex act, but the act could nonetheless reach, with some practice, a satisfying climax for both partners. In colonial New England the technique was commonly referred to as "the pull back." In one case a man charged in court with being the father of an illegitimate child admitted intercourse but denied paternity on the grounds that "I minded my pullbacks."

Coitus interruptus did, obviously, require a considerable degree of candor and explicitness about the mechanics, or the physiology, of the act of intercourse itself, and after the Great Repression it is doubtful if it was widely used as a method of contraception. When John Humphrey Noyes founded his Perfectionist communities, he instituted the practice of free selection of sexual partners. The Perfectionists were against every form of selfishness or exploitation. Noyes and his followers believed that the "possession" of an exclusive sexual mate as in marriage was another instance of the selfish and materialistic spirit which along with the ownership of private property was destructive of the full development of the individual. *Coitus interruptus* was the official technique that members of the community were instructed to follow in order to prevent the birth of children who were not planned additions to the community. Public opinion was of course scandalized by the sexual practices of the Perfectionists and most conspicuously by their birth control technique.

The birth control movement called initially the Neo-Malthusian Movement which Margaret Sander publicized so successfully in America had a long history. Francis Place, an English tailor, labor leader, and writer, published a book in 1822 called *Illustrations and Proofs of the Principle of Population* in which he advocated the use of contraceptives by every workingman. Robert Dale Owen, the English reformer who established a utopian community in America, published in 1830 a work called *Moral Physiology* dealing with methods of contraception. Everything Owen took up was designed to transform society and contraception was no exception. It would, he proclaimed "improve the equality of marriage and the status of women, reduce prostitution, and create a eugenically sounder race." Two years after Owen's book Charles Knowlton applied medical knowledge to the problem in a work entitled *Fruits of Philosophy*. Knowlton described four methods of contraception: *coitus interruptus,* the condom, the use of a saturated sponge in the vagina, and the use of chemical solutions by syringe. It is hard to estimate the sales and circulation of the book in the United States but when Charles Bradlaugh and Annie Besant republished it in 1876 it sold over 400,000 copies in England alone.

By the end of the nineteenth century birth control as the avenue to sexual emancipation had become the battle cry of the more advanced feminists. The generation of Margaret Sanger took up the cause as a great crusade. Like present-day advocates of the Pill they assumed that contraception had just been discovered. Ralcy Bell assured her readers that means of preventing conception were available and that they were "harmless as a tepid bath and pure as a drop of dew."[11]

Contraception, supplementing divorce, promised a new freedom. Nature, "by decreeing that the result of a free emotional life should be negligible and momentary for a man, but permanent and devastating for a woman . . . [had] made all talk of equality between the sexes laughable." The masculine opposition to the dissemination of birth control knowledge was the "last and bitterest battle waged by man to keep woman in subjection." In terror "of what should happen to their vested interests should this last security fail," men were fighting for their very lives. Birth control had two goals, one social, one individual. On the social side it was a means of enabling the poor to limit the size of their families and thus, it was hoped, avoid destitution. On the individual side it was the "new woman's" passport to richer sexual experience. The diaphragm in the purse was the symbol of emancipation.

In the nineteenth and the early decades of the twentieth century, virtually all of the women who wrote, even in the most elliptical terms, of sex and sexuality, viewed it as a blight or illness which must somehow be suppressed or cured. It was a disease peculiar to men and a few depraved women. One of the most persistent arguments of the reformers from the earliest days through the Sanger era was that when women achieved equality a wholesome companionship between men and women would replace that abnormal sexuality which so distorted the relationship between the sexes. Beatrice Hale looked for a "new man of the faithful monogamous type," a proper companion for the new woman, "so tired of the old-fashioned man's preoccupation with her sex that she hails the advent of the new man, with his sincere and unforced respect for women, his friendliness, and lack of either condescension or flattery, with inexpressible relief."[12] Sex, the reformer insisted, must be spiritualized.

It was plain that "spiritualized" meant sublimated. It is a theme that we have already taken note of, one that runs through virtually every feminist tract, a persistent and irrepressible anxiety. To Ralcy Bell, "The average man too long has looked upon the female of his kind principally through the little pig-eye slit, which sees only sex. His eyes are no better than buttonholes burned in a blanket — they are just about as perceptive. His cunning little primitive eye is no improvement on the brute's; his optical evolution ceased in a fringe of lashes. When he sees sex, he thinks he sees all there is to a woman."[13]

Every projection of the new, enlightened community of the future emphasizes the diminution of the sex urge as a primary goal. As we have seen, the new pantheisms, the religions of the mind, have as a central tenet the banishing of sex. The utopian communities of the nineteenth century, from those avowedly committed to free love like

Stephen Pearl Andrews's venture to John Humphrey Noyes's Perfectionist communities, struggled to devise systems to control the ravenous sexual appetites of men. The men and women who founded utopian communities wished to banish competition and excessive sexuality (which it sometimes seems was almost any). The conjunction is significant. It suggests an inability to cope. The desire to escape from the strains and tensions of life into a kind of nirvana is obviously one of the very basic human impulses. Nineteenth-century Americans suffered from two complementary tensions: individualistic, competitive, exploitative capitalism and the essentially tragic sexual muddle. The utopian communities represented both authentic and self-conscious impulses to reform, and an exhaustion of nerve and will. They, like the science of mind cults, could be taken to measure the "nervousness" produced by American life.

Women often took a pitying or sympathetic attitude toward masculine sexuality that was not, in its inner quality, much different from that of the sentimental female novelists. To Beatrice Forbes-Robertson Hale, it was clear that men were "so constituted temperamentally as to be almost incessantly conscious of sex, and this is no more their fault than if they were born with defective sight." It may, indeed, be "many thousands of years before the whole race has learnt the finest use to which to put its superabundant sex energy."[14]

To Florence Guertin Tuttle feminism was, above all, an effort to establish a truer equilibrium between men and women, especially in regard to the past overemphasis of sex. "The all-round, symmetrically developed woman of today wishes to be loved for her human, social value, rather than for her face and sex value as of old." Mrs. Tuttle was especially anxious to free feminism from the stigma of free love, a doctrine propounded in every age by high-minded but misguided souls who proposed "a form of promiscuity more disastrous than anything they condemn." "Spiritual selection" must regenerate the race "since it is the only power that will overcome the materialism that still beclouds marriage."[15]

John Langdon-Davies displayed a classic form of the "disappearing sex" credo when he wrote that "the control of maternity [contraception] is setting women for the first time on a level with men," and that "since men and women are purely relative terms, long before the tendencies of our times work to their logical conclusions, men and women, as we know them, will have ceased to exist; and the human nature will have forgotten the 'he' and 'she.' "

One final, up-to-the-minute solution to the problem of sexuality is proposed by Elisabeth Mann Borgese. Mrs. Borgese's science-fiction utopia is worth noting because like so many nineteenth-century utopias it projects a society where sex is no longer a cause of anxiety and tension. Love between men and women in her "post-individual community" will indeed be Platonic, in that "it will unite physical and spiritual love and will be aimed at creating beauty immortal, rather than mortal children [who will be produced in a state-run children factory]. Love will be harmony, the reconciliation of elements that are not opposite, but harmonized. For men and women, in our society, cannot be considered as opposite elements."[16] Through the use of chemical and surgical techniques, all people between the ages of twenty and forty-five will be female. From forty-five to seventy-five, everyone will be male. They will be the masters, the teachers, the inspirers of women. They will be the great inventors and explorers. They will be the great artists and architects. The great historians, prophets, and high priests will be "sexless superindividuals" over seventy-five. The scheme has, beside ingenuity, little to recommend it. However, it does represent very well the anguish that many women have felt — perhaps increasingly during the last two hundred years — over "the burden of sex"; over not being men, and over the ways in which the sex issue beclouds and complicates almost all human relations.

It is clear that most of the reformers wished to diminish the importance of sex. In many of their tracts the call for the emancipation of women was supported by the argument that it would result in a moderating of sexual desire, primarily of course in men, but, incidentally, in women as well. Only a small radical splinter group ever promoted free love doctrines and here again many of these did so on the grounds that in a system of "free alliance" sex itself would become less central to the relationship between men and women. The sex emancipators ultimately carried the day; but the results were hardly what they would have anticipated. The emphasis on feminine sexuality brought with it a vastly increased emphasis on sex generally and made it, if anything, a greater preoccupation of men and women alike.

17

The New Prophets:

Ellis, Freud and Marx

Science was the god of the nineteenth century and the advocates of feminine equality looked confidently to it to support their claims that they were not only deserving of equal rights with men, but were in physical, moral, and intellectual qualities virtually identical with them. Women sought from that Delphic voice an unequivocal endorsement of their claims. "There is not a jot of difference between masculine and feminine minds," Florida Pier wrote.[1] And Teresa Billington-Craig saw feminism as seeking "a reorganization of the world upon the basis of sex-equality." It was a movement which would reject "every differentiation between individuals upon the ground of sex, would abolish all sex privileges and sex-burdens."[2]

Florence Guertin Tuttle, writing in 1915 of *The Awakening of Woman: Suggestions from the Psychic Side of Feminism,* stressed, like so many others, the "scientific" side of the woman's movement. "Running parallel with accepted laws of human growth" it was "distinctly scientific . . . In cosmic history . . . of all events the most significant and far-reaching."[3] Marriage itself came under attack. Earlier the free love movement attacked marriage primarily on the basis that by subordinating the wife to the husband it compromised the deep and tender relationship between a man and a woman that could only be based on genuine mutuality. Now, as the emphasis in

American society shifted from achievement and action to personality and behavior, some women revived Mary Wollstonecraft's argument that love was transient and that any permanent relationship was thus, of necessity, a cruel distortion of the proper relationship between the sexes. "Fulfillment" became the battle cry of the reformers. For the first time the issue of woman's place was separated from the larger context of Protestant Christianity. Men found satisfaction and, presumably, "fulfillment" in sexual relations with a variety of women. Woman should enjoy the same fulfillment in the act of intercourse itself.

There were also hints that in fact women had available to them sexual pleasures more intense than those of men. This word came from the English "sexologist," Havelock Ellis, Margaret Sanger's "god-sent liberator." Ellis, though the major prophet of the orgasm, was not himself successful as a lover; he admitted that he had not had a satisfying sexual encounter until he was in his sixties. A friend described him as "unusually timid, excessively cautious, secretive, preoccupied with private fantasies of sex and religion, faintly exotic even in his appearance."[4]

Ellis and his wife lived in separate establishments and developed a relationship which Edith Ellis called a "semi-detached marriage." Semi-detached or not, it was seriously deranged and Ellis's biographer finds evidence that Ellis encouraged his wife to have homosexual relations. However, when Mrs. Ellis lectured in America she spoke of "the continued buoyancy and widening hopes of their life" as the "outcome of an experiment in the perfect equality of the sexes." She had discovered that "love gains most of all from the opportunity to flourish in freedom when, separated from marital ties, it suffers scrutiny and grows in sunlight."[5]

Ellis in his program of sexual liberation was an enthusiastic supporter of erotic play, the first prominent Western advocate of lovemaking as a game full of novel positions and experiments. The most devout champions of sexual emancipation had not dared to go so far. In breaking down sexual inhibitions, Ellis felt, even the orgy had its proper place. An orgy could relieve "the high tension, the rigid routine, the gray monotony of modern life," although Ellis was vague about the "precise form that orgiastic relief" should take.

Ellis's lesser-known coadjutor, another Englishman named Edward

Carpenter, wrote *Love's Coming of Age,* and *Civilization, Its Cause and Its Cure* which became treasured texts for the sex emancipators — or the New Moralists, as they came to be called on both sides of the Atlantic. Carpenter was of the old school in that, while he preached sexual liberation, he placed great emphasis on the sublimation of gross sexuality into a higher spiritual love. "How intoxicating, indeed, how penetrating," he wrote "— like a most precious wine — is that love which is the sexual transformed by a magic of will into the emotional and spiritual. And what a loss on the merest grounds of prudence and the economy of pleasure is its unbridled waste along physical channels."

Carpenter, like the modern guru, Paul Goodman, espoused homosexual love as well as heterosexual love and proposed as the ideal marriage one free of possessiveness, "so free, so spontaneous, that it would allow of wide excursions of the pair from each other, in common or even in separate objects of work and interest, and yet would hold them all the time in the bond of absolute sympathy, would by its very freedom be all the more poignantly attractive . . ."[6]

It was perhaps inevitable that in the age of technology, the technology of sex should have its day. Ellis fathered a vast progeny of books which promised their readers new sexual delights in marriage through the use of the new technology. "How-to" books on sex became as common as how-to books on exotic cookery or backyard barbecues. For all the anxious, the timid, the frigid, the despairing and forlorn, those bored with each other or trapped in loveless marriages it was promised that some new positions, some advanced techniques, would bring marital joy.

More and more the emphasis shifted to the sexual act and its mechanics. As the means of salvation, or as a "tranquilizer," a release from the tensions of everyday life, the sex act was discussed, analyzed, recommended, longed for, celebrated, and overburdened. It was perhaps as much tragic as ironic that one solution to the bleakness of American life was to abolish anxiety by, in effect, abolishing sex, while a much publicized alternate was to make sex an androgynous deity, intercourse a kind of religious rite.

Initially, of course, only a few of the most advanced took up such ideas. The temper of the great majority of suffragettes can be gauged by Kitty (daughter of Nette) Blackwell's protest to Alice Stone Blackwell (Lucy's daughter) over the *Women's Journal,* the leading suffragette paper, printing a picture of Havelock Ellis. His books, Kitty wrote her friend, were disgusting. Alice replied a little sharply: "I am sorry if his books are disgusting but they deal with a disgusting subject, and perhaps under the circumstances can't help being so."[7]

Although the daring days of the woman's rights movement were long over, the word of Ellis and his fellow "sexologists" got around. The sexual encounter, which women had been gritting their teeth and enduring, a mark of their subordination to masculine lust, could in fact be something quite agreeable, even ecstatic. It was thus through books written by men that women learned the exciting news about the female orgasm. I have found no book (though there certainly may be some) written by a woman before 1930 which did more than vaguely hint at the subject. Men (almost invariably "doctors") wrote the explicit, "scientific" manuals of sexual technique.

One of the pioneer sexologists was Dr. William J. Robinson, editor of the *American Journal of Urology* and founder of "Dr. Robinson's Famous Little Monthly," the *Guide and Critic,* which discussed "the larger, social aspects of medicine and physiology in a fearless and radical manner . . . birth control, venereal prophylaxis, sex education in the young, and free discussion of sexual problems in general." In addition, under the imprint of the Critic and Guide Press, Dr. Robinson poured out tracts in the modern spirit: *Never-Told Tales: Graphic Stories of the Disastrous Results of Sexual Ignorance* (whose reception, we are told, was "extravagantly and unanimously enthusiastic"); *Woman: Her Sex and Love Life: For Men and Women* ("How to hold the love of a man, how to preserve sexual attraction, how to remain young beyond the usually allotted age"); *Sex Knowledge for Men* ("Absolutely free from any cant, hypocrisy, falsehood, exaggeration, compromise, or any attempt to conciliate the stupid and ignorant"); *Sex Morality: Past, Present and Future* ("Will monogamy or variety prevail in the future? Is continence injurious? Are extramarital relations ever justifiable? . . . Will our present moral code persist? These and similar questions discussed by original and unbiased thinkers").

As time passed the how-to-do-it sex manuals became bolder and more explicit. One of the inhibiting factors in sexual relations and

thus in marriage, they told their bemused readers, were prim and outmoded notions of what was proper or permissible in the sex act. Ignorance and prudery had identified as perversions perfectly normal and natural patterns of sexual behavior. "Foreplay" had been under the ban and husbands and wives thus avoided such ingenuous romps or felt guilty if they indulged in them. They should rather approach the sex act in a free and experimental spirit; many a jaded marriage could be revived if the partners got out of the rut of sex-as-usual by experimenting with different "positions"— upside-down, inside-out and round-about. It is, of course, impossible to estimate how many sexual acrobats were produced by such advice (anything published in a book, especially a book written by a "doctor" carries some authority), but one might be excused for doubting that many marriages were saved by these calisthenics. Such feats of sexual prowess are, to be sure, enterprising tricks but they have about as much importance for what used to be called the development of race as the ability, say, to have intercourse while hanging suspended upside-down, a "position" doubtless mastered by some amorous acrobats.

A current magazine carries an advertisement for a work entitled *Sexual Lovemaking* by, of course, a doctor, which is typical of hundreds of such works. The book offers "64 pages of male/female positional photographs" which enable you to swiftly master "the positional attitudes, intercourse innovations and sexual variants which best satisfy a seeking mate's *orgasmic need* . . . It transforms same-old-thing "bedroom encounters" into *excitingly different* LOVE AFFAIRS — again, again and again . . . Every night a 'new' lover — uninhibited, inventive, incredibly sensitive, deliciously delightful! Yet a lifelong mate whose lovemaking repertory, complemented by yours, passionately banishes the sameness of old-hat sex. Can any marriage, anchored to this solid *bed*rock of unsuppressed *voluptuous sexual variety* fail to become stronger?"

People too sophisticated to be taken in by the cruder of such works nonetheless came to believe in salvation through sex. Vigorous and uninhibited sexual play, it was argued, could cure "American nervousness" and all the other tensions of twentieth-century urban industrial society. Such literature has had the unhappy effect of creating the mythology that the proper end and object of marriage is the female orgasm. A society which comes to believe that the health and soundness of a marriage is somehow to be measured by the frequency and duration of the female orgasm is, one suspects, in trouble. The simple fact is that the discovery and exaltation of the female orgasm has not been accompanied by a notable increase in happy marriages. It is perfectly apparent that marvelously adjusted sexual partners may have bitterly unhappy marriages. It is also clear enough that there have been very happy marriages where the wife has very infrequently or never had an orgasm. The female orgasm, pleasant as it is, and important as it is, seems to be the means of neither personal nor marital salvation.

A new and more authoritative prophet of sexual liberation than Havelock Ellis was the Viennese doctor, Sigmund Freud. Freud's emphasis on the harmful effects of repression encouraged some women to look on him as a valuable ally in the fight for sexual emancipation. Elsie Clews Parsons, writing in Harold Stearns's *Civilization in the United States,* drew on Freud to support her advocacy of sexual freedom. The sublimation of the sexual instinct had led, Miss Parsons charged, to a rise in homosexuality and perversion. Not only that but American bad manners and the "cheerlessness and aridity" of our intellectual circles could be traced to "failure of one kind or another in sex relations." The "hard sense" had made most Americans blind conformists. It was the selfishness and timidity of American husbands which kept their wives from having creative sexual adventures outside of marriage. Miss Parsons looked hopefully to the day when "artists in love" were tolerated and when society, freed from sexual inhibitions and restraint, became wholesome and healthy.

In fact Freud had remarkably little to say about women, perhaps the most notable being his comment: "The question that has never been answered, and which I have not yet been able to answer despite my thirty years of research into the feminine soul, is: What does a woman want?"[8] Freud's psychology was to prove by no means an unambiguous asset to the cause of sexual emancipation. In 1944, Helene Deutsch, a student of Freud, offered a weighty analysis of feminine psychology in a two-volume study entitled *The Psychology of Women, A Psychoanalytic Interpretation.* The modern girl, Dr. Deutsch pointed out, faced bewildering choices. " 'What shall I be?' This means: 'With whom shall I identify myself? Shall it be father, mother, some other ideal figure? Shall I be a *femme fatale* or a career

woman, an artist, scientist, or a mother of many children, an ascetic or a believer in free love?' "

The woman who is intellectual, "ambitious, pedantically conscientious" seemed to the author, "the most miserable feminine type in existence . . . often an excellent but usually an incomplete man . . ." Such females have abandoned "the treasure of intuition, the source of woman's genius . . . Their affective lives are dry, sterile and impoverished . . . for woman's intellect, her capacity for objectively understanding life, thrives at the expense of her subjective, emotional qualities." Dr. Deutsch insisted that all the forms and kinds of human cultural aspiration that require a strictly objective approach are, with few exceptions, the domain of the masculine intellect, or of man's spiritual power, against which women can rarely compete. . . .

Only the truly feminine woman can hope to be popular with men, "thanks to their intuition and their lack of envy, competitive feelings, and other forms of aggression." Woman wants to be fought for and conquered and "awaits her final 'defeat' in joyful excitation . . ." The "passive-masochistic" woman is Dr. Deutsch's heroine, provided she is also monogamous. "Experience teaches us that manifestations of a too great sexual freedom are not found where there is harmonious femininity . . . The woman who is harmoniously erotic, who is most 'feminine' and represents the best achievements of her Creator" really loves only once.

Three years after Dr. Deutsch dropped her Freudian bombshell, an American journalist and a female psychologist collaborated on a book that gave its attention to the social implications of female character that the Deutsch volume had analyzed. *Modern Woman, The Lost Sex* gave a devastating answer to all the champions of feminine "equality." It was simply a "scientific truth" that women are "endowed with a complicated reproductive system with which the male genito-urinary system compares in complexity not at all, a more elaborate nervous system and an infinitely complex psychology revolving about the reproductive function. Women, therefore, cannot be regarded as any more similar to men than a spiral is to a straight line." All the historic contentions over woman's rights and woman's capacities were, the authors suggested, academic. Woman was trapped in biology and her destiny was, after all, the kitchen and the nursery.[9]

Modern woman in her struggle for parity with man, having abandoned her primary function as housewife and mother, had lost her way amid the perils and pitfalls of modern society. Her status had once rested solidly on her capacities as homemaker. Man's competitor, rather than his help-mate, "now she has no certainty of status . . . She consequently no longer has security of position as a *woman, a female being.*" Having renounced that which is her true essence, having denied her real self, she is empty, disconsolate, despairing. Engaged in competition not only with men but with other women, she is not "in sober reality, temperamentally suited to this sort of rough and tumble competition, and it damages her, particularly in her own feelings." Men, being "of tougher grain, simpler structure . . . are better able to endure competition."[10]

The authors are most deeply concerned with the social effects of the American woman's "unhappiness and deep discontent." The birth rate is falling because many women decline to have any children or have very few. The price they pay for such denial of their instinctual life is neurosis, the "ghostly epidemic" of modern society.

The authors are not satisfied with assessing the plight of modern woman. They retrace in some detail the long fight for woman's rights. It is clear to them that the female combatants have been motivated by the subconscious desire to become men, impelled by envy, and by unacknowledged resentments at their own sexual failures which gave them "castration complexes." By this reading feminism, in demeaning the masculine role, sought to emasculate the male: "*It was out of the disturbed libidinal organization of women that the ideology of feminism arose . . .*" The feminists were women who felt their "sexual life" as women threatened and who "fought back as men." "Basically," the authors state, "the feminists were out after nothing other than sexual gratification."[11]

Man is the aggressor. "He penetrates; woman receives." And education, too, is a villain in the piece, for education makes woman dissatisfied and neurotic, reduces her potential as a mother and distracts her with vain ideas of a career. In the authors' words, "the more educated the woman is the greater chance there is of sexual disorder, more or less severe."

If scientific Freudian psychology turned out to be a bitter disappointment to the traditional feminist, there was still hope from another famous "scientist." By the end of the nineteenth century a conspicuous new ingredient in American feminism were the dogmas of Karl Marx. Marx, drawing on Bachofen, had argued that in early society women were the equals if not the superiors of men. They had been enslaved by the institution of private property which destroyed the communal, matriarchal society and replaced it with an individualistic, competitive one. In the words of Marx's follower, Frederick Engels, this "overthrow of mother-right was the world-historical downfall of the female sex."

The earliest and most ingenuous feminist discipline of Marxian doctrine was Charlotte Perkins Gilman who examined the reasons for the "sexuo-economic" dependence of women and went on to propose the most radical solution. Mrs. Gilman was a great-niece of Harriet Beecher Stowe. She had been married and divorced. In 1898 her book on *Women and Economics* was published and two years later she married Houghton Gilman. Mrs. Gilman is an important figure in part because she provided a link between the earlier generation of reformers and the "modernists" and in part because of the trenchancy and originality of her most significant book. She displayed the same anxiety about marriage that had characterized the earlier generations of woman's rights champions but to this she added a Darwinian notion of social progress and a Marxian emphasis on woman's economic condition as underlying all her difficulties. She considered herself a scientific thinker, a cool-eyed sociologist, but she seldom refers to men without indignation: their qualities are "pride, cruelty, and selfishness . . . the vices of the master . . . unspeakable injustice and cruelty . . ."; they are creatures of "destructive energy, brutal, combative instinct . . . intense sexuality." No real life is possible for women until they are freed from their sexuo-economic dependence on men.

Mrs. Gilman carried the issue of feminine freedom further than any of her predecessors by forthrightly attacking motherhood and the family. But the real villain was an "over-sexed" society. Since woman's only way of winning security was by ensnaring a husband, every feminine need and quality was subordinated to this quest. Woman was in fact the only species of female in the animal world that did not secure her own food and was thus dependent on the male. It seems clear she yearned for the time when woman "ran about in the forest and helped herself to what there was to eat as freely as [the male] did." Thereafter, as civilization advanced, women felt the "increasing constriction of custom closing in . . . like the iron torture chamber . . ."[12]

Dependence on man for food meant an absurdly exaggerated emphasis on sexuality in both men and women: "the economic status of the human female is relative to the sex-relation." With the general process of social advancement had gone "an unnatural process, an erratic and morbid action, making the sex-relation of humanity a frightful source of evil." "Excessive sex-indulgence is the distinctive feature of humanity . . ." An excessive sex-distinction, "manifesting the characteristics of sex to an abnormal degree," had given rise to a degree of attraction "which demands a degree of indulgence that directly injures motherhood and fatherhood," she wrote. And in one of the many incisive phrases that characterize her book she noted that "the feeding sex [the male] becomes the environment of the fed." Economic dependence combined with the sex-relation had produced the monstrous sexuality of modern society and the excessive indulgence of the male did "direct injury to reproduction," left the wife weak and debilitated, and led to "the enormous evil . . . produced by extra-marital indulgence . . ."[13]

"Man," she wrote, "is the human creature. Woman has been checked, starved, aborted in human growth; and the swelling forces of race-development have been driven back in each generation to work in her through sex-functions alone." While Mrs. Gilman was an emphatic supporter of "the virtue of chastity, the sanctity of marriage," she was convinced that true love between husband and wife was only possible when women were independent economically and freed from the slavery of housekeeping.[14]

Woman's sexuo-economic dependence drives the male, in turn, to make the marketplace a battlefield and display qualities of "unnatural greed generated by the perverted condition of female energy." Thus women "as priestesses of the temple of consumption" have a "reactionary and injurious" economic influence. They encourage debilitating struggle and ruthless competition in their behalf, a competition which is as damaging to their partners as to themselves, fostering the "savage individualism" which is so characteristic of American society.

The "over-sexed woman, in her unintelligent and ceaseless demands, hinders and perverts the economic development of the world."[15]

Specialization and organization are the means by which male-dominated modern industrial society has subdued the world and produced, for the first time in history, a genuine abundance. But this specialization and organization, unless participated in by women, will simply drive a deeper wedge between the sexes and further stimulate already excessive sex-distinctions. These techniques must be applied to the home so that women can escape its endless demands and deadly routines. Women "confined absolutely to this strangling cradle of the race, go mad by scores and hundreds."[16]

Much of Mrs. Gilman's sharpest invective is directed at "that relic of the patriarchal age — the family as an economic unit," and, especially, at home cooking. Housewives must specialize just as much as plumbers or engineers. The family is becoming "individualized," members have less and less in common and this is highly desirable. Man is ready for a higher form of social life than the family: "the belated home industries" [cleaning, cooking, sewing, washing] must be "elevated and organized, like the other necessary labors of modern life."[17]

Cooking, another aspect of the sexuo-economic slavery of women, is "in the helpless hands of that amiable but abortive agent," the dependent woman. And she, by catering to her husband's gastronomic whims is slowly poisoning the race. "Cooking is a matter of law, not the harmless play of fancies . . . while every woman prepares food for her own family, cooking can never rise beyond the level of the amateur's work." Kitchens, archaic survivals of primitive times, must be removed from homes. Cooks must be trained experts and families must go out to eat. Mrs. Gilman imagined huge apartment houses with common dining halls, or, for those who insisted on clinging to single family residences, a common center or pavilion where all nearby families dined. For a wife to cook meals meant mixing sex and food, thereby producing an "unnatural race between artifice and appetite, in which body and soul are both corrupted." It was evident that "this affectionate catering to physical appetites" led directly to "unchecked indulgence in personal tastes and desires, in drug habits and all intemperance." In scientific kitchens healthy food would be prepared and self-indulgent males would come in time to like it and to subordinate their personal tastes to a wholesome common menu: "The stomach should be left to its natural uses, not made a thoroughfare for stranger passions and purposes." The way to a man's heart must not lie through his stomach. The "Cupid-in-the-kitchen arrangement" had produced nothing but vice and indigestion, "fat, greasy" husbands, "pampered with sweetmeats."

The vehemence of Mrs. Gilman's attack on cooking (the "unutterable depravity of gluttony and intemperance") and her intermingling of food and sex suggest either something a bit pathological in her own background or her sense that she was assaulting an almost impregnable redoubt. But assault it she must if women were to be freed from the "clumsy tangle of rudimentary industries that are supposed to accompany the home." When cooking and housework have been suppressed we will have a world "of pure, strong, beautiful men and women, knowing what they ought to eat and drink . . . capable of much higher and subtler forms of association" than at present.[18]

The woman had, of course, an initial and inherent superiority over the man. Enslaved as she had been, she had, nonetheless, tamed man and made him socially useful, moderating his "naturally destructive tendencies." Through the long process of humanization the male has passed from being "merely a reproductive agent . . . to full racial equality with the female." The woman has made the man "the working mother of the world." However, the bitter price woman had to pay for elevating the male was her own subordination. If she had remained, as she was initially, superior to the man "both would have remained stationary." Now that man had been civilized through the efforts of woman it was time for woman to cast off the shackles which she had assumed. Evolution had reached a point where the sexuo-economic dependence of women no longer served the race. That day must inevitably, in response to the laws of social progress, come. Women were growing "honester, braver, stronger, more healthful and skillful and able and free, more human in all ways."[19]

"When the sex-relation is made pure and orderly by the economic independence of women, when sex-attraction is no longer a consuming fever, forever convulsing the social surface, under all its bars and chains," then human relationships will be based on mutual interest and affection instead of "one great overworked passion; . . . only kept from universal orgies of promiscuity by being confined in homes." Shallowness, exploitation, waste, and ostentation will disappear; women specialized in industry "will develop more personality and less sexuality; and this will lower the pressure on this one relation in both women and men." Women will then shed their "childish, wavering, short-range judgment, handicapped by emotion."[20]

Despite the influence of Mrs. Gilman's writings it was not until the Great Depression that Marxism became a conspicuous feature of feminism. In 1931 Samuel D. Schmalhausen and V. F. Calverton edited an ambitious volume entitled *Woman's Coming of Age*. The book, an anthology of writings on the place of women in American society, was dedicated "to the promising future of the new woman." The introduction set the tone of the volume, an almost pathological hatred and contempt for men combined with high hopes for the reform of American society along the lines of Soviet Russia. The editors spoke acidly of man's "vast repertory of techniques and cunnings for holding woman in a mindless inferiority that somehow produces in his dwarfish brain the exhilarated consciousness of superiority." Humanity could not rise above an "exploitative economics" or a "sadistic psychology of the sexes," the editors insisted, until competition, laissez faire, "go-getting and will-to-power" were replaced by "proletarian humanism" and "communal comradeship." Only with the overthrow of "male-infected competition" will true love between the sexes — "proletarian love" — be possible. To another contributor "the deep emotions aroused by pregnancy" must be made to "flow into scientific channels" so that mothers may come to care less for their own children and more for the children of others. The "petty bourgeois" view of life "in which small separate families are reared (however perfectly) in prideful scorn and competition one with another" must be broken down and replaced by the agencies of a collective society.

To Samuel Schmalhausen, "woman's plight on earth is tragic." They were "doomed females" whose agonies have been witnessed by man with pleasure "since out of [woman's] unhappy pain he has somehow managed to extract a bitter-sweet essence of superiority with which upon appropriate occasions he could poison the joy of living for her." Man was indeed, "fiendish," a "cunning worm," and a malicious tyrant; to Schmalhausen, if there had been in modern times "any genuine love" between the sexes, it could only be found in the "beautiful audacity and life-conserving sincerity" of Soviet Communism. Schmalhausen perceived that women have been the chief victims of the social dislocations and tensions of modern industrialism: "Anxiety surrounds the sexual relation in a sense more harrowing than it has ever known before." And there was more than a little truth in his observation that "while man runs society he has at his disposal many ways of keeping woman subordinate and infantile, that is, of rejecting her: his most recent and most subtle way is to grant her equality sexually and then to use her more lightheartedly and trivially — with her sportsmanlike consent — than he has ever dared to do before."

The insight was an important one. The feminists who proclaimed sexual equality had fallen into a trap of their own making. Their freedom was full of dangers to themselves as individuals and as women, and yet to admit it would be to abandon one of the cardinal points of their faith — that sexual freedom for male and female was the only sound basis for a healthy society. The discovery was full of pain and astonishment. The new freedom did not bring new harmony and new wholeness; it brought if anything more anguish and despair than the old bondage of home and children. Man had won again. The more women fled the full implications of their womanhood, the more they indulged in "neurotic moods and hysteric flight from reality."

Throughout the anthology runs the classic concern about female frivolousness, the concern that women will frustrate all hopes for a better day by remaining "parasites and dumbbells and whorish darlings." The "idiot god, fashion," in his alliance with man, sought constantly to trivialize and debase women thereby preventing them from realizing their true potentialities.

Ethel Mannin, whose *Women and the Revolution* was dedicated to Emma Goldman, preached a similar doctrine. To her, however, it was not man who was woman's hereditary enemy, "frustrating, exploiting, and oppressing her." Woman's enemy was the same as man's — "the capitalist state, which exploits Man and Woman alike." Miss Mannin looked to the day when women would be "free in the social system of a classless society, and free in their own souls, with . . .

time to savour life as the vast luxury it is capable of being, not for the privileged few, but for the masses . . ."[21] Engels in 1884 had argued that when economic causes disappeared from marriage true monogamy would appear for the first time. "For with the transformation of the means of production into social property there will disappear also wage-labour, the proletariat, and therefore the necessity for a certain — statistically calculable — number of women to surrender themselves for money. Prostitution disappears, monogamy, instead of collapsing, at last becomes a reality — also for men."[22]

The problem of masculine sexuality was met, if not for a certainty solved, by the discovery of a female sexuality more intense and, as regards specific encounters, more prolonged, rising, indeed, to a peak at a time in life when men's potency was on the wane. Feminist writing had, as we have seen, been obsessed with the question of how to reduce, modify, diminish and/or somehow contain the inordinate sex drives of men. Suddenly and rather alarmingly it appeared that the question might have to be turned about: were men able to satisfy the sexual needs of women? The issue was aggravated by the fact that men have always had this secret anxiety; were they sexually potent? It was perhaps easier to buy reassurance from a woman who was in the business of pleasing her customers than to win it from a wife, convinced that sexual delight was one of her inalienable rights and determined not to be shortchanged. The fact that the issue of sex had been removed from the problems of "adjustment" in the typical nineteenth-century marriage may have made such marriages a good deal simpler and, in certain ways, more pleasant. There is something more than slightly comic in the transformation of the American man from a sexually ravenous male animal to an anxious and uncertain practitioner of the new sexual techniques.

To many feminists, Freud became an embarrassment. The best hope for the "scientific" emancipation of women seemed to lie in a judicious combination of Havelock Ellis and Karl Marx.

18

Women's Organizations

Perhaps the earliest antidote to the isolation and the disintegrative effects of American life was the Masonic order. Other fraternal groups were formed during the course of the nineteenth century, many of them local in character. Hundreds of thousands of Americans found a sense of companionship in reform organizations, antislavery, woman's rights, peace and temperance societies, spiritualism and phrenology, and in utopian communities, but the vast majority of women found the center of social as well as their spiritual life in their church. Having gotten a taste of the pleasures of organizational activity in the rights movement, women soon displayed an extraordinary fertility in spawning innumerable clubs and societies. Obsessed in many instances by a feeling of powerlessness, they discovered in such organized activity a sense of purpose and of modest power which was obviously rewarding.

Men were always organizing things, retreating to masculine preserves, to clubs and lodges; women soon demonstrated a talent for such activity that put men in the shade. It seems evident that women respond every bit as much as men to associational activity, to reports, committees, minutes, and all the tedious paraphernalia of voluntary groups. The vast majority of such groups were designed to do good, to rescue fallen women, to aid indigent seamstresses, to support foreign missions, to protect the family, to prohibit the sale and consumption of liquor, to establish world peace, or, failing that, to at least keep America out of war.

Temperance had a long history in the United States stretching back to the early days of the Republic. By 1855 thirteen states had passed prohibitory laws. Then the tide receded; a number of states repealed the laws forbidding the sale or consumption of alcohol. At the end of the 1860's the Prohibition Party was founded to work for a constitutional amendment and five years later the Woman's Christian Temperance Union was started, in the town of Hillsborough, Ohio, where a group of women inspired by Dr. Dio Lewis and led by the daughter of a former governor of the state, met to pray and sing hymns in front of the saloons of the town. The movement spread to nearby Washington Courthouse where the women formed a "Committee of Visitation" and appealed to the liquor dealers "in the name of our desolate homes, blasted hopes, ruined lives, widowed hearts, for the honor of our community, for our happiness, for the good name of our town, in the name of God who will judge you and us, for the sake of our own souls which are to be saved or lost." The dealers were called upon to "cleanse yourself from this heinous sin, and place yourselves in the ranks of those who are striving to elevate and ennoble themselves and their fellow men." The church bells were tolled and women and children knelt in the snow chanting and praying. This was all too much for the saloon keeper who turned over his stock to the ladies to be emptied into the streets with loud hosannas.

One of the early crusaders, Fannie Leiter, recalled her first campaign. In a company of four hundred women she marched down the main street of Mansfield, Ohio, stopping outside of each saloon to hold services on the windy sidewalks. When the vanguard entered a notorious tavern she was appalled by "the dark, damp, underground retreat, redolent with the fumes of whiskey and beer, made doubly hideous by the jeers and shrieks of those who had rallied around the proprietors . . . the very embodiment of all that was evil." Feeling she might never have such an opportunity to redeem the fallen, Mrs. Leiter stepped on a chair and began to pray. "So long as reason remains," she wrote, "I shall never lose the impression made by that multitude of upturned faces, bearing unmistakable evidences of the hold of the tempter upon them."[1]

Similar scenes were repeated in hundreds of towns and cities in the decade following the Hillsborough crusade. It was the last great outpouring of the Protestant passion, the last and one of the most dramatic attacks against "the man's world" symbolized by that classic masculine preserve, the saloon. The tarnished hopes for a redeemed world were burnished a final time. The passion that had ignited the abolitionist movement and the crusade for woman's rights flared up once more, drawing together new legions of Christian ladies. The fight was, in part, directed against a genuine evil, almost endemic drunkenness, and in part against the image of the male — rough, sodden, bestial, and above all, disappointing — that had a strong appeal to so many nineteenth-century wives. Under the leadership of Frances Willard, the W.C.T.U. enlisted women by the tens of thousands.

The social side of the temperance movement was perhaps as important as the mission itself. The Thornton, Indiana, meeting in July, 1890, began by singing "All Hail the Power of Jesus' Name." Then came an "impressive and energizing prayer," and a reading from Scripture. An elocution and singing contest followed, featuring such topics as "Prohibition, the Hope of Our Country," "The Rumseller's Legal Rights," and "Save the Boy," interspersed with renditions by a mixed quartet of "Sleeping on Guard," "Lift the Temperance Banner High," and "A Child's Pleading."

At the height of its success, the W.C.T.U. counted hundreds of thousands of women among its members. Praying, marching, and occasionally employing more militant tactics, they descended on bars and taverns across the land armored with the righteousness of Christian mothers. For a time it seemed as if a man could hardly enjoy an undisturbed beer at the corner saloon without a band of temperance ladies coming down on him quite literally like the wrath of God.

But the union had an importance that went far beyond the issue of temperance. It was the first national woman's organization that drew into one large society numbers of women from all levels of American life and from virtually all sections of the country. It was militantly Christian — it had for its object "the enthronement of Christ's spirit in the world — its customs, its habits and its legislation" — and its reformist zeal extended to woman's suffrage where it made common cause with the two suffrage associations and was, at the same time, more respectable. It campaigned for kindergartens, police matrons, "social purity," and child labor laws and prided itself upon its catholicity in bringing "upon one platform" Jew, Catholic, Methodist, Universalist, Unitarian and Baptist joined in "the one pulse, a protected home and a redeemed America." There was a measure of truth in its claim that it had "developed the brain of woman as no schooling ever did before, has broadened the sympathy of her heart until it takes in all humanity, has educated her will until it has become a mighty power, and has exalted to supreme heights her faith in God."[2]

Forty women in the "great society" each with a helper in every state, officered forty departments and "ten thousand local unions." Hardly an American woman remained untouched directly or indirectly by its network of unions and its indefatigable energy in doing good. Even the "solid South" was stirred to new life by the W.C.T.U. Anne Scott writes that "no group did more to subvert the traditional role of women, or to implant in its southern members a sort of unselfish-conscious radicalism which would have turned the conservative southern male speechless if he had taken the trouble to listen to what the ladies were saying. Between efforts to secure prohibition laws, the women of the W.C.T.U. worked in various southern states for prison reform, child labor regulation, shorter hours of labor, compulsory education — and cheered Frances Willard to the echo when she announced that the industrial revolution must be made to benefit the average working man and added 'If to teach this is to be a socialist, then so let it be!' " As one Southern woman put it, the W.C.T.U. was "the generous liberator, the joyous iconoclasm, the discoverer, the developer of southern women."[3]

Not satisfied with evangelizing at home, the W.C.T.U. reached out to form an international union made up of women of all nations "interested in temperance or social purity or *any other form of Christian, philanthropic, or reformatory work* [italics mine], without respect to nationality, class, or creed."[4] Certainly the "brotherhood" had no organization to compare in size or complexity with that of the "sisterhood." In terms of organization, men ran a poor second.

The union rescued wayward girls and lost boys, conducted research into the causes of alcoholism, started hospitals to care for chronic drunks and societies to look after their wives and children. It cherished its description of being "like a million mothers over the land." Deciding that drunkenness was the result of faulty education, the union started numerous kindergartens where temperance principles were taught along with the ABC's; it provided Sunday school literature which taught that "this body is the 'Temple of God' and poisons have no place there," and promoted scientific temperance teaching in public schools. In some instances the W.C.T.U. even paid the salary of police matrons when municipal governments declared themselves unable to afford the expense.

Doctor Mary Weeks Burnett, a delegate from the National Temperance Hospital and Medical College Association, described the causes of alcoholism in 1880 as including "The climate of America, its form of government, its mixed population and its numberless race crossings, its exciting political and business life into which our people are drawn as into a maelstrom." All these elements made Americans "a peculiar and complex people" especially susceptible to all forms of narcotics.[5]

In the popular mind the W.C.T.U. is associated with Carry Nation and the Anti-Saloon League, with ax-wielding battle-axes destroying good booze, and with the grimmest kind of Protestant fundamentalism. In the reaction to the Volstead Act which was its penultimate and, as it turned out, most disastrous achievement, cartoonists fixed the image of sour-faced ladies in formidable hats, clutching menacing umbrellas. In fact the Woman's Christian Temperance Union was probably the most extensive agency of social reform in our history and one of the most enlightened. As its origin was in the Middle West so was its greatest strength, and there was undoubtedly more than a tinge of anti-Easternism in it. It partook of the spirit of Populism; the East was selfish, decadent, materialistic, abandoned to creaturely comforts, saturated with spirituous liquors. There was also doubtless some anti-immigrant sentiment in its overwhelmingly WASPish constituency; disapproval of the whisky of the Irish, the beer of the Germans and, later, the wine of the Italians.

The 1880's and 90's were the most important years for American women in terms of their emergence into professions and occupations to which a handful of aggressive and determined ladies had won admission prior to and in the years immediately following the Civil War. Thousands moved into the professions, into medicine, law, and college teaching; thousands into the missionary field, and tens of thousands into offices and factories. They found a foothold in government agencies and federal bureaus; they formed women's organizations by the hundreds until it seemed as if every middle-class American woman was caught up in a national and, in many instances an international organizational network, extending from Maine to California and across the ocean to England, France, Germany, and Western Europe. Women's conventions and congresses blossomed everywhere.

In 1888 Susan Anthony and Mrs. Stanton called together under the aegis of the National Woman's Suffrage Association the International Council of Women at Washington, D.C. The meeting was called to celebrate the fortieth anniversary of the Seneca Falls' Convention. It was intended to "rouse women to new thought . . . intensify their love of liberty, and . . . give them a realizing sense of the power of combination." No matter how nations might otherwise differ they were all alike "on one point, namely, man's sovereignty in the State, in the Church, and in the Home."

"Much is said," the call to the meeting continued, "of universal brotherhood, but, for weal or for woe, more subtle and more binding is universal sisterhood."

Delegates came from England, Scotland, Ireland, France, Denmark, Norway, Finland, India, Canada, plus "thirty-one different associations of moral and philanthropic reforms." The convention opened with a religious service. Six ordained women participated, including, of course, the first to be ordained in the United States, Nette Brown Blackwell. The Reverend Annie Shaw delivered a sermon on the Heavenly Vision, comparing the Lord's call to women to that which came to Paul on the road to Damascus. For ages men had tried, without success, to turn back the "tide of base passion and avarice," meanwhile "Patient, sphinx-like, sat woman, limited by sin, limited by social custom, limited by false theories, limited by bigotry and by creeds . . . patiently toiling and waiting, humbly bearing the pain and weariness which seemed to fall to her lot." At last she lifted her eyes to the heavens, and saw the sign of deliverance, "full of wonder that her soul burst its prison-house of bondage as she beheld the vision of true womanhood. . . . She remembered the words of prophecy, that salvation was to come to the race not through the man, but through the descendant of the woman."

"Recognizing her divinely-appointed mission, she cried out: 'Speak now, Lord, for thy servant heareth thee.' And the answer came: 'The Lord giveth the Word, and the women that publish the tidings are a great host.' " The great day had arrived: "From every land the voice of woman is heard proclaiming the word which is given to her, and the wondering world . . . has at last learned that wherever the intuitions of the human mind are called into special exercise . . . wherever heroic conduct is based upon duty rather than impulse, wherever her efforts in opening the sacred doors for the benefit of truth can avail — in one and all of these respects woman greatly excels man. . . . The Spirit Omnipotent" will "in these last days, fall especially upon woman." She will be the instrument of "human redemption." Now, "in this sunset hour of the nineteenth century" women had gathered "from the East and the West, the North and the South, women of every land, of every race, of all religious beliefs . . . with one harmonious purpose — that of lifting humanity into a higher, purer, truer life."[6]

Miss Shaw ended her sermon by reminding her listeners how the woman's movement had started years ago in London when men in their pride and arrogance excluded from the World Anti-Slavery Congress "the women whom God had moved to lift up their voices in behalf of the baby that was sold by the pound." In that cruel and heedless gesture was "the key-note of woman's freedom. . . . Out of a longing for the liberty of a portion of the race, God should be able to show to women, the still larger, grander vision of the freedom of all human kind."

Susan Anthony introduced Mrs. Stanton who reminded her audience that "half a century ago the women of America were bond slaves. . . . Their rights of person and property were under the absolute control of fathers and husbands. They were shut out of the schools and colleges, the trades and professions, and all offices under government . . . and denied everywhere the necessary opportunities for their best development. Worse still, women had no proper appreciation of themselves as factors in civilization. . . . Like the foolish virgins in the parable, women everywhere in serving others forgot to keep their own lamps trimmed and burning, and when the great feasts of life were spread, to them the doors were shut."

The older leaders had, like the children of Israel, wandered in the wilderness for forty years. All this had been changed and now only the vote remained to give women their full rights as citizens and as human beings. "The true woman is as yet a dream of the future," Elizabeth Cady Stanton told her listeners. "A just government, a humane religion, a pure social life await her coming. Then, and not until then, will the golden age of peace and prosperity be ours."[7]

The convention then proceeded to its work sessions on education, philanthropies, temperance, industries, professions, organizations and legal conditions, social purity, political conditions, and a nostalgic session on pioneers, a tribute to the old leaders who, like Frederick Douglass, Lucy Stone, and Nette Blackwell, had labored so long in the vineyards.

When Chicago held the World's Columbian Exposition in 1893 a congress of women opened the fair. Representatives from twenty-seven countries attended and two hundred and nine women served as delegates from a hundred and twenty-six organized groups, fifty-six in the United States. Thirty of the organizations were primarily religious and thirty-four committed to "civil and political reform." During the week of the congress as many as twenty meetings a day were held for a total of eighty-one, some of them laid on in response to enthusiastic overflow crowds. An estimated 150,000 persons attended the sessions. Eight hundred and thirty women joined in the planning and the meetings themselves. Throngs of ten thousand or more people packed elbow to elbow poured daily through the Art Palace to hear the news of the new day proclaimed by three hundred and thirty women presenting papers and discussing contemporary issues. The papers ranged from such topics as "Cholera in Hamburg," and "Assyrian Mythology," to "The Glory of Womanhood," and "The Financial Independence of Woman." Julia Ward Howe gave a paper on women in Greek drama and Miss Agnes Manning made a plea for "Complete Freedom for Women."

Madame Blanc, the touring French lady, arrived in Chicago at the time of the world's fair. She was not taken by the architecture of the Woman's Building, designed by a female architect, and she was uneasy at a tendency which she observed in American life to mark off a kind of special category for women in the arts. "Competition with men is indispensable for the elimination of rubbish," she noted shrewdly, "and also to set forth, not always the inequality, but the profound difference in the gifts and aptitudes of the two sexes." But she was much impressed with what went on inside the building, with the organizational abilities of the women and with the variety and quality of their discussions and exhibits. "All who had, or thought they had, new ideas to express, found a hearing."[8]

A number of addresses dealt with clothes reform and exercise as means of improving the health of women: "Harmonious Adjustment Through Exercise." The vast majority dealt with the condition of women in America and in the world — in Turkey, Egypt, India, Italy, Bohemia — many of the latter delivered by women representatives of the countries and all paying special tribute to American women missionaries for having raised the status of women and given foreign, and particularly Eastern women, the hope of a better condition for their sex.

The statistics were omnipresent and impressive. It seemed clear that woman's influence was increasingly geometrical. The last two decades had witnessed such a dramatic access of woman power that, if one viewed the future as a projection of present trends, the prospect was dazzling indeed. Some speakers were at pains to make clear that women, having freed themselves from masculine domination, had no desire to rivet chains on men; men should have full equality. Mrs. Laura Gordon reminded her audience that while men could do virtually everything women could do, it was not true that women could do everything men could do. If men were suddenly withdrawn from all practical affairs women would be hard put to it to operate the complex technological world built by masculine genius.

Cara Reese, a reporter for the *Pittsburgh Commercial Gazette*, went further and touched a particularly sensitive nerve in warning of the danger that women in pursuit of a career might neglect their primary responsibilities as wives and homemakers. "The dusty parlor, the cluttered kitchen, the half made beds, the hurried meals are familiar objects," she noted, "in the homes where the women have gone over to the hustling world."

On the other hand the skillful and industrious housekeeper often was made to feel that she was, in some way, betraying her sex by keeping a home "in true gospel fashion," rather than becoming a "money-making woman." "The unappreciated home-makers of to-day," Miss Reese continued pathetically, "and, oh men and brothers, how many there are! watch the career of the wage-earning woman with hungry eyes. . . . Both are discontented and in that discontent lies the leaven that will work future destruction." While the home becomes a prison for the increasingly restless and frustrated house-wife, the career woman's "reserve wears away, feminine graces vanish, the cold practical atmosphere in time dulls the sensitive nature, and the woman worker becomes a money-making, fame-seeking machine; an ingrate, often forgetful of friends and favors; a cold, selfish, calculating automaton, and above all, a chronic dis-content."

Miss Reese ended her address with a dramatic plea: "Courage, women of America, you have fought great battles, you have won great victories. Now look to the homes and firesides. The present is yours, the future belongs to God."[9] That Miss Reese had touched a sensitive nerve was perhaps indicated by the fact that in the "Histori-cal Résumé for Popular Circulation" her speech was omitted. But if the conflict between home and career could be suppressed it could not be banished. It was to remain the American woman's most persistent and often agonizing problem.

Aside from the cautionary words already noted, men seldom appeared in the papers and discussion of the Women's Congress except as the rather shadowy "opposition." An exception was Mrs. Martha Cleveland Dibble whose paper "The Nervous American" dealt primarily with the nervous male. America had accomplished great things through the expenditure of vast amounts of nervous energy. In this sense "nervous" meant agile, restless, quick, active. But he had also paid the price in "nervousness," in the disordering of his nerves, in nervous exhaustion, and nervous illness. "How many of our men live, or seem to live," Mrs. Dibble asked, "only to do business? The man seems lost, submerged under its exactions. The thing he created to serve him as a means to an end is transformed into the master, to which he is chained. He no longer seeks amusements; home sees little of him; wife and children are small incidents in his daily life; friendship is an almost forgotten word; general reading is out of the question; and the grind of the counting room or office goes on year after year, till the wheels stop, utterly worn out . . . Does money-making — for that is the great incentive in most cases — does this constitute the only legitimate and worthy employment of time? Is there not today a large field in philanthropy, science, art, literature, and healthy recreation of many kinds, which can profitably and agreeably occupy one's powers. . . ."

The consequence was, in part, increasingly early death for American males "killed by overwork . . . the victims of nervous exhaustion" leaving no "grand old men," full of years and wisdom, to guide the young and strengthen the councils of the nation. "The tremendous strain upon the nervous system" which was wearing out "our people in business, social and domestic life" must somehow be counteracted. It would, if not checked, produce increasingly "feeble offspring," and foster insanity. Mrs. Dibble's remedy was a modest one: "rowing and running and tennis and bowling, riding, swimming and base-ball." If the Republic is to be preserved young men must be "virtuous and temperate" and get plenty of exercise.[10]

Women, of course, were as prone as men to "nervous prostration," but the remedy was as simple: homes that were "less an object of care and anxiety," dress that was loose and comfortable, and healthy food. Certainly the Victorian parlor was designed to represent and produce anxiety. It contained a thousand knickknacks from shells to ormolu clocks, it was festooned in suffocating draperies and hangings, in fringes and furbelows. Between dusting such a room and avoiding smashing the glass case with the stuffed birds or the figurines from Bangkok a poor maid was between the devil and the deep. The petticoats and stays, the antimacassars and marble statues on pedestals really told the whole story.

There are two things worth noting about the World Congress of Woman: it marked the high point of the woman's rights movement in the most general sense; it marked also the passing of the movement in a diminished form into the hands of wealthy and socially prominent women. The international council five years earlier had been dominated by all the great figures of the women's movement — Elizabeth Cady Stanton and Susan B. Anthony, most particularly. Mrs. Potter Palmer, a rich and beautiful Chicago socialite, dominated the World

Congress of Women. Mrs. Stanton was not even present and Susan B. Anthony played a distinctly minor role.

The promise of the congress was, in a sense, a false one. The genuine social radicalism that lay behind the woman's rights movement in the pre-Civil War era and even, to a degree, behind the two principal postwar suffrage organizations, the National Association and the American Association, was quite dissipated by 1890. Concentration on the vote obscured the more basic issues of the relation of women to American life. The euphoric mood of the congress focused on triumphs rather than problems. The spirit of radical reform dwindled, by and large, to a charitable impulse kept alive by socially prominent women. "Social work" became an activity of upper-middle-class women, the more intelligent of them plainly bored with the quality of their lives. And the vote itself, that capstone of the long struggle, was interminably delayed. It was to be another twenty-seven years before it was won.

The delay could not be blamed on the distractions offered by the temperance movement or on the remarkable proliferation, after 1900, of women's peace organizations. A major part simply had to do with a conservative reaction which, beginning at the very time when the woman's rights movement seemed to be sweeping to its final triumph, overtook it, as it overtook so many other reform impulses in American life. The rising tide of "undesirable" immigration also worked against women being granted suffrage. The conservative upper-middle-class women into whose hands the movement largely passed were not inclined to radical measures in behalf of the cause. Margaret Sullivan, a journalist for the *Chicago Herald* made a shrewd analysis in 1893 of women reformers. Their power, she wrote, "lies in the fact that they have always personally deserved public esteem; not one of them has dipped into eccentricities of base quality, such as advocating free love, or making a parade of dangerous socialist theories." Even in the early days the more aggressive reformers "were, without exception, irreproachable from the point of view of morals. The Stantons, the Anthonys, the Lucy Stones, those apostles of the emancipation of woman, may have been berated as fanatics and ranters at first, but they were always respected as honest women. The most advanced members of the Woman's Club are good wives and mothers."[11]

Like the W.C.T.U. the woman's club movement helped to liberate Southern women. Under its influence they founded clubs for every conceivable purpose (and some inconceivable ones). "They organized libraries; expanded schools, tackled adult illiteracy; organized settlement houses; fought child labor; supported sanitary laws; juvenile courts; pure water; modern sewage systems; planted trees; and helped girls go to college."[12]

There were, of course, two types of women's organizations. There were the primarily local woman's "clubs" which were social and sometimes, like the Junior League, established branches in large cities which had, in the view of the League's officers, "a society" in the Social Register sense. And then there were specific women's reform societies such as the Woman's National Committee for Law Enforcement, the Southern Woman's National Committee for Law Enforcement, the Southern Woman's Educational Alliance ("To help Southern girls and women secure the best preparation for life. . . ."), The Wheel of Progress ("dedicated to the progress of mankind in the pursuit of happiness and prosperity"), and almost literally innumerable others. The difference between the two was often more formal than practical. Upper-middle-class or "society" women like Mrs. Potter Palmer belonged to great numbers of organizations; the membership was very largely overlapping especially in national organizations. Perhaps the principal distinction between those clubs which like the Junior League were made up of society women and those directed at various specific reforms was that the local women's clubs directed their energies very largely toward municipal reform. Since most of them were, by a process of natural selection, the wives of successful and important men, they had considerable political leverage. To a remarkable degree the leaders of "society" were also the leaders of reform. While the distinction that I have described existed and was significant, the woman's club movement was a generic term which was taken to include all female associational activity from the period of the 1880's on. The phrase included groups as diverse as the Daughters of the American Revolution and the Chicago ladies who supported Hull House.

Charlotte Perkins Gilman hailed the woman's club movement as "one of the most important sociological phenomena of the century, — indeed, of all centuries, — marking . . . the first timid steps toward social organization of these so long unsocialized members of our race." "Now the whole country is budding into women's clubs. The clubs are uniting and federating by towns, States, nations: there are even world organizations. The sense of human unity is growing daily among women." The movement is restoring a new heroism to modern life, filled as it is with cowardice and self-seeking.[13] Madame Blanc was much impressed by the ubiquitous women's clubs. They were "a school in organization" everywhere well attended, hospitable, intelligent, and animated. She "admired the ease of manner shown (at one meeting) by all the ladies who spoke in turn, the precision of their opinions, the critical sense which they displayed." It was apparent to her "that periodical meetings of this nature have a strong influence on the mind of women, on their powers of conversation, banishing frivolous and too personal subjects, accustoming them to listen attentively, to refute an argument logically." The Fortnightly Club of Chicago was a model of such organizations. It had five hundred members divided into committees on reform, philanthropy, education, housekeeping, art and literature, science and philosophy. The topics discussed ranged from "Evolution of the Modern Woman," to "Should Emigration be Restricted," "Industrial Co-operation," "Co-education," "Dante and the Divine Vision."

She was equally impressed by the family protective agency, a voluntary organization started and staffed by women, which devoted its attention to helping families in need: "Here are not only frauds and injustice redressed, wages paid, cases of cruelty or violence punished, guardianships assumed, divorces obtained . . . illegitimate births made regular . . . strangers in the city directed and helped" at a remarkable expenditure of "sympathy, exertions, and advice. . . . In short, behind every reform we find the dauntless Woman's Club; and if they strive to reform the streets, they also wish to improve the general manners."[14]

Madame Blanc visited Hull House started by Jane Addams and run on principles of "Christian humanitarianism," with "men, women, and children joining in one family as God meant them to be." Immigrant men belonged to the German club, the gymnastic club, the drawing club, or the political economy club. She attended a

lecture given by a professor followed by a lively and even acrimoni-
ous debate between the workingmen in the audience and the speaker.

The woman's club movement might be divided into roughly three
aspects: (1) the purely organizational activity which, as we have
observed, women thrive on; (2) lectures, interminable, inevitable
lectures on every subject under the sun from Hottentot courting
rituals to Japanese flower arrangement; Beatrice Forbes-Robertson
Hale, who was entirely in sympathy with the movement, noted: "No
class in the world will so willingly listen to so many lectures as will
these club women";[15] (3) work of humanitarian reform of every
conceivable description (there was supposed to be an organization of
ladies in Boston to agitate against plopping lobsters in boiling water
without killing them first). The selfishness of man in his greedy
pursuit of gain, of his extravagant material dreams, his restless and
insatiable acquisitiveness, could only be softened by the ultruism of
woman. "She cannot reach her full stature," a prominent feminist
wrote, "save in a humanitarian age; and a socially conscious age must
have her help in order to attain its fullest growth."[16] Feminism
would only come of age when it developed into humanism. Social
reform became, in this view, the avenue by which women were to
redeem a materialist society and in doing so realize their own
potential.

Such women were the principal promoters of all social reforms.
Madame Blanc, visiting Chicago, was astonished to find "the domin-
ion of women in that great centre of vigorous manhood, in that focus
of traffic and trade, where everything at first seems rough. . . ."[17]
There was, of course, no city where "the feminine element is better
represented than in Boston." The city had been the breeding ground
of virtually every reform movement of the century. In the 1890's the
ladies of Boston, led by the now ancient but still charming Julia
Ward Howe, were active in all efforts for the improvement of human
society.

There was, moreover, in the club movement a remarkable solidarity between women of different classes, ethnic groups, and sections.
"In no country," Madame Blanc wrote "are individual friendships
nobler and more devoted."[18] Typical of the alliance of upper-middle-
class WASP women and their immigrant working-class sisters was

the relationship between Mrs. Raymond Robins, a member of the Boston elite, and Mary Anderson, a Swedish immigrant who rose from domestic service to become the secretary of a union of women shoemakers and later the first head of the woman's division of the Department of Labor. Mrs. Robins was always "Dear Mrs. Robins" to Mary Anderson, but Mary was "Dearest Mary" to her Boston friend. Mary visited the Robins's winter home in Florida; the two women remembered Christmases, birthdays and anniversaries, exchanged gifts and endearments — the classic relationship of women devoted to each other and to common causes. There were many such relationships in the various movements of the day. They were, it is safe to say, uniquely feminine relations that had very few if any masculine counterparts. Of course such relationships were not free of class attitudes as the differences in the salutations of Mrs. Robins and Mary Anderson suggest. But the ties of mutual affection clearly transcended all such divisions.[19]

While the total number of women involved in organized social and political activity increased greatly from the 1880's on, their efforts were fragmented. Much of the coherence and effectiveness of the older phase of the movement was due to the fact that its destinies were directed by several dozen men and women who were closely bound by ties of friendship and, not infrequently, of marriage. As women's activities proliferated they inevitably lost much of their unity and, paradoxically some of their power. One might thus ask whether the woman's rights movement was not at its most potent in the decade following the end of the Civil War. Growth meant diffusion and diffusion loss of momentum. Moreover, the vote became primarily a secular issue. Although the Woman's Christian Temperance Union remained strongly prosuffrage it was not its primary concern, and the enormous force of the Protestant passion could not be effectively mobilized behind the suffrage drive.

For the middle-class ladies of the Eastern cities the peace movement turned out to have a powerful attraction. Starting in the 1880's and 90's and given a powerful impetus by the Spanish-American War, peace organizations grew like mushrooms. Ironically the decade immediately prior to World War I saw the greatest peace activity. The peace activities of Fannie Fern Andrews indicate the remarkable proliferation of women's organizations. Mrs. Andrews belonged to:

WOMEN'S ORGANIZATIONS

International Peace Congress of 1910–11
International Commission for Permanent Peace, 1915–1919
Woman's Peace Party
International Peace Bureau, 1911–1924
Neutral Conference for Continuous Mediation, 1916–17
Woman's International League for Peace and Freedom, 1920–24
American Union Against Militarism, 1916–21
Association to Abolish War, 1920
Women's Committee for World Disarmament
National Student Committee for Limitation of Armament, 1922–24
Committee on Militarism in Education, 1926–27
International Peace Brotherhood, 1915
World Peace Foundation, 1910–24
Central Organization for a Durable Peace
Massachusetts Peace Society, 1911–1916
American Peace Society, 1911–15
American Society for Judicial Settlement, 1911–17
Intercollegiate Peace Association, 1908–1915

Other peace groups which women dominated or in which they were prominent were the Fellowship of Reconciliation; No More War Movement; War Resister's International; War Resister's League; The Women's Peace Union of the Western Hemisphere.

In addition to the peace movements listed above Mrs. Andrews also belonged to:

Committee on National Outlook and National Goals, 1933–35
Loyal Coalition, 1919–1920
American Association for Labor Legislation, 1911–26
Playground and Recreation Association of America, 1915–24
National Americanization Day Committee, 1915–16
Mexican Cooperation Society
World Court League
League for Constructive Immigration Legislation
League for Democratic Action
Pro-League Independents, 1920
Our World Institute, 1922–1926
Uncle Sam's Voters, 1923
National American Council, 1923
The Liberal League
National School Club, 1924

Friends of Mexico Committee, 1924–25
Children's Foundation, 1924
National Committee on American-Japanese Relations, 1924–27
Geneva Federation
Pathfinders of America
League for the Organization of Progress
Foreign Policy Association
League of Women Voters
American Woman's Association
National Institute of Social Science
National Education Association
National Economic League
National Committee on Prisons and Prison Labor
National Conference of Jews and Christians

In the National Congress of Mothers, Mrs. Andrews served on the Marriage Sanctity Committee. As this list of organizations would suggest, much of the membership of such groups was overlapping; nonetheless they indicate a kind of organizational mania, a faith that the world could be redeemed from intolerance and aggression by bands of enlightened women.

In the Red scare that followed World War I, women's peace societies were charged with acting as fronts for the Communists: "Do Bolshevists 'Use' our Women's Clubs?" The *Dearborn Independent* (March 15, 1924) promised its readers in scare headlines an "Amazing Account of How the Propaganda is Spread Thro' American Organizations." The editorial went on to charge that the resolutions adopted by the Annual Conference of the Women's International League for Peace and Freedom calling for the abolition of the army and navy had been dictated by the Communist Third International. The resolution against the chemical warfare department was another example of Red influence, "since gas may be used to quell riots, and they (the Reds) plan the beginning of the Revolution in the United States with riots." The plans of the International called for the infiltration of Chautauquas, churches, and peace societies. As the *Independent* continued its "exposé," headlines warned that the "Socialist-Pacifist Movement In America" was "an Absolutely Fundamental and Integral Part of International Socialism." At the end of a lurid account of Red infiltration came a poem:

Miss Bolsheviki has come to town
With a Russian cap and a German gown,
In women's clubs she's sure to be found,
For she's come to disarm America.
She uses the movie and lyceum too
And alters text-books to suit her view;
She prates propaganda from pulpit and pew,
For she's bound to disarm America.

The ideological basis of a great part of the work of women's clubs was a kind of pragmatic socialism which the ladies did not hesitate to speak of. We have already noted Frances Willard's challenge —"if to teach this be socialist, then let it be." Many other women were equally candid.

Beatrice Forbes-Robertson Hale was convinced that the solidarity of women and the solidarity of labor were the two great hopes of the world. Margaret Robins spoke for a considerable company of like-minded women when she told Mary Anderson that the day when Americans could *"escape* from economic, political and religious pressure and tyranny" by moving West in covered wagons was over. "Social condition must be met and mastered at our own front doors and in our own back yards." The convergence of "Lenin's Revolution," Gandhi's technique of passive resistance, and the techniques of mass production had transformed the world. "Unrestricted competition with individualist control of production and distribution cannot master the economic forces of this modern world," she added. This was hard doctrine for "those who love the individual responsibility and self-reliance that was the crowning virtue of the days of the pioneers." Voluntary cooperation was the best way of preserving freedom in the coming age; Gandhi and Lenin must be reconciled.[20]

The peace story is one story; there are dozens of others. It is indeed difficult to identify an area of social reform where clubwomen did not take the lead. Beatrice Hale, praising their "disinterestedness," called them in 1915 "an enormous reservoir of power almost untapped, a vast potential force for good." American men were "grotesquely overworked," the nation's "civics . . . a pathetic muddle." Since there was "no adequately large class of men of leisure and integrity to undertake the duty of setting that muddle straight," the job had fallen to organized clubwomen.[21]

The fact is that women's clubs and individual women working through organizations like Hull House developed virtually all of the voluntary social services that blossomed so luxuriantly in the 1890's and in the early decades of the twentieth century. From the institution of police matrons to "the modernization of . . . garbage plants" and the creation of juvenile courts, women, and more particularly, women's associations for civic reform and social betterment, were the moving force. It was of such women that Lord Bryce was thinking when he wrote that "the influence of the American system" with its remarkable emphasis on the status of women "tells directly for good upon men as well as upon the community." While the "brightness and vivacity of American ladies" was coming to be much appreciated and admired in Europe, the real story was what America owed "to the active benevolence of its women, and their zeal in promoting social reforms. . . . No country seems to owe more to its women than America does, nor owe them so much of what is best in social institutions and in the beliefs that govern conduct."[22]

By the 1930's the transfer of social services to municipal, state and federal welfare agencies deprived women of their most important and rewarding area of public activity and one for which they were obviously well-suited. It would be interesting to know what one suspects: namely, if these social services, while perhaps somewhat more efficiently run by public agencies, are less humanely run. Like the lady missionary, the lady bountiful, leaving her handsome mansion to work for the poor suggests a kind of social condescension that is uncongenial to the modern temper. But it must be remembered that while such attitudes certainly existed they were balanced by a very strong feeling for what Beatrice Forbes-Robertson Hale called "sex-loyalty" or feminine solidarity, and reading of Hull House one can only be astonished at the remarkable empathy between Jane Addams and her female allies on the one hand and the immigrants, both men and women, whom they served.

In any event the professionalization and absorption of social work in large bureaucratic structures was by no means an unmixed blessing. One is inclined to speculate that if social services had remained on a volunteer basis (and of course they obviously could not have done so on a large scale because of the enormous sums of money that came to be involved) the marginal population of our great cities might not have become so alienated from the "white power structure" or "the establishment." The social work done by middle-class ladies was humanizing both for the ladies and for the poor they concerned themselves with. The functions of the most enlightened and well-intentioned bureaucracy soon become routinized and the bureaucracy itself a vast kind of defensive system responding only in terms of its conditioned reflexes, the deeply incised circuitry of operating procedures. It is plain, for example, that much of the hostility of the big city ghettos is directed against professional social workers. Human beings rebel against being "cases." But what is more important is that the professional social worker acts as a buffer between the indigent and depressed segment of society and that portion of the middle class whose social conscience is most readily stirred by human misery and suffering. In other words, if the social services offered by public agencies to impoverished urban Negroes had been provided by women volunteers there is reason to believe that their inevitable moral outrage might have resulted, as it did in the case of the immigrant poor, in a program of legislation designed to meet the "Negro problem" far more promptly and intelligently than in fact has been the case.

There were, then, as a consequence of the professionalization of social work, two losses: a loss in what we today call "communication," a break in the contact between the comfortable and the deprived elements in society; and the disappearance of an important field for intelligent feminine activity. The reform spirit has diminished to the League of Women Voters, the Parent-Teacher Association, and similar organizations of comparatively low social voltage.

One of the most stirring speeches at the Solidarity Day rally during the Poor People's March on Washington in the spring of 1968 was that of the recently widowed Mrs. Martin Luther King. Mrs. King called for a "campaign of conscience" among the women of America in behalf of the American Negro: "Women, if the soul of the nation is to be saved, I believe that you must become its soul." A national columnist entitled his comments on the speech "Women Are An Awful Failure," and poked mild fun at an editorial in McCall's magazine which declared: "The women of this country have heard enough about black power, white power, student power, senior-citizen power. The greatest power of all for good is theirs — woman power. No force on earth can stand against it."[23] There are several revealing things about the column. The writer upbraids women because the Nineteenth Amendment did not result in a purification of American society as many champions of woman's suffrage had claimed it must; he shows no awareness of all the remarkable reforms promoted primarily by women in the nineteenth and early twentieth centuries; he does record simply by his attitude the fact that women today play a negligible role in the social and political life of the country.

Of course it is not only the professionalization of social work that has so dramatically reduced the involvement of women in American public life. "The Great Withdrawal" with its emphasis on the home and family to the virtual exclusion of all other feminine roles has played a very important part. But we must keep in mind that the Great Withdrawal followed rather than preceded that retreat. It is hard not to suspect that what we might call the "privatization" of American life — the shift from the Protestant passion with its redemptive mission and its accompanying if less important ethic of thrift, piety, and hard work to the Passion for Self Fulfillment (and the Ethic of Cheerful Consumption) — is the real culprit.

The ranks of women reformers grew from a small but courageous advance guard in the 1830's and 40's to a sturdy band in the 1870's and then to a great army organized into regiments and brigades of women's clubs in the 1890's. After the passage of the Nineteenth Amendment the army was gradually demobilized. Many useful and enterprising cadres remain but the great campaigns which did so much to ameliorate the harsher aspects of American life were over.

Women and Capitalism

We have seen that in colonial times, women, in the absence of any theory about what jobs were appropriate, were everything from blacksmiths to newspaper editors. After the Great Repression they were restricted to those jobs thought to be suitable for their sex. According to Harriet Martineau who visited the United States in the 1830's there were only three occupations open to women, "teaching, needle-work, and keeping boarding houses or hotels." Of course girls had been working as mill hands since the textile factories at Lowell and later Lawrence were started. Most women who had employment were elementary school teachers or seamstresses, and the condition of the latter was a symbol of the wretched pay and miserable life of women who had to work for a living. "During the present interval between the feudal age and the coming time," Harriet Martineau wrote, "when life and its occupations will be freely thrown open to women as to men, the condition of the female working classes is such that if its sufferings were but made known, emotions of horror and shame would tremble through the whole of society."[1] From the beginning of the woman's rights movement, wider job opportunities for their sex was a major goal of the reformers. The effective barring of women from virtually all jobs and careers was to them a symbol of their hopelessly dependent state. Even the more conservative reformers like Catharine Beecher placed great emphasis on training girls for an occupation.

Prior to the Civil War little progress was made in opening up jobs to women. In fact with the flood of Irish immigration in the forties and fifties many women were forced out of industrial jobs. With the war women had an opportunity to make modest inroads into what had formerly been masculine preserves. In addition, they disproved by their labors as nurses and war workers the notion that they were too delicate to undertake many of the jobs traditionally performed by men. After the war the problem of what might be called "the female surplus" gave greater force to the agitation for jobs for women. Granted the proper place for women was in the home, but if hundreds of thousands of women had no hope of marriage, they must receive charity, have jobs, or presumably become prostitutes.

According to the census of 1880 women outnumbered men in sixteen Eastern states. In Massachusetts, with 70,000 more women than men, the imbalance was the most acute. There was a widespread conviction that the disparity would remain or increase due to "the desolating wars of the world, drunkenness, and other ruinous excesses peculiar to men, and at the present day, the waste of lives consequent on the reckless and absorbing rush of men into dangerous businesses in pursuit of wealth." Dio Lewis in *Our Girls* wrote: "My hopes of the future rest on the girls. . . . I believe America's future pivots on this great woman revolution." The surplus female problem must be met directly if the purity of the home was to be preserved. Women must be trained to take suitable jobs. They would make excellent amanuenses and photographers, copyists and bank clerks (especially the latter since they would not be tempted "by gambling, fast horses, and other forms of dissipation to steal," and would thus save banks those considerable sums purloined by male employees); they would make first-rate brokers, dentists ("her gentle touch, the size and flexibility of her fingers, her quick sympathies, her instinctive sense of proportion and beauty, and her conscientiousness present," Lewis wrote, quite carried away, "singular qualifications for the dental profession").[2] They would also make good lawyers and "inevitably cleanse and elevate" that debased profession; they had already proven themselves skillful lecturers and they might be, in addition, librarians, physicians, preachers, publishers, teachers, teachers of gymnastics and dancing, watch repairers (again those flexible fingers), makers of pens and "aquaria," architects, engravers, photographers, cooperative farmers, merchants, carpenters. Indeed, any of these occupations were to be preferred to the current mania for playing the piano.

Mrs. M. L. Rayne in her volume *What Can A Woman Do; or Her Position in the Business and Literary World* was more enterprising than Dio Lewis. She began by giving her readers an idea of the wages they might expect in New York and other major cities. Good sales-women got from $6.00 to $10.00 a week with a few veterans being paid as much as $12.00. Lady cashiers received somewhat more and bookkeepers from $10.00 to $12.00 a week although many well-trained women considered themselves fortunate if they made $8.00 a week. Eight hundred dollars a year was a large salary for a teacher. At the Palmer House in Chicago the head cashier, a woman, received a salary of $2,000.00 a year and a stenographer at the same hotel got $1,500.00 a year and board. In such positions a woman was superior to a man. An employer could be sure "she will not embezzle his money in gambling or in late suppers. She will not smoke his cigars, or bestow them on her impecunious friends."

The profession of literature presented special problems. Miss Burney was, properly speaking, the inventor of the modern novel. Before her entry into the field in the latter part of the eighteenth century, most novels "were such as no lady could, without confusion, own that she had read. The very name of novel was held in horror among religious people." But Miss Burney restored the novel to respectability and Harriet Martineau and George Eliot used it for instruction and entertainment. Writing offered many opportunities for talented women. Rosa Hardwick when only seventeen had written a poem that insured her fame—"Curfew Must Not Ring Tonight." There were, Mrs. Rayne assured her readers, "a large number of women in New York who support themselves by writing for the newspapers, daily or weekly; . . . some write short sketches; others furnish long serial stories; . . . household departments, fashion letters . . . children's columns, market articles, art criticisms, book reviews — these are nearly always the work of women."[3]

In the early 1890's there were some ninety women lawyers in the United States, most of them graduates of the University of Michigan law department. Similarly in medicine women made progress in the 1880's. Of one hundred and ninety-eight medical students in the Boston University School of Medicine in 1886, seventy-nine were women. In Chicago several women held chairs as professors of medicine and more than a hundred and fifty practiced in the city. Detroit also had a number of women doctors. Three hundred and ninety women were engaged in active practice in twenty-six states; eleven with medical degrees never practiced and twenty-nine retired after practicing for a period. A hundred and forty-four had practiced less than a year; one hundred and twenty-three between five and ten years; twenty-three over twenty years. Dr. Emily Pope, reporting the survey, made much of the fact that the health of women doctors was above average and many declared that their health had improved during their practice. There were nonetheless only a handful of institutions that accepted women and three of these were medical schools for women. The fact was that as late as the mid-1880's the United States lagged behind Czarist Russia and Italy in admitting women to medical schools.

Mrs. Rayne went on to list "the profession of music" where, of course, singers like Patti, Modjeska, and Langtry were cited as examples of the fortunes that could be made by women of unusual talent. On a somewhat different level women clerks were in demand in government offices because they were "punctual and docile," and not given, like men clerks, to "nocturnal dissipation."

The female entrepreneur, offered as an encouraging example to ambitious young ladies, was Mrs. Sarah Ray who ventured into Leadville, Colorado, when that town was one of the toughest mining spots in the West. Mrs. Ray "took in washing and made a fortune of $1,000,000. . . . She is now fifty years old, weighing one hundred and fifty pounds, and is rugged and well. She educated her handsome daughter in an Eastern school, and although deprived of it herself, she is a firm believer in the advantages of higher education." (Taking in washing has perhaps never been so lucrative.)

In dentistry, Mrs. Elizabeth Morey of New York City practiced with her husband and invented the first "skeleton tooth" or cap. Mrs. Morey was of the opinion that men "use too much force, and often crush a tooth or injure the jaw, taking it out. When I am obliged to pull a tooth," she added, "I take it out whole." By 1890 there were between four and five hundred "lady dentists" as well as thousands of "assistant operators" for male dentists. At a commencement of the Pennsylvania College of Dental Surgery of one hundred and three graduates, nine were women all of whom ranked among the top twenty in the class. The first women received their dental degrees from the institution in 1867 and between 1878 and 1892 the Pennsylvania College of Dental Surgery graduated forty-eight women.[4]

Stenography and typewriting were especially recommended for those nimble fingers. Our heroine here is Miss Bertha Louise Parker who was employed by the American Writing Machine Company as "a stenograph amanuensis" and, using their calligraph, dashed off 194 words in one minute. "The perfect ease and grace . . . the entire absence of contortion or effort so common to fast writers, adds a charm to the performance that makes it especially enjoyable" Mrs. Rayne observed. There were over five thousand women in New York and Brooklyn in 1892 who were working as stenographers. Telegraphy was a most appealing job because it did not soil women's dresses, keep them standing, or compromise them socially. Moreover, young ladies working for Western Union reported that they were treated with "sedulous courtesy," and it was possible to knit or crochet between messages, although many operators are subjected to telegrapher's cramp, a temporary paralysis of their hand and arm. Lady book-canvassers and commercial travelers also enjoyed good opportunities. Some women made $20.00 a week selling corsets door-to-door, in effect a feminine monopoly.

"Reading and declaiming poems and prose selections now offers a really important field of labor in the smaller towns and cities where there are no theaters, giving a fair remuneration to the public reader," Mrs. Rayne wrote, adding reassuringly, that there was "nothing derogatory to the dignity of any lady in giving these readings or recitations." In Detroit there was a large training school in elocution to prepare young ladies for such a career. It had "sent its pupils out as readers north and south, east and west, and they have the capacity of filling halls wherever they go with a paying audience." The properly trained elocutionist "can imitate a bird singing, a chicken piping, machinery creaking, a child laughing or a piano playing . . . she can whistle like a boy or a steam engine" and make her audiences "cry or laugh at will."[5]

Bellevue Hospital in New York founded a training school for nurses in 1873 and in twenty years turned out four hundred and twenty-four pupils. These thoroughly trained, efficient young ladies have replaced "the despotic nurse of the past, the stupid, ignorant and opinionated woman, who, in her superannuated days, [went] out nursing."

Mrs. Rayne, following in the footsteps of Catharine Beecher, pushed gardening and farming enthusiastically as healthy, outdoor occupations ideally suited to the temperament of women. Poultry raising and bee-keeping had made modest fortunes for a number of enterprising ladies. "Scientific bee culture" was a rapidly growing field aided by the movable comb-hive and the discovery that bees were "susceptible of education and control, the same as other farm stock."[6]

Dressmaking, housekeeping, cooking, keeping boarders, were all appropriate tasks for energetic ladies. Indeed, it might be said that cooking in America was emerging from the Dark Ages. While America has never been distinguished for its cuisine, there is some evidence that in the nineteenth century, it was, in most social classes, particularly abominable. But cookbooks and cooking schools, home economics, domestic science and scientific cookery, pressed into the curriculums of schools and colleges by the indefatigable Beecher sisters marked the dawn of a new gastronomical era. Wholesome diets and palatable if not inspired food could not in themselves rescue the American intestine from an ancient flatulence whose origins were not simply gustatory, but they undoubtedly did much, in an unspectacular way, to improve the miserable health of both men and women.

There were dozens of books such as those of Dio Lewis and Mrs. Rayne, quaint to read today but often instructive as well, since one discovers that women had notable starts in fields such as dentistry and medicine which they have since virtually abandoned. Full of sentiment, indeed, of sentimentality, of instructive little anecdotes, homilies, Christian morality, of cloying verse, of blurred lithos and wretched typography, they contained a considerable amount of practical information on wages, working conditions, training schools, and institutes where girls might prepare themselves for occupations. Along with the ubiquitous etiquette books and the popular novels, they to a large degree formed the mental world of young women in the last quarter of the nineteenth century. If they seem archaic to a modern reader, they represented for women who lived in that era a world of marvelously expanded range and opportunity, and this sense of liberation that a great majority of women felt is, I suspect, hard to overemphasize. It is only if we keep very much in mind the extraordinary constriction that characterized the situation of middle-class urban women in the period from roughly 1780 to 1880 that we can begin to understand that this new age, an age often thought of as marking the high tide of Victorian artificiality, the Gilded Age or the Mauve Decade, was, for millions of American women, the dawn of a truly new day.

Again, in this emergence, there is considerable evidence that the sympathy and support of a father was critical for most women. My copy of Mrs. Rayne's volume was given to Mabel Vaughan by her father, and many of the sketches of professional women and successful female entrepreneurs make particular mention of a father's encouragement. Of course, the widely accepted notion that a woman who failed to marry or whose husband died and who had no training could only choose between a life of destitution or prostitution undoubtedly helped to override resistance to women entering areas that had earlier been considered entirely unsuitable. But perhaps the most important element was the insatiable need of a rapidly expanding capitalism for more and more manpower or womanpower. If there were several dozen women doctors in New York City, they were in fact only a token number among several thousand men. But the five thousand stenographers of New York and Brooklyn virtually monopolized the field. It became clear by the mid-eighties that women were much better suited than men to a wide range of essentially clerical and secretarial jobs. These were jobs that men, by and large, neither occupied nor wished to occupy. The majority of them were, in fact, new positions for which suitably trained men could not be found. The frequent references to the liabilities of men clerks — speculation, gambling, drunkenness, unpunctuality — were doubtless quite accurate and indicated the type of man that could be recruited for such jobs.

In these areas, therefore, women were welcome and soon actively recruited. But in areas where they competed with men or in jobs which men traditionally held and had every intention of retaining as essentially masculine preserves, women found the same resistance or sometimes increasing resistance after an initial, often sentimental, receptivity. Thus Elizabeth Blackwell had no successor at Geneva Medical College and more than twenty years passed before women made appreciable headway in entering the medical profession. Against the stubborn opposition of most men, a few determined women became lawyers. Typical of the attitude of lawyers themselves were the comments of the liberal and reform-minded George Templeton Strong who wrote in his diary in 1869: "Application from three infatuated young women to Law School [Strong was connected with the Columbia Law School]. No woman shall degrade herself by practising law, in New York especially, if I can save her. . . . 'Woman's-Rights Women' are uncommonly loud and offensive of late. I loathe the lot."[7]

At the law school commencement a speaker delivered "ultra-radical theories, among them, that women ought to vote and possess a natural, inherent right to the elective franchise. This produced an interesting little contest between hisses and applause."[8] The Pennsylvania College of Dental Surgery graduated the first woman dentist in 1867 but in 1874 it barred women and almost five years passed before the college accepted them again.*

Half of all married women work outside the home but less than one percent of working women earn $10,000.00 a year or more and their median income is $3,145.00 compared with $5,308.00 for men. Or put another way, women make up a third of the labor force but receive one-fifth of its wages and salaries.

However, to approach the problem of women's work from the perspective of particular jobs obscures a more central issue: the relation of women to the so-called capitalist system. We would argue here that the development of industrial capitalism was peculiarly congenial to women; that they provided a most valuable human resource for capitalism and that it, in turn, facilitated their emergence

---

* The Los Angeles *Times* for Tuesday, March 12, 1968 ran an article headlined: "Wanted: Women to Fill Dentistry Gap." The article pointed out that dentistry was an especially appropriate field for women and that while there were innumerable women dental technicians there were only a handful of female dentists. Since the University of Southern California Dental School was founded in 1897 it has graduated only fifty-five women dentists. The peak year was 1927 with four women graduates. The article points out that in most South American countries approximately 75 percent of the dentists are women.

from the home. We are very conscious since Weber and Tawney, of the effect of the Protestant ethic on the creation of American capitalism. We have paid far less attention to its role in shaping the "American woman." The reason she was such a wonder to the world, that she enjoyed such remarkable freedom as an unmarried girl and sank so resignedly into domestic labor as the wife, the reason she asserted herself as an independent and equal human being with man, all this is to be found in the feminine version of the Protestant ethic. The ethic enabled her, as we say, to "internalize" all those restraints and inhibitions with which, to put the matter plainly, female sexuality had been surrounded in every other culture or society (whether for the protection of the female or of the male is not entirely clear, but the presumption is strongly to the latter).

Werner Sombart, with more eloquence than accuracy attributed the rise of capitalism in Europe to the growth of luxury, and credited women with being the principal inspirers of that luxury. "Luxury . . ." Sombart declared, "itself a legitimate child of illicit love — as we have seen — gave birth to capitalism."[9] In this luxury, refinement, and sensuality, the key figure is the woman. She is the conspicuous consumer *par excellence*. She creates a house, a room, a seductive trap to capture the male. She expresses her power by stimulating the expenditure of enormous sums of money on her clothes, furniture, decor, jewels. She thus provides a critical incentive to the development of capitalism. So runs Sombart's argument which is an interesting counter-theory to Weber's Protestant ethic. *

Sombart's insight into the relation between sex and money, or more specifically, sex and capitalism is a suggestive one but he seriously misstates the case. Sexuality follows on leisure; the availability of large amounts of disposable income makes possible lavish display and this often, though not invariably, centers on women. What Sombart based his theory on was the behavior of an obsolete and

* Sombart says further: "In the last analysis, it is our sexual life that lies at the root of the desire to refine and multiply the means of stimulating our senses, for sensuous pleasure and erotic pleasure are essentially the same. Indubitably the primary cause of the development of any kind of luxury is most often to be sought in consciously or unconsciously operative sex impulses. For this reason we find luxury in the ascendant wherever wealth begins to accumulate and the sexuality of a nation is freely expressed. On the other hand whenever sex is denied expression, wealth begins to be hoarded instead of spent; thus, goods are accumulated, especially in such abstract forms as precious metals and, in more recent periods, money." 60–61

parasitic class of French courtiers who, infinitely bored, became infinitely ingenious in devising sensual excitements, many of them sexual. Far from giving rise to capitalism through insane luxury, this class gave rise to the French Revolution and contrasted dramatically with the austerity of the Huguenots who were the true French capitalists. But a point is made which might properly be applied to the development of capitalism in the United States. The desire of American women, particularly working-class girls, to dress in the height of fashion was one of the basic incentives that from the first decades of the nineteenth century drew an endless supply of skilled, energetic, docile young women into American factories and provided a large and important portion of the labor force in certain American industries prior to the last decades of the century. And it is certainly the case that the extraordinary expenditure of the Robber Barons, the new industrial and financial elite of the Gilded Age, both provided a stimulus to capitalism and dramatized its almost Oriental opulence. But capitalism itself, as Marx, Freud, and a host of others have argued, was based on repression, not on exuberant sexuality.

"Individualism" (that is to say preoccupation with the individual and, more especially of the individual with himself or herself) was one of the consequences of the "individuality" of the person with internalized values, David Riesman's "inner-directed man," a person free of loyalties to external structures, institutions, even, to a degree, to clan, family, or friends. That this "individual" should wish to appropriate an increasing quantity of "things" as a method of self-authentication was inevitable. It was the means whereby they were rendered tractable instruments or integuments of the industrial system; the means whereby "independent individuals" were prepared for absorption into the dependent collectivity.

Needless to say, a very large portion of these "independent individuals" were women. For the most part they did not need enough money to "make a living," only enough to bedeck themselves in hope of attracting a husband. They had no interest in unions or organization; they were too "independent" for such efforts. Their treasured independence was in fact a kind of double dependence; as wage earners they were more or less independent of their families, and as girls who "didn't need to work" they were more or less independent of the factories. If conditions became intolerable, they might strike, which they did with surprising success; since they were not working "for a living" they could go home to their families and outwait the most obdurate employer.

In the early years of the twentieth century, two Philadelphia society women, sisters-in-law Marie Van Vorst and Mrs. John Van Vorst, disguised themselves as "working girls" and entered a number of different factories employing women. Their comments on their experiences are extremely revealing. "In America," they wrote, "where tradition and family play an unimportant part, the great educator is the spending of money. It is through the purchase of possessions that the Americans develop their taste, declare themselves, and show their inherent capacity for culture." Among factory girls the Van Vorst women found "the idolizing of material things . . . a religion. . . . The love of self, the desire to possess things, the cherished need for luxuries," these were "but one manifestation of the egoism of the unmarried American woman."[10]

The Van Vorsts argued that in a country where conditions changed with startling rapidity and each generation was in consequence "a revelation to the one which preceded it, it is inevitable that the family and the state, should be secondary to the individual. . . . We substitute experience for tradition. Each generation lives for itself during its prime. . . . This detaching of generations through the evolution of conditions is inevitable in a new civilization. . . . But it means a youth without the peace of protection; an old age without the harvest of consolation. . . . The American woman is restless, dissatisfied. Society, whether among the highest or lowest classes, has driven her towards a destiny that is not normal. . . . For natural obligations are substituted fictitious duties of clubs, meetings, committees, organizations, professions, a thousand unwomanly occupations." The enemies of a stable and harmonious life are, in the view of Marie Van Vorst, "the triumph of individualism, the love of luxury . . . the passion for independence."[11]

The Van Vorsts found that the great majority of factory girls in the mill towns of New England lived with their parents, made a point of the fact that they did not have to work, and used the greater part of their very low wages on clothes, dressing, as we have seen, in the latest Paris fashions. Many of the girls encountered by the Van Vorsts spent the present-day equivalent of two or three thousand dollars a year on clothes. In the ladies' opinion, two or three months of "polishing" would allow most of them to pass in Philadelphia society. Independence and fashion were thus the twin gods of the American working girl. These gods were, to a degree, the products of capitalism and they made her the system's willing slave.

From the beginning, capitalism (and especially that aspect of capitalism dealing with industrial production) was most hospitable to the entry of women into the labor market. From the time of the Lowell girls to the present, mill owners have displayed a splendid indifference to the question of a woman's proper place. It has seemed to them that their proper place was running looms or making shirts at wages from a third to a half of those paid to men. Women thus were, from the beginning, scab labor of a kind. They came into the labor market most often to fill in the years between girlhood and motherhood, to get away from home, to be "independent," to make money to spend on adorning themselves in the latest fashion. The passion of American women for independence and for self-adornment have been constants in her temperament from the earliest years of the Republic. Girls constituted an almost inexhaustible pool of available cheap labor, drawn from farms and small towns, from the daughters of artisans and skilled workers, and later from the daughters of immigrants. These girls, of what we would call today lower middle- and working-class origins, with their independence and mobility had little interest in woman's rights or the suffrage. They were, for the most part, entirely conventional in their thinking; but they nonetheless provided the foundation or substratum upon which the woman's rights leaders could build. The fact of this independence, non-ideological and primarily selfish as it was, was a critical element in the social climate of the United States. The independence that the working girl found in the factory, the middle-class woman fought for in the wider ranges of the nation's social and political life. Moreover, it turned out that women were even better equipped than men to take advantage of the democratic egalitarianism that came to be an increasingly conspicuous part of American society, that is to say, of American industrial capitalism.

Since women are essentially classless, industrialism provided them with jobs which provided them with money which provided them with clothes which provided them with that middle-class appearance which was the wonder of foreign visitors. Thus the fluidity of American society was in large part the consequence of the fluidity of American women. The wives of workingmen, adopting a middle-class style, dragged their husbands along with them and thereby helped to create that ample and commodious catchall, the American Middle Class, which includes, with a truly splendid lack of discrimination, everyone from judges to plumbers, leaving out only Negroes, Mexicans, Puerto Ricans, and those whites below the so-called poverty line.

One of the paradoxes and certainly one of the principal sources of tension in American history has been the conflict between the individual and the collectivity. The individual was supposed to be autonomous, inner-directed, potent, aggressive, successful, but he was increasingly absorbed into an anonymous collectivity where powerlessness, impotence, and alienation were his lot. Hermann Baumann in *Das Dopplelte Geschlecht* has argued that "sex antagonism always reflects a crisis in the relation between the individual and the collectivity." There is certainly a great deal in the history of the hostility between the sexes in nineteenth-century America to support such a thesis. The development of a collectivized society was a serious threat to men and in many ways a remarkable opportunity for women. Elisabeth Mann Borgese argues that women are naturally drawn to collective forms of society. If this is true it would help to account for the attraction that modern cities seem to have for women.

The masses, Mrs. Borgese contends, are feminine, the elites masculine. In proof of the point she states that the masses remained bound to feminine deities while elites created and struggled to impose on the masses masculine gods who are always more rational and more predictable. In this same spirit it might be argued that Protestantism, as an elite and masculine version of Christianity, had to dispense with the Virgin Mary as a major deity. Women in this same line of argument have a special affinity with the faceless crowd so characteristic of modern society because they show "diminished individualism and variability." They are, therefore, ideally suited for the collectivized society of modern times; they have, in fact, emerged most conspicuously wherever society has been most thoroughly collectivized. Correspondingly "women, during the individualistic to the post-individualistic phase, are more repressed, more frustrated, and more alienated than men."[12]

Applying Mrs. Borgese's thesis to the situation of women in America in the late eighteenth and the nineteenth centuries, one might argue that the disruption of the original Puritan communities and the shift of the middle-class elites to the rapidly growing urban centers, produced the "sex antagonism" of which Baumann speaks and which we have identified with the Great Repression. Moreover, it appears true that the more collectivized our society has become the larger has become the role of its women. In the most highly collectivized societies of our time, Russia and even more, China, women play a far more important role than they do in America, a less collectivized society.

The problem is that the difference in the degree of collectivization in American society, on the one hand, and Russian and Chinese society on the other, does not seem to be enough to account for the great discrepancy between the roles of women in the different countries. Women already makeup, as we have observed, one-third of the labor force in America and the proportion of women to men is still increasing quite rapidly. The difference between the countries is not so much in terms of the number of women in the basic labor force (in this respect the figures are roughly comparable), but rather in the number of women in important professional careers and here the difference between America and the Communist nations is so startling that we must account for it on ideological rather than social grounds.

In 1880 women formed 13.5 percent of the total labor force in the United States and by 1920 they constituted 21.2 percent. In 1960 one-third of all married women and more than half of all women between eighteen and fifty-five were working full-time or part-time and making up some thirty-three percent of the total labor force. Three-fourths of all teachers below college level are women; 6.8 million are office workers, and another 3.5 million are service workers — waitresses, cooks, beauticians, etc. One and a half million are salesgirls. In 1958 the Soviet Union had 12.6 million women industrial workers, 2 million agricultural workers; 283,300 engineers, or some thirty percent of all engineers; over 3 million women in public education and over 2.5 million in public health. Sixty percent of all economists, statisticians and merchandising specialists are women. Twenty-six percent of the total membership of the Supreme Soviet are women and twenty thousand village soviets are headed by women.

As early as 1914 Beatrice Forbes-Robertson Hale had predicted that "a very large part of the sedentary administrative and executive work of government offices and business enterprises, which now devolves upon men, will be performed by women. . . ."[13] Mrs. Hale was a wise prophet. The more the nation has shifted to a "service economy" the more women have been drawn into the labor force. Through the decade of the 1940's two contradictory movements could be traced. Under the pressure of manpower needs, hundreds of thousands and eventually millions of women entered the labor force, the overwhelming majority in industrial assembly-line positions and clerical jobs. The vast majority of women in the labor force were assembly-line workers (they were cleaner, neater, faster, and more dependable than men). They virtually took over assembly-line duties in light industry, in food processing, in appliances, and in the rapidly growing electronics field. Similarly they completed the rout of men from clerical and secretarial positions and virtually took possession of the field of elementary education.

Women's instinct for neatness and order, for creating "a family" made her ideally suited to occupy the ubiquitous "office." Women are, in some ways, natural bureaucrats. Indeed, a bureau might be compared to a vast, complex "home," stressing the orderliness and "duties" of the home, while foregoing most of those human aspects that distinguish a true home. A "bureau" is a kind of pseudo-home where many feminine rituals are entrenched — birthday parties for the girls in the office, celebrations for the engaged, showers for the pregnant. Those who graduate, or defect into marriage, bring their infants back so that they may be fondled and admired by the girls in the office. In the most efficient offices there is always an undercurrent of the conspiracy and intrigue that characterize feminine societies.

Women thus provide most of the connecting tissue in the modern bureaucratic structure. At the apex of virtually every major business enterprise is a woman, often called "an administrative assistant" who has a position of considerable importance. She is attractive, efficient, discreet, selfless, the mother superior of corporate order, ranking only below the Chairman of the Board; presidents come and go but she remains. She knows everything and, what is perhaps more important in the long run, she remembers everything. Just as she remembers her nieces' and nephews' birthdays she recalls the details of the Tung Oil deal in 1938 or the problems with the Wiskom Company in 1947.

These anonymous ladies are essential elements in American capitalism. No man could do their job nearly so well and certainly not as cheaply. They are doubtless the most systematically exploited workers in the vineyards of American business enterprise. Quite literally married to their jobs, they are the modest but indispensable votaries of Mammon.

Industrial capitalism, with the closing off of immigration, discovered an enormous, docile, highly productive native labor force, and after absorbing women by the tens and then by the hundreds of thousands, began, in the 1940's, to absorb them by the millions. This integration of enormous numbers of skilled and efficient women into the labor force received its greatest impetus from World War II. It is an additional irony that this supply of inexpensive and readily trained labor undoubtedly delayed by a number of decades the integration of American Negroes into the skilled jobs created by mid-twentieth-century capitalism. The great Negro migration to the industrial centers of the country began at the same time as the influx of women into industry. If women had not been available, the Negroes, as the largest pool of inadequately utilized labor in the country, would almost certainly have been drafted into the industrial army. As it was there were other recruits.

Capitalism has clearly benefited from the entry of women in very large numbers into the labor market. They have supplied a large, docile, skilled labor force. They have spent their wages faithfully and thereby provided a vast market for what we might call low-grade democratic luxuries, principally clothes and beauty aids. Their political influence has been in the aggregate very largely conservative. We could also say that by their devoted reform activities they have modified the harsher features of industrial capitalism and thus prevented the development of dangerous resentments and revolutionary upheavals.

Today women largely control and finance the "culture business" in America: book clubs, art museums, galleries, theaters, symphonies, and opera which is an increasingly lucrative part of a middle-class "leisure society." As we have seen, busy and overworked American males have left culture largely in feminine hands. In addition, women own almost three-fourths of the stocks and bonds (thus reaping most of the unearned increment of capitalism), seventy percent of the insurance policies, sixty-five percent of all savings accounts. They outnumber men by some five million (mostly in the older age brackets) and, of course, as housewives they dispose of the greater part of their families' incomes.

Women have been content to let the male expend his physical and psychic energy in creating the most powerful technological and collective society in history. They have been its active abettors and, in purely material terms, its principal beneficiaries. They have not become, for the most part, its doctors, lawyers, professors, dentists, scientists, engineers, and politicians; they have not occupied the high-paid, high-prestige positions they fought so hard to establish their right to. They have left these to be filled by their Russian, Chinese, Polish, Indian, and African sisters. Cocreators and primary beneficiaries of capitalism, American women seem to have lapsed into a traditional role — Margaret Mead's "desperate cave-dwellers."

20

The Great Withdrawal

It was only sixteen years between *Woman's Coming of Age,* published in 1931, and *Modern Woman, The Lost Sex,* which appeared in 1947, but the two books were generations apart in their thinking. *Woman's Coming of Age* was the culmination of a hundred-years-long dream of a society feminized and thereby redeemed. Marxist in its ideology, it was profoundly American in its millennial spirit. Since the years immediately following the Civil War and to some degree before the war, there had been a strong vein in the woman's rights movement that was hostile to the increasingly competitive industrial capitalism that was developing so rapidly in the United States, an economic system with, it was felt, exploitive tendencies and excessive emphasis on material values. This theme was prominent in the writings of the Claflin sisters and in the woman suffrage journals, especially in *Revolution,* the voice of Elizabeth Cady Stanton and the National Woman's Suffrage Association. It became much stronger in feminism, expressed most emphatically by Charlotte Perkins Gilman and Ethel Mannin.

A society redeemed by the power of women, or, more familiarly, woman power, would be a society free of competition and exploitation. Woman was thus not simply equal to man, she was clearly his superior. Eliza Farnham had declared that the female had "in her ovum the entire living germ of any future offspring." All that men contributed was the "food which the germ requires to start it into life." Woman's brain was, moreover, finer than man's as were all her other tissues. "In the male animal the apparatus of the lactatory office is hinted at by a rudimentary form." For Mrs. Farnham women constituted "the highest grade of development of the highest type of living creature here." They possessed the most perfect, "complex, varied, refined, beautiful and exquisitely endowed organization, comprising, with its corresponding faculties, the most susceptible, sensitive yet enduring constitution; and also the purest, most aspiring, progressive, loving, spiritual nature of any being that inhabits the earth."

Mrs. Abbey Price expressed the conviction that with the triumph of woman's rights would come "a new era, glorious as the millennial morning . . . an advent only less radiant than that heralded by angels on the plains of Bethlehem,"[1] and Ralcy Bell declared: "In her personality [women] behold the most of human hope . . . woman symbolizes an endless avenue of evolution . . . she may be likened to a poem of promise . . . she represents progression . . . she is double-wombed, being psychical as well as physical . . . she is double-germed, having spiritual as well as protoplasmic possibilities . . . she stands for infinity, because she suggests endless development, whereas man represents only a blind alley branching off the highway of progress, and symbolizing power rather than promise. . . . Once man's spiritual vision shall be broad enough to encompass these things, his attitude will change. . . ."[2]

Because temperance was a failure, the peace movement was a failure, spiritualism, phrenology, free love, the Fourier movement, Brook Farm, the emancipation of the slaves — because nothing had worked, nothing had fulfilled the American Dream, perhaps it was time to try women. Lester Ward, the father of American sociology, was convinced that "the equality of the sexes" would "mark the regeneration of humanity,"[3] and C. Gasquoine Hartley wrote of the coming twentieth century as "the golden age, the dawn . . . of feminine civilization."[4]

Woman's Coming of Age thus represented the merging of two utopian streams, one the older redemptive and millennial current suffused by the Protestant passion; the other the new scientific socialism of Karl Marx. *Modern Woman, The Lost Sex* was, as we have seen, a thoroughly reactionary document. To the authors the whole woman's rights — woman's suffrage — feminist revolution of the preceding three generations was an unhappy mistake: penis-envy projected onto the stage of world history. They brushed it aside as being not merely an irrelevance but a disaster.

That two people should have such views was in no way remarkable; the views were in many respects as old as civilization and they were not entirely mistaken or perverse. But that such views should have found a large and responsive audience in the middle of the twentieth century *was* remarkable. While *Modern Woman, The Lost Sex,* with its slightly hysterical dismay over the de-maternalizing of modern woman, did not initiate the Great Withdrawal, it did symbolize it.

Women, having established their right to professional training in virtually all fields, failed to capitalize on their opportunities. The percentage of women earning professional degrees reached its peak in the second decade of the twentieth century and by the 1930's had begun to decline. A smaller percentage of advanced degrees were awarded to women in each succeeding decade after 1920. (In 1930 two out of five B.A.'s and M.A.'s were awarded to women; and one out of seven Ph.D.'s. By 1962 the figures had dropped to one in three and one in ten.) The percentage of women dentists, doctors, architects, lawyers, and professors dropped or made, in some instances, insignificant gains. Currently some six percent of all lawyers are women and an approximately equal percent are doctors. As we have seen in the preceding chapter, these figures are in sharp contrast to those of most of the other countries in the world. In England the number of women doctors, while still only twelve percent, has increased steadily from six percent in 1940. In Russia 75.5 percent of all doctors are women as are 42.3 percent of all advanced degree holders. In Italy and Germany there are a number of outstanding women architects; in Japan many dentists are women. Much the same is true in the underdeveloped countries where women are prominent in many professional areas. In France the percentage of women in the labor force and especially in the professions is increasing rapidly.

It might be illuminating to look briefly at a professional area where women established themselves quite early in the fight for women's rights and one for which they were long considered to have a special aptitude — college and university teaching. At present women make up the vast majority of elementary and secondary school teachers in the United States but the percentage of women in the college academic community has declined from a high of some thirty-eight percent in 1879 to slightly over twenty percent in 1959, and even this latter figure needs to be qualified: a majority of that modest twenty percent have very marginal academic positions. They teach beginning language courses, remedial English, and are assistants in laboratory courses or in large lecture courses. Only a handful are recognized scholars in major institutions.

Improving the educational opportunities for women was one of the major preoccupations for the reformers in the years following the Civil War. By 1886 there were 266 colleges for women, 207 coeducational institutions (hence the dreadful name of "co-eds" for women students) and fifty-six agricultural, mechanical, medical, and scientific institutions which accepted women for a total of 529 institutions of more or less higher education enrolling 35,976 female students. By comparison there were 802 institutions of higher education with 78,185 men (there were actually more girls than boys in school at the high school level, because many male students dropped out to go to work and this has remained true up to the present. As late as 1962, 966,000 girls graduated from high school as opposed to 872,000 boys) a very impressive ratio in view of the fact that thirty years earlier there had been only a few hundred women in college.

Many of the colleges founded for women in the nineteenth century were headed by women and had large numbers of women on their faculties. Some, like Wellesley, had only women professors. In addition a great many able and devoted women with Ph.D.'s in conventional academic fields helped to found and presided over home economics colleges which were originally staffed exclusively by female teachers. Yet even here male professors and deans have replaced the pioneering women who began the movement. But the home economics colleges are still directed toward the ideal of service; while the older "elitist" women's colleges of the East (Smith, Vassar, Wellesley, etc.) stress the "adjustment problems" of their alumnae.[5]

Jesse Bernard, in her study of academic women, makes clear that most of the women who enter the academic world are those "who have time for students, who do not think of them as natural enemies robbing them of time they need for their own research; these are the women who sponsor clubs, entertain students in their homes, accompany them on trips. These are the women who are married to their careers."[6]

I am afraid we must agree with Jesse Bernard when she remarks that academic women by performing "some of the hardest work that has to be done by academic institutions, the grinding drudgery of unchallenging introductory courses have . . . released academic men for the more rewarding assignments, graduate courses in new and more exciting areas. . . ."

Professor Bernard has deduced considerable evidence to show that women collect in those academic specialties where the emphasis is on transmission of conventional knowledge or specific information (anatomy in medicine, languages in the liberal arts) and avoid the rapidly changing fields, where originality and instability are characteristic. In her view women do best where "they have behind them the weight of definitive bodies of knowledge about which relatively little controversy or few differences in interpretation exist." Pieced together from a wide variety of sources, "the modal picture of the academic woman that emerges is of a very bright person so far as test-intelligence is concerned, but compliant rather than aggressive, from an above-average social class background, and with a major interest in the humanities."[7]

Two problems might be mentioned in regard to the supposed lack of creativity in women academics who, incidentally, have perhaps done their most creative work in the sciences, especially in the biological sciences. There are always lots of ideas around; the problem is not so much to have ideas as to persuade other people to take them seriously. This is much harder for a woman to do than for a man. A variety of personal and professional pressures work against her winning acceptance for new ideas which, in any event, are seldom cordially received if they run counter to existing scholarly prejudices. Harold Urey has spoken of courage as being the most important quality for a scientist to have, the courage to believe your own insights even when they are opposed to generally accepted views. It is not that women are lacking in moral or intellectual courage — quite the contrary — but rather that their marginal position in the academic world makes it much more difficult for them to persist successfully in an unorthodox or unpopular scholarly position. Moreover, studies have shown that the most creative students have strong tendencies toward "aggression and violence," a classic part of man's competitiveness. If this is so, the fact that most women register considerably lower in these qualities may help to account for a lower degree of creative productivity.[8]

In the last analysis academic women are playing a game whose rules have been devised by men for men. Like the upper levels of the corporate executive jungle, the academic jungle is "red in tooth and claw." Male academics expend vast energies in political maneuverings designed to win preferment for themselves, or perhaps more typically, just to make the system work. These intricate and demanding strategies are uncongenial to women. The fact that men can survive at all in such an atmosphere is due to their capacity to submerge the personal, at least to a degree. For women this is far more difficult and is, indeed, a kind of violation of their deepest instincts. Their feelings of loyalty and justice inhibit them. To smooth over a bitter contention with a smile and a handshake seems to a woman simply hypocrisy; to a man a measure for survival.

One other matter must be mentioned which is of profound importance in all those professions which require a prolonged and exacting training. Beginning in the late 1930's and the early 40's American women launched themselves on what Jesse Bernard calls rather acidly, "a reproductive mania." She notes that in the early days of the female academic it was considered inadvisable if not slightly immoral for a woman professor to marry. In the present age, the reverse is true. Virginia Gildersleeve, head of Barnard, observed that "from a tradition which, in effect, forbade academic women to be married, let alone to become mothers, to one which, in effect, required them to, was a remarkable jump to take. One moment she was having to protect married women; the next, unmarried women."[9]

There is no doubt that the absence of women in higher education is due in part to the new ethic which placed great emphasis on marriage and, more significantly, on a large family. Between 1940 and 1960 the birth rate for third children more than doubled, for fourth children almost tripled, for fifth children more than doubled, for sixth and seventh children increased by half. Again in Jesse Bernard's words: "For women the change in values [the new attitude toward the feminine role at the beginning of World War II] was to mean a headlong flight into maternity. Whether they wanted babies or not, they felt they should want them. Even motion picture actresses who had once kept their motherhood secret now flaunted their pregnancies. . . . The woman who had four babies could patronize the women who had only three, and the woman with five or six could condescend to the women with four."[10]

"The mania for reproduction" affected the entry of women into all professional fields. If it was difficult to pursue a career and raise one or two children it was that much more difficult to combine a career with four or five. Earlier, able and energetic women who desired a career preferred, if they could not find a husband sympathetic to their ambitions, to remain single. Now they preferred to give up the career rather than go without husband and children, but the matter was clearly more complicated. For one thing, middle-class women had been spurred on to prepare for careers by the chronic economic insecurity of the nineteenth century. Many were haunted by the specter of poverty should a father or husband die, or, indeed, should they fail to marry at all. In this atmosphere, the ablest women sought to protect themselves against penury by earning professional degrees. They were constantly reminded that there were more women than men and that their chances of finding a suitable mate were thus lessened. In addition, the prospects of marriage were decreased for women with strong feminist sentiments. They must find husbands with similar views about feminine equality or else abandon their own principles.

Above all, there was the stimulus and excitement of being a pioneer. A woman who became a doctor or a lawyer or a minister or professor, while she might be viewed as a freak by many traditional-minded men and women, enjoyed enormous prestige among the constantly growing company of women sympathetic to the campaign for woman's rights.

The increasing economic stability of the twentieth century (excepting of course the decade of the 1930's); the appearance on the American scene of retirement benefits and old age security, lessening the fear of poverty in old age; the increase in life insurance coverage; the improved chances of the appropriate marriages due to more enlightened attitudes on the part of men and the better ratio of men to women at the marrying age; the rise in pay for the work women could do, if necessary, without professional training — all these combined to lower the purely economic incentive to a career. On what we might call the psychological side, the ease of divorce and the increasing tolerance of it was also very important. Marriage did not appear for bright and well-educated women such a dubious alternative to a career.

With the thrill of pioneering gone, the labors and hardships involved in professional training loomed larger and larger. The most serious deterrent of all, however, was the increasing rigor and constantly extended period of time required to gain professional authentication. This alone would have been enough to discourage all but the most determined. A recent study shows that on the average, seven years are required to win a Ph.D. in most academic fields. Moreover, much of the training is tedious and irrelevant having more to do with some kind of professional mystique than with genuine intellectual or scholarly achievement. The rule seems to read "the more mediocre the quality of the degree and the larger the number of persons who need it for purposes of employment the longer it takes to get it, and the more disheartening the whole process becomes." This is true of carpenters and electricians as well as of professors and doctors. Few women are prepared to spend seven years beyond their undergraduate college careers earning a degree that they are practical enough to know they may never use. Since an unsuccessful marriage can be escaped from and indeed can be used, through alimony, to finance an independent life, there is every reason to get married rather than to go through the interminable routine of acquiring an advanced degree. Since undergraduate education has become less and less truly liberal education and more and more a specialized preprofessional training, women, coming into undergraduate institutions in ever increasing numbers, have found themselves in a cruel dilemma. Clearly as bright, and often brighter than their male classmates, they are subjected to a training (one can again hardly call it an education) fashioned for the special needs of men while they themselves have less and less incentive to go the long and tedious route to professional careers. This would be a relatively minor problem if it were not for the unhappiness and frustration produced in the women concerned, and for the fact that their intelligence and energy are, in consequence, largely unavailable to a world which very much needs those qualities. In a society where everyone is authenticated by a "degree" (and increasingly by an "advanced degree") those without them are severely limited in finding tasks commensurate with their abilities (the authentications are in any event, largely irrelevant to the talents they purport to verify).

Another factor which should be mentioned is less tangible but not less important. Marxist countries have a positive ideological stand on the role of women. As we have seen, Marx and Lenin adopted Bachofen's thesis that the fall from a matriarchal society to a patriarchal one was a fall into competitive male society where "woman right" was ruthlessly subordinated. In a true Marxist society, women, like labor, would cease to be an exploited class and enjoy full equality with men (a consequence of this dogma was the launching of a female astronaut into space by the Russians). Communist states have thus taken very specific steps to facilitate the professional training of able women, viewing them as a valuable resource for the state. Whatever it is that we call capitalism has no such specific ideological position on the role of women in our society. Capitalism is, indeed, very vulnerable to the charge that it uses sex as a commercial product and that its interest in women centers on the opportunity to exploit them as a sexual commodity. Such a view is, of course, ridiculous in the sense that capitalism does not exist as a coherent body of doctrine about anything. But that loose and highly complex system of more or less independent industrial and commercial activity has nonetheless proved remarkably successful in subordinating human values to monetary ones; women, embodying sex, are plainly a commodity.

On the side of "psychological" rather than practical deterrents to women's entry into the professions we must place the most depressing fact of all. A respondent in a study of "educated women" in American society, believes that "intellectual ability, professional skills, and ambition in women is treated with envy, distrust, scorn and outright hatred by many men." It can be said with some assurance that a woman who enters medical school today encounters more resistance from her fellow students than Elizabeth Blackwell did when she enrolled at Geneva College in the 1840's.[11]

This complaint runs as a steady undercurrent in the comments of

career women: "The major problem with which intelligent and educated women must contend is vain and pretentious men," says a
woman lawyer. The authors conclude: "The fact that a college girl
understands that her life in the decades ahead will be largely determined by a man she has not yet met and children she has not had does
not enable her to plan soundly for the specific contingencies she will
meet in the years ahead." Whether or not she is able to marry and
carry on a career will depend almost entirely on the attitude of the
man she marries.[12]

What is equally depressing is that women who embark on careers
encounter almost as much resistance from members of their own sex
as they do from men. Under such circumstances it is hardly surprising
if some career women become strident or defensive.

In America the various professions have tended to a monolithic
character. Thus in England you have only a handful of professor-
ships, supplemented by tutors, readers, lecturers, etc., who in fact
make up the great majority of academics. In America, professors of
various ranks, all of whom expect to be regularly promoted, make up
by far the larger proportion of academics. Similarly, in England there
are various grades in the legal profession — barristers, attorneys, and
solicitors. In America all are lawyers but again, of course, with a very
high degree of specialization. Much the same may be said for the
medical profession in Russia and architecture in Italy. The at least
potential advantage to women of such distinctions as obtain in English law or in Russian medicine is that professional training can be
geared to the actual function that will be performed by the individual. Thus it can be shorter and more specialized. The fact that
American professions are gathered under a single title is almost certainly due to our democratic ethos which wishes to confer on every
practitioner an equally respectable title. However, by requiring all
"lawyers" to master a standardized law curriculum the period of legal
training is inevitably prolonged. The same is true in the extended
training of psychiatrists who have to take a conventional medical
degree *before* they may begin their psychiatric training. The question
here is not whether the greatly extended, enormously expensive (and
probably very wasteful — in human terms and in money) American
system of professional training is a "better" system but that it works
to the great disadvantage of women with professional interests. It is

not too much, I think, to say that it is the single most important
deterrent to the entry of women in large numbers into the various
professional fields, especially medicine where it is generally observed
that they have a special gift in pediatrics, obstetrics, and general
practice.

If we followed the argument of Lundberg and Farnham we might
be inclined to say that women, having finally gained the most important right of all — the right to the orgasm — simply retired to the
home to enjoy it. But this would hardly account for the large size of
middle-class families. After all, contraception had been acclaimed as
offering wives a way to enjoy sexual intercourse without the nagging
fear of pregnancy. Middle-class women clearly had children because
they wanted them or because they did not sufficiently care about *not
having them* to take the by now fairly simple precautions necessary to
prevent conception. At the same time it must be kept in mind that the
women who, in a sense, retreated into domesticity did so on entirely
new terms. The actual situation of the wife who never had the slightest interest in suffrage or emancipation was greatly changed by the
simple fact that a few thousand women had become lawyers, doctors,
missionaries, or professors. Her husband could never look at her,
simple and doll-like as she seemed, without the uneasy suspicion she
might herself contain a hidden lawyer or business executive. Certainly
he could never think of her the way his grandfather had thought of
his wife, as a delicate, spiritual creature too fragile for the hard
knocks of the world, with a brain and a "nervous organization"
radically inferior to his own.

The anxiety of women in the feminist tradition over the return of
the American wife to the home was clearly expressed in a collection
of essays entitled *American Women: The Changing Image.* In the
introduction, Margaret Mead reminded her female readers that they
are inheritors of a tradition which encouraged women to leave their
homes "to extend the services once performed within the home to the
wider world outside." How do women stand in relation to this tradition, she asked, and answered the rhetorical question: "We stand very
badly indeed." Most of the traditional duties of women such as bathing and preparing the dead, midwifery, and caring for the ill are in
the hands of professionals, most of them males. "Dedicating one's
life to God or human welfare is becoming steadily more unpopular,

the teaching and nursing orders depend upon bringing in women from the less sophisticated parts of the world. . . . The care of the infirm old has been put as far outside the home as possible and delegated to institutions in which gadgets replace tenderness and the television set the friendly personal voice. Meanwhile some 500,000 surplus older women, many of them with more than adequate means are not extending their activities on behalf of mankind, but shrinking them to the preservation of their own private, and often boring existences. Neither their fortunes, nor their hearts nor their imaginations are placed at the service of the wider world. . . . If, after the children are grown, women look for some greater meaning in life, their eyes are turned towards a hobby, self-fulfillment, seldom towards activities on behalf of the larger community."[13] Margaret Mead speaks scornfully of this "retreat into fecundity" encouraged by a self-centered attitude which is "stifling the ethical life of the nation." As long as women "in desperate cave-women style, devote their whole lives to narrow domesticity, first in schoolgirl dreaming and searching for roles which make them appealingly ignorant, then as mothers and then as grandmothers, our scientific activity will remain one-sided, with an overemphasis on power, and an underemphasis on human values."[14]

Agnes Meyer, writing in the same vein, deplores the failure of college girls especially to undertake careers of service. "In former days women went to college to develop their minds and personalities. Today many of them frankly go to coeducational institutions of learning to find a husband as early as possible. This is a frivolous attitude at a time when our nation is threatened with destruction unless we develop more highly skilled people and more leadership. . . ." She finds young women "profoundly influenced by the overemphasis on sex now so prevalent in our whole culture."[15]

Why the Great Withdrawal? One is tempted to a too easy quasi-Freudian explanation: much of the remarkable energy and reforming zeal displayed by American women from the early decades of the nineteenth century to the early decades of the twentieth was the consequence of repressed sexual drives; when these drives were no longer repressed, the reforming zeal evaporated. There is undoubtedly something in this proposition but not much. Two profoundly important historic events influenced the Great Withdrawal: (1) The passage in

1919 of the Eighteenth Amendment, prohibiting the sale of intoxicating liquors (it went into effect in 1920), and (2) the almost simultaneous passage of the Nineteenth Amendment giving the suffrage, at long last, to women. Certain practical consequences followed: two of the most powerful and important women's organizations — the Woman's Christian Temperance Union and the American Woman's Suffrage Association which, to be sure had been on the decline for a decade or more, with their objectives attained — virtually dwindled away.

The collapse of the Great Experiment was thoroughly demoralizing to hundreds of thousands of reform-minded women. Nine years after the passage of the Eighteenth and Nineteenth Amendments the Great Depression struck the country. Instead of the new era so devoutly hoped for, the country was plunged into one of the worst crises in its history. Every significant movement of women into professional areas had taken place in periods of prosperity. The prolonged depression destroyed the "economic margin" and every important extension of their rights which was so essential to women's entry into masculine fields. When there were few jobs they must go to the primary breadwinner in the family — the man. When there was little money it must be used to educate the prospective breadwinner, the boy rather than the girl. The corrosive anxieties about making a living distracted attention from reform activities of all kinds. The economic and social crisis was so severe that private charity (with shrinking funds) could no longer make any pretense of coping with it and the government moved in on a massive scale to establish the basic framework of the welfare state.

In addition, the passage of the Eighteenth and Nineteenth Amendments marked the virtual end of the Protestant passion and the beginning of the Age of Personal Fulfillment; the end of the Protestant ethic (thrift, piety, and hard work) and the rise of the Ethic of Cheerful Consumption (consume, consume, consume). Social theorists decided that the era of reform was over. They no longer called for a reform of American society in obedience to the teachings of Jesus Christ. Where authority was invoked it was more apt to be that of Karl Marx than the Nazarene. Tinkering with the decrepit machinery of capitalism could only briefly prolong the life of a creaky and clearly disintegrating system. Revolution not reform was the order of the day and revolution is by and large antithetical to the feminine temperament.

World War II which brought an expensive end to the depression, created an instant job market. Women poured into it. The desperate austerity of those years was at last over. Patriotism was reinforced by the exhilarating experience of making money. There was no time to undertake extended professional training. Hands were needed in every industry to replace men called up by the draft and to expand production. Middle-class girls who several decades earlier might have dreamed of professional careers took pride in operating a station on an assembly line making army tanks or bombers. On the domestic scene America experienced the war as a period of almost unparalleled prosperity, harbinger of the "good life." Children reared in the thirties (boys and girls alike) thought far more of getting a job than of the prolonged and arduous training required for a career at which one might, in any event, be unable to make a living.

So a mixture of factors, social, economic, psychological, produced by a series of events that followed on in rapid succession — the amendments of 1920, the Great Depression, and World War II — transformed almost every aspect of American life. Among the multitudinous changes that accompanied this transformation, none was more conspicuous or important than the change in the ideals and aspirations of American women.

The Nature of Women

Anyone who writes about women has to confront, sooner or later, the question of the "nature" of women. Few have gone as far as John Langdon-Davies in declaring that "man" and "woman" are simply relative terms and that in time all distinctions between the sexes will disappear; or Samuel Schmalhausen who hoped for alternating pregnancies so that men could experience the "white torment of parturition"; or Elisabeth Borgese with her scheme of sexual change from man to woman and then back again. But a considerable number of both men and women have argued that the apparent differences between men and women are "culturally" produced and not inherent. That is to say that women are taught by their man-dominated culture, and especially by their parents as the agents of that culture, to behave "like a woman." It is certainly true that the "nature" of women may not be part of the inalterable order of the universe — there apparently is little that is — and we have observed enough change in that nature and enough misapprehensions about it to approach the issue with some caution.

Virtually all men and most women in the nineteenth century were confident that they understood very well the nature of women. Alexander Walker who in 1840 wrote a work entitled, rather ambitiously, *Woman Physiologically Considered as to Mind, Morals, Marriage,*

Matrimonial Slavery, Infidelity and Divorce, put forward the view that "nature, for the preservation of the human species, has conferred on woman a sacred character, to which man naturally and irresistibly pays homage, to which he renders a true worship." Nature has given to woman "prompt and infallible instinct as a guide to all her gentle thoughts, her charming words, and her beneficent actions, while man has only slow and often erring reason to guide his cold and calculated conduct."

But what Walker gave with one hand he withdrew with the other. From the physical nature of woman, "and the varying states of her vital system, result woman's incapability for reasoning — generalizing, forming trains of connected ideas, judging, persevering. . . ." Moreover, "great mental exertion is injurious to her. . . . Her friendship, her philanthropy, her patriotism and her politics, requiring the exercise of reason, are so feeble as to be worthless."[1] So in effect she should stay home and mind her own business.

It just may be possible that what we think of as characteristically feminine is after all the consequence of cultural conditioning, of the fact that mothers persuade their daughters from infancy that there are certain ways of behavior, of response, of gesture, glance, and manner which are appropriate to the female and certain which are appropriate to the male. Obviously a great deal of such conditioning does go on. The question is whether the conditioning simply reinforces a profound biological and psychological difference or creates it; in other words if little girls were raised like little boys would they be as adults, certain biological differences aside, just like men? Some homosexuals show secondary female characteristics. Men have by hormone treatments and operations been turned into "women" and women have been turned, apparently, into "men," a transformation if anything even more inscrutable. Proponents of the "no difference" school always say "aside from certain gross physical differences." But of course there is no "aside from." The profound center of a woman's nature is the capacity to give birth. Even if she were in every other way like a man that single fact is so radical a difference that every other secondary sex characteristic could perfectly well flow from it and, in my opinion, does.

It may well be that all man's "creativity" is an effort to compensate for that archetypal creative act of the woman — birth. Freud believed

that women were obsessed with penis-envy, seeing man's genitals as a symbol of his power and dominance. By this time we know enough of the disturbed libidinal life of women in the nineteenth century to be ready to concede that this may well have been true *in the nineteenth century* but I see no reason to believe that such envy is a constant in woman's nature.

It is logical to assume that as women have emerged from their state of dependence and subordination, their envy of the penis, which is after all, in purely aesthetic terms, a rather poor object, has greatly diminished. I believe that I have observed the reverse: womb-envy in men, or at least envy of the woman's monopoly of the reproductive function. Certainly anyone who has seen a mother with her infant can hardly doubt that it is the primal act of creation and suspect that all of man's restless creativity is not entirely satisfactory compensation for it.

One of the leading feminists put the matter rather accurately if somewhat floridly. Beatrice Forbes-Robertson Hale wrote that women "have this enormous advantage over men as disciples of Eros, that the apotheosis of their love comes after mating, in the child, which is its symbol, and which demands service, tenderness and faith. Unhappily for men, they have little part in that miracle, so that for them all that follows on the supreme moment of mating is in the nature of an anticlimax. They can only serve love in one way, whereas women can give first love, then life, and then sustenance, three separate joys. . . . Women should pity men for this disability, realizing that as they give more, so they have more than men — that it is easier for them to win love's thorny crown."[2]

In order to talk about the nature of women it is, of course, necessary to say something about the nature of man and since the differences between the sexes are the consequence in very large part of their different sex functions we must start with these. It has, for instance, been generally observed that men are inherently promiscuous and woman monogamous. In the animal world the male's willingness, in most species, to mate promiscuously serves a very useful function by guaranteeing the impregnation of the maximum number of females, a necessary aspect of herd life where females often outnumber males. In primitive human society male promiscuity was also undoubtedly an asset although it is not unlikely that "bonding" or some primitive form of marriage existed in a very early stage of human development. It may well be the case that masculine promiscuity developed as a consequence of the effort to cope with feminine sexuality.

We have seen that in early societies women's basic functions were separated which made promiscuity, in the modern sense of the word, inevitable. In order for man to be properly promiscuous, he must have a generalized sexual drive; that is to say he must be excited by the idea of sex activity in and of itself. This means a highly developed sexual fantasy life, in a large degree abstract, and it may well be this capacity to abstract sexual experience, in a sense, from a particular partner which is the beginning of that richly expressive imaginative (or fantasy) life which lies at the root of most masculine creativity. In the words of Ortega y Gasset: "Nine-tenths of that which is attributed to sexuality is the work of our magnificent ability to imagine, which is no longer an instinct, but exactly the opposite: a creation." Certainly in modern times sexual fantasies loom far larger in the imaginations of males than of females. Women dream of homes and children, of handsome and devoted, and above all, faithful lovers; men enjoy fantasies of wildly seductive females in marvelous profusion, i.e., of the procession of voluptuous dames that parade through *Playboy*.

Much of man's sex is in his mind, while woman's is more centrally located. Pornography is thus a preeminently masculine invention. There is no feminine counterpart of the "girlie" magazines and related materials which constitute a billion-dollar business in the United States, nor do women write "hard core" pornography. In recent years magazines featuring nude males have appeared on newsstands but these are primarily for the homosexual trade. Women find relatively little sexual stimulus in erotic pictures, descriptions or objects. The reverse is true with men. They are highly susceptible to every kind of erotic fetish, and their fantasies exist apart from their physiological capacity to satisfy them in any normal way. Portions of the female body have the power to excite them and this excitement is transferable, so to speak. It need not be directed at the object which caused the arousal.

Women can and do exploit this susceptibility. A man can be sexually excited by a glance from a woman, quite clearly by the way she dresses and even her smell (and it might be said, parenthetically, that the consciously seductive dress of girls and women imposes a strain on the masculine psyche primarily because it promises so much and delivers so little. Women persistently dress like sexual objects but expect to be treated more or less like ladies). Yet a woman's sexual experience may be more intense than a man's and she is capable, as a man is not, of a prolonged orgasm. In man's attitude toward woman's sexual experience there is thus a touch of envy and astonishment.

Autoeroticism or, more plainly, masturbation is a peculiarly though by no means exclusively masculine involvement. It is related to man's ability to fantasize his sex life. Although figures are difficult to procure, the creation and distribution of pornography (that is, material without redeeming social importance intended to stimulate sexual desire) in the United States has become a billion-dollar industry. Millions upon millions of pornographic books, magazines, films, and pictures are turned out every year. Millions of men buy this material and it seems safe to say that the sexual fantasies aroused by this torrent of dreary erotica are not expressed in normal heterosexual relationships but in masturbation. Masturbation, which need involve no one else, is perhaps the classic form of sexual release in an impersonalized but sex-saturated society. Even if we were to assume that the result of this stimulation were heterosexual contacts, it would be disconcerting to discover that such stimulation was desired or necessary.

Modern man, despite his considerable ingenuity did not, of course, invent autoeroticism. But it is unlikely that it was a major element in the total sexual experience of nineteenth-century males for two reasons. The first was that prostitutes were readily and reasonably available. The other was that from an early age boys were warned against the terrible dangers of masturbation. Dr. E. C. Abbey's book on *The Sexual System and Its Derangements* represented the attitude of the time very well when he described the consequences of masturbation. It would, boys were warned, destroy an immature power and prevent them from being sexually potent upon reaching manhood. It would also produce nervousness, languor, "tiresome feelings," despondency, unfitness for business, unsociability, cowardice, bashfulness, irritable temper, lack of confidence, unfixedness of purpose, broken sleep, trembling dizziness, staggering, soft muscles, weak back, pasty skin, hollow eyes, blunted senses, eruptions, scanty beard, and, ultimately, such ailments as epilepsy, palsy, idiocy, insanity, and nervous break-down.[3] Such prospects were surely a severe deterrent.

In addition, there was much less direct sexual stimulus. Porno-graphic books, pictures, and drawings certainly existed and in small towns were vended by enterprising youths, but they were not avail-able at every drugstore and newsstand. Of course, it is also true that a Victorian male might be as aroused sexually by the sight of an ankle or calf as a modern youth by a topless go-go girl (perhaps more). But the typical sexual outlet for nineteenth-century males was plainly through prostitutes. Today, when prostitution has greatly diminished it would seem likely that masturbation is by far the most common sexual outlet outside of marriage (and perhaps a more common one within than is generally thought). Thus the amount of money spent in the United States in a year for material inducing a state of sexual stimulation, typically relieved by autoeroticism, may be not entirely disproportionate to the money spent on prostitutes in a particular year of the mid- or late-nineteenth century. Moreover, this amount of masculine sexual activity over and above heterosexual experiences is certainly a measure of the fantasy life of men.

A great part of man's erotic reaction, then, is highly imaginative, fantasized and inclined in consequence to be general. While he may be devotedly monogamous, usually at some cost, he is very aware of a wide variety of sexual stimuli; for example he constantly "looks at other women." And women of course are tempted to exploit this masculine reaction.

The sexual response of women is more practical, direct, specific, and intense. These very basic differences color, in decisive ways, the respective life experiences of men and women. I would like to discuss in the remainder of this chapter some of the "secondary" sexual characteristics of women and their significance for the race.

The breast is the most powerful erotic object in the world; it is also the original source of food and the symbol of a woman's function as the feeder. The fact that the feeding of the infant is such a sensually and psychologically satisfying experience for the mother must surely be closely related to her classic function as the feeder of the race. Charlotte Perkins Gilman very shrewdly observed the relation be-

tween sex and food and inveighed against "the unnatural race between artifice and appetite" and "the Cupid-in-the-kitchen." The fact
is that they are quite natural; a woman's cooking and a man's eating
have an erotic undertone. How many cinematic seductions have begun
with a candlelit meal!

But while women may be great cooks, very few are great chefs. A
woman's cooking is personal. She cooks for those she loves and
wishes to nurture; her cooking is thus sacramental. The famous chef
is a culinary artist which is something quite different. He takes pride
in the food per se and is able to detach it from the eater.

The woman is the comforter — "the shelterer, the nourisher, the
life-giver . . . the medicine woman, the potter of cosmic vessels, the
spinner of the threads of life . . ." — above all the primal source of
consolation.[4] The breast is the feeder, the comforter, the mandala as
well as the erotic object, and hence the symbol of woman's ambiguity.
What is ambiguous is dangerous — "Next to the wound, what
women make best is the bandage" — they hurt and heal. It has always
been man's temptation to render them powerless to hurt, while having them available to heal.

Erik Erikson has rediscovered the "life cycle." Earlier generations
have, typically, seen life as extending from "cradle to grave," each
age with its own particular duties and pleasures. We have largely lost
that understanding. There were functions and opportunities appropriate to each age (I have before me a typical admonitory and instructive volume of the late nineteenth century: *Woman's Work and
Worth in Girlhood, Maidenhood & Wifehood*). Little girls were
little girls, not precocious vamps or nymphettes, "maidens" were
girls, ideally at least, in training for and anticipation of "wifehood"
and "motherhood." Courtship preceded marriage and performed the
essential role of dramatizing the approaching union of a boy and a
girl, representing the transformation into man and woman, of two
young people, ready to enter history as father and mother.

The marriage ceremony summons all the powers of heaven and
earth to fortify and support this strange venture on which two frightened and uncertain people embark. Adorning the bride is the primal
act of art. The bridesmaids offer their own at least theoretical virgin-
ity in testimony to the great event, to the putting off of girlhood and

the taking on of womanhood. They represent the company which the bride is leaving, as the married guests and the respective parents represent the world into which she is entering.

The girl who wishes the pleasures of marriage without entering the institution of marriage makes marriage unimportant (and often, when it comes, unsuccessful). The wife who wishes to still be a girl, "kidding with the fellows at the office," rejecting the dignity of a married woman, demeans herself.

One of the particular losses women have experienced in America is in their function as grandmother. As late as the nineteenth century the grandmother was deemed to have an essential role in the nurture of her grandchildren; she was a living repository of traditional wisdom, of painfully accumulated experience that touched every aspect of domestic existence. She knew how to limit the size of family by contraceptive techniques, how to make bread rise, or remove warts, when to plant potatoes and when to wean an infant. Most important, the grandmother mediated the child to its parents. The relation of parents to child is an intense and often emotion-charged one; the grandmother was an intermediary. She had *time;* time that a busy mother or harassed father did not have, and her time spans coincided with the child's. Her stories of the child's parents' childhood made the parents understandably human for the child, gave them a stronger reality as people whose lives had a depth and texture not readily revealed in day-to-day relations within the family. It is always an enthralling experience for a child to discover the childhood of its parents.

Many of the tensions of the modern "nuclear" family are the consequence of the absence of this traditional mediator, the grandmother. And grandmothers, tolerated and endured, must often find a quarter of a century of busy work to hold off, as best they may, feelings of futility. Old-fashioned, outmoded, obsolete, they have, thanks to geriatrics, the dubious blessing of a long life. Children in consequence have no sense of old age as anything but unplanned obsolescence. The whole dimension of old age, a classic life experience of earlier generations of the race, is missing for modern children. How are they to know what growing old means if they see no old people except out of context as pathetic misfits in a culture where only the new and young are prized or thought to be relevant? Old people become childish in seeking to remain young.

America, I believe, needs grandmothers more than Indians. We need them for our souls' sakes and for theirs. We cannot continue to write off a quarter of our population and remain a viable society. Most of us, after all, will be old much longer than we are young. If we consider that the life expectancy of women today is in the neighborhood of seventy-five years, that "youth" might be said to last somewhat more than a decade — from fourteen or fifteen to the late twenties — and that we qualify as "senior citizens" after fifty or fifty-five, it is plain enough that we all have a vested interest in the fate of the aging and aged. Unless women respect this order — childhood, girlhood, wifehood, motherhood, and grandmotherhood — they will end up frustrated and unhappy wayfarers in the valley of the dolls.

As in the fairy story, love is capable of conquering all, if only people could learn to love. There is an extraordinary range in successful marriages. They transcend differences of race, class, nationality, religion, potency, education, temperament, illness, age, and most difficult of all, the differences of sex. Marriages between two people who seem, on the surface, ideally compatible, frequently fail while those between a man and wife of the most diverse possible backgrounds quite as frequently succeed. Indeed, it may well be that those marriages are often most successful in which the partners, aware of a wide difference in background, make from the beginning a particular effort to encompass each other's "otherness." This difference is a symbol of that deeper difference of the sexes, the reconciling of which is the model for all reconciliations.

Sexual adventures outside of marriage are certainly a betrayal of the most intimate commitment that two human beings can make to each other and it is absurd to pretend otherwise. If the sexual encounter is treated as something with a validity "in itself," something that exists as an independent value, like a fine wine that two congenial people may share, rather than as the ultimate commitment of two people to each other and, potentially at least, to the future of the race, then it is increasingly difficult to confine it to the marriage relationship. If intercourse is simply a way of "identifying," "relating," "empathizing," and all the other cant words of our time, it can be treated as of no more consequence than an affectionate handclasp or friendly embrace. But I believe the matter is very different. We dare not detach sexual relations from the particular context of the monogamous marriage, actual or prospective.

I have discussed the roles of mother and grandmother. We might focus here primarily on the woman as wife. Husbands tease wives about female characteristics which, while insignificant in themselves and often emphasized with an air of affectionate condescension, nonetheless contain important clues to their function in the great enterprise of history. Thus a woman's ability to remember the birth dates of the three children of a school mate or what she had for dinner twelve years ago at the Thompsons' are pointed out as amusing examples of the trivialities with which women concern themselves. Actually, the memory of such details is the mark of woman's historical sense, her feeling for the importance of the specific if minor details of life, details upon which civilized existence is based. It seems to the husband simply amusing that his wife should recall such things while his mind is on important matters of a business deal or a promotion. The remembered birthday is a symbol of the woman's concern for the occasions and ceremonies of life. That she remembers allows the husband to forget. Because she devotes herself to conserving what must be conserved of the past, he is free to be concerned about the future. Birthdays are, in any event, more important in the eternal scheme of things than promotions.

Women are unforgiving to anyone who has offended someone towards whom they feel love and affection. She: "I wouldn't have so-and-so set foot in this house after what he said about you." "What did he say?" "He said you were an incompetent fool." "But that was ten years ago. He was nervous and upset." "I don't care. I won't have him in my house." First of all, the wife remembers. And then her loyalty, which is one of her strongest traits is touched, and, finally, her task is to uphold standards. She is unforgiving of stupidity or meanness and intolerant of evil. She at once is too practical and too principled to be casual about or indifferent to wickedness. With her devotion to principle and fairness she has, at the same time, no sense of honor. Honor is a masculine concept which seems simply silly to a woman's practicality. She is used to fighting with all the weapons at her disposal and the notion that it is dishonorable to use certain ones is, in her view, childish. Honor is a masculine luxury. The same thing, I fear, must be said about honesty, that offspring of honor. Women are fearful liars though it must be said that the lying is often to protect some precious kernel of truth and life, someone's pride or self-esteem or, more simply to avoid an unpleasant scene.

Homemaker and wife-of-the-house are rather old-fashioned and opprobrious terms. Much of the discontent of middle-class women seems to be related to the notion that men go off and do something challenging whereas women "just stay home and take care of the children."*

The problem with all such discussions of men's versus women's spheres is that the cards are invariably stacked: fascinating job as opposed to prison-like home. On the other hand we have a large body of literature which describes the terrible boredom and sterility of most masculine jobs. If masculine jobs are so great, one is tempted to ask, who has them?

Women are "bountiful"; they are the world's greatest creators of surplus, of an unearned increment, and whoever has experienced this bounty cannot doubt its reality; the margin between existence and life is, in large part, the consequence of women doing more than is necessary. Necessity is the mother of masculine invention: prodigality is the offspring of the feminine mystique. This indeed is close to the proper definition of grace — that which cannot be bought or earned but which is freely given and so given is the means to the soul's salvation; we exist by the necessary and live by the unnecessary.†

Women are "private," men are "public." A woman's life turns inward. Her "internality," her privateness, is symbolized if not directly related to the fact that her sex organs and above all, her womb,

* One is reminded of H. L. Mencken's description of man's "mental equipment" as "that mass of small intellectual tricks, that complex of petty knowledges, that collection of cerebral rubber stamps." It was Mencken's cynical opinion that the very capacity of men "to master and retain such balderdash" as that required to run a business or pursue a profession was the best proof of their "mental inferiority" to women.

† This feminine "bountifulness" has, in American society, a particular institutional manifestation — the charitable foundation. There are eight thousand foundations in the United States. The classic American impulse to endow, to bestow a dowry, has fallen not so much on daughters but on eleemosynary foundations designed to improve some aspect of individual or social life. They are an almost uniquely American phenomenon and in a real sense they embody daughterhood. The endowing of daughters is extended through them to the endowing of society as a whole.

are interior. Man's external organs symbolize his "externality," his outwardness, his "publicness." He must be authenticated by an audience, listeners, critics, acclaimers, otherwise he has, ultimately, no power to sustain his creativity. A woman can go on creating for a lifetime for her own private pleasure. Her acts are thus much "purer," the symbols of her bountifulness. It seems most likely that the greater part of what women have done, the poems they have written, the pictures they have painted, the music they have composed, has simply been lost to history because it was not essential to them to receive "public verification." Emily Dickinson is, of course, a classic example; she wrote extraordinary poetry all her life without any substantial recognition. If she had not had a devoted amanuensis, if her papers had been burned or destroyed, one of the most remarkable poetic talents in literature would never have been known. It is fruitless to speculate on the lost Emily Dickinsons of history but it is very difficult not to believe many have existed in all fields of the arts; perhaps the vast majority of them would be rated minor figures if their work was known but there must have been a respectable number whose work was very nearly of the highest order.

But the point I would come back to is that women (or perhaps I should say uncorrupted women) generally speaking do things for their pleasure and the pleasure of those they love; men seek fame and are thus far more ambitious and competitive. To be public means certainly to be competitive and while this competitiveness undoubtedly very often improves the quality of the work done, it makes men much more susceptible to fads and fashions. If they are to gain recognition they must work in the currently fashionable style. Women are free to work as they wish, though by this very fact they are less apt to gain widespread recognition. If Emily Dickinson had felt impelled to be published she would have had to write what the critics of her era considered "poetry." If she had done so she would not have been Emily Dickinson.

A woman "is"; a man is always in the process of becoming, and this latter process as we have suggested elsewhere is a much more precarious one; hence the need for support, admiration, authentication. A man wishes an audience of millions, a woman will create for one man she loves.

Take the environment that an aesthetically sensitive woman creates, most typically a home. It is notably private. It cannot be packaged, reproduced, displayed, sold over the counter or in any substantial way commercialized. Yet it may be a higher form of "art" than much of what passes under that name. Certainly the psyches of those relatively few individuals for whom it constitutes a major part of their environment are much more deeply affected by it than they could be by most formal works of art.

Women are cosmopolitan and metropolitan; and the sense of international sisterhood is, in practical fact, stronger than that of brotherhood. A white American woman for instance feels a greater affinity with her African counterpart than does an American male for *his* African counterpart. Women everywhere are bound together by a sense of common cause, and by that subtle but unmistakable flow of sympathy that indeed makes all women sisters. The primary functions — feeding and child-bearing — are both more basic and more universal than the roles or functions of men from different races and cultures. Men are parochial and national. Women are international. They marry into other races and nationalities more readily than men do and transfer their national allegiance much more freely. It is a rare American male who will marry a French, English, or Japanese woman and settle successfully in his wife's native land. It is not at all uncommon however, for a woman to marry a man of another country or culture and settle quite happily into the ways of her adopted homeland. Women are, at the same time, more place-oriented, more bound to a particular locality. Conversely, they are strongly attracted to the city as opposed to the village or town. While they have far more influence in the town than in the city, while the city is much more clearly man-created and middle-class-dominated, women almost invariably prefer the metropolis to the commune. Men are better able to cope with the isolation of rural life, women feel more keenly the absence of friends and neighbors. The frontiersman who picked up stakes and moved further west when another family moved into his valley always carried with him a lonely and reluctant wife. A zoologist recently pointed out that certain "wild" animals thrive in quite thickly populated rural areas; such animals, most typically deer, according to our zoologist, like a "disturbed environment." Without, in any sense, comparing women to wild animals, it seems rather as though they, too, are attracted by the "disturbed environment" of big cities. Most men who have grown up in small communities and who have, in order to make a living, to reside in a city or suburb, yearn for the warmth and intimacy of the town of their childhood. I have, literally, never talked to a woman from a small town who felt any nostalgia for the town, or at least enough to wish for a moment to return, although I do not doubt that there are ladies of such sentiments. We are inclined to think of rural or small town life as ideally suited to the feminine temperament while the noisy, impersonal, crowded, dirty life of the city would seem thoroughly uncongenial to the female psyche. One answer may be that the sense of community is more important for a man than a woman. She wants neighbors, but despite her involvement in community life and activities, "the small community" has little attraction for her and the rural scene even less (one writer has noted that all books extolling the simple life are written by men).

The primary concern of women is with order; the primary concern of men is with disorder, disorder not simply in the form of war and strife, but disorder in the form of change and revolution. For a man to be excessively preoccupied with order is to be compulsively (or repulsively) neat. For a man to be sloppy and a woman neat, seems to us quite natural. It is a classic source of domestic friction. The wife is typically after her husband to put the caps back on the toothpaste, to pick up his socks, hang up his coat, etc., etc. That is manageable and it is safe to say that few marriages break up on these grounds alone. But for the wife to be untidy and the husband neat is quite another matter (this turnabout is unfortunately quite common in our society due, we are told, to bad toilet training which produces a high percentage of anal men) and it is almost invariably disastrous.

Women perform routine tasks better than men. A housewife may become frustrated and periodically despairing over the interminable routines of household work — endless dishes and clothes to wash, floors to sweep, meals to prepare — but she is far better able to cope with such repetitious jobs than the male. (It has been suggested that her constant physical change represented in her menstrual cycle accounts in part for her ability to transcend routines.) As far as the home is concerned it is a kind of model of the order in the external world. Therefore, in "ordering" the home, as in giving birth to children, the woman is performing one of the most potent symbolic acts in all human experience. The home is a means of grace because it is an arena where much may be done with love, and by this "loving order" which a woman creates, all life is enhanced. Detached from this order or turned out from it most men are poor lost souls, exiled from the garden. This fact helps to explain their low tolerance for divorce. In divorce actions the wife not only gets the children, *she gets the home as well.* A bachelor apartment is more apt to resemble one of the stages of hell than the gleaming pads of *Playboy*'s heroes.

All our higher life is built on a foundation of routine. Large areas must be routinized so that other areas can be free. We perform the tedious routine of learning a foreign language so that we may be liberated from the limitations of a single language and enter a world of wider potentialities. The notion then, that routines are at all costs to be avoided is hopelessly superficial and condemns those who subscribe to it to lives of aimlessness and futility. As true as it is that routines have to be transcended, it is equally true that they have to exist in order to be transcended. The household routines of women have in them a profound source of consolation in their symbolically "ordering" character.

In addition women protect a substantial center of life which makes possible man's action in the world. Women create an intimate order which men usually are powerless to effect and which is essential to all larger (though not necessarily more important) orders.

The ordering of life begins in the home and in a sense justice (which is one of the important forms of order in the world) grows out of it. Antigone is determined to bury her brother in the face of all man-made laws or kingly edicts because the proper order of the world depends on his having a decent burial. This is the source of justice, as opposed to arbitrariness, and of the notion of a "higher order." Against all the disorder of life, this basic order must be constantly reasserted. The home is its paradigm, the wife its votary, the guardian of its rites.*

The woman is repetitious in order that the man may be innovative, but the repetition, while it may contain a very considerable amount of

---

* Novalis wrote: "Whenever there is a group of young people there is a republic. With marriage the system changes. Married couples want order, safety, peace and quiet; they wish to live as a family in a family, as an orderly household; they seek for a genuine monarchy," — also, "the state is not founded upon single individuals, but upon couples and groups."

the dull and monotonous, is susceptible to infinite variation. Every vase of flowers is a fresh episode, every meal, every new touch of beauty is a kind of parable on the inexhaustible richness of the commonplace. It is the wearying routines of business and professional work that are often most truly stultifying. What may be needed is an existential philosophy of the home.

There is a sense of course in which women view most of men's frenetic activity as a kind of play. "From the greater part of men's acts," Beatrice Forbes-Robertson Hale wrote, "the deep soul of women stands aloof with a puzzled tolerance, as a mother watches the ingenuous make-believe of her little son. . . . To women it seems that men play with life."[5] It is the game and not the prize that captivates them. It is the particular function of women, on the other hand, to create happiness and most of the happiness a man knows is the gift of a happy woman. Women by the sensuous intensity with which they live in the moment, may teach the restlessly aspiring male the renewing pleasures of living a day at a time, of celebrating those things which are humble or useless. In such ways, in a happy vivifying uselessness, a woman can save a man's soul and sanity.

Against all those things that must be done over again forever, the daily renewal of life, are those things which must be done for the first time. Man can only have the stamina to do this terrifying "for-the-first-time" if he has experienced the order and renewal that are the unique qualities of woman. Women will have to relearn this and teach it to men. Spengler said "women are history, men make history," by which I understand him to have meant that women represent the continuity of generations, the ongoing of life, while men take action *in* history. This is one of the most basic rhythms of our existence.

One should perhaps also speak of the corruptibility of women. A woman is most often corrupted by a man. On the other hand, she can do corrupting things (or at least things that for a man would be corrupting, like marrying for money) without herself being corrupted. Having married a man she does not love in order to avail herself of his money or to have financial security she may prove an unselfish and devoted wife. The tender-hearted and the reformed prostitute are real-life figures. There is a kind of moral resiliency in women that is much less apparent in men. Once on the "skids" a man seldom recovers his moral equilibrium. Moreover, his personality is more volatile. A new job, a new environment, a new wife can change a man's character almost beyond recognition. He may become pompous, arrogant, uneasy, and inept; he may discover new powers within himself or undertake tasks that, by revealing his limitations, shatter his ego beyond repair. Women while infinitely adaptable have a kind of solid center of character or personality which is usually formed by the time they are in their late teens. One can often see the grandmother in the face and temperament of the eighteen-year-old.* But the facade that conceals that core of fully-formed character is astonishingly changeable, various, and multiform. Aided by clothes, coiffures, and makeup, women can change their appearance in a most disconcerting way. This gives emphasis to the fact that women not only are never quite what they appear to be (or at least one can never count on it), but in fact consciously exploit this quality.

As G. K. Chesterton has put it: "Variability is one of the virtues of a woman. It obviates the crude requirement of polygamy. If you have one good wife you are sure to have a spiritual harem."[6] Even without the aid of cosmetics, the same woman can be homely or beautiful by turns. It has been often observed that happiness has the power to transform a homely woman into a beautiful one. Girls, or at least American girls, have a time between the ages of, roughly sixteen to twenty, when they are on the edge of womanhood, which is like the fragrance of a flower, a marvelous and transient perfume of the spirit, of boldness and delicacy. Carl Rogers compares their sexuality in this period to Sleeping Beauty, a charmed slumber before wakening. They are truly virginal in that their future lies before them in a form not yet disclosed. It is a future which has a particularly compelling character about it, a future not made, but, in a sense, awaited. The issue is simple enough but absolutely determinative: who is to be the father of their children? Sometime, somewhere between the ages, most generally, of sixteen and thirty the great majority of women will be married. This act will very largely determine their economic status, their happiness or unhappiness, the color of their children's eyes and hair, to a large degree their friends, and the whole quality of their lives. They have, at the beginning of their lives, to make their most

---

* "All women become like their mothers. That is their tragedy. No man does. That is his." Oscar Wilde, Auden and Kronenberger, 175.

important decision. A boy is engaged in a series of choices and decisions, which often go on most of his adult life, among these the choice of a wife is certainly of great importance but it is not nearly so crucial or so determinative as the woman's choice of a husband. The male has a far wider margin of error. He may marry a pretty, frivolous woman who will make a devoted wife and mother, provide him with a charming home and attend loyally to his every need. A woman may marry an appealing but inept male whose life is a series of small or large disasters and defeats through which she must suffer. The risks of course are not all on one side; a man may marry a selfish wife who may make him miserable. He may marry a woman who will give him no peace of mind; or an aggressive and competitive woman who will make him feel inadequate; or a petulant and dissatisfied one. But he has a career, a role, modest or important, to play, action to take in the world which keeps him from being wholly dependent on the character of his wife and the nature of his marriage.

It was this sense of ultimate dependence, mitigated to a degree, by the availability of divorce, which continued to obsess many bright and able American women over the past one hundred years. It prompted Charlotte Perkins Gilman to write her work on *Women and Economics* in which she emphasized the sexuo-economic dependence of women.

But even this is not the basic issue. Let us suppose husband and wife both earn more or less the same amount of money (and many, of course, do) and accept the notion of complete mutuality and "equality." The husband's job is, in a sense, what he is; it is essential to him. It is what he does; how he appears in the world. The woman's job, however well she does it, is to a degree ancillary. If she does not wish to do it, she need not do it. If she had never done it or if she stopped doing it, she would, in most cases, be substantially the same person. But with the man the case is obviously quite different. And of course it is this feeling on the part of the woman for a man's role or function in the world, for his power or potency, that attracts her most strongly to him. It is very common for a woman to be drawn to a man because he is a "success" or because he promises "success." A woman's attractions for a man rest on quite different grounds, the most familiar being, I suppose, physical beauty. Only a very silly and immature girl is going to give any weight, fortunately, to masculine beauty. In a man, handsomeness is quite irrelevant; handsome men are often vain and spoiled.

Despite Benjamin Franklin's highly practical advice to choose an old mistress, the vast majority of men prefer a young one, presumably gaining thereby a sense of renewal. Actually since men die, on the average, ten years earlier than women, it would make sense for them to marry women approximately ten years older than themselves. The sexual life of such couples would also be more "in phase" if we accept the aforementioned Kinsey proposition that women's sexual needs and capacities increase in middle age at the time when men's diminish.

On the other hand if one partner to the marriage has to be widowed, it is clearly better that it should be the woman. The husband who is "predeceased" by his wife is, as we have already noted, a pathetic figure. A widow is much better able to cope with what remains of single existence than a widower. And if she were given back her "grandmotherhood" she would usually make out very well indeed.

The extraordinary preoccupation of men with guns and violence is perhaps too neatly Freudian. While there are some women marksmen, most women fear and dislike guns. American men cling to them with an almost pathological vehemence; witness the efforts to block passage of any kind of adequate gun control legislation. Do men, stripped of most of their masculine symbols and prerogatives, feel that women, who are the principal supporters of gun control legislation, are trying to castrate them?

Even in jokes there are marked sexual differences. Women will seldom tell "dirty" jokes. While they enjoy the same "humor" as men, the same cartoons and often the same stories, their notion of "playing a joke" on someone is quite different from the male's. The young male wishes "an explosive" joke, a frightening noise, the threat of violence, an apparently mangled thumb, a hideous nose; the girl wishes some "distance" from the "joke." She will devise one that is less frightening but sometimes more cruel and humiliating — calling another girl and inviting her to a nonexistent party at someone else's house is a typical "joke" for a young female. She does not have to "see" the effect of the joke. For the male this is usually the whole point. There are, moreover, relatively few women "humorists" or cartoonists and the creation of verbal jokes or funny stories seems to be virtually a masculine monopoly.

On the level of the community most of the intelligent and useful things done are done by women; but they also make much of the mischief. And this relates to their political role. While women could not, I suppose, have invented parliamentary procedure (it is the kind of formal and abstract system in which the masculine mind is so fertile), they discovered an immediate affinity for it when they began to organize into various societies and associations. Parliamentary procedure offers at once the quality of order congenial to the feminine mind with an opportunity for strategic maneuvers, to defer or refer, to offer a privileged motion and thereby take the opposition in the flank — all these are obviously very satisfying to ladies. They are natural plotters; having, for the most part, a suspicious turn of mind (which has been very necessary to prevent themselves from being gulled by glib males), they are extremely ingenious in mapping campaigns and constructing almost Borgian plots to overturn a rival faction in the PTA.

At the same time there is an intractability about women that greatly complicates democratic politics which are, traditionally, based on compromise. Women are upholders of principle, not compromisers. To compromise goes very much against the grain; for example, they will rarely admit that they are in the wrong. W. B. Yeats has made perhaps the most astute analysis of this quality of the irreconcilable in women: "Women, because the main event of their lives has been giving themselves and giving birth, give all to an opinion as if it were some terrible stone doll. Men take up an opinion lightly and are easily false to it, and when faithful, keep the habit of many interests. We still see the world, if we are of strong mind and body, with considerate eyes, but to women, opinions become as their children or their sweethearts, and the greater their emotional capacity, the more do they forget all other things. They grow cruel, as if in defense of lover or child, and all this is done 'for something other than human life.' "[7]

Jean Paul Richter had the same quality in mind when he wrote that "with women all ideas become human beings," and thus evoke the same passionate feelings that people do. Women are, plainly enough, intensely personal. They react in terms of particular people. This combined with their loyalty and their lack of honor often affects their judgment and inclines them to intrigue. One aspect of this is the promptness with which women enter into the most confidential relationships with members of their own sex whom they barely know. After an acquaintanceship of ten minutes many women will exchange confidences that a man would not reveal to a lifelong friend. Perhaps it can be accounted for in large part by woman's centuries-long position of inferiority in male-dominated society, which has accustomed her to achieve her ends by guile. There is a similar quality, in any event, among Negroes who encounter each other in largely white company. They are instant "soul brothers" by virtue of their traditionally subordinate role in a white-dominated society.

Needless to say, this conspiratorial quality in women is unnerving to men. They are simpler and more direct and less inclined to harbor resentments. This in turn may be due to their habit of dominance.

Women are great reformers and even, on occasion, great revolutionaries, but they are, by and large, poor politicians. And this is related to the speech of women. Passionate speech is a woman's proper mode of discourse. This puts her at a marked disadvantage in politics which is marked by bombastic or equivocating speech (and in the academic world which is characterized by stale speech, desiccated speech, pseudo-speech, or merely reasonable speech).

Moral indignation gives women, as we have seen, great power and enables them to command attention through speech. The same thing, of course, is true of the black power movement. In a time of dried-up, conventional speech, passionate speech is irresistible. We *must* listen, though we may not like what we hear.

The fact that passionate speech is a woman's true voice is often baffling to man who complains that when she speaks of the matters of everyday life, she is "too extreme," "overstates things," "exaggerates," is "unreasonable." That is her native language. And it is also the language of love which is, fortunately for the male, "immoderate." Poetry is in essence, I suppose, the effort of man to speak this passionate language of woman.

Women are not theorists but they are peculiarly susceptible to human suffering and need. They are thus a profoundly conservative force in political life. Their impulses are always to ameliorate the harsher conditions within a political and social system; the instincts of the men are to preserve it inviolate or change it radically. Wherever women are active in social reform, the society is apt to be essentially a conservative one. When women are inactive, reaction on the one hand and revolutionary change on the other are usually the most pressing alternatives.

If passionate speech is the natural speech of women they are also the mistresses of silence, indeed of silences, as men are masters of talk. Silence is one of a woman's most potent weapons. In the words of Malcolm de Chazal: "A woman knows how to keep quiet when she is in the right, whereas a man, when he is in the right, will keep on talking."[8] In addition, when a woman is offended or furious, she knows how to create a silence so dense that it is palpable. She can be more eloquent by a particular silence than the most expressive male by torrents of words. This is, I think, because she understands much better than the man that life is systolic and diastolic, that one breathes in and out. Silence, so baffling to most males, is a refuge as well as a weapon for women. Again it may also have been mastered as the weapon of the weak and powerless, those who cannot hope to prevail by disputation or through authority.

Related to the passionate speech of woman is her undividedness. And this quality is also related to her unwillingness to compromise. Man is basically divided and thus wishes to divide things; women are whole. As Balzac put it "women are afraid of things that have to be divided." It took men to develop such concepts as "body and soul," "mind and matter," "spiritual and the material"; these have no reality for women. Men all have in them an element of the schizophrenic — a disease which is much more a masculine than a feminine one (except in periods of extreme feminine demoralization). Men are constantly tempted by various forms of dualism, and trinitarian schemes are an effort to avoid the danger of dualistic thinking. On the other hand man is a natural specialist. Woman is a generalist. The woman is happiest who represents a various but harmonious whole — wife, mother, creator, social activist. That man is most deeply himself (one would not say necessarily happiest) who pursues a single passion.

Men are natural compromisers because they have to compromise their own different "selves." Division precedes analysis and organization. The world must first be divided and classified before it can be organized, and man's impulse to do this lies deep in his nature (it was men after all who divided women into various functions). Solomon's challenge to the competing mothers to divide in half the baby they both claimed was a thoroughly masculine notion. Compromise is based on division; it is a recognition that under certain circumstances things must be divided and these divided and disparate things cannot be reconciled and must exist side by side without resolution.

"Manners" are not held in great repute these days. They are thought to be the superficial coverings of our "true" emotions and feelings. Rudeness is proclaimed as candor and honesty, lack of respect for age or office an antidote to middle-class hypocrisy. But manners, though they can surely be false and pretentious, are the principal agency by means of which decent and civilized life is maintained. They are the training which lead us to thoughtfulness. And they are the particular province of women. As Remy de Gourmont has put it: "What is truly indispensable for the conduct of life has been taught us by women — the small rules of courtesy, the actions that win us the warmth or deference of others; the words that assure us a welcome, the attitudes that must be varied to mesh with character or situation; all social strategy. It is listening to women that teaches us to speak to men."[9] Life is made up more of small occasions than great events. How we meet the small occasions usually determines how we respond to the great events; it is thus a mistake to separate the two. Women, who instruct us in the small occasions enable us to rise to the great events.

Most seers and predicters have been women. They have a special affinity for the occult (prophecy is largely a male function). The Delphic Oracle was a woman; Cassandras foretell specific evil. We go to fortunetellers and palmists (invariably women) to learn about our private destinies but for that of the race we consult prophets, columnists, and more recently, computers. This represents woman's concern with the "personal" future.

Perhaps the most basic difference between the sexes is that women are made of "sugar and spice and everything nice," while men are made of "snips and snails and puppy-dog tails." Thus a man with any sense or sensitivity must feel that it is a kind of miracle that a woman will love him. He feels or should feel himself unworthy to be loved, incapable of winning or earning a woman's love. He is conscious that he is uncouth and that she is couth; that he is ugly, awkward, smelly, generally unlovable, whereas a woman is beautiful, graceful, smells good, and exudes some indefinable *amarosa* that is more intoxicating than any liquor. That such a person should choose to love someone so basically unlovable is a great mystery to a man. Since grace is, by definition, something freely given, undeserved and unearned, men perceive women as a source of grace.

This feeling is expressed in classic form by Boris Pasternak in a letter to Nina Tabidze: "Ever since my childhood I have nourished a timid feeling of adoration for women, all my life I have remained stunned and stupefied by her beauty, by her place in life, and by my pity of her and fear for her. I am a realist who has a thorough knowledge of the earth not because, like Don Juan, I have frequently had a lot of fun with women on earth, but because since childhood I have gathered pebbles from under her feet on the path she had trodden. The few women who have had an affair with me were magnanimous martyrs, so unbearable and uninteresting am I 'as a man,' so often am I incorrigibly and inexplicably weak, so much do I not know myself even now. . . ."[10]

There are powerful reasons why we dare not diminish the difference between the sexes. That difference is the archetypal encounter of otherness; it is the model of all reconciliations, of all the mystery of the person other than oneself into whose life one enters in fear and trembling as into paradise or hell; the origin of drama; the center of religion. If that basic encounter is denigrated or avoided, the psyche can never grow, can never make an entry into the dimension of transcendence. The dimension represented by the woman who is not the man is what truly rescues us from our "one-dimensionality." The unutterable otherness of women which has dazzled men from the earliest time stands for the mystery which must be lived with, which has in it always something hellish and threatening, something to which man yearns and which he fears, which probably must always be under masculine divinity for just that reason. Sexuality is the heart of it but it is by no means the whole of it. The desire to escape from the tensions of sexuality are part of the desire to escape from all those tensions inherent in life of which the sexual tension may be taken as the paradigm.

There is finally the question of the "superiority" of women. The question is quite meaningless except for polemical purposes. It is only conceivable in a highly competitive society oriented towards notions of dominance and subordination. Can it have any "historical" meaning? I think not. It reeks of justification, defensiveness and aggression. We hardly need to perpetuate it. Women are, quite clearly, more intelligent than men. In H. L. Mencken's words, "Women, in truth, are not only intelligent; they have almost a monopoly of certain of the subtler and more utile forms of intelligence."[11]

Cliché though it may be, women are, in fact, more "life-oriented" than men — if there is a death-wish it is primarily a masculine demiurge. They are more open, more responsive, more religious, more "giving," more practical than men; more loyal, far more the natural enhancers and celebrators of life; more passive or more capable of passivity, more elemental, more passionate. But then men are "more" a lot of other things and who is to say what is superior? The question is rather what is necessary; what, at *this moment of history,* must be emphasized? Certainly I should properly be the last to denigrate the capacities and achievements of man (I trust I am without that malice toward my own sex that has so often accompanied masculine espousals of the cause of women). But masculine achievements, remarkable as they are, have almost wrecked us. In man's cruel overorganization of all life he has done a terrible violence to the human spirit and it is certainly a hopeful sign that in a confused, inchoate, and rather dangerous way we are at last beginning to recognize this.

I believe that it is to women primarily that we must look for the opening up of those areas of our life which touch the spontaneous, the joyful, and the responsive. Moreover, we make a serious mistake if we believe that this aspect of our repressed life must be expressed sexually. Our symbolic life can be far richer than we imagine. The present-day dances devised by teenagers are classic expressions of sexual play acted out socially with a consequent release of sexual tension. The orgiastic quality which dismays so many adults is, of course, the whole point. There could be no more dramatic contrast than that between the formalism of the waltz or fox-trot and the abandon of the boogaloo or any of the free-form gyrations of these innocent bacchanalians. I suspect that the dances are far more the creation of girls than of boys.

Women who wish to be as much like men as possible (as opposed to having as much worth and dignity as men) will resist such exhortations on the grounds that the intention is to trap them in traditional feminine roles. What they fail to see, however, is that this very masculinization of the world, to a portion of which they aspire, is just the trouble with it. The world is so sadly in need of being enhanced, adorned, and celebrated, so in need of rituals, pageants, processions, and similar delights, that women must serve these needs. If they simply battle their way into all the dreary and routine tasks performed by men (and this is indeed so far exactly what they have done, taking over the vast portion of the least interesting and most poorly remunerated jobs in our society) they will have won that famous hollow victory.

It will appear from the above that, clumsily as I fear I have argued the case, I do believe that women have "a nature" and I believe that this nature, powerfully and confidently expressed, is essential to any harmonious personal existence and to any hope for a better human society.

The Future of Women

We might briefly review the major theses of this book. Men, in an effort to cope with feminine sexuality, divided women into different functions: wife and mother on the one hand; mistress, concubine, priestess, seer, custodian of mysteries on the other. The Judeo-Christian tradition restored the unity of women under a single deity and much of the subsequent history of the relationship between the sexes can be understood as an effort by men to deal with the multiformity of women, a multiformity in which sexuality was, of course, a dominant quality.

Puritan New England was notably successful in containing feminine sexuality in marriage without repressing or distorting it. Women enjoyed an almost unparalleled status and importance in early New England. Part of this status came from their scarcity and their economic importance but a major part came from the new relationships in the reformed family where daughters, perhaps for the first time in history, had as much worth and dignity as sons.

The constriction of the physical relationship between men and women that went on from the middle of the eighteenth century to the end of the nineteenth (and indeed almost to the mid-twentieth) had its counterpart in the narrowing of the range of intellectual, and even social contacts between, most typically, husbands and wives. There are many remarkable letters between married couples throughout the seventeenth and eighteenth centuries. Revolutionary statesmen like John Adams wrote to their wives as to intellectual equals, discussing complex points of political strategy, describing military engagements, arguing moral philosophy, referring to literary and historical works of which both husband and wife had firsthand knowledge. Abigail Adams would have been a rare wife in any era but she was by no means atypical of women of the revolutionary era, nor was John Adams's attitude toward her by any means unique. However, at the time of the Civil War one will search in vain to find the same kind of candor and openness, of mutuality, in the correspondence of statesmen and public figures with their wives. The vast portion of it is stilted and perfunctory.

There were, however, several important residues of the earlier Puritan attitudes toward women: young unmarried women continued to enjoy remarkable freedom throughout the course of American history; American men, however much they may have at times falsified and sentimentalized their relationship with women, continued to regard them with a degree of deference and respect that astonished visitors from other countries of the Western world. By the same token American women impressed these same visitors as a remarkable breed, representing in many ways the best achievement of our culture. Captain Marryat thought it "unquestionable" that American women were "physically, as far as beauty is concerned, and morally, of a higher standard than the men." The best hope for America was that the women should raise the men "to their own standard."[1] Mrs. Trollope, though more critical than Marryat, was also convinced "that the American people will not equal the nations of Europe in refinement till women become of more importance among them."[2] Eighty years later it was clear to Lord Bryce that American women had a predominating influence, "for in America the balance inclines as much in favour of the wife as it does in England in favour of the husband."

Bryce also observed that "no country seems to owe more to its women than America does, nor to owe to them so much of what is best in its social institutions and in the beliefs that govern conduct." The remarkable influence of women was due in large part to the fact that "the American man is exceptionally deferential to women, and

the American statesman exceptionally disposed to comply with every request which is urgently pressed upon him." This was "the kernel of the suffragist case."[3]

The emergence of women has, it is evident, created new kinds of sexual anxiety. That there is presently an impulse toward "depolarization" of the sexes seems evident. But I do not see much chance that woman with her recently discovered sexual potentialities is apt to find this a congenial development. Her sexuality may be repressed but her primary needs will still center around her reproductive function.

The ambivalence, indeed what one might call our primary schizophrenia on the question of feminine sexuality, is demonstrated most vividly by the contrasting styles of the female hippie, whose passive promiscuity is deliberately desexed, and *Playboy*'s "playmate." With her lank hair, absence of makeup, torn jeans and T-shirt, the hippie is the antithesis of the seductive female. She scorns the manipulation practiced by more artful girls. She wishes to be a companion, freely and generously and indiscriminately available to anyone who needs her. She doesn't belong to anyone. A boy does not have to pay elaborate court to her, does not have to pass through the frustrations, delays, and perhaps disappointments of courtship. Passive, drug-saturated, available, she represents a noncompetitive, non-anxiety-producing, undemanding low-level sexuality. She is the antithesis of the aggressive "manipulative" female. She is neither "Mrs. P.T.A.," smart, confident, "managerial," nor is she the playgirl-of-the-month. She takes the classic part of the passive-masochistic female, and of the mother. Infants are much featured in hippie communities. One feels they are presented as symbols of this society, "nonviolent" responsive, flower-like, simple, spontaneous, affection-needing and affection-giving and relatively undemanding since they *are* infants. So the feminine style is perhaps more important and more revealing than the masculine style; both are clearly an effort to deal with some of the most severe anxiety-producing aspects of contemporary society.

Transient as the hippie society seems to be it is symptomatically important. It has, of course, already been eclipsed by a new wave of youthful violence and hostility. It is clear that the styles, the activities and the individuals interpenetrate, and that not infrequently the nonviolent hippie experiences a conversion to the style of violence.

In sharp contrast to the torn blue jeans and dirty T-shirt syndrome we have the mini-skirt and boot style which is certainly the most flamboyantly erotic female costume of modern times (most girls, of course, play both parts). I am sometimes startled at the resentment expressed by middle-class boys towards what they call "manipulative girls." It is a new word for "vamp," that traditional bane of the male. The "manipulative girls" are those who take some pains to make themselves attractive and desirable but who are not ready to tumble into bed with the first aggressive boy. The problem is, in part at least, that the average young male wants sexual experience without, usually, a very deep personal commitment; the average young girl wants and needs for her own sense of self-esteem and confidence as a woman, masculine attention but does not need sexual release nearly so much as her masculine counterpart. The paradox is that while under the proper circumstances her sexual pleasure may be much more intense than that of the man, it is not, generally speaking, nearly so urgent a matter with her. As we have seen, the Puritans solved this problem by accepting extensive premarital sexual relations that were contained within rigid social controls. The nineteenth century solved the problem quite unsatisfactorily by confining masculine premarital sexual relations for the most part to prostitutes and mistresses and denying them entirely to unmarried young women, or at least trying to.

A considerable number of middle-class boys and girls, most of them of college age, now live together as husband and wife. These alliances are of two kinds. In one, the partners feel themselves to be in love and intend to get married: it is simply not presently convenient. Parental pressures or the need to complete their education make it simpler to postpone marriage. Such an arrangement approaches most closely the practices of the young Puritans of New England with two important qualifications. New England couples under pre-contract, while they were allowed remarkable freedom, did not live together as husband and wife. Secondly, modern unmarried couples do not experience strong sanctions impelling them to marry if sexually compatible. With more effective methods of contraception they can more readily avoid the pregnancy which so often made marriage necessary for their Puritan ancestors. Moreover, modern youngsters have a greater incentive to avoid pregnancy because they are not as certain that their relationship will or should eventuate in marriage.

Furthermore, the reasons of convenience which induce them to delay marriage equally incline them to avoid having children. The danger of such a relationship is that, given the strains and tensions attendant upon two people of the opposite sex living together (and especially under semiclandestine circumstances), they may, after having entered into very deep emotional involvements, end by breaking off their "marriage." Such a break is often devastating to the girl involved. Two or three such "failures" are not the best preparation for a stable and enduring marriage.

A similar alliance specifically disavows all thought of marriage. It is thought of from the beginning as a transient union, based on mutual physical attraction and "respect for each other as individuals," as we say these days. It has a pretentious and rather touching jargon all its own. Common assurances of a determination not to let the relationship become confining or "possessive," pleasure in their ability to "relate" to each other, pride in their sexual emancipation, etc. Since human emotions are not to be controlled like water in a tap, such alliances sometimes ripen into marriages. Others when dissolved leave a considerable residue of bitterness. In any event it seems safe to say that the emotional or psychological hazards of premarital sexual relations are much greater for women than for men. Sexual emancipation, so far as it involves nonmarital sexual relations, works almost exclusively to the advantage of young males. To the extent that they are inherently promiscuous it requires some effort on their part to observe a monogynous relationship. However, married to a wife who will not tolerate philandering, they often adapt themselves good-naturedly to the requirements of a monogamous union. (The classic prescription for the sex drives of young males — cold showers and lots of exercise — has never proved an adequate remedy for the distemper.)

In the face of the disintegrative forces of modern life, early marriages suffer from a disastrous mortality rate. They also are against the best interests of the girl because a young male is so unformed that the element of risk in an early marriage is disproportionately high for her. Furthermore, the premarital sexual encounter is in a sense far less important today than it was in the seventeenth century when it was necessary to counteract the repressive tendencies which characterized Reformation doctrine. Few such inhibitions exist today. The tendency is certainly not to underrate the importance of the sexual encounter but quite the reverse, as we have seen. Sexual relations between a couple prior to marriage certainly can be tolerated by any society and would be indicted only by the most rigid code. But it would be unrealistic not to face the fact that the impermanence of most relations in our society poses severe problems for those who engage in sexual relations outside of marriage. These relations are by no means the simple or easy answer to the problem of sexual imperatives that their proponents so glibly make them out to be.

When our problem is to restore the unity and wholeness of human experience, such attachments dissipate our psychic energies and further fragment our lives. Loyalty, continuity, integrity, responsiveness, courage, and tolerance are qualities of which our time stands in special need. Our "torn-to-pieces-ness" — that almost universal schizophrenia which is the wound and illness of our age — must be healed. That healing involves the reconstruction of all human relationships.

The problem of sex in marriage is that marriage is concerned essentially with the perpetuation of the race. It looks to the future. A marriage of self-indulgence whether in milkshakes or sex is a falsification of the true "I — Thou" because however much some may try to persuade us that the sex act is a kind of sacrament it is nothing in and of itself; it is ambiguous. The church has always resisted contraception because it has understood that in a sense contraception destroys the future or, at the very least, threatens it because it makes private pleasure the center of that relationship upon which the race depends for survival. The nurturing of children is the most basic reason for the monogamous marriage. One of the dangers of placing sexual play at the center of a marriage is that there is a kind of radical insatiability in the sex instinct; it is one of those appetites "that grows by what it feeds upon"; rather than satisfying sexual desires it augments them and is one of the things which leads to the suburban "wife-swapping" that currently engages the attention of some of our playwrights and novelists. In other words, sex, made the consuming preoccupation of marriage, breaks out of marriage and threatens the good order of the entire community.

Benjamin Franklin — "old Daddy Franklin" D. H. Lawrence called him — gave the classic American prescription for sex: "Rarely use venery but for health [the modern word might be "pleasure"] and offspring, never to dullness, weakness, or the injury of your own or another's peace or reputation." Lawrence's reply was: "Never 'use' venery at all. Follow your passional impulse, if it be answered in the other being; but never have any motive in mind, neither offspring nor health nor even pleasure, nor even service. Only know that 'venery' is of the very great gods."[4]

The point is, none of the crucial acts of life are to be "used" or played with or "taken out of context." The Christian church has tried for two thousand years to put sexual relations "in context." That context is the monogamous marriage which stands *between* past and future; it is social *as well as* private. It has to mediate the past and envision the future. Its own indulgences and appetites have to be subordinated to this greater task. And this, in a sense, is what many of the feminists and the reformers were saying. Their touching desire to subdue or abolish sex, to "spiritualize" it came out of their instinct that if indulged it could destroy the future. Sex can only be a harmoniously balanced aspect of life when that life itself is directed towards the future. Discipline fortifies the ego; indulgence erodes it. These issues have nothing to do with morality per se: morality here is uninteresting and irrelevant. They have to do with the future of the species.

Those marriages concerned exclusively with the present are doomed to misery and decay. The problem with the middle-class American husband and wife is not their preoccupation with sexual experimentation or with material things but their boredom. Most are desperately bored, desperately searching for this false dream of "fulfillment."

It is this restless passion for "personal fulfillment" that disfigures our age. Life and liberty seem to have taken a backseat to the pursuit of happiness which is everyone's inalienable right. If one no longer believes in duties and responsibilities, in obligations and loyalties, or in a future state of rewards or punishments, then, of course, one must get everything NOW. It is this passion, not materialism as such, that has revolted the younger generation; but they too are trapped for the most part in the same old rhetoric. We can only say that their instincts are better than their vocabularies or their concepts.

As we come to the end of this remarkable story we confront women (are they a "problem" still?) in contemporary American society. This book has not set out to "explain" American women or indeed to "understand" them for it is the author's conviction that history cannot be "understood" or completely grasped in the sense of a rational order, and women certainly least of all. But it has been my purpose to try to understand women's role in American history and of course to insist that they cannot be, as they have been, simply subsumed under the history of men. Today when people no longer belong to orders, institutions, and corporate bodies (except General Motors, Ford, *et al.*) or even to true communities, a large part of our identity is to be found in our history, our "autobiography" as Rosenstock-Huessy has called it. Men have deprived women of their history, and, in consequence, of an important part of their identity, by the simple expedient of not telling it. (Again there is analogy between the situation of women vis-à-vis men and that of white society vis-à-vis the Negro.)

But what of the future of women? That is part of their history. Indeed, the only reason I am interested in their history is because I am interested in their future; they have a future to the degree that they have a history.

There is, of course, no lack of seers prepared to tell us what women and what the world will be in the next century. The *Futurist,* published by an organization called the World Future Society, predicts that there will be more women senators and public officials, housework will take less time, kitchens will be computerized (the housewife will feed her menus into a computer which will get out frozen foods, cook, and serve them), robot maids will dust the furniture and keep the house, intelligent apes will serve as chauffeurs, dresses will be worn once and thrown away, and a wife will put "antigrouch" pills in a grumpy husband's food. Men and women of the future "will be able to enjoy sex at will, thanks to birth control pills, sex education, and cosmetic bio-engineering (refashioning of the body to make everyone sexually attractive). If we add to all of these potentialities for the enhancement of heterosexual stimulation the likelihood that techniques may be developed for more rapid seminal regeneration in men and easy arousal of the sexual appetite by hormone control in both sexes, we have it made, so to speak. . . . Every variety of *sexual soma,* the aphrodisiacs of the future, will be available to men and women."[5]

We are presently witnessing a recrudescence of semi- or demi-feminism. Betty Friedan, whose book *The Feminine Mystique* was an old-fashioned feminist attack on the notion that there are specifically feminine qualities and functions or a classic feminine "role," is one of the leaders in the National Organization for Women (NOW) which seeks "full equality for all women in America, in truly equal partnership with men." NOW is a kind of catchall of neo-feminists ranging from those whose concern is primarily with equal pay for equal jobs to those who foresee "the demise of marriage." Every traditional feminist theme is represented but the "movement," extremely modest in numbers, is for the most part lacking in the evangelical spirit of its predecessor.

A more practical venture is Catalyst, a national organization designed to "work with colleges and universities to motivate the female student to direct her talents and education toward *individual fulfillment with a real purpose"* [italics mine]. The phrase is significant; all the activities of women today have to be directed toward "self-fulfillment" or "individual fulfillment," because this is the ideal of a decadent society, but now to it we find appended "with a real purpose" which hints at useful social activity. Further, Catalyst wishes to "stimulate the college student to think of her future in realistic, far-seeing outlines and, recognizing that child-raising will occupy only a small fraction of her time, plan for a sensible sequence of family and work." The organization also seeks to find part-time jobs for wives and mothers (since only a "small fraction" of their time is to be given to child-rearing) and encourage programs of continuing education such as that already in operation at Radcliffe. This program is, I fear, much too modest to succeed. We live in an apocalyptic age. There are many indications that we are ready to be moved once more by calls for the redemption of a fallen world rather than by shrewd appeals to self-interest or "self-fulfillment," whatever that *ignis fatuus* may be.

But here I must say something parenthetically about the careers of women in our society lest I be misunderstood. An anonymous eighteenth-century lady wrote "What business do women turned forty have to do in this world?" The question has as much and perhaps more urgency today than when our lady asked it. Today a woman of forty is at the height of her powers; often a person of unusual intelligence and energy she has no clearly marked tasks or careers available to her. The federal government which so often seems to spend our money in addled and ineffective ways (when it is not spending on military hardware capable of exterminating most of mankind) could very profitably spend several billion dollars a year to assist married women with families (since it's plain enough that most women wish to be married and have families) to continue their education with a view to entering active professional careers when their families can spare them.

Women enrolled in such a plan would receive quarterly or biannual journals designed specifically to keep them informed of the important developments in the field or fields of greatest interest to them. In addition they might attend monthly lectures (or receive them on tape) and have every summer (or winter when the children were in school) week- or two-week-long sessions of intensive study and discussion. After fifteen or twenty years of such a program (or certainly sooner if they wished), they would, without having to be subjected to the dreary and interminable routines of graduate school receive the appropriate professional degree or certification and be launched in full- or part-time careers. This is substantially what is done in the Army Reserve program and in the National Guard. The same technique could be adapted much more successfully to the continued training of career-oriented women who wished to have both family *and* career.

This scheme is so simple and so sensible that it will have, in time, to be undertaken, the sooner, of course, the better. But the problem of women in American life goes considerably deeper. It is more "social" than "personal."

There are signs that the civil rights and black power issues and the Vietnam War have stirred women out of their thirty-year slumber. Dagmar Wilson's Women Strike For Peace roused the echoes (unheard of course) of ancient women's battles for peace and is perhaps the most effective woman's organization of recent years. The Jeannette

Rankin Brigade is another woman's peace movement and recently the "third force," the "national liberation" and anti-draft movements have spawned feminine counterparts made up primarily of girls who do not care to be ordered about by boys or relegated to answering telephones and making sandwiches.

It is entirely possible that since the destinies of the woman and the Negro have been so intertwined in American history, the appearance of the Negro as the most dramatic, powerful, and problematical figure in American life will trigger a widespread revival of a feminism of which the modest ventures described above may be the harbingers.

In the Peace Corps, in the ghettos, in many forms of service, young couples are learning once more, perhaps in a certain sense for the first time, what a true marriage is, how it looks both inward and outward, backward and forward, how it lives within the "cross of reality" or, if unable to achieve that alternation, is crucified upon it.

Amid all the sickness of soul, the shallowness, the falseness, the simple perverseness that characterizes our time there is new growth and hope; it is a tender vine that has put down roots in stony and arid soil. Masculine sexuality cannot be "cured" by female sexuality. They are good gifts of God and they are not to be abused. We could take heart from the fact that they existed harmoniously in our own society when the "thou shalt" was stronger than the "thou shalt not," when the future was a more powerful reality than the present. And so they shall again when our "torn-to-pieces-ness" is healed by the imperatives of the future. And this means women must know that there are tasks for them in the twenty-first century as significant and compelling as those they performed so notably in the nineteenth.

Sex and race are the two most profound issues confronting mankind. They are inevitably intermingled. America is a "racist" society but so is every other society. Racial arrogance is a human not simply an American sin. America happens to be the country where this issue is being fought out and worked out, but it is a universal drama, an event not simply of importance to America but of world historical significance. The same was true of women's fight for their rights as human beings. Now taken for granted and little understood or appreciated, it, too, was an event whose implications reached far beyond the boundaries of the United States. In the words of Karl Marx,

"Every emancipation is a restoration of the human world and of human relationships to man himself."

Because of their very tendency to oversimplify (the Madwoman of Chaillot's famous declaration: "Nothing is ever so wrong in the world that a sensible woman can't set it straight in the course of an afternoon"), women have a peculiar power. It is true that at the heart of almost every human dilemma is some simple moral principle that must at last be grasped. The antislavery movement had become encrusted (by men) with the most elaborate, ingenious and unworkable proposals for gradual emancipation. It was paralyzed by the variety and complexity of these schemes. Women saw that the issue was not primarily political or social (it was indeed insoluble by political or social means), but moral; the slaves must be freed, and, once freed, they must be made part of American society. That was simple enough. The cause of slavery having been espoused, the cause of women followed inevitably. Women were enslaved. They were the slaves of men. They had to "gain possession of their own bodies." Again, simple enough, but also revolutionary. So there is something, after all, to the madwoman's conviction.

Missionary women, seeking to save souls, seeded the world with Western values and ideals and by so doing substantially forwarded the most profound revolution of modern times — the emergence of the non-Western peoples into world history.*

The reformers released female energy and enterprise into the world with an effect more profound than the release of nuclear power. Women, fired by the Protestant passion, were behind every significant social reform of the late nineteenth and early twentieth centuries. In most instances their initiative or support was crucial. Without careful attention to their actions American history cannot be properly understood.

And it must, of course, be remembered that without devoted masculine allies they could hardly have accomplished anything. The male abettors of the woman's movement are heroes in their own right.

---

* The issue of population control is a feminine issue in essence. It is women who control the size of their families. The population of the world will not be controlled until women in underdeveloped countries gain enough status and enough confidence to limit the size of their families by "gaining possession of their own bodies."

THE FUTURE OF WOMEN

When all is said and done, it is evident that much as the champions of woman's rights overstated their case at times, and as extravagant or ridiculous as they sometimes seemed, they belong to our future as much as to our past. As a historian I started out to treat them as "history," interesting and touching curiosities from an earlier age, but they broke through my scholarly defenses and became what I had not at all anticipated or intended, the heroines of this book. Their vigor, their intelligence, their charm and, perhaps above all, their courage made me their attentive, indeed devoted, admirer.

Since we all need ancestors, the young women of our time will do well to claim these ladies. One of the most basic accomplishments of those women who were pioneers in such fields as law, medicine, and scholarship was simply the fact that *women could actually do these things.* There was accumulation of theory and prejudice which had maintained that women were intellectually and constitutionally unable to enter into fields reserved for men, thus the bare fact that women did succeed had an enormous impact on the thinking of both men and women about the appropriate roles of the sexes. Since the great majority of women believed what they were told about the limits of their capacities — their smaller brains, delicate and nervous constitutions, etc. — the achievements of their ambitious and energetic sisters disclosed new potentials in themselves, led indeed to a widening discovery of self. Even the woman who scoffed at the female lawyer or doctor knew something hitherto unknown about herself. It was this sense, intangible, difficult to document, but nonetheless profoundly important, which made the period from the late eighteen-seventies through the first decades of the twentieth century an enormously exciting and stimulating epoch for American women. They were, in fact, in the process of developing a new consciousness of themselves and their relation to the world. A new kind of woman had begun to emerge in the English colonies of North America as early as 1620. She took form throughout the seventeenth, eighteenth, and early nineteenth centuries, but it was a form without a very sharp focus of self-consciousness. The new consciousness came to a handful of women in the era prior to the Civil War; it was passed on to American women generally in the last decades of the nineteenth century. It completed their transformation and it obviously transformed the larger society. At the same time modern women are still very far from attaining the promise that American life once seemed to hold for them. Our common existence will never be made whole until that promise is more nearly achieved and it will never be achieved until the lazy hearts and consciences of men and women alike are roused out of a slumber of complacency and self-esteem.

I have, I trust, made it plain that I am not resourceful enough to imagine a richer human experience between the sexes than a monogamous marriage. I believe that men and women are different, and I think it unimportant and undiscoverable whether this difference is biological or cultural. I believe that it is, in any event, functional, and that society could not endure without the peculiar qualities that men and women most typically represent in the distinctiveness of the respective sexes; that these qualities do, in fact, so complement each other, that life without them would be infinitely less rewarding than it presently is.

Common enterprises are the channels of redemption. In the words of Saint-Exupéry: "Love does not consist in gazing at each other but in looking together in the same direction."[6] We must pay proper homage to the extravagant visions of the early reformers. They dreamed of a new kind of human relationship and helped to make it come partway true. They freed man from the curse of his domination over woman, for however tender and sentimental that domination may have been it did in effect deny woman her full humanity. Nor will the future yield to fantasies of perfect sexual adjustment; man's (and certainly woman's) needs and dreams go beyond such private pleasures. They yearn toward a better human order, a finer race, as the feminists would say. What is needed most is a recovered faith and the stamina to take up the burden that the misunderstood and ridiculed feminists laid down.

It is also true that our culture seems to be more receptive than it has ever been before to those feminine qualities which are so at odds with a highly organized technological society — responsiveness, openness, celebration. The world needs both the "gifts" of woman and her remarkable social energies. We must have secular missionaries, men and women who will, with an understanding of the intractability of history that yields only to labors capable of being sustained over the span of at least two generations, take up the task of reconstructing human society. There is no solution to the "woman problem"; there are only tasks which require all the intelligence, skill, and patience that men *and* women together can bring to them. American men and women must, as Rosenstock-Huessy has put it, re-immigrate into the world. The epoch of America is over, that of the world has begun. American women must play a central role in the next chapter of human history.

A Bemused Postscript

This manuscript was substantially finished in the spring of 1968. Since then the rather tortuous editorial processes have afforded me ample opportunity for second thoughts. These second thoughts have, of course, been stimulated by the startling growth of various brands of neo-feminism of which the most prominent is perhaps the women's liberation movement. When I finished my manuscript neo-feminism was a cloud on the horizon no bigger than a man's hand. Now it looms like an angry thunderhead.

I have viewed this escalation of the discussion about the place of women in American society with mixed feelings. Will my book, I have wondered, enter in some salutary way the increasingly noisy debate over the nature and destiny of women? Or will militant women, following the lead of militant blacks, declare that no man has a right to speak or write about women since only a woman can understand the problems of women?

Above all, as the debate increases in intensity, I have a strong sense of *déjà vu*. I have been there before and I find myself somewhat unnerved and slightly defensive in the face of the charge by female militants that admiration for women, belief in their "nature," pleasure in their company is simply a masculine put-down, an insidious attempt to confine women to a role which is convenient to males, a role which serves their comfort and their selfish interests.

Here I must become autobiographical, and not apologetically so, since I believe that all theory, all understanding, all "objective" research begins (and usually ends) in autobiography. I would thus be less than candid if I did not state frankly that this is basically an autobiographical work. It is based upon my knowledge of those women to whom this book is dedicated and, above all, on twenty-eight years of married life. I find I must ask myself, most insistently, if my emphasis on the life-enhancing role of women as their "natural" role is based on a selfish exploitation of their sex? The answer is not one that I can properly give. Protesting the purity of one's motives is rarely convincing, and mine are, I am sure, no purer than the next man's. I can only say that I cannot imagine that my wife could do so graciously and gracefully the things she does if they were not as much of a delight to her to do as they are to me as the principal though by no means exclusive beneficiary of them.

If she does all these things so marvelously well under the illusion that she enjoys them, tricked by the masculine-dominated culture's notion of her proper role, then, I can only say, we should all be happier in the shadow of such illusions.

There is much, as I hope this book makes clear, that is seriously amiss with regard to the situation of women in America but I can hardly believe that the remedy is to be found in a fretful and vindictive spirit on the part of women or, indeed, of men who clearly have much to answer for. Many men and women in American life lead truncated and diminished lives, but surely the solution is not to be found in women insisting upon living the man's life in every possible particular. She has every right to expect the best of *both* worlds, "her" world and the world she identifies as "his"; home and children if she wishes and whatever career her interests and talents draw her to. Many women will wish to explore what Ben DeMott calls "the rich freedoms of a subsidized life."

The same author has, I think, stated the issue as well as it is likely to be stated: "The case is that the [women's liberation movement] idea has great honing powers — and whether or not marriage is, as the wise man said, the only adventure open to the cowardly, it plainly ought to have an edge. And an edge sharpens when unconscious assumption is confronted, and when truths of possibility, both the risk and the promise, come clear." The women's movement can be a "means of opening ourselves, sounding the depths of our still insufficiently acknowledged personal responsibility for the terms of our daily life" (*The Atlantic*, March, 1970, page 117). For that is, after all, the arena where all these issues must ultimately be decided and here patience and love and a capacity for mutual sacrifice are, finally, our best guides. In the lingo of the youth culture I wish, with certain cautious, middle-aged qualifications, to "make love, not war," for of all the wars the species can wage, that between the sexes is certainly the most futile and the most dangerous.

Chapter Notes

CHAPTER 1

1. Robert Briffault, *The Mothers* (New York and London, 1927), II, 430–432. A law of Manu, the Hindu lawgiver, states: "The wisdom, the energy, the strength, the might, and the vitality of a man who approaches a woman covered with menstrual excretions, utterly perish. If he avoids her while she is in that condition his wisdom, energy, strength, might and vitality will all increase." G. Buhler, "The Laws of Manu," *Sacred Books of the East* (Oxford, 1879–1910), XXV, 135.
2. Briffault, *The Mothers*, II, 432.
3. M. Esther Harding, *Woman's Mysteries: Ancient and Modern* (Los Angeles and New York, 1955), 38.
4. L. W. King, *Seven Tablets of Creation* (London, 1902), I, 223.
5. Harding, *Woman's Mysteries*, 142.
6. Briffault, *The Mothers*, III, 207–208.
7. John A. Wilson, *The Burden of Egypt* (Chicago, 1951), 94.
8. Werner Jaeger, *Paideia* (Oxford, 1939), I, 21.
9. Jaeger, *Paideia*, I, 95.
10. Jaeger, *Paideia*, I, 131–132.
11. Humphrey D. Kitto, *The Greeks* (Baltimore, 1965), 221.
12. Aristotle, *Politics* I.2.183, quoted in *The Philosophy of Aristotle* edited by Renford Bambrough (New York, 1963), 74.
13. J. P. V. D. Balsdon, *Roman Women* (New York, 1963), 63.
14. Tacitus, *Annals*, XIV, 1ff., quoted in Balsdon, *Roman Women*, 212–213.
15. Balsdon, *Roman Women*, 207.
16. Juvenal 6.82–113, quoted in Balsdon, *Roman Women*, 212–213.
17. Balsdon, *Roman Women*, 242, 237.
18. J. J. Bachofen, *Myth, Religion and Mother Right*, selected writings translated by Ralph Manheim (Princeton, 1967), xlix.

CHAPTER 2

1. Frederick Heer, *The Medieval World* (New York, 1963), 173.
2. Emily James Putnam, *The Lady: Studies of Certain Significant Phases of Her History* (New York, 1910), 71.
3. Heer, *The Medieval World*, 114.
4. Heer, *The Medieval World*, 172.
5. Johann Huizinga, *Waning of the Middle Ages* (London, 1948), 95.
6. Heer, *The Medieval World*, 181.
7. Dante Alighieri, *The Divine Comedy*, translated by Dorothy L. Sayers and Barbara Reynolds (Baltimore, 1967), Canto XXXI, 82–90.

CHAPTER 3

1. South Carolina Magazine, XXIII, 86–88; quoted in Julia Spruill, *Women's Life and Work in the Southern Colonies* (Chapel Hill, 1938), 136.
2. Quoted in Spruill, *Women's Life and Work*, 137.

3. Quoted in Spruill, *Women's Life and Work*, 137.
4. Frederick Gay, "Rev. Francis Marbury," Mass. Hist. Soc. *Proceedings*, XLVIII (Boston, 1915), 281; quoted in Emery Battis, *Saints and Secretaries* (Chapel Hill, 1962), 8.
5. John Winthrop, *Journal* (New York, 1908), 133.
6. John Calvin, *Institutes of Christian Religion* (Philadelphia, n.d.), II, Chapter VIII, 41–43.
7. Calvin, *Christian Religion*, II, Chapter VIII, 44.
8. Jonathan Edwards; quoted in Perry Miller, *Edwards* (New York, 1948), 201–202.
9. Thomas Clap; quoted in Louis Leonard Tucker, *Puritan Protagonist* (Chapel Hill, 1962), 36.
10. Margaret Fuller, *Women in the Nineteenth Century* (Boston, 1855), 38–40.
11. Quoted in George Willison, *Saints and Strangers* (New York, 1945), 324.
12. Emil Oberholzer, Jr., *Delinquent Saints* (New York, 1956), 39–40.
13. Oberholzer, *Saints*, 63.
14. Oberholzer, *Saints*, 137.
15. "Boundary Line Proceedings," *Virginia Magazine*, V, 10.
16. Spruill, *Women's Life and Work*, 236.
17. Elizabeth Dall, *College, Market and Court* (New York, 1867), 226.

CHAPTER 4

1. Page Smith, *James Wilson* (Chapel Hill, 1956), 32–33.
2. Quoted in Smith, *James Wilson*, 34.
3. John Adams, *Adams Papers, Diary and Autobiography* (Cambridge, Mass., 1963), III, 265.
4. *Lady's Magazine*, May, 1773, 238; quoted in Julia Spruill, *Women's Life and Work in the Southern Colonies* (Chapel Hill, 1938), 167.
5. John Quincy Adams; quoted in Page Smith, *Adams* (New York, 1962), II, 657.
6. Benjamin Rush to Rebecca Smith, *Letters of Benjamin Rush* (Philadelphia, 1792), I, 617.
7. Moreau de St. Méry, *Moreau de St. Méry's American Journey, 1793–1798*, translated and edited by Kenneth Roberts and Anna Roberts (New York, 1947), 287–288.
8. Spruill, *Women's Life and Work*, 243.
9. Alexis de Tocqueville, *Democracy in America* (New York, 1945), II, 201.
10. Paul Achard, *A New Slant on America* (Chicago and New York, 1931), 137–138.
11. Spruill, *Women's Life and Work*, 154.
12. Quoted in Spruill, *Women's Life and Work*, 155.
13. Frederick Marryat, *A Diary in America*, edited by Sydney Jackman (New York, 1962), 425.
14. Smith, *Adams*, I, 225.
15. John Adams to Mercy Warren, *Warren-Adams Letters* (Boston, 1917), I, M.H.S. Collections, LXXII, 221–224.

16. John Adams to Abigail Smith; quoted in *The Adams Papers, Adams Family Correspondence,* edited by L. H. Butterfield (Cambridge, Mass., 1963), I, 2.
17. John Adams; quoted in *The Adams Papers,* I, 3.
18. John Adams; quoted in *The Adams Papers,* I, 4.
19. John Adams; quoted in *The Adams Papers,* I, 24.
20. Charles Francis Adams; quoted in *The Adams Papers, Diary of Charles Francis Adams,* edited by Aida DiPace Donald and David Donald (Cambridge, Mass., 1964), II, 107.
21. Charles Francis Adams; quoted in *Diary of Charles Francis Adams,* II, 118.
22. Charles Francis Adams; quoted in *Diary of Charles Francis Adams,* II, 124.

CHAPTER 5

1. James Fullerton Muirhead, *The Land of Contrasts: A Briton's View of His American Kin* (Boston, New York and London, 1908), 46.
2. Captain Frederick Marryat, *A Diary in America,* edited by S. W. Jackman (New York, 1962), 420.
3. Marryat, *A Diary in America,* 366.
4. Alexis de Tocqueville, *Democracy in America* (New York, 1945), II, 213–214.
5. de Tocqueville, *Democracy in America,* II, 212.
6. Muirhead, *Land of Contrasts,* 49.
7. Muirhead, *Land of Contrasts,* 59–60.
8. Muirhead, *Land of Contrasts,* 54–55.
9. James Bryce, *The American Commonwealth* (New York, 1912), II, 600, 795.
10. Bryce, *American Commonwealth,* II, 797.
11. Beatrice Forbes-Robertson Hale, *What Women Want* (New York, 1914), 162.
12. Paul Achard, *A New Slant on America* (Chicago and New York, 1931), 136.
13. Achard, *New Slant on America,* 135–138.
14. Moreau de St. Méry, *Moreau de St. Méry's American Journey, 1793–1798,* translated and edited by Kenneth Roberts and Anna Roberts (New York, 1947), 283.
15. Frances Wright, *Views of Society and Manners in America* (Cambridge, 1963), 24–25.
16. de Tocqueville, *Democracy in America,* II, 198–200.
17. de Tocqueville, *Democracy in America,* II, 205.
18. Bryce, *The American Commonwealth,* II, 801.
19. Bryce, *The American Commonwealth,* II, 804, 802.
20. Marquis de Chastellux, *Travel in North America in the Years 1780, 1781 and 1782* (Chapel Hill, 1963), I, 68.
21. Madame Blanc, *The Condition of Women in the United States* (Boston, 1895), 26–27.
22. Achard, *New Slant on America,* 133–135.

CHAPTER NOTES

23. Muirhead, *Land of Contrasts*, 50, 51, 53.
24. Chastellux, *Travel in North America*, II, 417–418.
25. St. Méry, *American Journey*, 283.
26. Marryat, *A Diary in America*, 340, 343–344, 418–419.
27. de Tocqueville, *Democracy in America*, II, 201.
28. Marryat, *A Diary in America*, 422–424.
29. Frances Trollope, *Domestic Manners of the Americans*, edited by Donald Smalley (New York, 1949), 413.
30. James Stirling, *Letters from the Slave States* (London, 1857), 155–159.
31. Marryat, *A Diary in America*, 424–425.
32. Mary Boykin Chesnut, *Diary from Dixie*, edited by Ben Ames Williams (Boston, 1949), 186.
33. de Tocqueville, *Democracy in America*, II, 201–202.
34. Trollope, *Domestic Manners*, 155–156, 299.
35. Hale, *What Women Want*, 154, 157.
36. Trollope, *Domestic Manners*, 285.

CHAPTER 6

1. Mary Wollstonecraft, *A Vindication of the Rights of Women*, edited by Charles Hagelman, Jr. (New York, 1967), 53.
2. Wollstonecraft, *Vindication*, Introduction, 19.
3. Wollstonecraft, *Vindication*, 33, 209, 247, 255.
4. Wollstonecraft, *Vindication*, 72.
5. Wollstonecraft, *Vindication*, 122.
6. Wollstonecraft, *Vindication*, 84.
7. Hannah More, *Strictures on the Modern System of Female Education* (New York, 1813), 155–157.
8. More, *Strictures*, 22.

CHAPTER 7

1. Sarah Grimké; quoted in Gerda Lerner, *Grimké Sisters* (Boston, 1967), 37.
2. Sarah Grimké; quoted in Lerner, *Grimké Sisters*, 52–53.
3. Angelina Grimké; quoted in Lerner, *Grimké Sisters*, 78–79.
4. Sarah Grimké; quoted in Lerner, *Grimké Sisters*, 251.
5. Angelina Grimké; quoted in Lerner, *Grimké Sisters*, 223.
6. Lerner, *Grimké Sisters*, 224–225, 242.
7. Lucretia Mott; quoted in *Eminent Women of the Age* (Hartford, 1868), 373–376.
8. Elizabeth Cady; quoted in *Eminent Women*, 334, 337.
9. Elizabeth Cady; quoted in *Eminent Women*, 338.
10. Lerner, *Grimké Sisters*, 95.
11. James Bryce, *The American Commonwealth* (New York, 1912), II, 602.
12. Nette Brown to Lucy Stone, Oberlin, September 22, 1847, Blackwell Papers, Schlesinger Archives, Radcliffe College, Cambridge, Mass.
13. Nette Brown to Lucy Stone, n.d. but apparently 1847, Schlesinger Archives.
14. Nette Brown to Lucy Stone, Oberlin, n.d. Schlesinger Archives.

CHAPTER NOTES

15. Nette Brown to Lucy Stone, Oberlin, September 28, 1847, Schlesinger Archives.
16. *Eminent Women,* 346–348.
17. Nette Brown to Lucy Stone, April 14, 1852, Schlesinger Archives.
18. Nette Brown to Lucy Stone, Henrietta, December 16, 1852, Schlesinger Archives.
19. Lucy Stone to Nette Brown, April 14, 1852, Schlesinger Archives.
20. Nette Brown to Lucy Stone, Henrietta, August 16, 1853, Schlesinger Archives.
21. Nette Brown to Sam Blackwell, n.d., Schlesinger Archives.
22. Nette Brown to Susan Anthony, January 28, 1856, Schlesinger Archives.
23. Nette Brown Blackwell to Susan Anthony, Newark, April 23, 1858, Schlesinger Archives.
24. Susan Anthony to Nette Brown Blackwell, Seneca Falls, May 2, 1858, Schlesinger Archives.
25. Susan Anthony to Nette Brown Blackwell, September 4, 1858, Schlesinger Archives.
26. Susan Anthony to Nette Brown Blackwell, April 28, 1858, Schlesinger Archives.
27. Lucy Stone; quoted by Elinor Rice Hays, *Morning Star* (New York, 1961).
28. Nette Brown Blackwell to Susan Anthony, Newark, March 12, 1856, Schlesinger Archives.
29. *History of Woman Suffrage, 1815–1902,* edited by Elizabeth Cady Stanton (New York, 1881–1922), I, ii.
30. *History of Woman Suffrage,* I, 15.

CHAPTER 8

1. Gerda Lerner, *Grimké Sisters* (Boston, 1967), 233.
2. Lerner, *Grimké Sisters,* 7.
3. Lerner, *Grimké Sisters,* 371–374.
4. Lillian O'Connor, *Pioneer Women Orators* (New York, 1954), 36.
5. *America Through Women's Eyes,* edited by Mary Beard (New York, 1933), 201.
6. Dr. Mary Walker, *Hit* (New York, 1871), 33.
7. Blackwell Papers, Schlesinger Archives, Cambridge, Mass.
8. D. C. Bloomer, *Life and Writings of Amelia Bloomer* (Boston, 1895), 106–110.
9. *The Diary of George Templeton Strong,* edited by Allan Nevins and Milton Halsey Thomas (New York, 1952), II, 130.

CHAPTER 9

1. Moreau de St. Méry, *New Travels in the United States of America, 1788,* edited by Durand Echeverria (Cambridge, 1964), 280.
2. Beatrice Forbes-Robertson Hale, *What Women Want* (New York, 1914), 244.

CHAPTER NOTES

3. Catharine Beecher, *Letters to the People on Health and Happiness* (New York, 1855), 211.

4. Beecher, *Letters,* 24, 124, 133.

5. Lyman Beecher Stowe, *Saints, Sinners and Beechers* (Indianapolis, 1933), 460.

6. Harriet Beecher Stowe to Calvin Stowe, Brattleboro, Vermont, May 27, 1846, Beecher Papers, Schlesinger Archives, Radcliffe College, Cambridge, Mass.

7. Harriet Beecher Stowe to Calvin Stowe, Brattleboro, Vermont, January 24, 1847, Beecher Papers.

CHAPTER 10

1. *America Through Women's Eyes,* edited by Mary Beard (New York, 1933), 230–231.

2. Alma Lutz, *Susan B. Anthony, Rebel, Crusader, Humanitarian* (Boston, 1959), 163. The Republican party flirted in 1870 with the notion of pushing for woman's suffrage through Congress and the courts rather than going the long and uncertain route of amendment.

3. *America Through Women's Eyes,* 231–232.

4. Emanie Sachs, *The Terrible Siren* (New York, 1928), 66–67, 71–73, 79, 81, 87, 94.

5. George Templeton Strong, *Diary,* edited by Allan Nevins and Milton Halsey Thomas (New York, 1952), 132–133, 244–245.

6. Tennie C. Claflin, *Constitutional Equality: A Right of Women* (New York, 1871), 143.

7. Claflin, *Constitutional Equality,* 27, 28.

8. Claflin, *Constitutional Equality,* 63, 64.

9. Claflin, *Constitutional Equality,* 21, 63.

10. Claflin, *Constitutional Equality,* 147, 148.

11. Claflin, *Constitutional Equality,* 71.

12. Claflin, *Constitutional Equality,* 75.

13. Sachs, *The Terrible Siren,* 218–219, 223.

14. Elizabeth Cady, *Newark Call;* quoted in Sachs, *The Terrible Siren,* 235.

15. Victoria Woodhull, *The Human Body, The Temple of God* (London, 1890), 29–31.

16. Woodhull, *The Human Body,* 51, 53.

17. Lawrence Lader and Milton Meltzer, *Margaret Sanger: Pioneer of Birth Control* (New York, 1969), 53.

18. Lader and Meltzer, *Margaret Sanger,* 28–30.

19. Lader and Meltzer, *Margaret Sanger,* 65.

20. Lader and Meltzer, *Margaret Sanger,* 71.

21. Lader and Meltzer, *Margaret Sanger,* 73.

22. Lader and Meltzer, *Margaret Sanger,* 88.

23. Margaret Sanger Papers, Sophia Smith Collection, Smith College, Northampton, Mass.

24. Alexander Berkman to Margaret Sanger, San Francisco, December 9, 1915, Margaret Sanger Papers.

25. Lader and Meltzer, *Margaret Sanger,* 79.

CHAPTER 11

1. Lucy Stone to Mrs. Stanton, August 14, 1853 and October 22, 1855; quoted in Nelson M. Blake, *The Road to Reno* (New York, 1962), 89.
2. Lucy Stone, December 10, 1867; quoted in Katherine Anthony, *Susan B. Anthony* (New York, 1964), 58.
3. Henry Blackwell in *Woman's Journal,* I (June 4, 1870); quoted in Blake, *Road to Reno,* 104.
4. *Revolution,* VI (October 27, 1870), 264.
5. Blake, *Road to Reno,* 106.
6. Nette Brown to Lucy Stone, Elizabeth, New Jersey, January 6, 1886, Blackwell Papers, Schlesinger Archives, Radcliffe College, Cambridge, Mass.
7. Nette Brown to Lucy Stone, August 1889, Schlesinger Archives.
8. Nette Brown to Lucy Stone, Elizabeth, New Jersey, February 10, 1888, Schlesinger Archives.
9. Catharine Beecher, *Woman Suffrage and Woman's Profession* (Boston, 1871), 3–4.
10. Beecher, *Woman Suffrage,* 4, 7, 11, 12.
11. Beecher, *Woman Suffrage,* 52.
12. Beecher, *Woman Suffrage,* 58, 181, 60.
13. *The Book of Woman's Power* (New York, 1911), xi.
14. *Book of Woman's Power,* 228, 230.
15. *The Woman Question in Europe,* edited by Theodore Stanton (New York, 1884), xv–xvi.
16. Dio Lewis, *Our Girls* (New York, 1871), 10.
17. Beatrice Forbes-Robertson Hale, *What Women Want* (New York, 1914), 227.
18. Charlotte Perkins Gilman, *Women and Economics,* edited by Carl N. Degler (New York, 1966), 168.

CHAPTER 12

1. Margaret Fuller, *Woman in the Nineteenth Century* (Boston, 1855), 37, 156, 176.
2. Frances Trollope, *Domestic Manners of the Americans,* edited by Donald Smalley (New York, 1949), 75. Frances Trollope described a typical social gathering of young married women. Eight ladies forgather and "stitch together for some hours. Their talk is of priests and missions; of the profits of their last [church] sale, of their hopes from the next; of the doubt whether young Mr. This, or young Mr. That should receive the fruits of it to fit him out for Liberia; of the very ugly bonnet seen at church on Sabbath morning, of the very handsome preacher who performed on Sabbath afternoon, and of the very large collection made on Sabbath evening." 282.
3. Julia Spruill, *Women's Life and Work in the Southern Colonies* (Chapel Hill, 1938), 248.

CHAPTER NOTES

4. Alexis de Tocqueville, *Democracy in America* (New York, 1945), II, 31–32.
5. Charles Fillmore, *The Twelve Powers of Man* (Missouri, 1930), 167; quoted in Donald Meyer, *The Positive Thinkers* (New York, 1965), 119.
6. Meyer, *Positive Thinkers,* 46.

CHAPTER 13

1. William E. Strong, *The Story of the American Board* (Boston, 1910), 143–144.
2. Fred Field Goodsell, *American Board of Commissioners for Foreign Missions* (Boston, 1959), 35, 19.
3. Goodsell, *American Board of Commissioners,* 35.
4. Goodsell, *American Board of Commissioners,* 50.
5. Goodsell, *American Board of Commissioners,* 51.
6. Goodsell, *American Board of Commissioners,* 42.
7. Sir Charles Napier; quoted in Fawn Brodie, *The Devil Drives* (New York, 1967), 64.
8. Goodsell, *American Board of Commissioners,* 160.
9. *Preparation of Women for Foreign Missionary Service* (New York, 1916), 20, 25, 27.
10. The quotations are all from Loanza Goulding Benton's diary in the Sophia Smith Collections at Smith College, Northampton, Mass.
11. Loanza Goulding Benton's diary, Sophia Smith Collections.
12. Loanza Goulding Benton, March 3, 1845, Sophia Smith Collections.
13. Katherine Pearce, September 17 and November 14, 1920, Sophia Smith Collection.
14. Rebecca Toy Lore's diary, Sophia Smith Collection.
15. Louise Snowden Porter, 1934, Mount Holyoke College Verse, Ada L. F. Snell, editor (New York, 1937), 88–90. This poem has an additional poignancy for me since it was called to my attention by my dear friend Douglass Adair shortly before his death.

CHAPTER 14

1. Frances Trollope, *Domestic Manners of the Americans,* edited by Donald Smalley (New York, 1949), 401.
2. Captain Frederick Marryat, *A Diary in America,* edited by S. W. Jackman (New York, 1962), 391.
3. Catharine and Harriet Beecher, *The American Woman's Home* (New York, 1869), 452.
4. Madame Blanc, *The Condition of Women in the United States* (Boston, 1895), 291.
5. Charlotte Perkins Gilman, *Women and Economics,* edited by Carl N. Degler (New York, 1966), 256.
6. Marryat, *A Diary in America,* 352.
7. Marryat, *A Diary in America,* 351.
8. *My Mother or Recollections of Maternal Influence* (Boston, 1856), 166, 152.

9. *My Mother*, 190.
10. Donald Meyer, *The Positive Thinkers* (New York, 1965), 54, 55.
11. Gilman, *Women and Economics*, 181, 189.
12. Gilman, *Women and Economics*, 193.
13. Ellen Keyes, *The Century of the Child* (New York, 1909), 84.
14. Beatrice Forbes-Robertson Hale, *What Women Want* (New York, 1914), 276, 277, 285.

CHAPTER 15

1. *America Through Women's Eyes*, edited by Mary Beard (New York, 1933), 34, 36.
2. Josiah Quincy; quoted in Julia Spruill, *Women's Life and Work in the Southern Colonies* (Chapel Hill, 1938), 177.
3. Mary Chesnut, *A Diary from Dixie*, edited by Ben Ames Williams (Boston, 1949), 122.
4. Chesnut, *Diary from Dixie*, 162–164, 165, 166.
5. *Secret Diary of William Byrd*, edited by Louis B. Wright and Marion Tinling (Richmond, Virginia, 1941), 68.
6. Marquis de Chastelleux, *Travel in North America in the Years 1780, 1781 and 1782* (Chapel Hill, 1963), II, 441–442.
7. *Secret Diary of William Byrd*, 107.
8. Charles Woodmason, *The Carolina Backcountry on the Eve of the Revolution, The Journal of the Reverend Charles Woodmason*, edited by Richard J. Hooker (North Carolina, 1953), 56.
9. Woodmason, *The Carolina Backcountry on the Eve of the Revolution*, 31–32, 61.
10. Alexis de Tocqueville, *Democracy in America*, edited by Phillip Bradley (New York, 1945), 203.
11. D. C. Bloomer, *Life and Writings of Amelia Bloomer* (Boston, 1895), 212.
12. Madame Blanc, *The Condition of Women in the United States* (Boston, 1895), 208, 214.
13. James Bryce, *The American Commonwealth* (New York, 1912), II, 803
14. *Report of the International Council of Women* (Washington, D.C. 1888), 77.

CHAPTER 16

1. Ralcy Husted Bell, *Woman from Bondage to Freedom* (New York 1921), 201.
2. Bell, *Woman from Bondage to Freedom*, 284, 287.
3. Elizabeth Blackwell, *Counsel to Parents on the Moral Education of Their Children* (New York, 1883), 72, 5.
4. Blackwell, *Christian Duty in Regard to Vice*, 4, 5.
5. Horace Greeley in *The Liberator*, November 24, 1865.
6. Beatrice Forbes-Robertson Hale, *What Women Want* (New York, 1914 247, 88–89.

7. *Report of the International Council of Women* (Washington, D.C., 1888), 250–251.

8. Elizabeth Blackwell, *The Moral Education of the Young in Relation to Sex, Under Medical and Social Aspects* (Boston, 1884), 6.

9. Bell, *Woman from Bondage to Freedom,* 194.

10. Hale, *What Women Want,* 257.

11. Bell, *Woman from Bondage to Freedom,* 204.

12. Hale, *What Women Want,* 260.

13. Bell, *Woman from Bondage to Freedom,* 228.

14. Hale, *What Women Want,* 257.

15. Florence Tuttle, *The Awakening of Woman: Suggestions from the Psychic Side of Feminism* (New York, 1915), 125, 150–151, 163.

16. Elisabeth Mann Borgese, *Ascent of Woman* (New York, 1963), 220–224.

CHAPTER *17*

1. Florida Pier, "The Masculine and the Feminine Mind," *Harper's Weekly,* September 24, 1910.

2. Teresa Billington-Craig, "Feminism and Politics," *Contemporary Review,* November 1911.

3. Florence Tuttle, *The Awakening of Woman: Suggestions from the Psychic Side of Feminism* (New York, 1915), 27.

4. Quoted in William O'Neill, *Divorce in the Progressive Era* (New Haven, 1967), 124.

5. Ernestine Evans, "A Woman Who Has Found Freedom," *Independent,* May 25, 1914, 135; quoted in O'Neill, *Divorce in the Progressive Era,* 125.

6. Edward Carpenter, *Love's Coming of Age* (London, 1903), 11, 103.

7. Kitty Blackwell to Alice Stone Blackwell, Dorchester, Massachusetts, March 1, 1912, Blackwell Papers, Schlesinger Archives, Radcliffe College, Cambridge, Mass.

8. *The Viking Book of Aphorisms,* edited by W. H. Auden and Louis Kronenberger (New York, 1960), 168.

9. Ferdinand Lundberg and Marynia F. Farnham, *Modern Woman, The Lost Sex* (New York, 1947), 3.

10. Lundberg and Farnham, *Modern Woman, The Lost Sex,* 77.

11. Lundberg and Farnham, *Modern Woman, The Lost Sex,* 173.

12. Charlotte Perkins Gilman, *Woman and Economics,* edited by Carl N. Degler (New York, 1966), 42, 60, 65.

13. Gilman, *Women and Economics,* 26, 30, 33, 38, 42.

14. Gilman, *Women and Economics,* 75, 95.

15. Gilman, *Women and Economics,* 119–121.

16. Gilman, *Women and Economics,* 267.

17. Gilman, *Women and Economics,* 156.

18. Gilman, *Women and Economics,* 231–233, 253, 243.

19. Gilman, *Women and Economics,* 129, 132, 149, 216.

20. Gilman, *Women and Economics,* 304, 306, 313, 317, 337.

21. Ethel Mannin, *Women and the Revolution* (New York, 1939), 289, 300.
22. *The Woman Question — Selections from the Writings of Karl Marx, Frederick Engels, V. I. Lenin, and Joseph Stalin* (New York, 1951), 68.

CHAPTER *18*

1. Phebe A. Hanaford, *Daughters of America or Women of the Century* (Augusta, Maine, 1883), 380.
2. *Report of the International Council of Women* (Washington, D.C., 1888), 110.
3. Anne Firor Scott, "The 'New Woman' in the New South," *South Atlantic Quarterly,* LXI, Autumn 1962, 477.
4. *Report of the International Council of Women,* 114.
5. *Report of the International Council of Women,* 118.
6. *Report of the International Council of Women,* 10, 33, 24–26.
7. *Report of the International Council of Women,* 29, 32, 35.
8. Madame Blanc, *The Condition of Women in the United States* (Boston, 1895), 39.
9. *The Congress of Women . . . World's Columbian Exposition, Chicago, U.S.A., 1893,* edited by Mary Kavanaugh Oldham Eagle (Philadelphia, 1895), 329–331.
10. *The Congress of Women,* 706–707.
11. Madame Blanc, *The Condition of Women,* 88–89.
12. Scott, "The 'New Woman' in the New South," 478.
13. Charlotte Perkins Gilman, *Women and Economics,* edited by Carl N. Degler (New York, 1966), 164, 166.
14. Madame Blanc, *The Condition of Women,* 44, 49, 52.
15. Beatrice Forbes-Robertson Hale, *What Women Want* (New York, 1914), 79.
16. Hale, *What Women Want,* 85.
17. Madame Blanc, *The Condition of Women,* 90.
18. Madame Blanc, *The Condition of Women,* 191.
19. The papers and letters which record this friendship are in the Schlesinger Archives, Radcliffe College, Cambridge, Mass.
20. Margaret Robins to Mary Anderson, December 4, 1931, Schlesinger Archives.
21. Hale, *What Women Want,* 81.
22. James Bryce, *The American Commonwealth* (New York, 1912), II, 809.
23. Clayton Fritchey, *San Francisco Chronicle,* Sunday, July 7, 1968.

CHAPTER *19*

1. Harriet Martineau, *Society in America* (New York, 1962), 307.
2. Dio Lewis, *Our Girls* (New York, 1871), 131, 134.
3. M. L. Rayne, *What Can a Woman Do* (Peterborough, New York, 1893), 21, 25, 42.
4. Rayne, *What Can a Woman Do,* 105–106, 108.
5. Rayne, *What Can a Woman Do,* 120–121, 159–161.
6. Rayne, *What Can a Woman Do,* 176, 197.

7. *The Diary of George Templeton Strong,* edited by Allan Nevins and Milton Halsey Thomas (New York, 1952), IV, 256.
8. Strong, *Diary,* IV, 136.
9. Werner Sombart, *Luxury and Capitalism* (Ann Arbor, 1967), 171.
10. Mrs. John Van Vorst and Marie Van Vorst, *The Woman Who Toils* (New York, 1903), 113.
11. Van Vorst and Van Vorst, *The Woman Who Toils,* 80–82.
12. Elisabeth Mann Borgese, *Ascent of Woman* (New York, 1963), 46.
13. Beatrice Forbes-Robertson Hale, *What Women Want* (New York, 1914), 290.

CHAPTER 20

1. Abbey Price, *Proceedings,* Woman's Rights Convention, Worcester, Massachusetts, 1850.
2. Ralcy Husted Bell, *Woman from Bondage to Freedom* (New York, 1921), 230.
3. Lester F. Ward, *Dynamic Sociology* (New York, 1897), I, 657.
4. C. Gasquoine Hartley; quoted in Ferdinand Lundberg and Marynia F. Farnham, *Modern Woman, The Lost Sex* (New York, 1947), 458.
5. Jesse Bernard, *Academic Women* (University Park, Pennsylvania, 1964), 98.
6. Bernard, *Academic Women,* 111.
7. Bernard, *Academic Women,* 125, 83.
8. Bernard, *Academic Women,* 173.
9. Bernard, *Academic Women,* 210.
10. Bernard, *Academic Women,* 62.
11. *Educated American Women:* Self-Portraits, edited by Eli Ginsberg and Alice M. Yohalem (New York, 1966), 159.
12. Eli Ginsberg, *et al., Life Styles of Educated Women* (New York, 1966), 120.
13. *American Women: The Changing Image,* edited by Beverly Cassara (Boston, 1962), xi–xii.
14. *American Women,* xiv.
15. *American Women,* 11, 17.

CHAPTER 21

1. Alexander Walker, *Woman Physiologically Considered as to Mind, Morals, Marriage, Matrimonial Slavery, Infidelity and Divorce* (New York, 1840), 6–7.
2. Beatrice Forbes-Robertson Hale, *What Women Want* (New York, 1914), 52–53.
3. Quoted in Lewis Atherton, *Main Street on the Middle Border* (Bloomington, Indiana, 1954), 91–92.
4. Elisabeth Mann Borgese, *Ascent of Woman* (New York, 1963), 55.
5. Hale, *What Women Want,* 304.

CHAPTER NOTES

6. *Viking Book of Aphorisms,* edited by W. H. Auden and Louis Kronenberger (New York, 1962), 173.
7. W. B. Yeats, *Dramatis Personae* (Dublin, 1935).
8. *Viking Book of Aphorisms,* 167.
9. *Viking Book of Aphorisms,* 171.
10. Boris Pasternak to Nina Tabidze, September 30, 1953; Boris Pasternak, *Letters to Georgian Friends* (New York, 1967).
11. H. L. Mencken, *In Defense of Women* (New York, 1928), 6.

CHAPTER 22

1. Captain Frederick Marryat, *A Diary in America,* edited by S. W. Jackman (New York, 1962), 418.
2. Frances Trollope, *Domestic Manners of the Americans,* edited by Donald Smalley (New York, 1949), 422.
3. James Bryce, *The American Commonwealth* (New York, 1912), II, 805, 809, 610.
4. D. H. Lawrence, *Studies in Classic American Literature* (London, 1937), 24.
5. *Futurist, A Newsletter for Tomorrow's World,* Vol. 1, No. 2, April 1967.
6. *Viking Book of Aphorisms,* edited by W. H. Auden and Louis Kronenberger (New York, 1962), 186.

Index

laws. *See* Israelites: laws; Puritanism
lawyers, in America, 89, 302: women
    as, 258, 276–78 *passim,* 282, 295
Leadville, Colo., 278
League of Women Voters, 273
Lease, Mary, 170
leisure: followed by sex, 283
Leiter, Fannie, 254
Lenin, Vladimir, 271, 301
lesbianism: in America, 88; in Eng-
    land, 95. *See also* homosexuality
Levy, Helen Solomon, 175
Lewis, Dr. Dio: supports woman's
    rights, 171; inspires W.C.T.U.,
    254; promotes women's occupa-
    tions, 276–77, 280
liberation, necessity of, 99. *See also*
    equality, feminine
Liberia, 106
Lincoln, Abraham, 141
Livy, 12
Lore, Rebecca Toy, 199
Lornez, Konrad, 4
love: in Greece, 10, 11; spiritualized,
    11; Christian, 24, 29; Platonic, 27;
    courtly, 28–31, 33; romantic, 31,
    42–45, 63, 65, 98; sacred and pro-
    fane, 29; necessity, for women,
    144; erotic, 161
Love's Coming of Age (Carpenter),
    239
Lucius Apuleius, 5
Lundberg, Ferdinand (*Modern
    Woman, The Lost Sex*), 303
Luther, Martin: initiates Reforma-
    tion, 33; language, 61*n.*
luxury: as basis of capitalism, 283;
    women's need for, 285

makeup: Puritan disapproval, 49;
    sale, 290
maiden name: retained in marriage,
    117–18
Mann Act, 231
Mannin, Ethel: theories on economic
    effects on women, 250–51; anti-
    capitalism, 293
Maori tribes: attitude toward men-
    struation, 4

marriage: passion in, 20, 98, 143;
    fidelity, 20–21, 64, 234, 315–16;
    as antidote to sexuality, 23–24, 41;
    monogamous, 24, 35, 97, 101, 150,
    234, 243, 251, 316, 337–39, 346;
    subordinate to social and religious
    purposes, 41, 61–62; romantic
    choice of mates, 41–42; mutuality,
    as ideal, 41, 43–47, 237; private
    choice of mate, 62–63; relation-
    ship of materialism to, 64–65, 89–
    91; as woman's weapon, 82;
    abolition advocated, 97, 150; equal-
    ity in, 97–98, 100; arranged, 218–
    19; role of, 313–14; successful,
    315; order in, 320–21, 321*n.;*
    importance, to women, 323–24;
    early, 337. *See also* courtship; di-
    vorce; marriage, historical per-
    spective; husbands; sexual rela-
    tions; wives
marriage, historical perspective: in
    Babylon, 8; in Egypt, 8–9; in
    Greece, 9–11, 15; Roman, 11, 13–
    15; Hebrew, 20–21; Christian at-
    titude toward, 24–25, 41, 62; Prot-
    estant attitude toward, 33, 41, 62,
    63. *See also* marriage
    PURITAN: sexuality, 40, 42, 44;
    aims, 41–43; romantic choice of
    mates, 41–43; precontract, 42, 44,
    50, 56, 61, 75, 219, 336; mutuality,
    41, 43–47; advice to wives, 48–49;
    adultery, 51, 52
    NINETEENTH CENTURY: loss of
    mutuality, 45, 75, 237; intolerable
    to women, 66, 151; male attitude
    toward, 70–71, 136–38; age, 74;
    wives' subordination, 91–92, 133,
    237; wives' fidelity, 64, 92; wives'
    constricted existence, 88–89, 121,
    126; failure, 131–32, 139, 143–44,
    148–49, 230–31, 333–34; female
    attitude toward intercourse, 132,
    138, 139, 149, 227–28, 230, 240;
    wives' strategies, 138; revision
    proposed, 148–50; men's restraint
    advocated, 230

sexual relations (intercourse)
(*continued*)

84, 336–38; extramarital, 64, 68–69, 71, 246, 315–16; age of consent, 231; "spiritualized" (sublimated), 234–35, 242; necessity for spiritual in, 239; mechanics, 239–42; twentieth-century status, 251, 338; role in future, 338–39, 340–41, 346. *See also* adultery; pregnancy; prostitution; rape; sexual rights, women's; sexuality

sexual rights (emancipation), women's: Mary Wollstonecraft's theories, 98–100, 143–44, 147, 238; devices to secure, 138–39, 144; issue in woman's rights movement, 143, 145, 157, 164–67, 238–40; free love issue, 144–48, 150–51, 163, 166, 231, 234–36 *passim*, 294; principles articulated by Clafins, 152–53, 156–57; "fulfillment" (orgasm), 153, 238, 240–42, 303, 310, 339; twentieth-century theories, 161, 237–51; through birth control, 233; through sublimation of sex ("spiritual sex"), 234–36, 339; outcome of issue, 236; dangers, 250. *See also* birth control; sexual relations; sexuality

sexuality: dancing as symbol, 50; threat to commercial elite, 60, 61*n.;* lack of, in religion, 180; complicates human relationships, 236; economic dependence as factor in, 246–50; follows leisure, 283–84; as commercial product, 301; overemphasis, 304, 311; ambivalence, 335; threat to community, 338; future, 343. *See also* repression, of sex; sexual relations; sexual rights, women's

FEMALE: reconciled with society, 6, 15; power, 6–7; function, 7; in feudal societies, 9; in Rome, 14; threat to Hebraic and Christian order, 16, 19, 21, 26; redeemed, in Christianity, 23, 28; Puritan anxiety, 49–50, 42; peak, 69, 325; in novels, 71–74; during meno-

sexuality (*continued*)

pause, 228; motherhood as objective, 228–29; emphasis on, 236; intensity, 251, 311; "internalized" by Protestant ethic, 283; monogamous, 309; "secondary" characteristics, 312; between ages sixteen and twenty, 323; quality in multiformity, 333

MALE: marriage as antidote, 41; in novels, 74; in eighteenth century, 99; nineteenth-century women's attitude toward, 139, 227–28, 234–36, 240, 251; in South, 218–20; aggressiveness, 220; restraint advocated, 230; confined to marriage, 231, 234; "fulfillment," 238; subordinate to female, 251; promiscuous, 309–10; role of imagination, 310–12; role of masturbation, 311–12.

Shatki, 7

Shaw, Rev. Annie, 258–59

silence, women's, 328

slavery: in Greece, 10–11; in Rome, 14; destroys family, 138; effect of *Uncle Tom's Cabin* on, 138; effect on South, 215, 217–18, 221. *See also* antislavery movement; slaves

slaves: sexual relations with, 52, 68, 74, 138, 216–21; women likened to, 126, 127, 149. *See also* antislavery movement; slavery

Smith, Gerrit, 110

social effects, of women's discontent, 243–44

social life: in Greece and Rome, 15; sexual segregation, in America, 92; dominated by church, 177–78; in West, 224; in temperance movement, 255

social service: professionalization, 272–73, 305

social work. *See* reform movements

socialism, 294–95

society, in America: imperils women's development, 68, 90, 99; supports women, 82, 84; based on materialism, 90; irrelevant to individual, 145; effect on family, 213;